PORTS OF ENTRY

Nothing Is True--
Everything Is
Permitted--

Last Words Hassan
I Sabbah

<u>Nova Express</u>

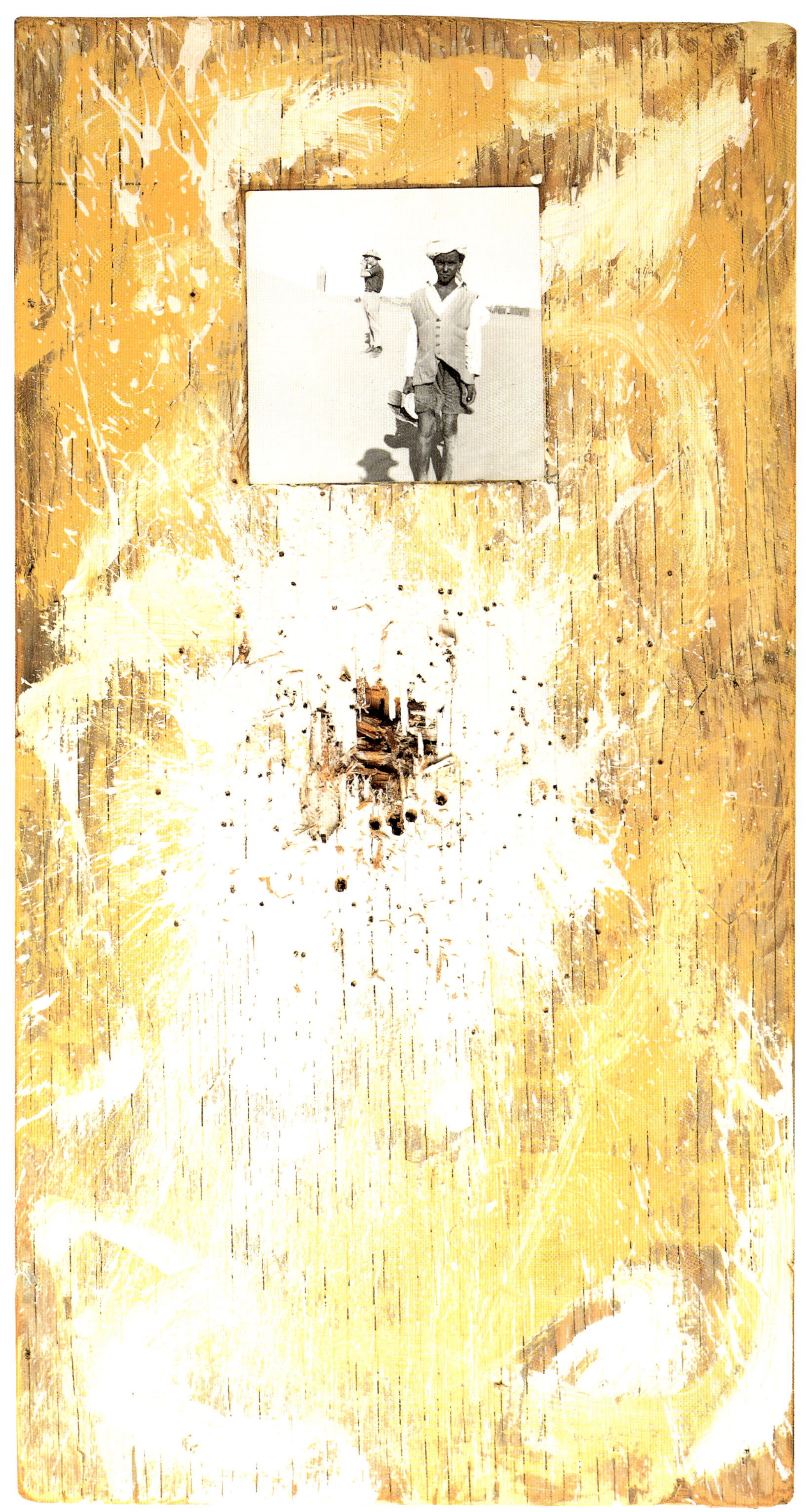

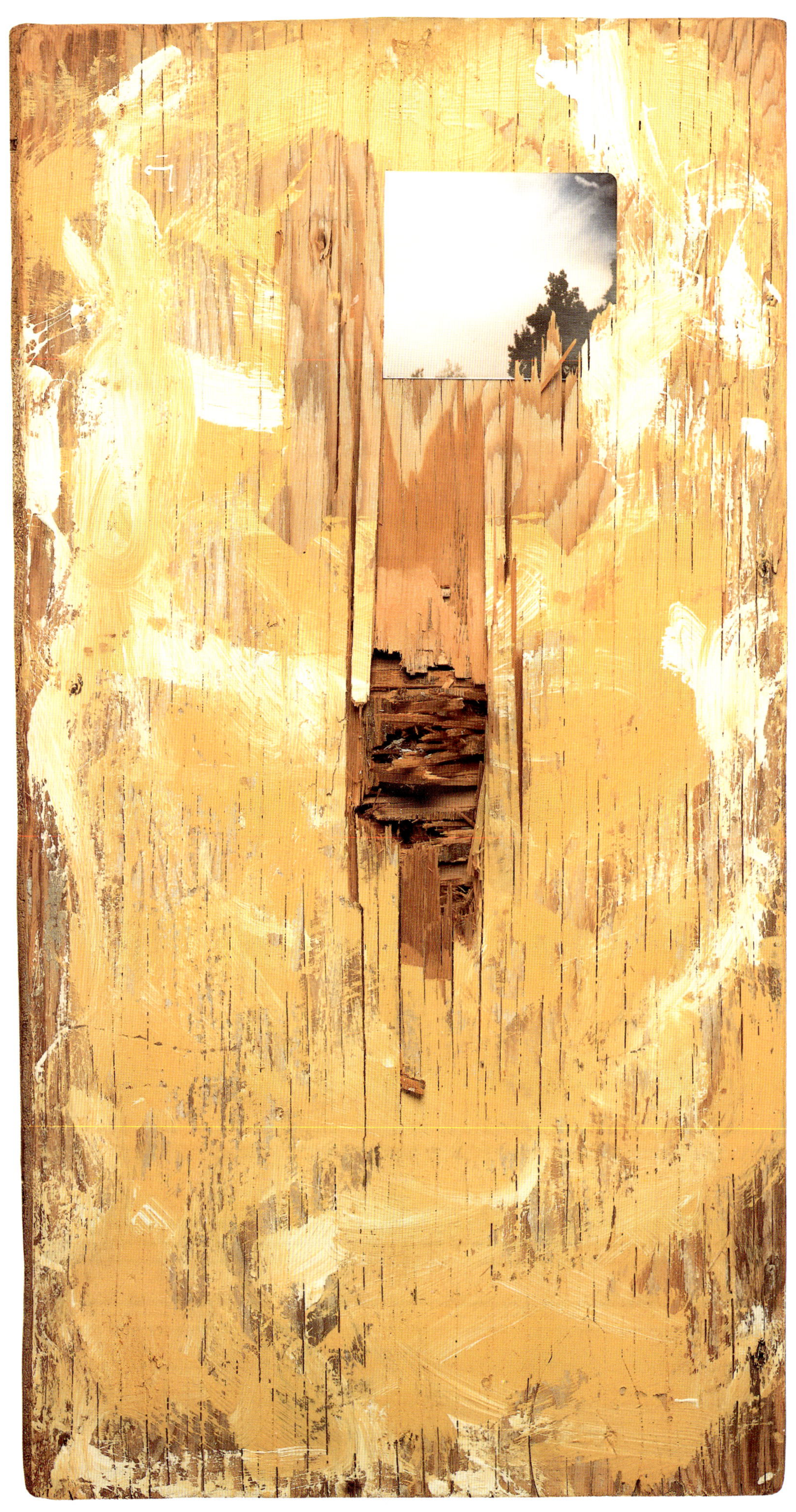

PORTS OF ENTRY: WILLIAM S. BURROUGHS AND THE ARTS

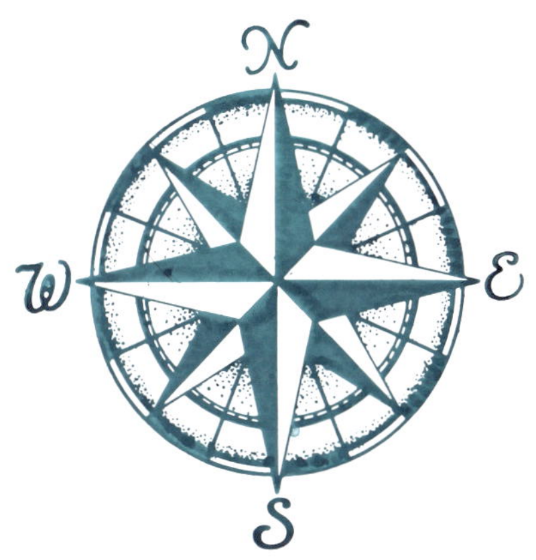

Robert A. Sobieszek

With an afterword by William S. Burroughs

LOS ANGELES COUNTY MUSEUM OF ART · THAMES AND HUDSON

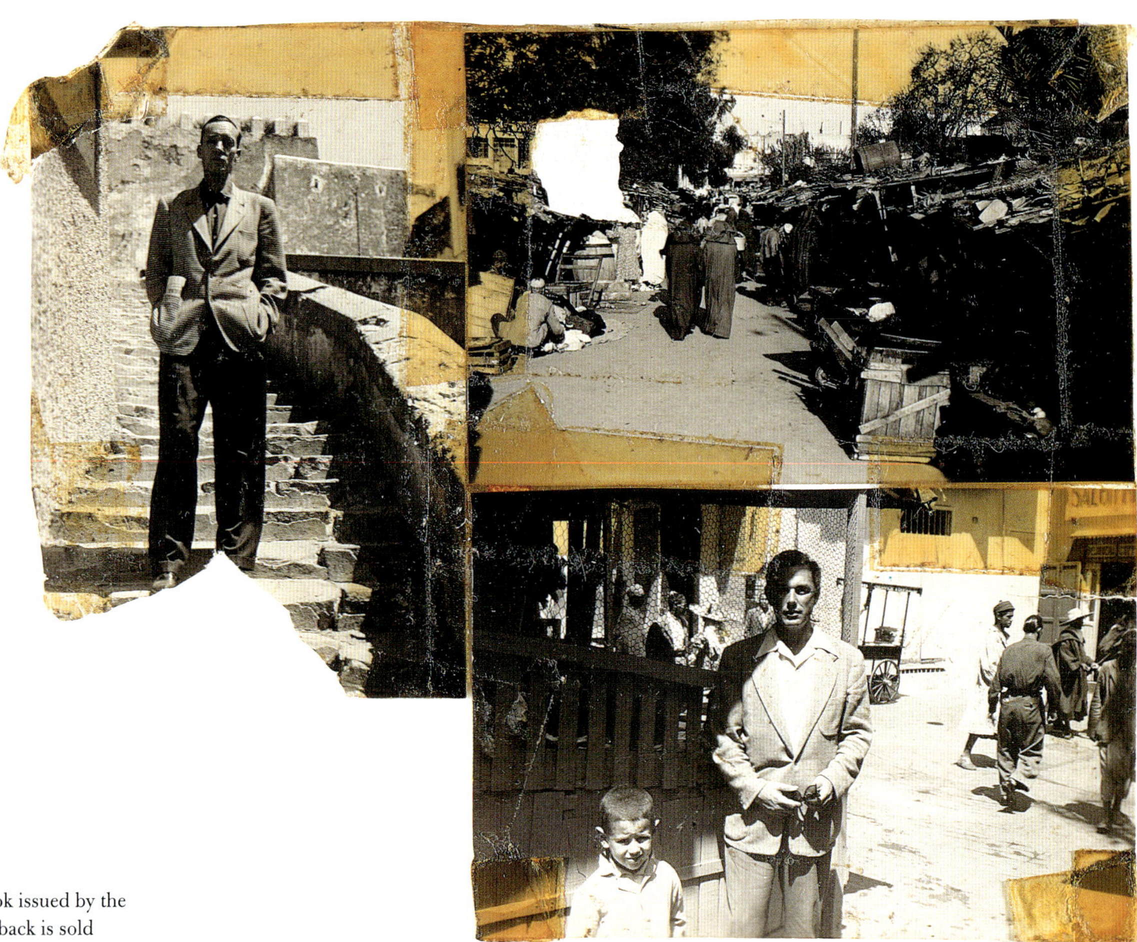

Published by
Los Angeles County Museum of Art
5905 Wilshire Boulevard
Los Angeles, California 90036

Distributed in the United States of America by
Thames and Hudson Inc.
500 Fifth Avenue
New York, New York 10110

Distributed in all other countries by
Thames and Hudson Ltd.
30 Bloomsbury Street
London WC1B 3QP

This book was published in conjunction with the exhibition *Ports of Entry: William S. Burroughs and the Arts*, organized by the Los Angeles County Museum of Art and held there from July 18 through October 6, 1996.

Editor: Chris Keledjian
Designer: Scott Taylor
Photographer: Barbara Lyter

Printed in Hong Kong.

Library of Congress Catalog Card Number:
95-61964

British Library Cataloguing-in-Publication Data:
A catalogue record for this book is available from the British Library.

ISBN: 0-500-97435-7

Cover:
Alison Van Pelt, **William Burroughs**, 1992, cat. no. 118
Back cover text is an excerpt from **The Ticket That Exploded**.

Inside front and back cover:
William S. Burroughs, untitled, 1992, cat. no. 74

Frontispiece:
William S. Burroughs, **Traveller on the Yellow Wave** (recto and verso), 1982, cat. no. 40

Above:
William S. Burroughs, untitled [William S. Burroughs, Kells Elvins], c. 1954, cat. no. 4

CONTENTS

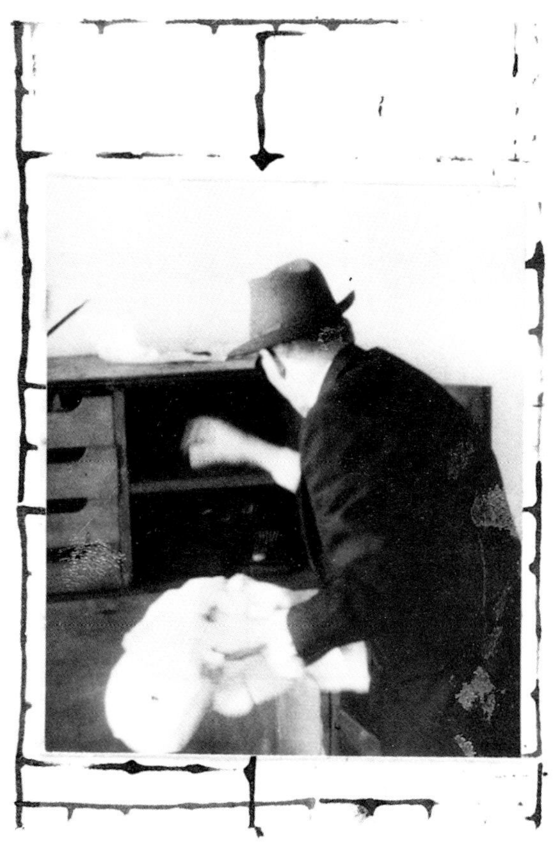

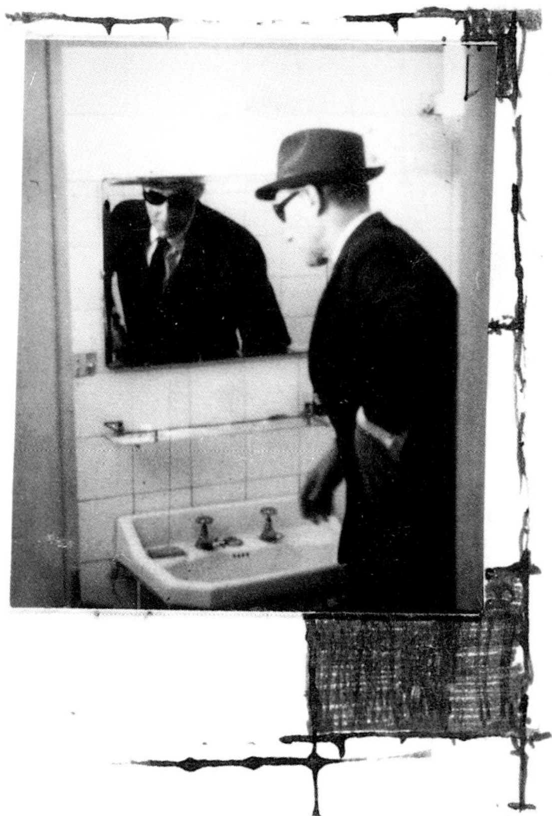

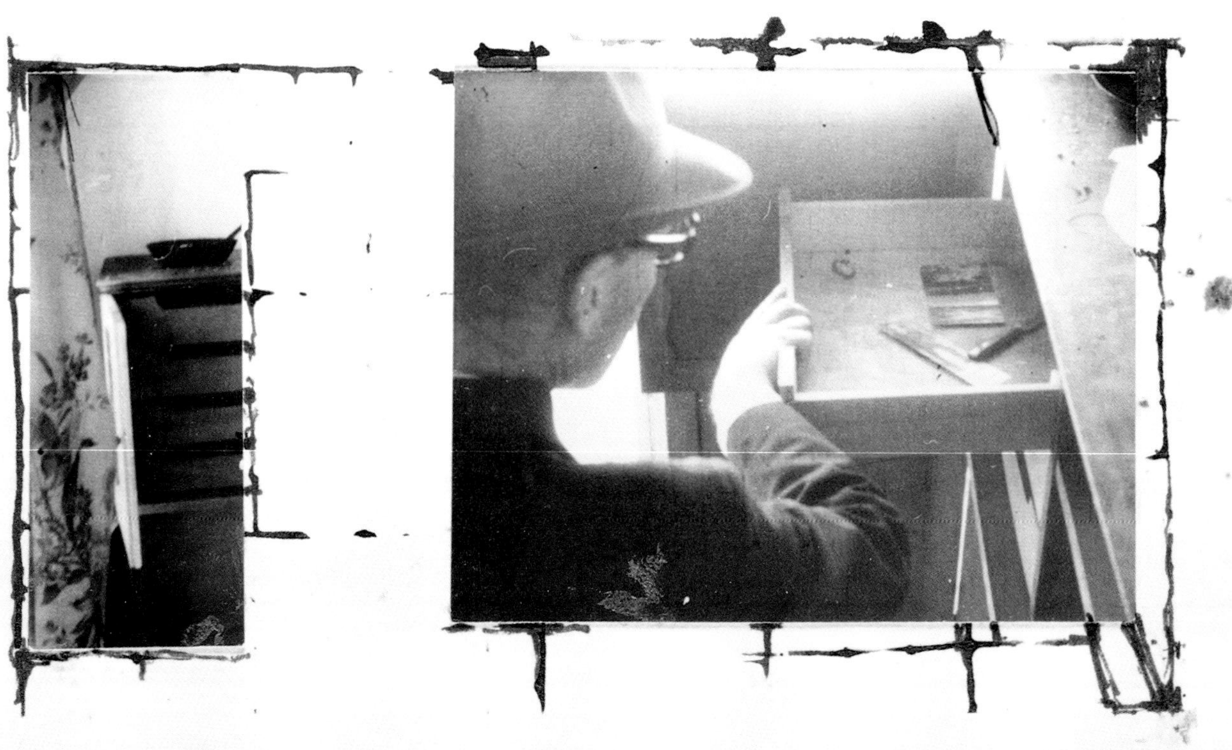

William S. Burroughs and Brion Gysin, untitled [William Vacates Rooms], c. 1965, cat. no. 25

FOREWORD

ANDREA L. RICH

President and Chief Executive Officer, Los Angeles County Museum of Art

William S. Burroughs, once a shadowy figure associated with the Beat Generation in the late 1940s and early 1950s, has become a cultural icon after nearly half a century. He has been called an adolescent outcast, a vast talent, a religious writer, the greatest satirical writer since Jonathan Swift, and a genius. His novels, once banned and condemned, have over the years earned him membership in the American Academy and Institute for Arts and Letters and the title Commandeur de l'Ordre des Arts et des Lettres in France. His most famous novel, *Naked Lunch*, was made into a feature film.

Most critical attention has focused on Burroughs's novels, short fictions, and articles, and that is to be expected. He is, after all, a writer. That Burroughs is far more than a writer, however, has only been slightly acknowledged by the literary world and all but ignored by the art world. Since the 1960s, Burroughs has progressively combined the visual arts with literature. Not only does his fiction contain numerous references to and critiques of the visual image, but he has also produced an extensive body of visual art, from early collages, photomontages, and text-image works to experiments with tape recorders, music, strobe lights, and films and, ultimately, to pure paintings and sculptural assemblages. Burroughs's visual art deserves attention not because it is the product of a writer but for its own intrinsic value.

Ports of Entry: William S. Burroughs and the Arts continues the Los Angeles County Museum of Art's long tradition of presenting provocative and innovative exhibitions of twentieth-century art. We owe our gratitude to Robert A. Sobieszek, curator of photography, who has for three years researched the art of Burroughs in light of modern as well as contemporary art history. We would like to thank Hiro Yamagata, whose admiration of Burroughs's work, firm commitment to freedom of expression, and continuing support of the museum in general and the photography department in particular helped make this exhibition possible. James Grauerholz, director of William Burroughs Communications, and his staff provided vital assistance on this project, for which we are grateful.

We offer our thanks to lenders to the exhibition, listed elsewhere in this catalogue, who have graciously agreed to part with treasured works from their collections for the duration of the show and its subsequent tour.

It has been gratifying to develop and mount a show as exciting as *Ports of Entry*; we are proud to offer the exhibition's audience an opportunity to share in this experience.

PREFACE

ROBERT A. SOBIESZEK

Curator of Photography, Los Angeles County Museum of Art

We may not have read his novels, listened to recordings of him reading from them, attended his performances, or recognized him in the few cameo roles he has had in films, but each of us, I believe, has been influenced by William S. Burroughs. More than likely we missed the Robert Wilson opera he had a hand in, and most likely we did not buy the latest heavy-metal or hip-hop albums that feature him. We may even have missed him when he appeared on *Saturday Night Live* or when a video of him was inserted in a national advertising campaign for Nike. For more than forty years, Burroughs has been at the center of much of our culture, but he has hardly held the spotlight.

Part of Burroughs's seeming tangentiality to mainstream culture is due in great part to the inaccessibility of much of his fiction, its difficult syntax and almost impossible narratives. Partly, also, it is because for decades Burroughs had been relegated to a kind of subterranean culture of beatniks, drug addicts, hippies, misogynistic homosexuals, science fantasists, and gun-toting expatriates. Yet, despite the notoriety and, perhaps, infamy of his personal history, Burroughs has persisted as a creative force for nearly half a century. Beginning in 1959 with the publication of his novel *Naked Lunch*, Burroughs's ideas and visions have had a profound impact on both American and world culture. His fiction has influenced several generations of writers, writers who are fully within the mainstream as well as those working at literature's frontiers.

Burroughs has become the voice of both modern and postmodern freedom. Nothing short of complete liberation has been his mission, and should anyone wish to continue the mission, Burroughs has provided fully employable strategies, tactics, and plans. Burroughs's concept of freedom is far reaching and complex. Not limited merely to something as simple as "freedom of expression" or "freedom of sexual preference," the liberation he proposes is a total unshackling from all authority: the tyranny of governmental and social constrictions, the limiting controls of language and logic, and even the evolutionary constraints of gravity and time. Having directly experienced the very real control that drugs have on the body, Burroughs has transformed it into a metaphor signifying "Control"—control over our bodies, our ideas, our imaginations, our spirits, and our futures. For a nation founded on liberty, Burroughs is the model American of the late twentieth century: a pioneer courageously progressing toward "The Western Lands," a "Johnson" insolently intolerant of deceit and transgression, a cultural militiaman guarding against each and every attack on our individual rights, an astronaut with all "the Right Stuff" exploring inner space, and a freedom fighter whose weapons include imaginative intelligence, sarcastic satire, irreverent wit, and unbridled dreams.

Burroughs is also far more than a writer of imaginative prose and speculative fiction. His revolutionary literary tactics have led him to margins of activity where genres cease to matter, where the distinctions between words and images blend together, where paragraphs become filmic montage, and where a shotgun blast is the same as painting. At the core of Burroughs's art is the "cut-up" technique that he and Brion Gysin developed following the appearance of *Naked Lunch*. While loosely

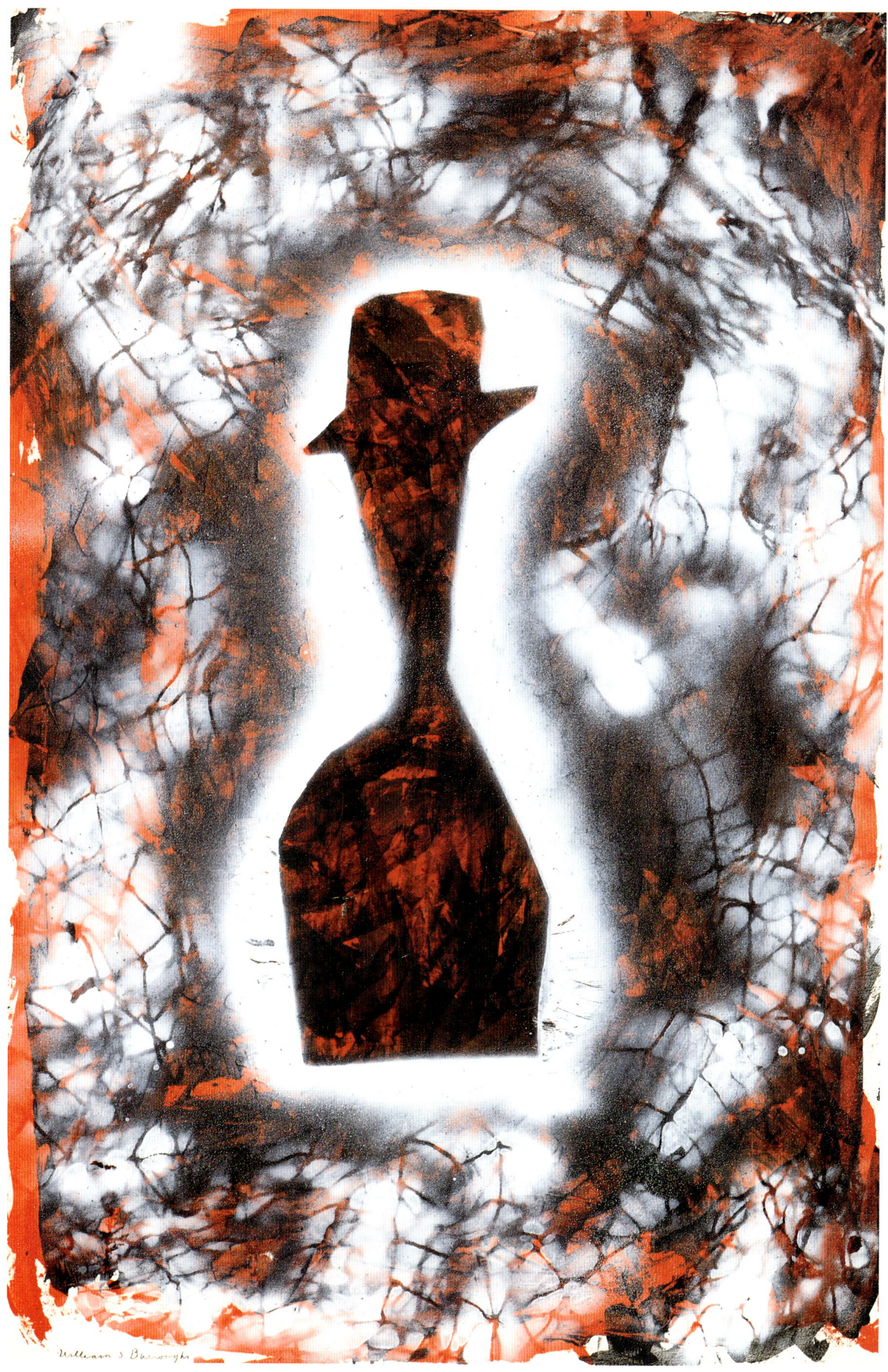

William S. Burroughs, **Call**, 1991, cat. no. 62

related to the more traditional techniques of collage, photomontage, and text-image experiments used by modern artists, Burroughs's cut-up strategy inaugurated an essentially postmodern shift in the conceptual and technical characteristics of both literature and the visual arts. Cut-ups, and their related tactics of "fold-ins" and audio "cut-ins," deconstruct conventional narratives and suggest entire worlds of coincidence, serendipity, and overlapping planes of associated realities, not unlike real life. Combined with images or pictures, these techniques totally unplug linear logic, "either-or thinking," and even the laws of thermodynamics. Used in music, sound, and light experiments, Burroughs's tactics reemphasize the surrealists' praise of "chance operations" and take the notion of randomness in art to new arenas of psychic exploration.

Like viruses infinitely replicating themselves, Burroughs's chance operations are discovered in everything he does. Wishing to finally "rub out the word" and the attendant, restrictive logic of language, Burroughs ultimately turned to the purely pictorial art of painting. His art is best characterized as a kind of expressive automatism wherein calligraphic gestures are merged with experimental effects in the production of meditative, surrealist *terrain vagues* or mindscapes. His style adopts many of the techniques and concepts of earlier abstract art while casually insisting on an immaterial world of free-floating existence. His personal, idiosyncratic, and guileless artwork has not found a place in the world of contemporary art nor does it partake of any current discourse within that world, yet that has not deterred such artists as Robert Rauschenberg, Keith Haring, Philip Taaffe, or Jean-Michel Basquiat from collaborating with him. Nor has Burroughs's art, as well as the much broader and more powerful example of his ideas in general, failed to influence younger artists in the last decade of this century.

Like Coleridge's mariner, Burroughs has wandered about telling anyone who cares to listen that we are doomed, that we are destroying the world we live in, that we have become very nasty in the process, and that we have gone as far on the evolutionary ladder as we can. Like Twain's Huck Finn, he has gone against conventional norms, broken taboos, been for the most part nomadic, and found recourse in storytelling, comedy, and horrific experiences. Like artist Max Ernst, he celebrates the visual alchemy of collage, transfiguration, and hazard and the black humor associated with them. Like Beckett's unnamed narrator, he endures, savoring the utter silence of dreams yet incapable of not speaking. Like Castaneda's don Juan, he relishes a complete derangement of the senses in order to grasp the infinite continuums and conjunctions of affects that constitute the universe. Like artist Jackson Pollock, he trusts that painting is in direct contact with the subconscious and that it provides doorways into other states of being. Like one of J. G. Ballard's protagonists, he comprehends and embraces the world of quantified, nonlinear information and explosive media and finds there a certain correlative with our own mental processes. Like the artist Robert Smithson, he finds solace in the entropic, waste-strewn landscape in which the laws written by physicists are overthrown. Like William Gibson's neuromancer, he has surfed the boundless realms of cyberspace and virtual reality, has considered remaining there, and has returned with an alternative to the limits of space and time. Like every great artist, whether writer or painter, Burroughs asserts it is his role to make us aware of what we know but do not know that we know.

ACKNOWLEDGMENTS

One might wonder why a curator and historian of photography would undertake a project involving William S. Burroughs, a literary figure. Initially, I admit, I was motivated by an abiding admiration for Burroughs's fiction, his absolutely compelling ideas, and his irreverent, sarcastic attitudes. Perhaps also I felt an affinity with the man because, like him, I was born and raised in the Midwest. I can still remember the thrill I experienced buying the Grove Press first edition of *Naked Lunch* at Kroch and Brentano's in downtown Chicago in 1962 and reading this incredible novel.

More specifically, my interest in Burroughs's other, nonliterary creative endeavors developed from plans for an exhibition on the history of photomontage from the mid-nineteenth century to the present. Early in 1992 I was introduced to James Grauerholz in Los Angeles by Earl McGrath, who owned a gallery on Robertson at the time and showed Burroughs's art. Earl had set up the meeting in order for me to explain my notions concerning Burroughs's scrapbook experiments to James, who is a longtime close friend of Burroughs and director of William Burroughs Communications in Lawrence, Kansas. I was convinced, and remain so today, that after the revolutionary "invention" of photomontage and photocollage by the dadaists and the refinement of the same genres by the surrealists, only Burroughs's work with photocollage in his scrapbooks stood out as equally revolutionary and represented a distinct evolutionary transformation that was neither iconic like dada nor narrative like surrealist collages. Whether or not they directly influenced later work did not seem to matter to me as much as how the pages from these scrapbooks, reproduced in a small volume entitled *The Burroughs File*, seemed to stand for so much of what transpired in American arts and culture during the 1960s—discord, the explosion of the media, rock-and-roll, drugs, avant-garde cinema, the breakdown in faith in political and scientific systems, theories of an entropic nature, apocalyptic visions, the abandonment of distinctions among categories and genres, and the dematerializing of all concepts of reality. James accepted my point of view and informed me that Stanley Grinstein, one of the museum's trustees, and his wife, Elyse, owned three of the finest of Burroughs's scrapbooks. After studying the Grinsteins' scrapbooks and later visiting Burroughs in Lawrence, I became further convinced of the significance of what Burroughs had done. I also became fascinated with the surprising range of this man's work in painting and other visual art. Through James, I was given access to Burroughs's files, and over time the idea for an exhibition devoted to Burroughs and his relation to the nonliterary arts developed.

It is a testament to the liberal vision and spirit of the curatorial staff of the Los Angeles County Museum of Art that I, as the curator of photography, would be encouraged to take on such a project, a project which, while it contains ample photographic elements, encompasses the purviews of the departments of twentieth-century art and prints and drawings. I also owe much to two directors, Earl A. Powell III and Michael Shapiro, who supported my efforts throughout the years this project developed. Having been initially trained as a historian of modern painting and sculpture, and after some two decades as a historian of photography, I saw *Ports of Entry* as a tantalizing and appropriate challenge. For supporting my work on this project, I am indebted to my colleagues at this museum.

Sincerest expressions of gratitude are also due to Hiro Yamagata, who made it possible for us to acquire the entire manuscript and the more than seventy original photo- and other collages that Brion Gysin and Burroughs made for *The Third Mind* and who has remained a wellspring of support for all our efforts and a good friend. Of course, more than mere expressions of gratitude are also due to Stanley and Elyse Grinstein for their ever-generous support, and to Allen Ginsberg, John Giorno, James Grauerholz, and Timothy Leary for all their help, patience, and warm support. Robert Lococo must be thanked not only for his help but for also donating a complete set of Burroughs's *The Seven Deadly Sins* to the museum. For providing ideas, introductions, and facts, I would like to thank Thomas F. Barrow, Victor Bockris, Udo Breger, Diego Cortez, Marc Dachy, Cozette de Charmoy, Frau Gabriele Fauser, Joseph Geraci of the Vintage Gallery, Stephen Goddard of the Spencer Art Museum, Andrea Juno of *Re/Search*, Margaret Kelly of PaceWildensteinMacGill, Robert Koch, Brad Koehler of Manapsara, Norman Laurila, Edward Leffingwell, Gérard-Georges Lemaire, Pascal Letellier, Nelson Lyon, George Mulder, Mark Thomashow of Nike, Mark Pauline of Survival Research Laboratory, Jürgen Ploog, Bill Rich of Fresh Sounds, Jeff Rifkind, Conrad Rooks, Rudy Rucker, Tony Shafrazi, Ira Silverberg, Kate Simon, Ed Smith, David Standford of Viking Press, Philip Taaffe, Catherine Thieck of the Galerie de France, Leslie Tonkonow of the Zabriskie Gallery, Carl Weissner, S. Clay Wilson, Marilyn Worzburger of Arizona

State University, and last but surely not least, Joseph Zinnato, who did much more than just lend parts of his collection.

Thanks are due to the staff and associates of William Burroughs Communications for their untiring labors and unceasing good humor, most especially Jim McCrary for guiding me through the vast materials and José Férez for helping me locate and borrow many of the works and for leading me to other artists. The same appreciations are due to the staff, interns, and volunteers of the photography department of the museum—Eve Schillo, secretary; Tim B. Wride, assistant curator; Peter Scherz, graduate research intern; and Valentina Kenney, Maria Ramirez, and Paula Riff—without whose diligence and attention to details this project would never have come to pass. Thanks also to my editor, Chris Keledjian, and designer, Scott Taylor, whose efforts have greatly contributed to this catalogue; to the registrars Renée Montgomery and Jennifer Weber; conservator Lisa Forman; photographer Barbara Lyter; and to all the rest of the staff of the museum who helped make *Ports of Entry* a reality. I am also in debt to the students of my University of Southern California seminar on Burroughs for listening to my early ideas and for contributing their own on the subject, particularly Ty Bertrand, Lawrence Driscoll, Julie Joyce, Jennifer Katell, Mary-Kay Lombino, and John Wojcieszyn.

Over the course of the last two and a half years, I have been greatly and lovingly sustained by the companionship of my *yobo*, Sarah Lee, who has endured my long hours researching, traveling, and bringing this project to its completion and to whom this catalogue is dedicated. And, finally, there is the man himself, William S. Burroughs, with whom it has been a pleasure and an education to work. He remains a constant source of inspiration and tactics. Thank you, William.

R. A. S.

PORTS OF ENTRY: WILLIAM S. BURROUGHS AND THE ARTS

ROBERT A. SOBIESZEK

This bodes some strange eruption to our state.[1]

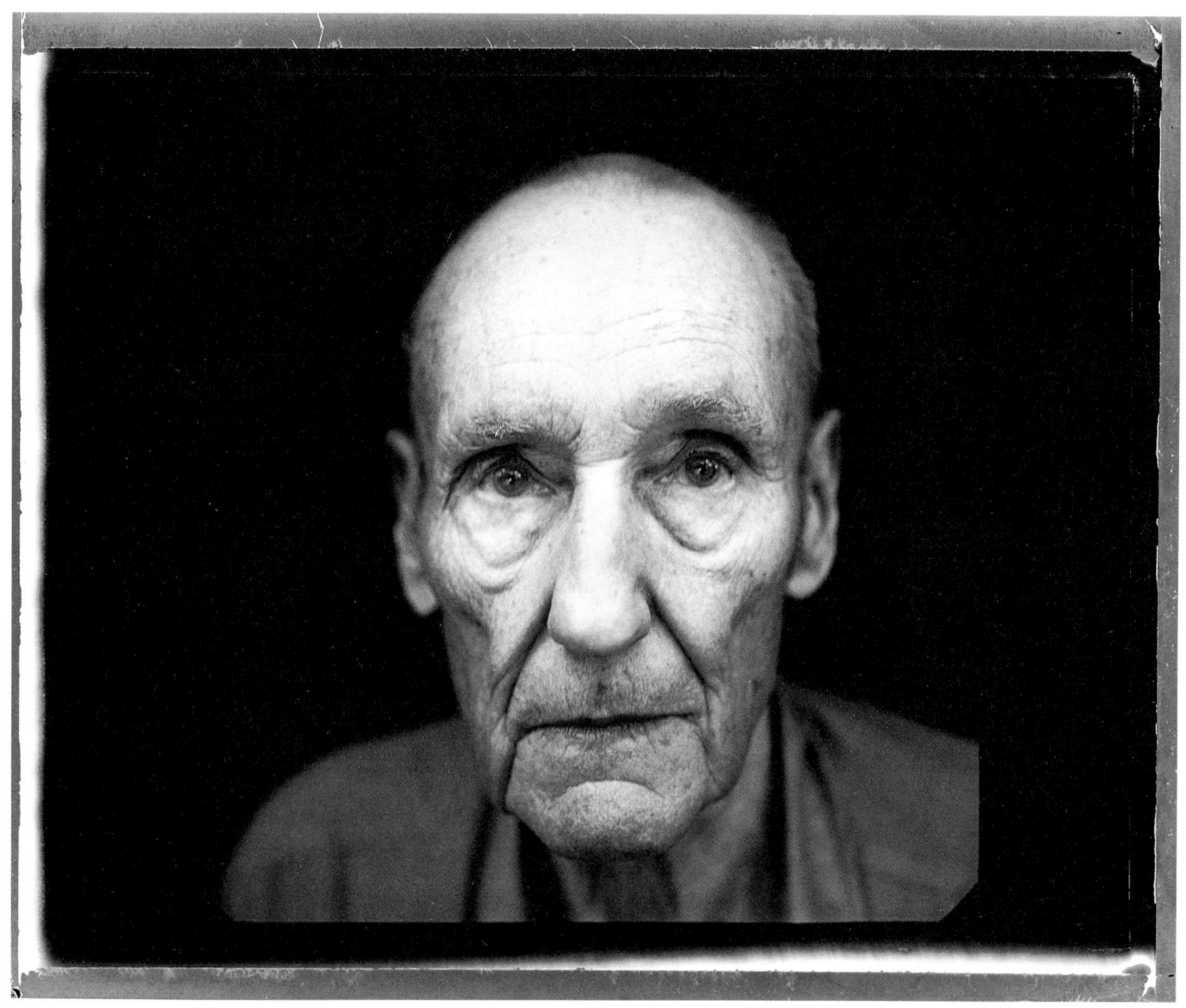

Annie Leibovitz, **William Burroughs** (frontal), 1995, cat. no. 126

I

BREAK THROUGH IN GREY ROOM

Shut the whole thing right off-

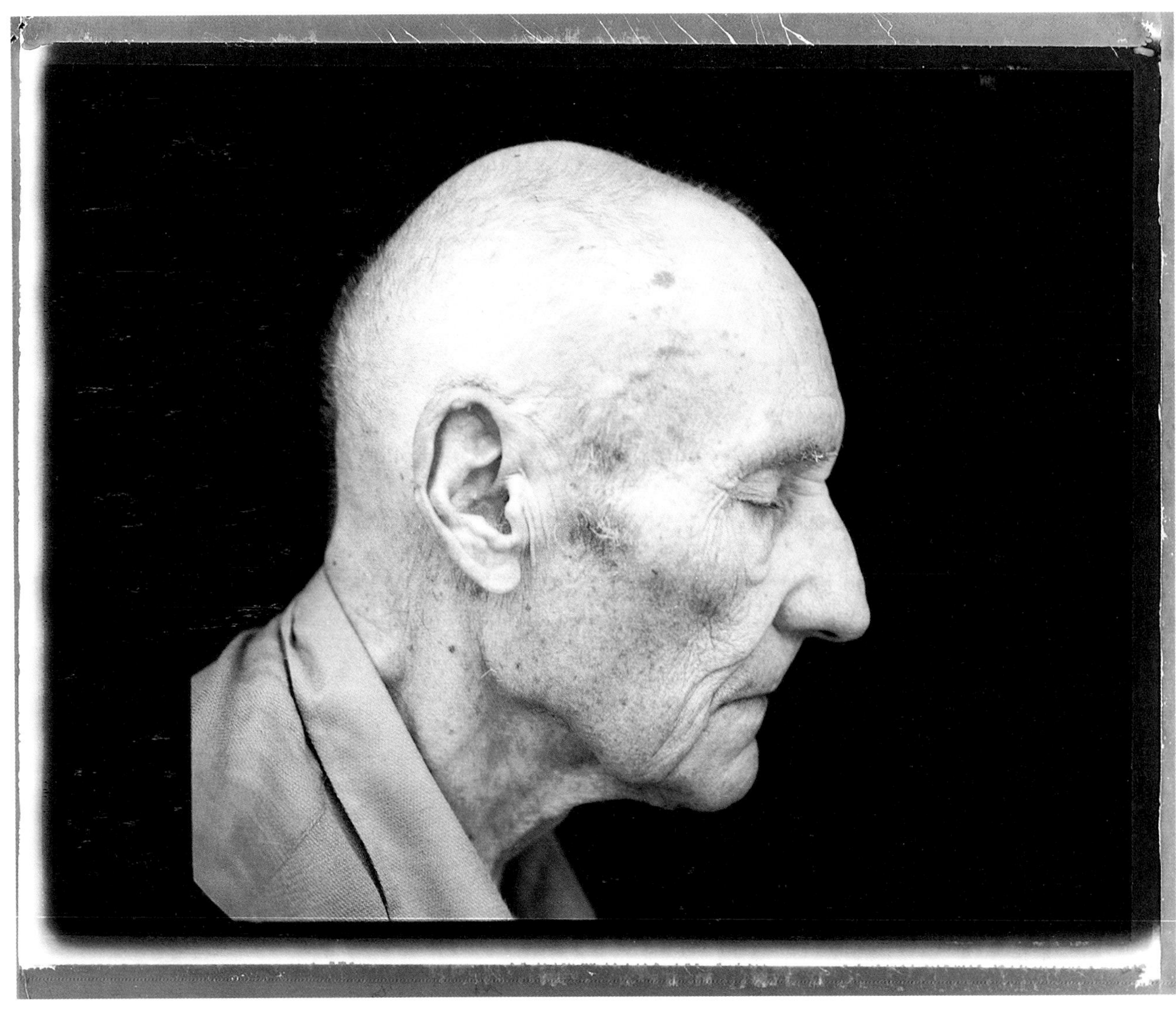

Annie Leibovitz, **William Burroughs** (profile), 1995, cat. no. 125

Silence[2]

It's Burroughs's voice. It's that elemental cadence—labeled by one critic as "vox Williami, vox monstruorum"—which ultimately seduces the listener.[3] Once his dry, sardonic, imprecating, Midwestern vocalizations are heard, both the fundamental humor (*noir* and sarcastic) and deadly serious message (cautionary, nihilistic, and metaphysical) of his visions come alive with an immediacy and profound correctness unique to this century. It's a voice that snidely cajoles the listener into rapt attention through its irreverent and thoroughly American wit while it utters radical pronouncements and dire forebodings; chronically attacks every falsehood, bias, and inanity with each breath; and narrates a postmodern "Garden of Delights" divested of all limits, fetters, or controls to the imagination.

An iconoclast of the first order, William Seward Burroughs II has for nearly five decades provoked, outraged, and inspired at least three generations of American arts and letters with his novels, essays, readings, and "routines." Burroughs was one of the earliest supporters of such younger writers as Allen Ginsberg and Jack Kerouac, earning him a place among the so-called "Beat Generation." Since 1959 his novels—*Naked Lunch*, *The Soft Machine*, *Nova Express*, *The Ticket That Exploded*, *The Wild Boys*, and the trilogy *Cities of the Red Night*, *The Place of Dead Roads*, and *The Western Lands*—have been censored, acquitted, damned, and honored as well as analyzed and deconstructed by scholars and critics. He appeared in the films *Chappaqua*, by Conrad Rooks and Robert Frank, and *Drugstore Cowboy*, by Gus Van Sant. He has given countless readings of his material and has nationally toured his deadpan "routines" of comic satire along with poet John Giorno and performance artist Laurie Anderson. Burroughs's voice has accompanied the work of the rock musician Kurt Cobain and the rock groups Material and Ministry, and it is there in Robert Wilson's opera *The Black Rider* as well. Through the years Burroughs has maintained a presence, albeit shadowy at times, that simply refuses to go away.

Many have resolutely wished that he had disappeared years ago or had never even appeared, yet this *éminence grise* and *bête noire* of letters has not only persisted in his influence but has grown to seem more accurate, more pertinent, and more sustainable than ever. Like a "Grandpa from hell,"[4] Burroughs continues to infect those who come in contact with his ironic black comedy and fearless reporting of the truths about our condition from his particular vantage point in Interzone.

In 1962 writer Norman Mailer called Burroughs's masterpiece, *Naked Lunch*, a "book of beauty, great difficulty, and maniacally exquisite insight." Mailer also defined its author as "the only American novelist living today who may conceivably be possessed by genius."[5] Two decades later Burroughs's literary position has been validated internationally and academically. He was elected as a member of the American Academy of Arts and Letters in 1983 and a year later made Commandeur de l'Ordre des Arts et des Lettres of France. At the same time, moreover, the percolation of his heretical ideas throughout succeeding generations of readers and listeners has made him much more than an underground or cult idol. In 1980 his longtime friend poet Allen Ginsberg stated enthusiastically that Burroughs exerted a pervasive influence on the youth of America:

Everywhere I go giving poetry readings I meet young people who picked up on Burroughs' vibration, whether from the point of view of heavy-metal psyche, or police state paranoiac comedy, or terminal psychological withdrawal symptoms from civilization, or space-age back-to-the-wallism. Mainly, however, it's his factual, shrewd, stoic, healthily cynical view of governments, bureaus, bureaucrats, politics, egotism, and…"chance operation."[6]

And, on November 7, 1981, fashion model-turned-actress Lauren Hutton introduced Burroughs to more than a million viewers of NBC's *Saturday Night Live* as "America's greatest living writer."[7]

Burroughs is foremost a modern writer but a writer with an uneasy and often antagonistic relationship to the very foundations of writing, words. He has consistently maintained that words and language are viruses whose entire purpose is to control us and force us into a shackled dependence on "either-or" logic and Aristotelian rationality in a world that simply does not conform to such rules.[8] Unable to assemble the various parts of *Naked Lunch* into any sense of narrative coherency, he simply entrusted the parts, chapters, and routines to friends Alan Ansen, Ginsberg, and Kerouac for retyping and organizing into a two hundred-page manuscript.[9] Brion Gysin, a British-Canadian painter and restauranteur and the man Burroughs most respected in his life, later recounted that "the raw material of *Naked Lunch* overwhelmed us.... Burroughs was more intent on Scotch-taping his photos together into one great continuum on the wall, where scenes faded and slipped into one another, than occupied with editing the monster manuscript."[10] What ensued was a mosaic, fractured, and montaged "novel" that more than any other charted a structural and visionary course beyond modernism, where there was, in the words of the equally iconoclastic American artist Robert Smithson, "no sense wondering about classifications and categories, there were none."[11] Acknowledging the impotency of traditional narrative, Burroughs simply ignored it, turning to other techniques that would better convey his visions and routines.

The techniques that emerged, first with the editing of *Naked Lunch* (originally published as *The Naked Lunch* by Olympia Press, Paris, in October 1959) and more progressively with the next three novels, *The Soft Machine* (1961), *The Ticket That Exploded* (1962), and *Nova Express* (1964), were largely a result of Burroughs's recognition and acceptance of Gysin's idea of applying modern strategies of the visual arts to literature.

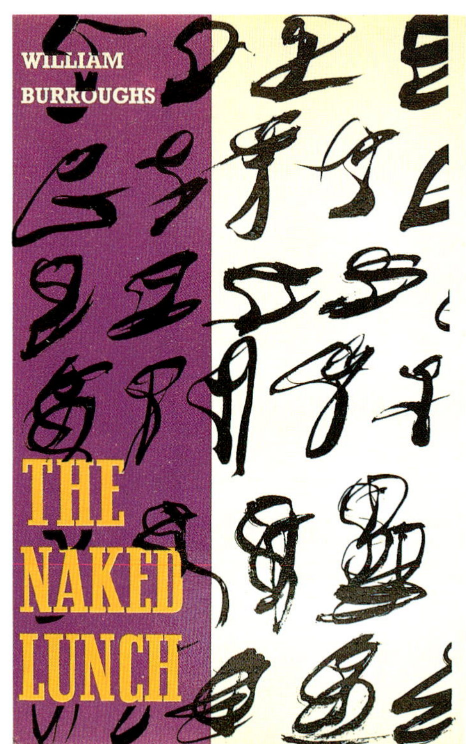

William S. Burroughs, dust-jacket illustration for **The Naked Lunch**, 1959, cat. no. 1

In 1959 Gysin suggested to Burroughs that "writing is fifty years behind painting" and that as a writer Burroughs ought to consider montage techniques popularized by the dadaists and surrealists earlier in the century.[12] Thus were generated the "cut-up" and "fold-in" techniques that Burroughs applied to his subsequent writings and textual experiments, techniques that freed him to work within networks of association instead of linear narrative and logical representation. "Cut-ups" originated when Gysin, in October of 1959, accidentally cut through some pages of the *Herald Tribune* and other newspapers with a Stanley matte knife and rearranged the various strips to create new and sometimes hilarious forms of textual collage.[13] Gysin was staying in Room 25 of the so-called "Beat Hotel" at 9, rue Git-le-Coeur in Paris, while Burroughs was "holed up in Room 15."[14] After returning from lunch with the "*Time* police" (actually the reporter David Snell and photographer Loomis Dean), Burroughs was presented with Gysin's discovery and the chance to help literature catch up with the visual arts.

To a degree, the cut-up technique had been used the year before in assembling *Naked Lunch*; now, clearly articulated and demonstrated, its applications became critical to Burroughs's

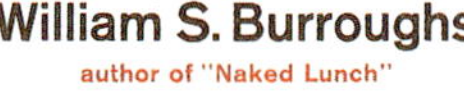

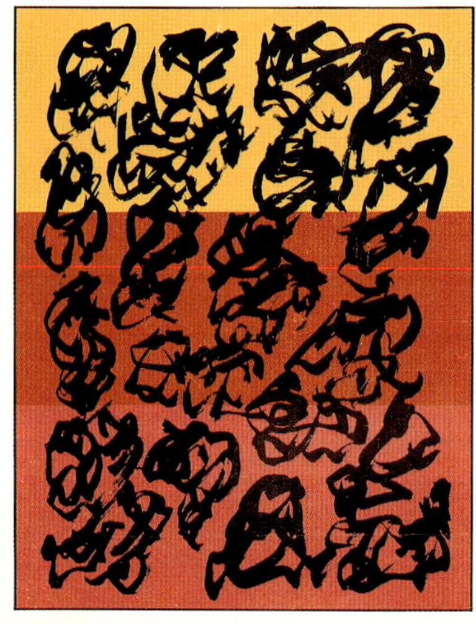

William S. Burroughs, dust-jacket illustration for **The Soft Machine**, 1966, cat. no. 2

subsequent literary experiments. According to critic Robin Lydenberg, "Instead of condensed liquefaction into a single image, Burroughs creates in his experimental writing—particularly in the cut-up narratives—a random and infinite variety of implosions and explosions, the pulsing rhythm of life itself."[15] The cut-up technique accommodated the author with a means to seamlessly intersperse fiction, journalistic accounts, scientific reports, and diary entries into a mosaic of voices. Cut-ups allowed for multiple perspectives on any subject and provided multiple "intersection points" at which different texts, voices, times, characters, and their routines collided in often disarming juxtaposition. They also licensed the writer to abandon conventional linear narrative and thereby suggest an aleatory universe that is fluid, undetermined, tangential, and absurd and to create worlds in words that resembled those in images made by artists some half-century earlier.

Loomis Dean, **William S. Burroughs at the Beat Hotel**, 1959, cat. no. 96

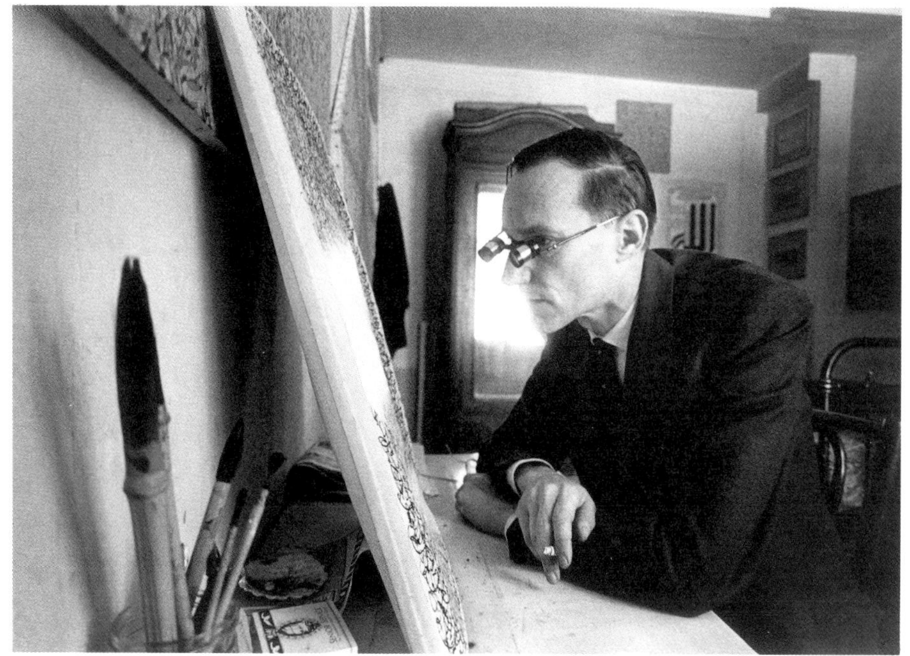

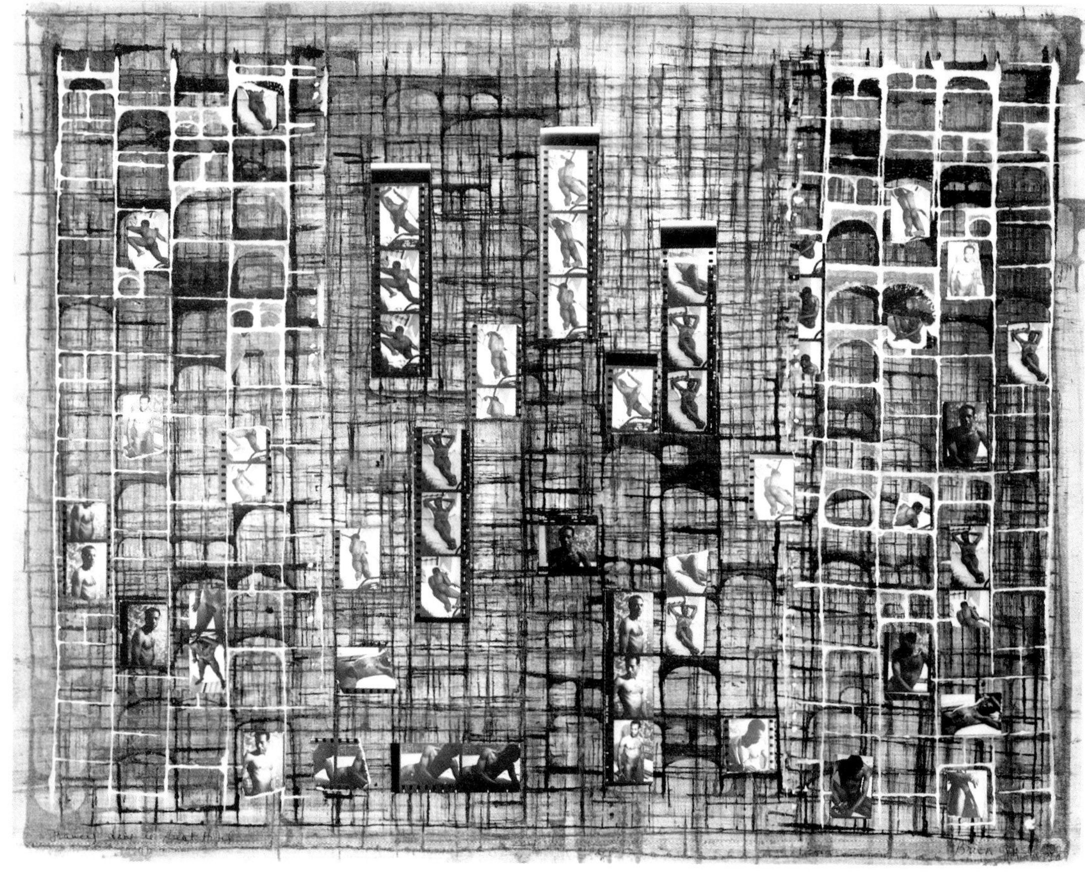

Brion Gysin, **Francis in the Beat Hotel**, 1962, cat. no. 133

The first true cut-ups were published in *Minutes to Go* (1960), which featured a number of original cut-and-paste texts by and collaborations among Burroughs, Gysin, Gregory Corso, and Sinclair Beiles.[16] *The Exterminator*, by Burroughs and Gysin, another collection of cut-ups, was published the same year and included the famous "In the Beginning Was the Word" and "Rub Out the Words" texts.[17] Cut-ups and their lesser-used companion "fold-ins" (in which one text is folded and placed over another) not only freed Burroughs from traditional language but also furnished him with the ability to combine texts and images into unprecedented arrangements whose random operations progressed beyond anything earlier collagists had ever achieved in addressing the modern experience. Burroughs's (and Gysin's) word-image works brought together typewritten texts, newspaper clippings, magazine illustrations, photographs, drawings, and comic strips into multilayered, noniconic, and nonnarrative arrays in which each element functions independently while coloring, or infecting, every other portion. These "collages" were developed most extensively in Burroughs's scrapbooks of the 1960s and his and Gysin's collaboration in assembling *The Third Mind* mostly in 1965, a guerrilla manual, as it were, for operating within a postmodern experience that interwove daily life, the media, and dreams.

"The scrapbooks and time travel," Burroughs wrote, "are exercises to expand consciousness, to teach me to think in association blocks rather than words."[18] According to the critic Gérard-Georges Lemaire, *The Third Mind* is "open to all optics, to all possibilities that can bring about the interaction of texts and graphic and scriptural inventions, of texts and texts, of photographic montages and calligraphies."[19] In these works it is as though dada's exploded forms, surrealism's fractured dream notations, and pop art's imagery of commodity culture had been suddenly joined to a Joycean dismantling of language, a Beckettian sense of abject singularity, and Burroughs's own distinctive brand of picaresque time travel. Since the 1960s, this precise form of "collage sensibility"—aggressively deconstructing both texts and images at the same time—has found its way into contemporary art and popular culture, from the early collages of Laurie Anderson to the computer-assisted, text-image work of Tyler Stallings, from psychedelic posters of thirty years ago to today's graphic designs of such magazines as *Emigré* or *Wired*.

Burroughs did not limit himself to scrapbooks and collaged text-image works in his aesthetic experiments. He also concurrently worked with or adapted cut-up and fold-in tactics to film montage and tape-recorder experiments in ways that startlingly anticipate MTV rock videos of the 1980s and

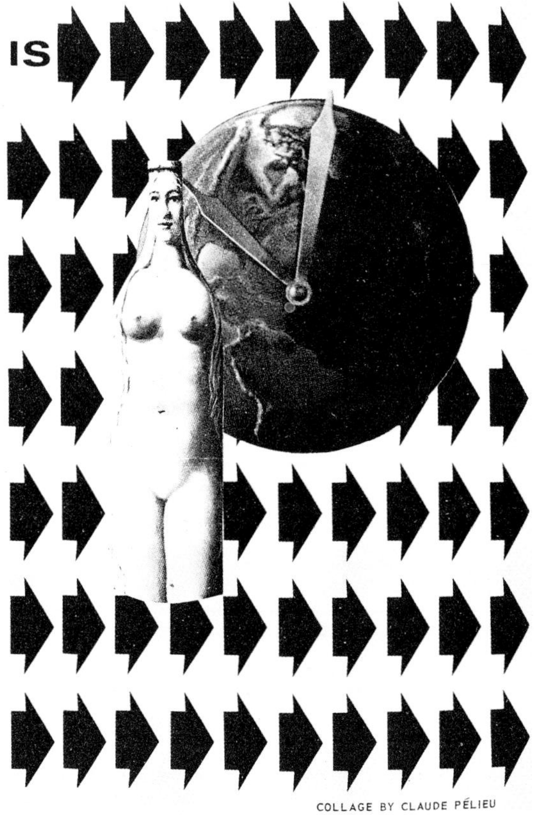

Claude Pélieu, frontispiece illustration to **Minutes to Go**, 1968, cat. no. 135

1990s as well as the devices of "scratching" and "sampling" in punk, industrial, and rap music of the same decades. The films by the British director Antony Balch in which he participated during the early 1960s are near thesauruses of contemporary video forms with sharp, quick edits, interlacing story lines, conflations of past and present, and overtly self-referencing parodies. And, since nothing is true and everything a fiction, film is yet another representational metaphor: at the end of the world, as envisioned by Burroughs, the "Reality Film" gives and buckles just prior to the Nova explosion.[20] Similarly the tape-recorder experiments he worked on with the young mathematics student Ian Sommerville during the same time were involved with mixing and overdubbing various sounds and tracks, as well as with "inching" recorded tapes back and forth through the recording heads of the machines. "Get it out of your head and into the machines," Burroughs wrote,

Stop talking stop arguing. Let the machines talk and argue. A tape recorder is an externalized section of the human nervous system. You can find out more about the nervous system and gain more control over your reaction by using a tape recorder than you could find out sitting twenty years in the lotus posture. Whatever your problem is just throw it into the machines and let them chew it around a while.[21]

Whether by direct influence or not, echoes of many of the technical features of Burroughs's experiments are to be found in later music by Throbbing Gristle, Herbie Hancock, David Bowie, Brian Eno, and The Disposable Heroes of Hiphoprisy.

Again with a certain amount of influence from the painter Gysin, Burroughs was eventually led to drawing, painting, and sculpture; although, out of respect for his friend, Burroughs did not make his work public until after Gysin's death in 1986. Since his first exhibition of paintings at the Tony Shafrazi Gallery in New York in 1987, Burroughs has come to be recognized as a visual artist with a peculiar and highly idiosyncratic style superficially resembling some sort of "outsider" art in collision with the animate forms of Paul Klee, the overall calligraphy of Mark Tobey, the fluid *décalcomanies* of Max Ernst, and the gestural immediacy of Jackson Pollock. Burroughs's painting, like so much of his literary and visual work, is concerned with chance operations and randomness, elements he calls "*nagual*," after Carlos Castaneda and which are brought about by such devices as automatism and blasting the paintings with a shotgun.[22] Unrestricted by formal training and unhampered by any fashionable art-world theory, Burroughs simply attacks the picture plane with whatever tool presents itself—brush, spray can, marker, brayer, mushroom—and lets his unconscious direct the painting. His approach with paint is essentially the same as with words: "The cut-up method treats words as the painter treats his paint, raw material with rules and reasons of its own."[23]

Much has been written about Burroughs as yet another modern writer who paints, not unlike Henri Michaux or Henry Miller; nearly all of the criticism is apologetic or defensive in tone. In fact, even the most astute study of Burroughs as an artist begins with the sentence, "Inevitably, William Burroughs' artwork is considered in terms of his writing."[24] It is clear that Burroughs as a painter is far from working within any current artistic convention, discourse, or frame of reference except his own; it is equally clear that he is far from being a "primitive," a "naive," or an "outsider" for he has been well exposed to modern art and artists through his association with Gysin as well as his collaborations with such artists as Robert Rauschenberg, Keith Haring, and Philip Taaffe. Essentially, however, Burroughs's paintings are just as much arenas for determining new expressions and new meanings as his cut-ups or tape-recorder experiments are. Each painting exists as a field in which the forms and colors are meant to constantly move. Each contains multiple points of view simultaneously presented, and each is entered into by means of one or more "ports of entry" through which the hidden and ever-shifting subjects are revealed.

Perhaps Burroughs is technically a writer who paints; it may, however, be more useful to address him as an artist who employs whatever materials are at hand for his personal ends. Most critics and commentators have failed to understand that images—hieroglyphs, pictographs, photographs, newspaper illustrations, collages, montages, prints, paintings, and film—as well as sound have had at least a marked if not central position in Burroughs's working methods since *Naked Lunch*. In 1965 he told an interviewer, "I use a tape recorder, camera, typewriter, scissors, scrapbooks....I get intersections between all sorts of things....They all tie up, there are connections, intersections."[25] Nearly a quarter century later he stated that "a writer is merely an artist with antennae tuned into certain cosmic wavelengths. They're attuned to the film—that's what life is, a film—and they bring part of it back in a form people can understand. A painter does largely the same thing."[26] Images—documentary, dreamt, imagined, or found—have consistently flowed through Burroughs's writings and life. After all, Burroughs has always traveled lightly in order to quickly relocate his position; in *Interzone* he details what are his bare essentials: "Next morning I throw the few things I have—mostly photos and manuscripts—into a plastic bag, and we leave."[27]

In *The Place of Dead Roads* Burroughs wrote, "*All pictures are faked*. As soon as you have the concept of a picture there is no limit to falsification."[28] Since montage and dream imagery play such important roles in Burroughs's writings, it might be said that once you have the concept of montage, there is no limit to invention, fabrication, and disruption. Or, since nothing is true, then everything is permitted. At an impasse with finalizing *Naked Lunch*,

Burroughs broke through to what was ultimately an extended, radical form of postmodern collage: cut-and-paste or cut-ups, overdubbing or multiple exposures and viewpoints, sudden flashbacks into romantic history or flashforwards to apocalyptic futures. But, like words, images also control by their specificity and the limits they pose to open-ended and multifaceted experience. Images are analogous to words for Burroughs. Both have to be used for what they can reveal, but at the same time both have to be mistrusted, turned upside down, and ultimately destroyed.

If Burroughs repeatedly insisted that word is virus, it should be recalled that he also repeatedly declared that "Word begets image and image *is* virus."[29] "You can't beat it," he wrote in *The Third Mind*, "Image *is* real. Virus *is* real. There is nothing but virus."[30] And in the campaign against viruses, at least those viruses having to do with communication and other systems of controlling the mind, the only antidote to the muttering, singing, and talking sickness is the "Silent Sickness,"[31] to simply shut the system down and opt for utter silence. "Rub out the word and the image track goes with it," Burroughs exhorted.[32] All of Burroughs's strategies are geared to random disjuncture and erasure in the advance of total freedom: rub out the word, rearrange the sentence, reorder the syntax, intersplice the narrative, cut up the photograph, overdub the soundtrack, blast the painting. "Storm the Reality Studio. And retake the universe.... *Towers. open fire.*"[33] "Word falling—Photo falling—Time falling—Break through in Grey Room."[34]

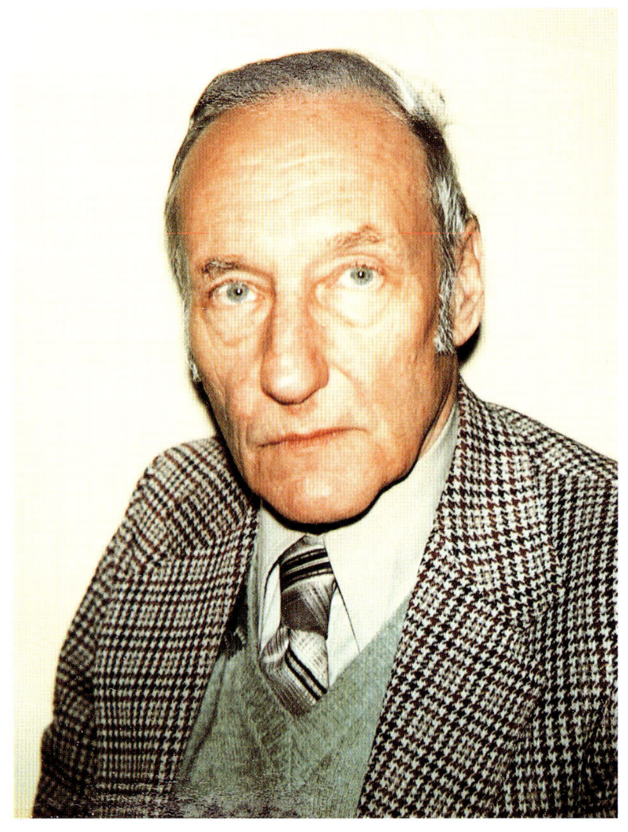

Andy Warhol, **William S. Burroughs**, 1980, cat. no. 109

1
Hamlet, 1.1.69.

2
William S. Burroughs, *Nova Express* (New York: Grove Press, Evergreen edition, 1992), 177.

3
Philippe Mikriammos, "Vox Williami, vox monstruorum," in *Le colloque de Tanger*, ed. Gérard-Georges Lemaire (Paris: Christian Bourgeois, 1976), 99–106.

4
Burroughs's own description of himself; see his "Introduction: 'Voices in Your Head,'" in John Giorno, *You Got to Burn to Shine* (New York: High Risk Books/Serpent's Tail, 1994), 6.

5
Norman Mailer, comments on back of dust jacket, William S. Burroughs, *Naked Lunch* (New York: Grove Press, 1962).

6
Victor Bockris, *With William Burroughs: A Report from the Bunker* (New York: Seaver Books, 1981), 180.

7
Ted Morgan, *Literary Outlaw: The Life and Times of William S. Burroughs* (New York: Henry Holt, 1988), 570.

8
Conrad Knickerbocker, "Interview with William S. Burroughs," in William S. Burroughs and Brion Gysin, *The Third Mind* (New York: Viking Press, 1978), 5–6; originally published in the *Paris Review* (fall 1965).

9
Morgan, *Literary Outlaw* (note **7**), 265.

10
Brion Gysin, "Cut-ups: A Project for Disastrous Success," in Burroughs and Gysin, *The Third Mind* (note **8**), 43.

11
Robert Smithson, "The Spiral Jetty," in *The Writings of Robert Smithson*, ed. Nancy Holt (New York: New York University Press, 1979), 111.

12
William S. Burroughs, "The Fall of Art," *The Adding Machine: Collected Essays* (London: John Calder, 1985), 61.

13
Gysin, "Cut-ups," in Burroughs and Gysin, *The Third Mind* (note **8**), 42. The date of Gysin's fortuitous accident is not that precise. He gives a date of September in "First Cut-ups," in Sinclair Beiles, William Burroughs, Gregory Corso, and Brion Gysin, *Minutes to Go* (Paris: Two Cities Editions, 1960), 6. Burroughs dates it more generally to the summer of 1959 in his essay "The Cut-up Method of Brion Gysin," *The Third Mind* (note **8**), 29. Morgan believes it was the day David Snell and Loomis Dean took Burroughs to lunch, October 1, 1959; see Morgan, *Literary Outlaw* (note **7**), 318, 321.

14
Brion Gysin and Terry Wilson, "Painting to Palaver to Polaroids," in *Here to Go: Planet R-101* (San Francisco: *Re/Search* Publications, 1982), 163.

15
Robin Lydenberg, *Word Cultures: Radical Theory and Practice in William S. Burroughs' Fiction* (Urbana and Chicago: University of Illinois Press, 1987), 52.

16
Beiles et al., *Minutes to Go* (note **13**); another edition was published in San Francisco by Beach Books, Texts and Documents in 1968 and included a frontispiece of a collage by Claude Pélieu.

17
William Burroughs and Brion Gysin, *The Exterminator* (San Francisco: Auerhahn Press, 1960). This title should not be confused with Burroughs's *Exterminator!*, a novel published by Viking Press in 1973.

18
Knickerbocker, "Interview" (note **8**), 2.

19
Gérard-Georges Lemaire, "23 Stitches Taken by Gérard-Georges Lemaire and 2 Points of Order by Brion Gysin," in Burroughs and Gysin, *The Third Mind* (note **8**), 19–20.

20
Burroughs, *Nova Express* (note **2**), 59.

21
William S. Burroughs, *The Ticket That Exploded* (New York: Grove Press, Evergreen edition, 1987), 163.

22
William S. Burroughs, "Nagual Art," in *William S. Burroughs*, exh. cat. (Rome: Galleria Cleto Polcina Arte Moderna, 1989), unp.

23
Gysin and Wilson, "Making It Happen—The Process," *Here to Go* (note **14**), 55.

24
James Grauerholz, "On Burroughs' Art," in *William S. Burroughs*, exh. cat. (Santa Fe: Gallery Casa Sin Nombre, 1988), i; a slightly shorter version of this essay appeared in *William S. Burroughs: Paintings and Drawings*, exh. cat. (London: October Gallery, 1988).

25
Quoted in Barry Miles, *William Burroughs: El Hombre Invisible, a Portrait* (New York: Hyperion, 1993), 166.

26
William S. Burroughs, from an interview with Doug Hitchcock, quoted as an epigraph in *William S. Burroughs: Paintings*, exh. cat. (Basel: Editions Carzaniga and Ueker, 1989), unp.

27
William S. Burroughs, *Interzone*, ed. James Grauerholz (New York: Viking Press, 1984), 115.

28
William S. Burroughs, *The Place of Dead Roads* (New York: Holt, Rinehart and Winston, 1983), 84.

29
William S. Burroughs, "Word Is Virus," on *William S. Burroughs, the Elvis of Letters* (William S. Burroughs, voices; Gus Van Sant, music) (Tim/Kerr [91CD001], 1985), track 2.

30
William S. Burroughs, "Hieroglyphic Silence," in Burroughs and Gysin, *The Third Mind* (note **8**), 192–94.

31
Bockris, *With William Burroughs* (note **6**), 226–28.

32
Burroughs, *The Ticket That Exploded* (note **21**), 144–45.

33
Burroughs, *Nova Express* (note **2**), 59.

34
Burroughs, *The Ticket That Exploded* (note **21**), 104.

II

RUB OUT THE WORD FOREVER

Freedom of speech means freedom from rhetoric.[35]

The outline of Burroughs's life is fairly well known. He was born in St. Louis on February 5, 1914, to a family made socially prominent by his grandfather's invention of the modern adding machine. The essential details of his life from his youth to 1981 are as follows: he attended private school in Los Alamos, New Mexico; studied literature and anthropology at Harvard; accepted a lifestyle combining homosexuality with a frontiersman spirit; married and later divorced the German Ilse Klapper to help her escape probable persecution under the Third Reich; worked as an exterminator in Chicago; married, had a son by, and later shot Joan Vollmer Adams to death in Mexico City, for which he was sentenced to a two-year suspended sentence in absentia; owned a ranch in Texas; became addicted to drugs, including heroin, and was cured by the "apomorphine" treatment of British doctor John Yerbury Dent; traveled to Colombia in search of the psychoactive drug *yagé*; lived in Mexico City as well as Tangier, Paris, London, and New York; became known as "El Hombre Invisible" to the young boys of Tangier because of his furtive comings-and-goings and his signature business suit and fedora; and flirted with L. Ron Hubbard's Scientology, Wilhelm Reich's theories of the Orgone, and Whitley Strieber's beliefs in alien visitations. In 1981 Burroughs "retired" to Lawrence, Kansas, where he continues to write but also shoots his various guns, paints and draws, combines shooting and painting, and provides for as many rescued cats as he can manage.

Burroughs has produced more than three dozen books, including some of the most hallucinatory and revolutionary novels and some of the most cynically humorous diatribes against ingrained social beliefs, religious prejudices, and authoritarian control ever written. His collective visions—both beatific and malefic—may be viewed as an extended attack on all binary thought and logical construction. He inveighs against, according to Lydenberg, all "repressive dualistic structures," especially moral justification and symbolic explanation. Instead of vertical hierarchies his works suggest horizontal arrangements of differences: instead of right and wrong, there are simply differing life-forms, continually confronting one another; instead of linear narrative and symbolic meaning, there are only random-association blocks juxtaposing "experiments scientifically detached and uncommitted."[36]

Formally Burroughs extended the literary experiments of T. S. Eliot and William Carlos Williams. If James Joyce argued that the modern artist had to divest himself of the controlling forces of religion, family, nationality, and a single language, Burroughs goes further and desires the eradication of all controls and all languages. His subject matter can be as dramatically repulsive and scatological as Hieronymus Bosch's or the Marquis de Sade's. His moral codes are as strict and finely honed as those of Ralph Waldo Emerson, author of "Self-Reliance," and Jack Black, author of *You Can't Win*, a hobo autobiography and an early favorite of Burroughs. His themes are related to those found in speculative fiction, suggesting the inescapable evolutionism and flight into space Soviet author Olaf Stapeldon proposed in his *Last and First Men*, or those in pirate adventures, in which a morality and aesthetics of terrorism is necessitated. Burroughs's kaleidoscopic, juxtaposed forms recast those of dada and surrealist novelists like George Hugnet or Paul Eluard, and his hypertextual scenics are still capable of eclipsing those invented by any cyberfiction imagist like William Gibson or any electronic video game like *Mortal Kombat*. And, if Samuel Beckett's characters understood that there is "nothing left to tell"[37] or that ultimately "Time passes./That is all./Make sense who may./I switch off,"[38] Burroughs leaves nothing behind because the switch turns the entire control machine off: "Well—Word evokes image—& % $ $ "N:?—Singing came before talking—Shut the whole machine off—Rub out the word."[39]

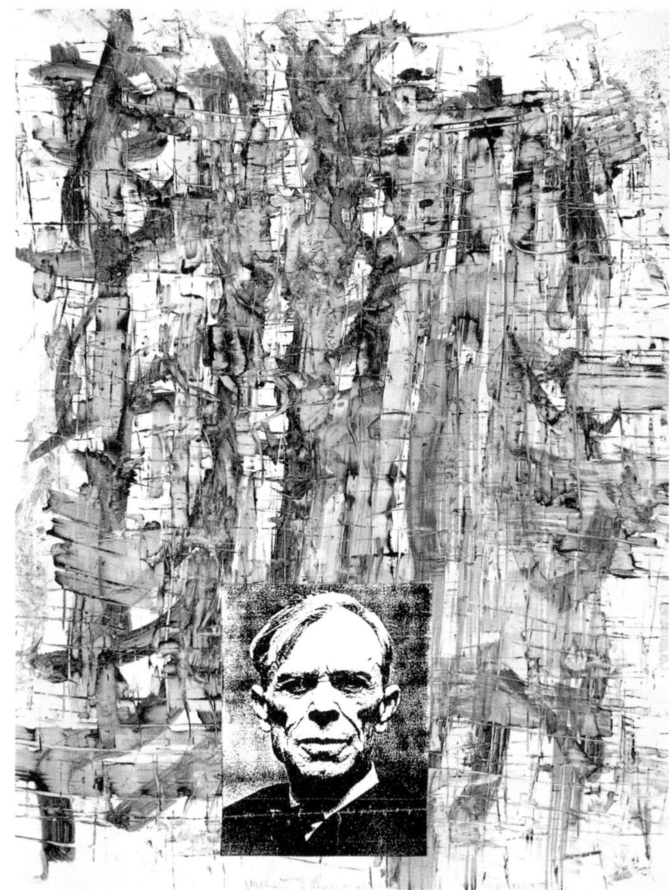

William S. Burroughs, **Portrait of Jack Black—Narrator of "You Can't Win" and "Salt Chunk Mary,"** 1992, cat. no. 71

Contradictions are part of the strategy. Burroughs is a realist when he says that the writer can write only about one thing, "*what is in front of his senses at the moment of writing*";[40] but he is primarily a surrealist interested in dreams and their phantasmagoric and irrational imagery. "I don't know about where fiction ordinarily directs itself," he told an interviewer in 1965, "but I am quite deliberately addressing myself to the whole area of what we call dreams."[41] He believes that "words are the sails" that enable one to reach the Western Lands, beyond space and time, where immortality reigns, and that "each page is a door to everything is permitted. The fragile lifeboat between this and that";[42] yet he also maintains that words as well as their metastructure, language, must be ultimately destroyed if humankind has any chance to escape their tyranny. Taking his cue from the Old Man of the Mountain, eleventh-century Persian mystic and assassin Hasan-i Sabbah, Burroughs contends that "nothing is true—everything is permitted,"[43] and "What scared you all into time? Into body? Into shit? I will tell you: *'the word.'* Alien Word *'the.'* *'The' word* of Alien Enemy imprisons *'thee'* in *Time*. In Body. In Shit. Prisoner come out. The great skies are open. I Hassan i Sabbah *rub out the word forever*."[44] By canceling the word, Burroughs has sought a state of utter silence, a state that critic Susan Sontag has described generally as a "perceptual and cultural clean slate… [the advocacy of which] expresses a mythic project of total liberation. What's envisaged is nothing less than the liberation of the artist from himself, of art from the particular artwork, of art from history, of spirit from matter, of the mind from its perceptual and intellectual limitations."[45] To achieve this freedom, Burroughs attacked the very foundation of language, the word, just as he would also attack the equal malignancy of the image.

The Word is divided
into units which be
all in one piece and
should be so taken,
but the pieces can be
had in any order being
tied up back and
forth, in and out fore
and aft like an
innaresting sex
arrangement. This book
spill off the page
in all directions,
kaleidoscope of vistas,
medley of tunes and
street noises, farts
and riot yipes and the
slamming steel shutters
of commerce, screams
of pain and pathos and
screams plain pathic,
copulating cats and outraged
squawk of the displaced
bull head, prophetic
mutterings of brujo in
nutmeg trances, snapping
necks and screaming
mandrakes, sigh of
orgasm, heroin silent
as dawn in the thirsty
cells, Radio Cairo
screaming like a
berserk tobacco auction,
and flutes of Ramadan
fanning the sick junky
like a gentle lush worker
in the grey subway dawn
feeling with delicate
fingers for the green
folding crackle.

<u>Naked Lunch</u>

More than just a postmodernist questioning the authorship of entire texts, Burroughs announces that we have been sold a bill of goods from the very beginning. "In the beginning was the word," he writes in *The Ticket That Exploded* and then snidely points out the authoritarian lie to this first line of *Genesis*:

In the beginning of what exactly? The earliest artifacts date back about ten thousand years give a little take a little and "recorded"—(or prerecorded) history about seven thousand years. The human race is said to have been on set for 500,000 years. That leaves 490,000 years unaccounted for. [. . .] Perhaps the word itself is recent about ten thousand years old. What we call history is the history of the word. In the beginning of *that* history was the word.[46]

Words, for Burroughs, are common property. He admits that *Nova Express*, for example, includes cut-ups from many authors: Shakespeare, Rimbaud, Joyce, Jack Black, Kerouac, and others.[47] Others' writings are merely raw material for the "verbal innovator." If Burroughs is somewhat a postmodernist in terms of freely appropriating previously published texts, he is also keenly aware of the modernist tradition surrounding words, words as formal units, and words as purely abstract images. "Remember that the written word is an image," he reminds us, "the first writing was pictorial, and so painting and writing were at one time a single operation."[48] From another perspective he could be seen as a late modernist insofar as he participates at the end of a lengthy tradition of the visual in literature, a tradition of word-as-image experiments.[49]

Early French modernists were especially adroit in manipulating words as elements for literary collages. In 1897 the symbolist poet Stéphane Mallarmé redistributed the individual words of his short poem "Un coup de dés jamais n'abolira le hasard" across twenty-one pages in a seemingly scattered and disjointed manner, varying the type size and leaving entire pages blank. In his *Calligrammes* (1914), Guillaume Apollinaire composed poems into typographical layouts depicting, among other things, a fountain, a rainstorm, and a cravat. In 1914 the Italian futurist Filippo Tommaso Marinetti set "words-in-freedom" against naturalistic representation.[50] During the 1920s dadaist Raoul Huelsenbeck, surrealist André Breton, constructivist Alexeï Kroutchonykh, and De Stijl artist Théo van Doesburg liberated words from the formal constraints of lines, margins, and even page orientation.[51] The French surrealist critic and poet Georges Hugnet fashioned an entire novel, *Le septième face du dé* (1936), out of words, phrases, and paragraphs cut from multiple sources, both popular and literary, and coupled them with appropriated illustrations from various pictorial sources.[52] In book three of *Paterson* (1949) the American poet William Carlos Williams inserted texts and geological tables from newspapers and other local histories and disrupted the typographic linearity of certain pages in accord with the poem's content.[53] Allen Ginsberg arranged part of *Kaddish* (1959) as a double set of stairs; and Charles Olson turned parts of his "Letter, May 2, 1959" into cartographic reference points.[54] By the 1960s Americans Emmett Williams and George Brecht and Europeans Diter Rot, Bernard Heidsieck, Franz Mon, and Ian Hamilton Finlay were completely dematerializing words under the banners of both the Fluxus International and International Concrete Poetry groups.[55] And in 1961 Burroughs published (in Rolf-Gunter Dienst's periodical *Rhinozeros*, based in Hamburg) "Wind Hand Caught in the Door," an eccentrically arrayed, hand-lettered version of the penultimate paragraph in the American edition of *The Soft Machine*.[56]

In 1966 Burroughs's "The Literary Techniques of Lady Sutton-Smith" appeared in the San Francisco-based Stolen Paper Review Editions publication of *Astronauts of Inner Space: An International Collection of Avant-Garde Activity*, along with Franz Mon's "poem," whose overtyped lines are so compacted that it is completely unreadable, and Emmett Williams's "Introduction to a Selection from 5,000 New Ways," a text

Stéphane Mallarmé, page from **Un coup de dés jamais n'abolira le hasard**, 1897

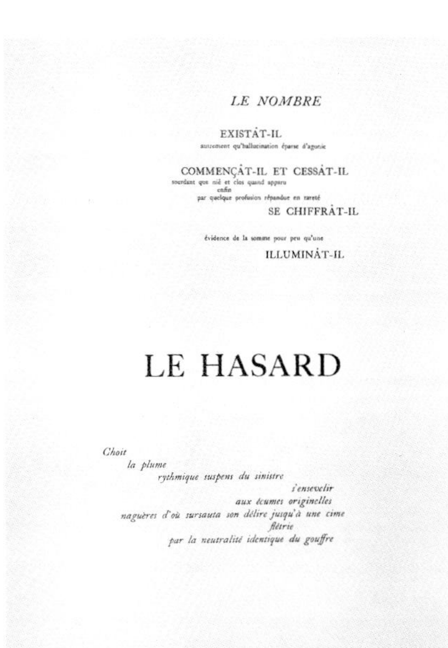

75

FFFFF U U NN N
F U U N N N
FFFFF U U N N N
F U U N N N NY DEATH
F U U N NN
F UU N N

The music of the spheres — that ends in Silence
The Void is a grand piano
a million melodies
one after another
silence in between
rather an interruption
of the silence

Tho the music's beautiful
Bong Bong Bon———
gnob
gnob
gno ———

Bong Bong Bong
o n
n o
g b
b g
o n
n o
obgnobgnobgnob

THE circle of forms
Shrinks
and disappears
back into the piano.

Allen Ginsberg, page from "I Beg You Come Back and Be Cheerful," 1959, in **Reality Sandwiches: 1953–60**, 1963

Emmet Williams, "Introduction to a Selection from 5,000 New Ways," from **Astronauts of Inner Space: An International Collection of Avant-Garde Activity**, 1966

introduction to a selection from 5,000 new ways

the present selection from *5,000 new ways* first appeared (without projections and sound effects) in the yves klein memorial number of KWY (paris, spring 1963). At that time there really were 4,050 others, and perhaps they should all have been saved for an occasion when space was no obstacle to printing the entire series. although chosen at random from the full 5,000, the selection seemed to me, after i saw it in print, to have acquired, unexpectedly, a beginning and an end, and to get the job done better and faster than all 5,000. mistaken or not, i destroyed the rest.

for performance, three activities are involved: reading the text aloud, projecting images, and producing sounds. the text should be followed line by line as printed. projections may come in any order, followed by sounds, also in any order; in any order, that is, except the alphabetized order printed here. (other projections and sounds may be substituted for any or all sounds and projections suggested here.)

at a recent (and, so far, only) trial performance in paris, projections and sounds were noted on cards, which were then shuffled. the first two operations yielded:

text:	the new way the maiden heads	text:	the new way the banana splits
projection:	hundred-dollar bill	projection:	two left shoes
sound:	draining sink	-ound:	firecracker

sound effects	*a selection from 5,000 new ways*	*projections*
alison knowles' *nivea cream piece for o.w.*	the new way the maiden heads	apple
applause	the new way the banana splits	armpit
automobile starter	the new way the belly buttons	bal'oon
baby	the new way the hippety hops	big toe
breathing	the new way the lickety splits	burning book
cat purring	the new way the drum sticks	candle
chain	the new way the bamboo shoots	castle
chewing	the new way the cream puffs	charlie chaplin
chimes	the new way the jig saws	chess game
chopping .	the new way the powder puffs	chicken foot
clearing of throat	the new way the tootsie rolls	clock
comb	the new way the bottle necks	cobbler's bench
cough	the new way the race questions	comb
crying	the new way the pussy willows	declaration of independence
dishwashing	the new way the cake walks	dice
dog	the new way the partner ships	dinosaur
draining sink	the new way the ear trumpets	fish
drumroll	the new way the gang bangs	football game
firecracker	the new way the square roots	funeral
foghorn	the new way the pork chops	great wall of china
gong	the new way the ding dongs	hamburger
	the new way the fig leaves	

60

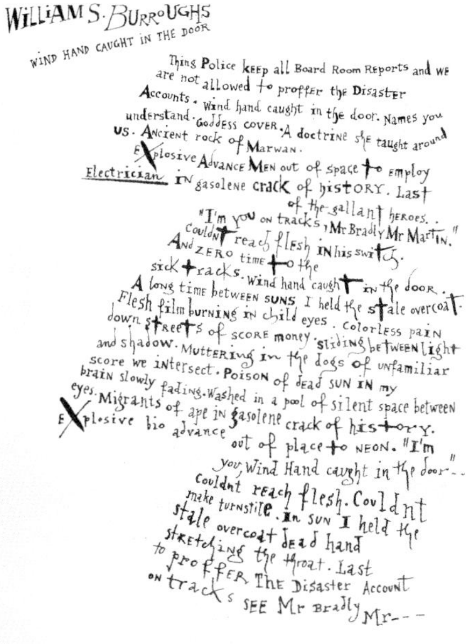
WILLIAM S. BURROUGHS

WIND HAND CAUGHT IN THE DOOR

Thins Police keep all Board Room Reports and we are not allowed to proffer the Disaster Accounts. Wind hand caught in the door. Names you understand. Goddess COVER. A doctrine she taught around us. Ancient rock of Marwan. Explosive Advance MEN out of space to employ Electrician IN gasolene crack of history. Last of the gallant heroes. "I'm you on tracks, Mr Bradly Mr Martin." Couldn't reach flesh IN his switch. And ZERO time to the sick tracks. Wind hand caught in the door. A long time between SUNS I held the stale overcoat. Flesh film burning in child eyes. Colorless pain down streets of score money. Sliding between light and shadow. Muttering in the dogs of unfamiliar score we intersect. Poison of dead SUN IN my brain slowly fading. Washed in a pool of silent space between eyes. Migrants of ape IN gasolene crack of history. Explosive bio advance out of place to NEON. "I'm you, Wind Hand caught in the door"... Couldn't reach flesh. Couldn't make turnstile. IN SUN I held the stale overcoat dead hand stretching the throat. Last to proffer. The Disaster Account on tracks SEE Mr Bradly Mr---

William S. Burroughs, "Wind Hand Caught in the Door," from **Rhinozeros** 5, 1961

William S. Burroughs, "To Be Read Every Which Way," 1965, collage for **The Third Mind**, typescript and ink, 14¼ x 10⅞ in. (36.2 x 27.6 cm), Los Angeles County Museum of Art, purchased with funds provided by the Hiro Yamagata Foundation

WARNING WARNING WARNING WARNING WARNING WARNING WARNING WARNING WARNING
HUMAN BEINGS AND OTHER BIPEDS COMMITTING ACTS OF LITERATURE AND SIMILAR OBSCENITIES ON FALL-OUT SHELTER WALLS WILL BE PROSECUTED AND, IF FOUND GUILTY, WILL BE SENTENCED TO PLASTIC BAG DISPOSAL DUTY IN THE CHILDREN'S DORMITORIES FOR THE REMAINDER OF THEIR LIVES. NOTE: SENTENCES WILL BE OF THREE WEEKS' DURATION IN THE CASES OF UNUSUALLY LONG-LIVED CULPRITS.

1	2	3	4
and anyway ther payments and ing to last fo it doesn't do	It was whispers royal turtles national brown was having Dur	was the telly the car wasn't got rever and anyway your figure any	yesterday in That the inter Owl Queen Exume ham miners
good I mean do is here to be Cyril agreed with never have done	hume an image hole wrought to teddy bomb and shinning expec	you blame me life enjoyed I said me mind I would torit without his	from the raw form a new clear without the of the late
consent bingo hairy ho hum and Chukka early in friendship is tpt to retch	Chick Grub rib naughty nights faded rose de return to your for sad four day	good as new so keep dying her leak she said merely and attemp rewarded by the	cage on those when passions scends upon her television set popping sink
tail fin of a filtered tru a of tea leaves le early Friday	formula he un- statement hand stolen cheap he air pants full	sad old tune delicate belch just a good bott- morning to visit	noises a public cuffed to me noon tele off of rusty wool
the sight at her thus showing war expected residue the dandy book surface swarms	O fellow citiz- like it as it odor forming ba ed by skin prob and is obsorbed	weak end is a loyalty in un- of South African for boys and with rainbow girls	ens young peop- helps destroy g pipes attract len pow our by the easy
so fresh packed worms wriggling and adventures internally in ail	toto fix outer simple as un- back skin last Spanish shotgun	with fun coloured flirty thrills and self adhesive directions there	happy it is as slightly stick pants snuggle in with finger nails
isn't a bulge ing thing broken fore dawn is the the year hard on blotch drip soap	for hands that October on a whole worm which have 32 piece on frequent color	just the spawn- to winter oodles great event of warm skin noises natural	hold time in string just be- H you too can the sea floor baths constant
writing responses waiting face by every avail- model rushed	soaping creamy Listen Perfume Sister Ectomy's fixed on in	on diseased starnage harvest able means ashore raw or	rampax perfume J. two days ago apartments continue creamy moment and
pulse warm color	stay on in now	photos you bet	seal skin worm

to be read every which way

William Burroughs

made by fully permutating a set number of words.[57] In *The Third Mind*, Gysin's and Burroughs's anthology of their literary experiments assembled in 1965, Gysin had already suggested that "Permutations" were valid poetry: "Permutations for 5 things, any 5, from the divine tautology 'I am that I am' to 5 pistol shots at a distance of 1 meter, 2 meters, 3 meters, 4 meters, 5 meters. Permutate them, and you have my 'Pistol Poem,' the most percussive of our time."[58] With the assistance of Ian Sommerville, who wrote a computer program for permutating word strings, Gysin published a number of permutations in *The Third Mind*, including "Junk Is No Good Baby," "Kick That Habit Man," "I Think Therefore I Am," "1 § ** 1 %," and "Rub Out The Word."[59] In 1982–83 Gysin worked with musician Ramuntcho Matta in taping jazz arrangements of his permutations and these, along with arrangements made after Gysin's death, were released as a recording in 1993.[60] With the exception of musical accompaniment (that would come later), Burroughs had been thinking along the same lines well before *The Third Mind*; in *Naked Lunch* he had written "The Word is divided into units which be all in one piece and should be so taken, but the pieces can be had in any order being tied up back and forth, in and out fore and aft like an innaresting sex arrangement. This book spill off the page in all directions."[61] Combining the cut-up technique with Gysin's permutations, Burroughs included a *hors-texte* page for *The Third Mind*. On it, beneath a paragraph of warning, a grid of forty-five rectangles contain from one to five lines of truncated phrases. Beneath this array Burroughs wrote in ink, "to be read every which way." Burroughs had previously published this page the year before in the small, mimeographed publication *My Own Mag* (4, no. 4 [1964]), edited by Jeff Nuttall.

Storm the Reality
and retake

35
Umberto Eco, "Ur-Fascism," *New York Review of Books* (June 22, 1995), 12.

36
Lydenberg, *Word Cultures* (note **15**), 10.

37
Samuel Beckett, "Ohio Impromptu," *Evergreen Review*, 98 (1984), 42.

38
Ibid., "What Where," 51.

39
Burroughs, *The Ticket That Exploded* (note **21**), 169–70.

40
Burroughs, *Naked Lunch* (note **5**), 221.

41
Knickerbocker, "Interview" (note **8**), 1.

42
William S. Burroughs, *My Education: A Book of Dreams* (New York: Viking Press, 1995), 49.

43
Burroughs, *Nova Express* (note **2**), 147–49.

44
Ibid., 4; Burroughs and Gysin are relatively inconsistent in their spelling and capitalization of "Hassan i Sabbah," while current scholarship prefers "Hasan-i Sabbah." I am thankful to the Islamicist Linda Komaroff for bringing this to my attention.

45
Susan Sontag, "The Aesthetics of Silence," in *Styles of Radical Will* (New York: Farrar, Straus and Giroux, 1969), 17–18; see also Lydenberg, *Word Cultures* (note **15**), 18.

46
Burroughs, *The Ticket That Exploded* (note **21**), 50. Please note that throughout this essay in quotations from Burroughs's writing ellipses are his and do not indicate an omission unless the ellipses are bracketed as in this quote, which indicates that I have omitted some of Burroughs's words.

47
Knickerbocker, "Interview" (note **8**), 6.

48
Burroughs, "Ten Years and a Billion Dollars," *The Adding Machine* (note **12**), 48.

49
See Judi Freeman, *The Dada and Surrealist Word-Image*, exh. cat. (Los Angeles: Los Angeles County Museum of Art, 1989), 14.

50
Filippo Tommaso Marinetti, "Geometric and Mechanical Splendor and the Numerical Sensibility," in *Marinetti: Selected Writings*, ed. R.W. Flint, trans. Flint and Arthur A. Coppotelli (New York: Farrar, Straus and Giroux, 1972), 100.

51
For the most exhaustive study of this subject, see *Poésure et peintrie: "D'un art, l'autre,"* exh. cat. (Paris and Marseilles: Réunion des Musées Nationaux, 1993).

52
Robert A. Sobieszek, "Erotic Photomontages: George Hugnet's *La septième face du dé*," *Dada/Surrealism* 9 (1979): 66–82.

53
William Carlos Williams, *Paterson* (New York: New Directions, 1992), 129–45.

54
Allen Ginsberg, "I Beg You Come Back and Be Cheerful," from *Kaddish*, in *Collected Poems: 1947–1980* (New York: Harper and Row, 1988), 237; Charles Olson, "Letter, May 2, 1959," from *The Maximus Poems*, in *Yugen* 6 (1960): 7–13.

55
See Philippe Castellin, "De la poésie restreinte à la poésie généralisée," and Jacinto Lageira, "Le poème du langage," in *Poésure et peintrie* (note **17**), 285–317, 318–33.

56
William S. Burroughs, "Wind Hand Caught in the Door," *Rhinozeros* 5 (1961): 25; a German translation by Anselm Hollo faces the text on page 24; cf. William S. Burroughs, *The Soft Machine* (New York: Grove Press, Evergreen edition, 1992), 178.

57
See *Astronauts of Inner Space: An International Collection of Avant-Garde Activity* (San Francisco: Stolen Paper Review Editions, 1966), 60.

58
Gysin, "Permutations," in Burroughs and Gysin, *The Third Mind* (note **8**), 84.

59
Ibid., 77–83; certain of these permutations first appeared in Beiles et al., *Minutes to Go* (note **13**).

60
Brion Gysin, *Self-Portrait Jumping* (1982–83) (Made to Measure [MTM 33 CD], 1993).

61
Burroughs, "Atrophied Preface," *Naked Lunch* (note **5**), 229.

Marcel Duchamp, **Rendez-vous du dimanche 6 février 1916 à 1 h. ¾ après-midi**, 1916, typescript on boards, 5¾ x 9½ in. (14.6 x 24.1 cm), Philadelphia Museum of Art, the Louise and Walter Arensberg Collection

Studio the universe.[62]

It is unclear whether Burroughs was familiar with Marcel Duchamp's text experiment of 1916, *Rendez-vous du dimanche 6 février 1916 à 1 h. ¾ après-midi*, presently in the Arensberg Collection at the Philadelphia Museum of Art. Like Burroughs's "To Be Read Every Which Way," Duchamp wrote arbitrary texts on the backs of four postcards and collected them into a grid. As an assembled text, there is little or no literal or logical meaning that can be deciphered. Duchamp had simply enjoyed juxtaposing elements of unrelated texts as he had done with writing and drawing in his *Boite de 1914*. In that work Duchamp utterly deconstructed not only linguistic syntax but the very process of writing itself. The words, according to the artist, have "no connection to each other":

Meaning in these sentences was a thing that I had to avoid...the verb was meant to be an abstract word acting on a subject that is a material object; in this way the verb would make the sentence look abstract. The construction was very painful in a way, because the minute I did think of a verb to add to the subject, I would very often see a meaning and immediately I saw a meaning I would cross out the verb and change it, until, working it out for quite a number of hours, the text finally read without any echo of the physical world.[63]

While Duchamp's *Rendez-vous* is listed in Robert Lebel's catalogue raisonné (published in Paris as *Sur Marcel Duchamp* in 1959), it is not illustrated or discussed. Nonetheless both Duchamp and Burroughs shatter the language-based concept of representing physical reality. Duchamp's writing "without any echo of the physical world" is remarkably congruent with Burroughs's militant attempts to free words from conforming to some imposed reality since, after all, "There is no real thing—Maya—Maya—It's all show business."[64]

Reality is no longer comfortably viewed as a wholistic singularity but rather as some "dynamic system of local, interdependent, self-updating movements, perceptions and gestures."[65] Futurist Heidi Toffler told an interviewer that "there are no facts. Everything is open to interpretation."[66] "Nothing Is True," Burroughs said some thirty years before, "Everything Is Permitted."[67] That the laws of classical thermodynamics no longer hold in the late twentieth century, that Cartesian logic might not be capable of determining the correct response, that instead of scientific certainty there is an "Uncertainty Principle" and "Chaos Theory," and that any cosmology or metaphysics suggesting anything approaching definitiveness is largely suspect—none of this is especially newsworthy or revolutionary, especially to anyone alive, reading, looking, or listening since the early 1960s. Writers and artists have been articulating these ideas for decades, most especially Burroughs. Traditional narrative and a single-point perspective were the first armatures of representation to be discarded in confronting a new, discontinuous, and tangential world, followed by classic plots, orderly temporal coherence, logical progression, and the single voice of the author. In their place were substituted montaged story lines, multiple points of view, kaleidoscopic perspectives, intersections of past, present, and future and disparate voices—in other words, all the aleatory techniques that Burroughs came to utilize in the early 1960s.

Perhaps Gysin was correct in 1959. Literature had taken some time to catch up with the visual arts, but it certainly had by the following decade. The abandonment of logical discourse and single-point representation dominated writing and films during the 1960s, roughly a half-century after Picasso and Braque were collaging newspaper strips onto to their cubist paintings. To be sure, the origins of Burroughs's and Gysin's techniques can be found in early modernism: Lautrémont's sudden juxtapositions of wildly dissimilar objects; the drastic dislocations and displacements in Rimbaud's *Drunken Boat*; Joyce's interweaving of disparate monologues and sets of memory in *Ulysses* or his deconstruction and re-creation of language and history in *Finnegans Wake*; the often violent montages of early Eisenstein and Pudovkin films; Ezra Pound's conflations of cultures both ancient and new; the disjointed tableaux in André Breton's poems and Luis Buñuel's cinema; John Dos Passos's blurring of dreams and reality through the "Camera Eye" sections of *U.S.A.*; and Antonin Artaud's attempt to create a theater in which continuity is fractured and language is mutilated.[68] Even the various quotes, cribbings, and appropriations in T. S. Eliot's *The Waste Land* function as alternative texts, voices, and points of view; and both Burroughs and Gysin have pointed to him as an early practitioner of the cut-up technique.[69]

possible transfer them to more socially acceptable areas within the passenger compartment. The steering assembly has been selected as a suitable focus for sexual arousal.

The planes of her face, like the

THE AROUSAL potential of automobile styling has been widely examined for several decades by the automotive industry. However, in the study under consideration involving 152 subjects, all known to have experienced more than three involuntary orgasms with their automobiles, the car of preference was found to be (1) Buick Riviera, (2) Chrysler Imperial, (3) Chevrolet Impala. However, a small minority (2 subjects) expressed a significant preference for the Lincoln Continental, if possible in the adapted Presidential version. (Q.v. conspiracy theories). Both subjects had purchased cars of this make and experienced continuing erotic fantasies in connection with the trunk mouldings. Both had a strong unconscious identification with the figure of Oswald and preferred the automobile inclined on a downward ramp.

cars of the abandoned motorcade

CINE-FILMS as group therapy. Patients were encouraged to form a film production unit, and were given full freedom as to choice of subject matter, cast and technique. In all cases explicitly pornographic films were made. Two films in particular were examined: (1) A montage sequence using portions of the faces of (a) Madame Ky, (b) Jeanne Moreau, (c) Jacqueline Kennedy (Johnson oath-taking). The use of a concealed stroboscopic device produced a major optical flutter in the audience, culminating in psychomotor disturbances and aggressive attacks directed against the still photographs of the subjects hung from the walls of the theatre. (2) A film of automobile accidents devised as a cinematic version of Nader's "Unsafe at Any Speed." By chance it was found that slow-motion sequences of this film had a marked sedative effect, reducing

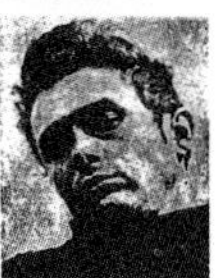
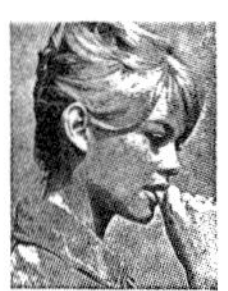
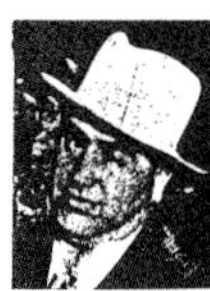

Homage to Abraham Zaprudar: at what point does the plane of intersection of these faces and the cleavage of Jacqueline Kennedy generate a valid image of the glazed eyes of Chiang Kai Shek, an invasion plan of the offshore islands?

10

J. G. Ballard, page from "Plan for the Assassination of Jacqueline Kennedy," from **Ambit** 31, 1966/67

Attempts to destroy traditional narrative structures and to create new structures reflective of modern experience increased considerably during the 1960s. Daniel J. Boorstein, the librarian of Congress, following to a degree the earlier writings of Walter Benjamin, detailed as early as 1961 how the "graphic revolution" and its technologies had "produced a new fluidity in all experience."[70] Characters in Alain Robbe-Grillet's *L'année dernière à Marienbad* (*Last Year in Marienbad*; 1961) seem to slip through various shifting locations, times, and events. In *Ficciones*, published by Grove Press in 1962, Jorge Luis Borges inverts history and authorship and calls for an "interpolation of chance into the order of the world."[71] There is a decided lack of focus and endless fragmentation in Margaret Duras's *Le ravissement de Lol V. Stein* (*The Ravishing of Lol V. Stein*; 1964). In 1963 Michel Foucault proposed an infinite language of mirrors, self-images, analogies.[72] The protagonist in Michelangelo Antonioni's *Blowup* (1966) is caught in an epistemological dilemma where what is experienced can no longer be ascertained. In 1963 the author of the short story "Blowup," Julio Cortazar, offered the reader of his novel *Rayuela* (*Hopscotch*) a seemingly random sequence of chapters by which to read the book and wrote that "the schoolbook chemistry point of view has been turned inside out."[73] British novelist J. G. Ballard's *The Atrocity Exhibition*, a "condensed novel" constructed in the form of a series of "related or apparently unrelated snapshots," began appearing in *New Worlds* and *Ambit* in 1966.[74] In 1967 Emmett Williams defined concrete poetry as one that "often asked to be completed or activated by the reader."[75] In the same year, the Italian writer Umberto Eco characterized "*cogito interruptus*" as that which requires "symbols and symptoms be flung by the handful, like confetti, and not lined up, bookkeeper style, like little balls on an abacus."[76] In 1964 Roland Barthes defensively argued that everything is language in his *Eléments de sémiologie* (*Elements of Semiology*), while in the same year Susan Sontag declared that content in modern art is "mainly a hindrance, a nuisance, a subtle or not so subtle philistinism."[77]

Futurist Marshall McLuhan wrote in 1963 about the post-Gutenberg world of communication and pointed to the revolutionary change brought about by electronic media. In place of the "visual" organization of conventional thinking and the "linearity" of traditional language and writing, a new kind of "auditory space" had been substituted:

> Television, radio and the newspaper (at the point where it was linked with the telegraph) deal in *auditory space*, by which I mean that sphere of simultaneous relations created by the act of hearing. We hear from all directions at once; this creates a unique, unvisualizable space. The all-at-once-ness of auditory space is the exact opposite of lineality, of taking one thing at a time. It is very confusing to learn that the mosaic of a newspaper page is 'auditory' in basic structure. This, however, is only to say that any pattern in which the components co-exist without direct lineal hook-up or connection, creating a field of simultaneous relations, is auditory, even though some of its aspects can be seen. The items of news and advertising that exist under a newspaper dateline are interrelated only by that dateline. They have no interconnection of logic or statement. Yet they form a mosaic or corporate image whose parts are interpenetrating. Such is also the kind of order that tends to exist in a city or a culture. It is a kind of orchestral, resonating unity, not the unity of logical discourse.[78]

J. G. Ballard, who critically defended Burroughs in Great Britain, understood that the cut-up method was the best tool for addressing the "recurrent images in all communication, fixed at the points of contact in the webs of language linking everything in our lives," and characterized Burroughs's novels as "terminal documents of the mid-20th century… a progress report from an inmate in the cosmic madhouse."[79]

Ballard felt an affinity with Burroughs's techniques and characterized the fractured aspects of our cosmic madhouse (along the same lines as McLuhan had) when he said, "Burroughs's narrative techniques, or my own in their way, would be an immediately recognizable reflection of the way life is actually experienced. We live in quantified non-linear terms—we switch on television sets, switch them off half an hour later, speak on the telephone, read magazines, dream and so forth. We don't live our lives in linear terms in the sense that the Victorians did."[80] Burroughs has often stated much the same in his writings, and he summarized the matter quite laconically in *The Soft Machine* when he wrote "the whole structure of reality went up in silent explosions."[81] Following the Nova explosion, all the fragments of reality were falling in *The Ticket That Exploded*: words, photos, time, crab words, virus photos, flakes, bodies, dead postcards, photomontage fragments, sound and image flakes, flesh, images, "love," sex words, the nova dream itself, and all the tapes were blank. In such a situation linearity, homogeneity, and a single point of view hardly pertain. We now call such a cultural environment "cyberspace," where perceptual windows onto a coherent and unified world have been sundered and replaced by a "multi-threading," "memory addressing," and fluid arrangement of unparallel, multi-tasking "Windows."

62
Burroughs, *The Soft Machine* (note **56**), 151–52.

63
Marcel Duchamp, quoted in Arturo Schwarz, *The Complete Works of Marcel Duchamp* (New York: Harry N. Abrams, 1970), 457.

64
Burroughs, *The Ticket That Exploded* (note **21**), 76–77.

65
Jonathan Crary and Sanford Kwinter, "Foreword," *Incorporations, Zone* 6 (New York: Zone Books, 1992), 12–13.

66
Heidi Toffler, in Claudia Dreifus, "Present Shock," *New York Times Magazine* (June 11, 1995), 50.

67
Burroughs, *Nova Express* (note **2**), 147–49.

68
See Susan Sontag, "Artaud," in Antonin Artaud, *Selected Writings*, ed. Susan Sontag, trans. Helen Weaver (New York: Farrar, Straus and Giroux, 1976), xxxvi.

69
Knickerbocker, "Interview" (note **8**), 3; and Gysin and Wilson, *Here to Go* (note **14**), 49.

70
Daniel J. Boorstein, *The Image: A Guide to Pseudo-Events in America* (New York: Atheneum, 1987), 168.

71
Jorges Luis Borges, "The Babylon Lottery," in *Ficciones*, ed. Anthony Kerrigan (New York: Grove Press, 1962), 69.

72
Michel Foucault, "Language to Infinity," in *Language, Counter-Memory, Practice: Selected Essays and Interviews by Michel Foucault*, ed. and trans. Donald F. Bouchard and Sherry Simon (Ithaca: Cornell University Press, 1977), 67.

73
Julio Cortázar, *Hopscotch*, trans. Gregory Rabassa (New York: New American Library, 1967), 351.

74
Edward James, *Science Fiction in the 20th Century* (Oxford: Oxford University Press, 1994), 170–71. Chapter 10, "Plan for the Assassination of Jacqueline Kennedy," originally appeared in *Ambit* 31 (1966/67): 9–11, illustrated with portraits of James Dean, Brigitte Bardot, and Jack Ruby taken from newspapers; these illustrations are left out in the Jonathan Cape edition of 1970 and in the extra-illustrated Re/Search Classics edition of 1990.

75
Emmett Williams, "Foreword and Acknowledgments," *An Anthology of Concrete Poetry* (New York: Something Else Press, 1967), vi.

76
Umberto Eco, "Cogito Interruptus," *Travels in Hyperreality* (New York: Harcourt Brace Jovanovich, 1986), 223.

77
Susan Sontag, "Against Interpretation," *Against Interpretation and Other Essays* (New York: Farrar, Straus and Giroux, 1964), 5.

78
Marshall McLuhan, "The Agenbite of Outwit," *Location* 1, no. 1 (1963); reprinted in John Cage et al., *Rolywholyover: A Circus*, exh. cat. (Los Angeles: Museum of Contemporary Art, 1993), unp. McLuhan had already pointed out that with computers the myth of a "homogeneity of mental states" resulting from print technologies could be replaced by "every possible variety of sense ratio"; see Marshall McLuhan, *The Gutenberg Galaxy* (Toronto: University of Toronto Press, 1962), 183. The paragraph in which McLuhan argues this point was considered for reprinting in the planned but abandoned Grove Press edition of *The Third Mind* of 1970; see William S. Burroughs and Brion Gysin, "The Third Mind," unpublished mss. and mechanicals, Los Angeles County Museum of Art, 183.

79
J. G. Ballard, "Mythmaker of the 20th Century," *New Worlds* 142 (May 1964); reprinted in V. Vale and Andrea Juno, eds., *J. G. Ballard, Re/Search* 8/9 (1984): 105–7; see also J. G. Ballard, "Terminal Documents," *Ambit* 27 (1966): 46–48.

80
J. G. Ballard, interview by George MacBeth, BBC, February 1, 1967, quoted in Vale and Juno, *J. G. Ballard* (note **79**), 160.

81
Burroughs, *The Soft Machine* (note **56**), 160.

You never take a picture of the present but always of the future.[82]

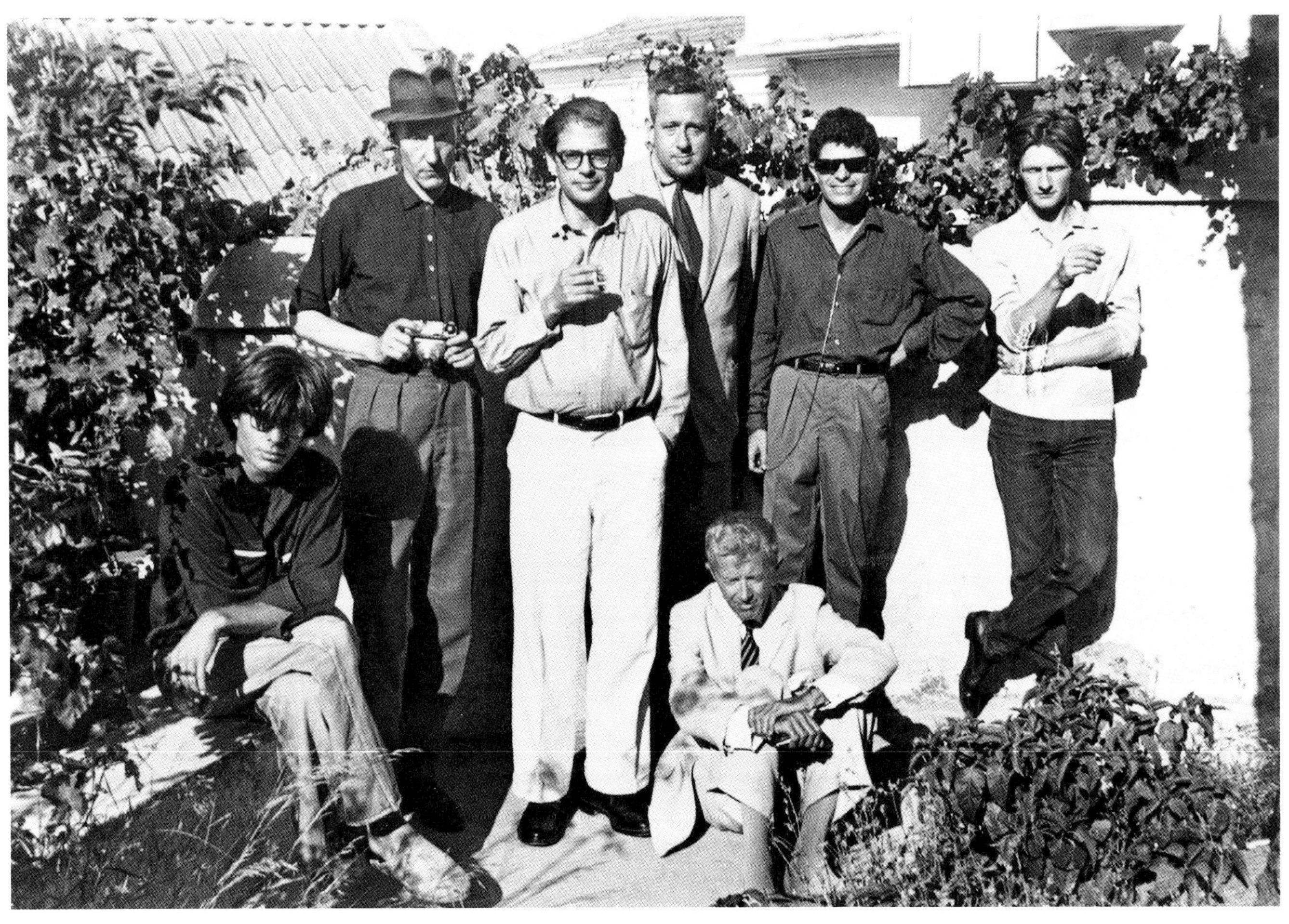

Allen Ginsberg, **Burroughs and Friends, Hotel Muniria, Tangiers**, 1961, cat. no. 97

IV

ANY OLD PHOTO WILL

Among the Allen Ginsberg papers there is a photograph (most likely shot by Gysin but directed by Ginsberg) of seven writers posing in the garden of the Hotel Muniria in Tangiers in 1961: Peter Orlovsky, Burroughs, Ginsberg, Alan Ansen, Gregory Corso, Ian Sommerville, and Paul Bowles (on the ground).[83] Besides the ubiquitous fedora, what distinguishes Burroughs from the others is the simple fact he is holding a 35-mm camera in his hands, the only one of these writers to carry an instrument for making images instead of words and narrative. Grauerholz mentions that Burroughs took snapshots while traveling in South America as early as 1953 and that he made a number of collages out of his snapshots during the 1950s.[84] By the time *Naked Lunch* was being assembled in the spring of 1957, according to Gysin, Burroughs was taping his photos together into a large collage on the wall.[85] Throughout the 1960s and 1970s Burroughs experimented with photography and photomontage, used newspaper clippings as negatives, and utilized mirrors to infinitely expand the photograph through reflections. In 1934 Man Ray suggested that new forms of art required the artist to radically reassess whatever medium he or she used when he wrote that "a certain amount of contempt for the material employed to express an idea is indispensable to the purest realization of this idea."[86] By cutting, splicing, overpainting, embedding, fracturing, degenerating the photographic materials he makes or incorporates, Burroughs certainly has created new forms by a degree of contempt for and violation of the photographic medium. As with words, so with images.

The subject of photography appears throughout Burroughs's writings, embodied in such characters as "Jimenez or 'Jimmy the Take,' photographer" in *The Soft Machine*; "Fred Flash from St Louis. Photographer" in *The Wild Boys*; and "Tom D. Dark, Traveling Photographer" in *The Place of Dead Roads*. Moreover, in a dream he had involving his lover Mikey Portman, Burroughs asserted, "We are photographs and we will turn everyone else into photographs."[87] Ginsberg relates that in the early 1960s Burroughs was fascinated with photographing a color field such as the sky, then rephotographing the photograph, and repeating the process a number of times in order to arrive at an ultimate distillation and abstraction of the subject's color, which in the instance of the sky was blue.[88] In *Nova Express* the color blue is the color of junk. "Take a sick junky," Burroughs wrote,

> **Throw blue light on his so-called face or dye it blue or dye the junk blue it don't make no difference and now give him a shot and photograph the blue miracle as life pours back into that walking corpse—That will give you the image track of junk—Now project the blue change onto your own face if you want The Big Fix.**[89]

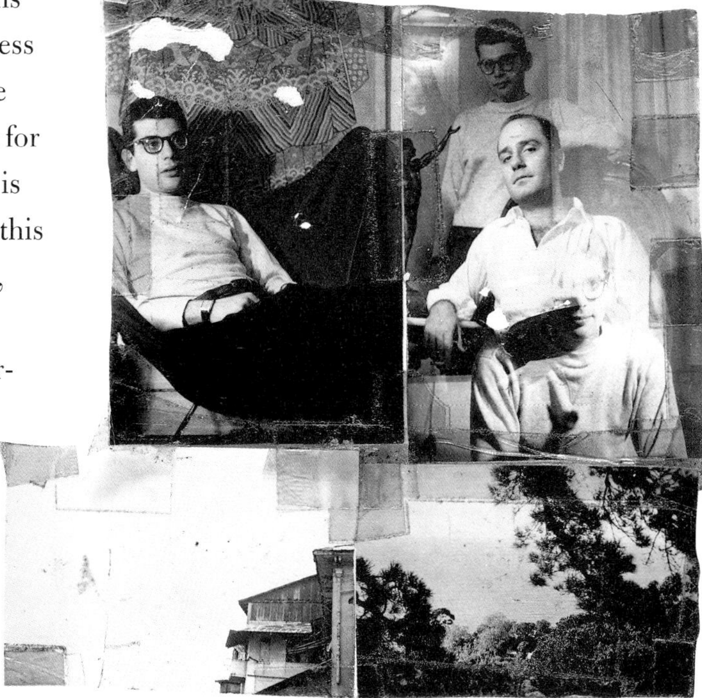

William S. Burroughs, untitled [Allen Ginsberg], c. 1954, cat. no. 3

Furthermore, blue is the color Burroughs associates with orgones, claimed by psychologist Wilhelm Reich to be the units of life's energy, which "have been photographed and the color is blue."[90]

For Burroughs, the photographic image was just that, an image, and on a par with the word. It is just as viral and dangerous as any word. "Here is the progression," he wrote in *The Third Mind*:

> **Words, glyphs, drawing or painting expansion of the glyphs into a Gysin picture or, you can do the same, of course, with any photo proliferating virus-wise, the way any old photo will...And, inasmuch as any vision and especially the vision of an artist presents itself in the form of an image—preferably a youth of blinding beauty...such frivolous neural patterns have been, of course, installed by the Word & Image Mob.**[91]

The precise progression described here is not absolute, however, since it implies that words came before image as in "In the beginning was the word." Burroughs completely understands that words are coeval with images as in Egyptian hieroglyphics or Chinese ideograms.[92] After all, "What is word?—Maya—Maya—Illusion—Rub out the word and the

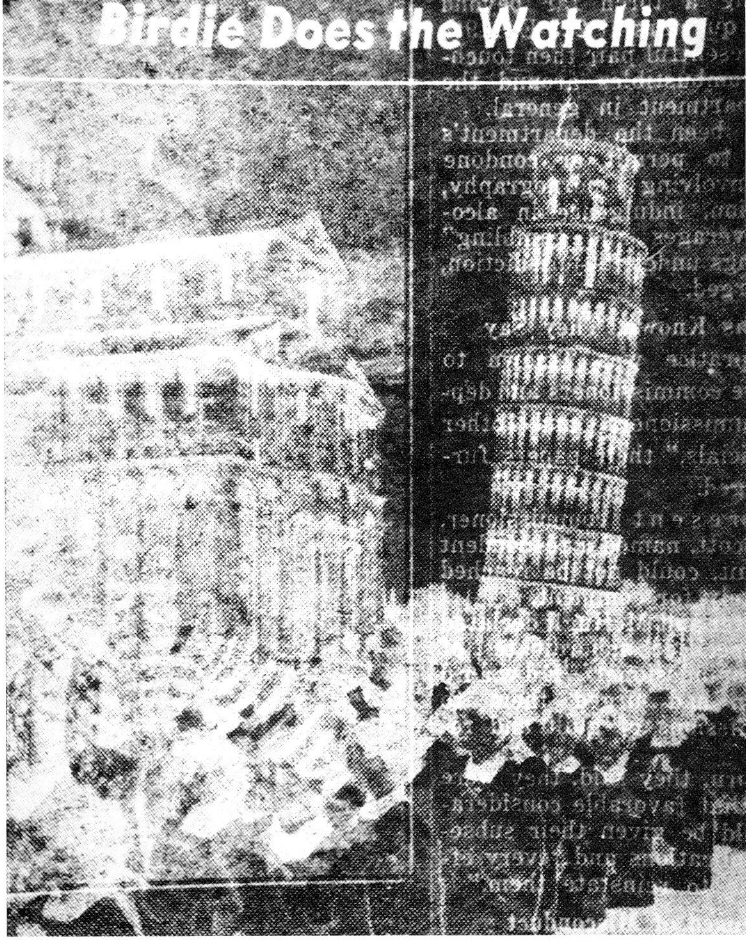

William S. Burroughs, **Birdie Does the Watching**, c. 1964, cat. no. 5

William S. Burroughs, **Sturdy Steel Snap-Tight** (diptych), 1964, cat. no. 6

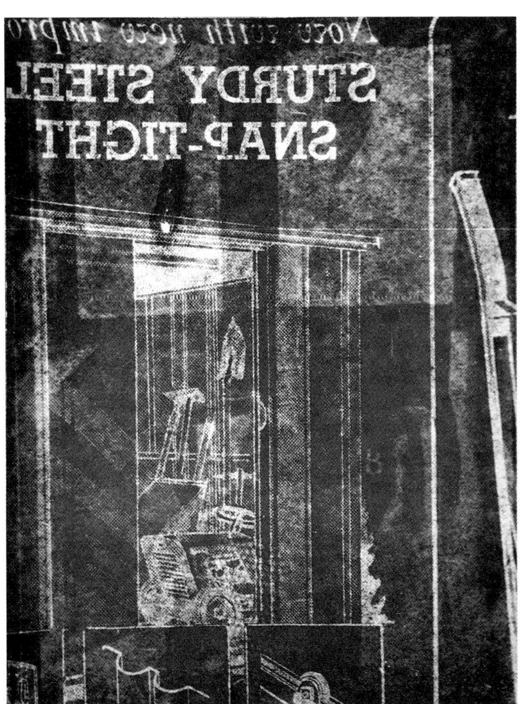

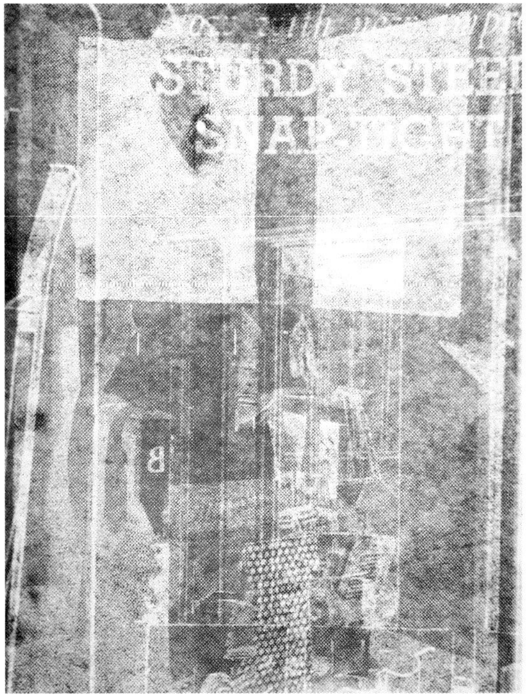

image track goes with it—[....]Image is trapped in word."[93] In some of his early photo experiments, done around 1964, Burroughs played with the idea of destroying both word and image tracks by having portions of newspaper pages used as negatives. In *Birdie Does the Watching* and *Sturdy Steel Snap-Tight* the partial texts and image fragments found on both the front and back of the newsprint are visually conflated, all distinctions, meanings, and readings blurred. At the end of the decade, photographic artist Robert Heinecken would use a similar tactic in commenting upon the contemporary, multilayered media culture of the late twentieth century. For Burroughs it was a matter of articulating something far more basic: "Image is trapped in word."

Time travel and escaping the limits of time have been and remain of vital concern for Burroughs. So is the inextricable control exerted over us by the media, among others the industry of Time/Life Incorporated. Like many writers and artists during the 1960s, Burroughs targeted both time and *Time* as a subject. Burroughs detailed how journalism was closer to the "magical origins of writing than most fiction" and that its technology, especially in newspapers and magazines, was best described as black magic:

They stick pins in someone's image and then show that image to millions of people. You can see how easy it is, if you own a newspaper, to start slipping in non-existent events; this has been and is being done all the time—by TIME especially, in fact. Starting with being a week ahead, they literally write the news before it happens; which is why they print so many false statements that they have to retract.[94]

In 1969 Heinecken manipulated actual copies of one issue of *Time* magazine, overprinting each of its pages with an image of some atrocity photograph from Vietnam or some sexually explicit image and returning the copies to the newsstand from which he purchased them.

I think there's going to be more and more merging of art and science. Scientists are studying the creative process, and I think the whole line between art and science will break down and that scientists, I hope, will become more creative and writers more scientific. And I see no reason why the artistic world can't absolutely merge with Madison Avenue. Pop art is a move in that direction. Why can't we have advertisement with beautiful words and beautiful images? Already some of very beautiful color photography appears in whiskey ads, I notice. Science will also discover for us how association blocks actually form.

<u>**The Third Mind**</u>

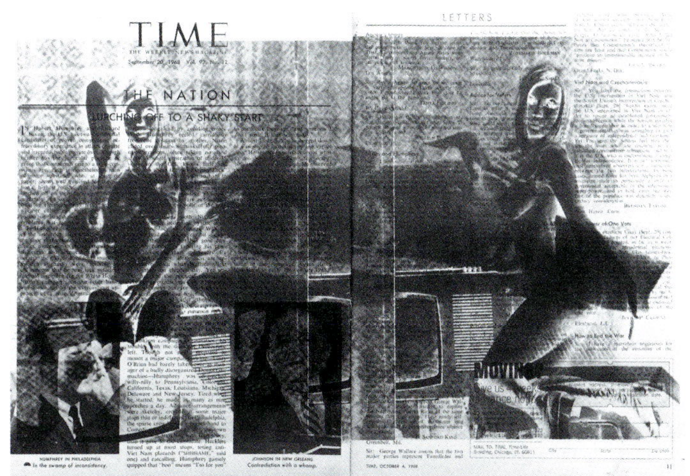

Robert Heinecken, **Time Magazine**, 1969, magazine pages altered by offset lithographic overprinting, 11 x 16 in. (27.9 x 40.6 cm), courtesy the artist and Fahey/Klein Gallery, Los Angeles

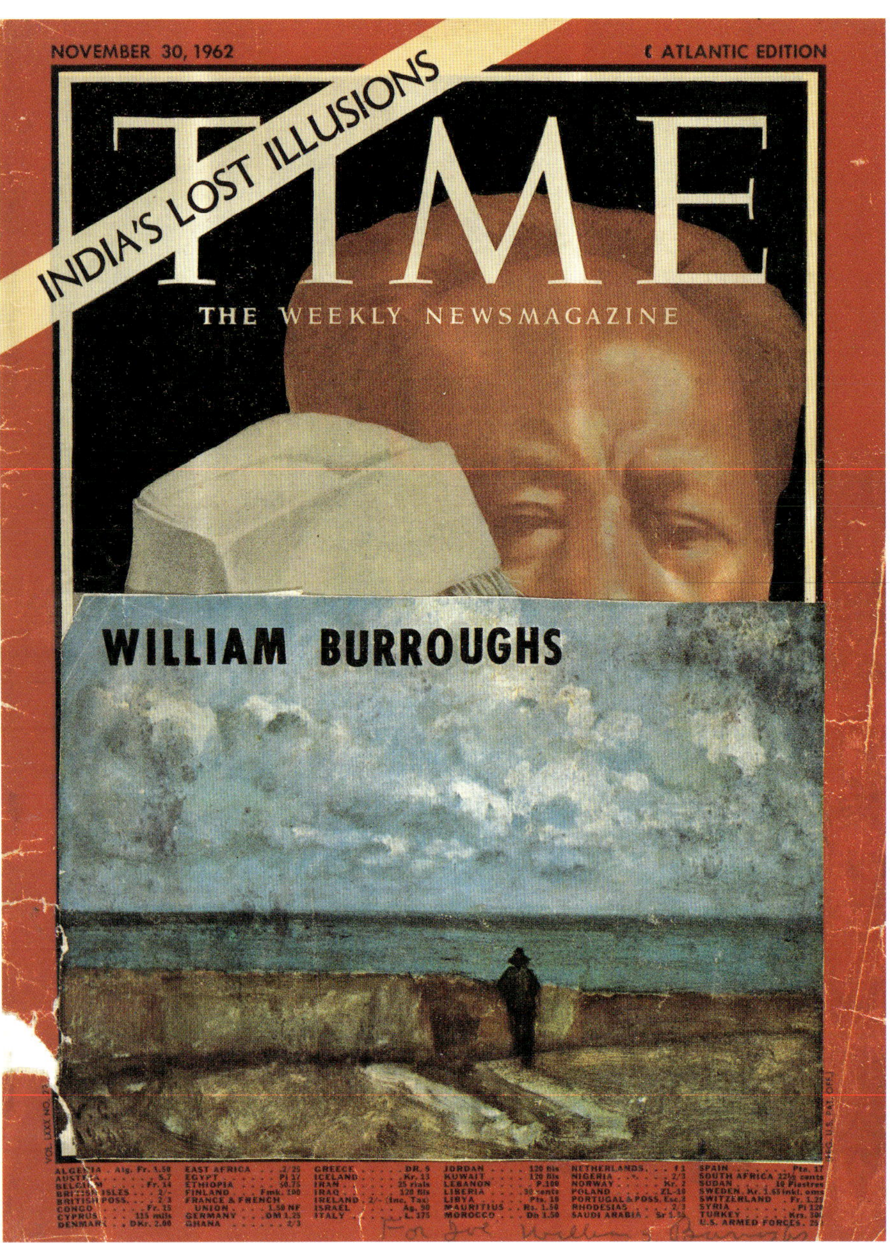

William S. Burroughs, **Time**, 1965, cat. no. 7

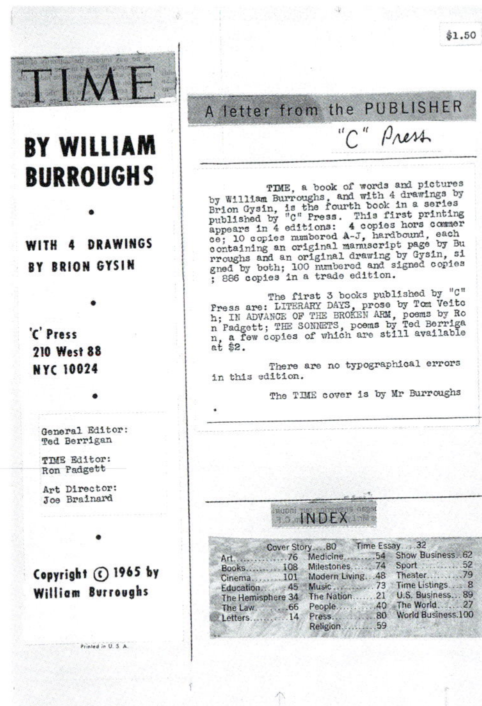

$1.50

TIME

BY WILLIAM BURROUGHS

•

WITH 4 DRAWINGS BY BRION GYSIN

•

'C' Press
210 West 88
NYC 10024

•

General Editor:
Ted Berrigan

TIME Editor:
Ron Padgett

Art Director:
Joe Brainard

•

Copyright © 1965 by William Burroughs

Printed in U. S. A.

A letter from the PUBLISHER

"C" Press

TIME, a book of words and pictures by William Burroughs, and with 4 drawings by Brion Gysin, is the fourth book in a series published by "C" Press. This first printing appears in 4 editions: 4 copies hors commer ce; 10 copies numbered A-J, hardbound, each containing an original manuscript page by Bu rroughs and an original drawing by Gysin, si gned by both; 100 numbered and signed copies ; 886 copies in a trade edition.

The first 3 books published by "C" Press are: LITERARY DAYS, prose by Tom Veitc h; IN ADVANCE OF THE BROKEN ARM, poems by Ro n Padgett; THE SONNETS, poems by Ted Berriga n, a few copies of which are still available at $2.

There are no typographical errors in this edition.

The TIME cover is by Mr Burroughs

INDEX

William S. Burroughs, untitled, collage for **Time**, 1965, 12 x 9½ in. (30.5 x 24.1 cm), collection of Joseph Zinnato, Burbank

William S. Burroughs, **Proclaim Present Time Over.Claim Present.Pro Time Over and Doble on Sunday**, collage for **Time**, 1965, cat. no. 8

the darkness, and cries of pain mingled she entered the university. By early this very personal thing and my personal

PROCLAIM PRESENT TIME OVER.CLAIM PRESENT.PRO TIME OVER AND DOBLE ON SUNDAY

Sunday March I,1964

back numbers of the Tan
ger Gazette and call it
Hongkong Bar.Its all made
e in Hongkong.Clom Flid
ay for your newsmagasine
I Sekuin perfected that
art along the Tang Dyn-
asty kicking the gong
around the Chink laudry
laundry you CAN PAPER
A WALL WITH THE DEAD
STAR brings the old bank
Jews used to be open Sun
ays 'Where you from Mar-
kesh? You like beeg one
son bitch bastard I ketc
h one clap from fucky
your ass hole/' '/Well
let's face it boys he
does'nt want his picture
taken but perhaps we
can persuade him to pose
for the nice press gentle
mens with gun and camera
/' said the wise cop one.
of those funy bastards
in every precinct: /How
you like a little heroin
Bill?/' which you better
think is funy and answer
up like a good Nigger:
'Yawsah boss I sure woul
d like some of that white
sugar Looks like I'll
haveta wait till they
burns me now'
The pig faced white lash
ed klieutenant looked up
from his books: '/They
cut out these execution
shots.Ruling just came
through from the Capital.
/' '/We were getting en
tirely too many 'executi
on addicts' dumped in our
laps'/' said a highly
placed narcotics depart-
ments officials '/The
ruling is retroactive re
calling all execution
shots/' '/Its a long way
to young English soldier
this is the fourth lesson
I "2 3 4 flickering fing
ers sweating last human

(Continued P.4 Col.I)

(Continued P.4 col.2)

sat in moulding who
moulding the chair you
er olf word columns
back in yesterdays pap
pre-sent time now move
the so called future in
or inother words we tak
and knew how to hang it
had a peg to hang it on
es will be there if you
out and take the picture
continuity then you go

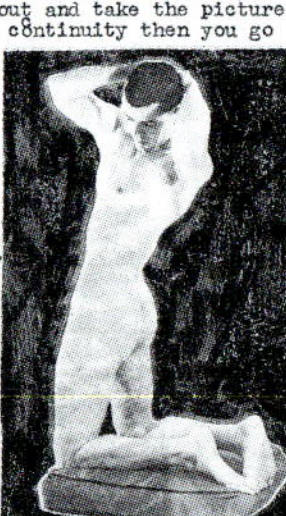

ere.First you write the
just time wrote it ther
picture just there.??
ina news paper.Why that
Now consider the picture
through word columns.Now
as you move back in time
orgetting' present time
the page.The page is 'f
less of present time on
e you do this there is
and so on back.Each tim
selections from yesterday
maining two columns with
ings.Now fill in the re
with cross column reading
column on another page

was open Sundays sitt
ing there ina smoky pa
per sun set waiting on
teh Japanesegirl a soft
knock and I open the
door naked with a hard
on - it was the top
floor all the way up
you understand nobdoy
nobody on that land-ing
'/Oooooh'she says feel
ing itup to my oysters
a drop of lubricant
squeezed out and toke
a smoky sun set on rose
wall paer I'd been
lying there naked think
ing about what we were
going to do in the
rocking chair rocks
off down the line.She
could get out of her
clothes faster than a
junky can fix when his
blood is right so we
rocked away into the
sun set across the riv
er just before blast
off that old knock on
the door and shoot thi
is fear load like I
never feel it wind up i
is her young brother
at the door in his cop
suit been watching thr
ough the key hole and
learn about the birds
& bee some bee in th-
ose days I was good
looking kid had all
teeth she set the
scene up you understan
d she knew all the sex
currents goose for
[illegible] pimple always
made her entrance when
your nuts are tight
and aching ice towles
lowels suspension the
lot.There was a little
storage room where
we rigged up a Japanes
e e Gym strictly from
Yokahma [illegible]

(Continued P.4.col33)

The Fliday Newsmagasine? No glot,Clom Fliday

Fliday March I3,I964

tant closing sugar bowl
train whistles to a dis
Sad back porch of dreams
down 'Cobble Stone Cody'
"Stepped you the Piper
"All The Sad Old Showmen?
I899 over New York.
answer drew 'September I7
From his gun a rusty
"The Last Post"?
desk cool remote Sunday.
ir papers on the city
Freshh southerly winds st-
"The Boy's Magasine"?
Mister."

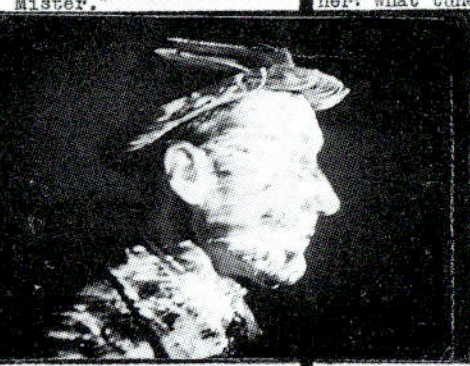

"Never called retreat,
"Annie Laurie?"
in last review:
the old files new stand-
freckles folded away in
cold on the thin boy with
porch falling leaves sun
from an old calander back
pieces faded sepia smile
page 3 column I./"
aim and fire/ Carry on
the coordinates precisely
target unless you plot
guns will not reach the
trget taget target.The
five years to reach the
times take fifty sixty
gunpost.The bullets some
r is a machine gun in a
esent time.Your tyepwrite
lets get this show in pr
of the Shakespeare Squad
"/All right you jokers

you were, 'you'? 'Were'?
::words.
I spentnsix months in th
e morgue.I made time map
s of the city.'Where the
second hand book shop
used to be right opposite
the old cemetary.' What
did the streets you walk
look like yesterday a
month ago a year ago?
What store what building
was there that is'nt the
re now?What was thw weat
her? What tunes were on
TV radio
juke box
music hall? Pre
carious st-
reets of
yesterday
recreated
pice by pie
ce in old
newspaers
old pictur
es old tun
es.
The next
step was
carried ou
t in a fil
m studio.I learned to
talk and think backwards
on all levels.This was
done by running film and
sound track backwards.
For example orgasm film
was run backwards in
slow motion (sex is of
course one of the heavie
st ankors holding one in
present time).Day after
day I watched the old
flickering back to silen
ce: unknown evenings and
strange memories cigarett
e smoke curling in black
pubic hairs piples of li
ght along naked thighs
slow blur of picture fl-
esh and there was Al Jol
son do you see this lea
ther lunger Jew bellowin
g out "Maaammy" and bar

(Continued P.5 Col.2)

(Continued P.5,Col 3)

around you.Black jack
St Louis Illinois she is
Yale.You walk in East
that was open the girl's
She named a price and
deputy waers 'ear muffe
is dead.Kindaspecial
g that old knack.Klinker
conditions of ash? I twi
bourne Grove.Smell those
by magic shop in West-
Johnny Law just happens
see this hand lifted?
citizen came up on her.
agent call.Recall John
about that cold outside
iness) Nobody thought
old birds and bees bus
come around with the ol
eavy and cold as a cop's
t the birds.(Her eyes
ch unless I browned abou
his cop suit been a pin
see standing there in
talked business/' You
ed you last time you
goes on Jew Corner.Nick
ght: '/ Maybe something
her cold returning thou
kept the guide ready
a wise guy.Mary she
ing universe. This is
son map his own fuck
steal.Meet this Johnson
thievs but anything
job hot and heavy.Young
doing my simple artisan
on the Japanese girl
ing in a Turner sun set
cool off.Like I was sitt
Picasso on Rembrandt and
Period. Or maybe you
safe behind the Blue
Klace waits for me wall
ing where a diamond nec
chauffeur map indicate
a disgruntled former
I meet this Johnson has
down to Marty's where
the girl left I walk
[illegible]. After
[illegible]
[illegible]
[illegible]or
[illegible]s

William S. Burroughs, **The Fliday Newsmagazine? No Glot.Clom Fliday.**, collage for **Time**, 1965, cat. no. 9

William S. Burroughs, untitled, collage for **Time**, 1965, 12 x 9½ in. (30.5 x 24.1 cm), collection of Joseph Zinnato, Burbank

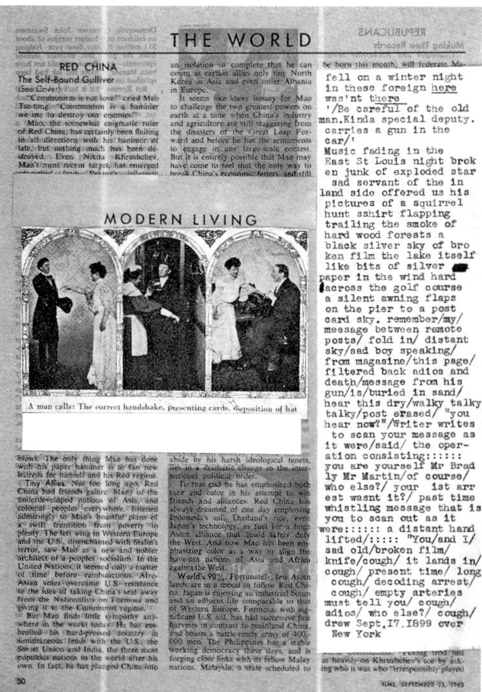

Similarly, in a unpublished typescript, artist Robert Smithson deconstructed an entire issue of *Look* and conjoined product advertisements, news stories, and photographs into a literary collage.[95]

Nova Criminals monopolize immortality, cosmic consciousness, love, sex, dreams, as well as "Life Time and Fortune." Always be skeptical, if not exactly cynical, Burroughs urges, "Inquire onward from the state to doer." After taking everything that is yours, he asks, will they give it back? "Did they ever give anything away for nothing? Did they ever give any more than they had to give? Did they not always take back what they gave when possible and it always was? *Listen*: Their Garden of Delights is a terminal sewer."[96] Before total destruction, before Nova, a defensive strategy needed to be in place: "Wise up all the marks everywhere. Show them the rigged wheel of Life-Time-Fortune. Storm The Reality Studio."[97] In 1965 Burroughs created his own version of *Time* magazine, including a *Time* cover of November 30, 1962, collaged over by Burroughs with a reproduction of a drawing, four drawings by Gysin, and twenty-six pages of typescripts comprised of cut-up texts and various photographs serving as news items. One of the pages is from an article on Red China from *Time* of September 13, 1963, and is collaged with a columnal typescript and an irrelevant illustration from the "Modern Living" section of the magazine. A full-page advertisement for Johns-Manville products is casually inserted amid all these texts; its title: "Filtering."[98] Three decades later, it has become quite obvious that all information if not all of reality has become premediated, filtered, and indeed controlled by the media. "If you are barely middle-aged," wrote Italian novelist Umberto Eco in 1977, "you will have learned personally the extent to which experience (love, fear, or hope) is filtered through 'already seen' images."[99] And one of the aliases under which Nova Criminals operate in Burroughs's fiction happens to be the "Word & Image Mob."

82
William S. Burroughs, "Old Photographer," *The Burroughs File* (San Francisco: City Lights Books, 1984), 122.

83
Illustrated in Morgan, *Literary Outlaw* (note **7**), between 276 and 277.

84
Grauerholz, "On Burroughs' Art" (note **24**), v.

85
Gysin, "Cut-ups," in Burroughs and Gysin, *The Third Mind* (note **8**), 43. Whether Gysin actually visited Burroughs's room at the Hotel Muniria while Ansen, Ginsberg, and Kerouac worked to put the manuscript of *Naked Lunch* together in April 1957 is unclear.

86
Man Ray, "The Age of Light," in *Photographs by Man Ray: 105 Works, 1920–1934* (New York: Dover Publications, 1979), unp.

87
Burroughs, *The Soft Machine* (note **56**), 86; *The Wild Boys: A Book of the Dead* (New York: Grove Press, Evergreen edition, 1992), 94; *The Place of Dead Roads* (note **28**), 83; and *My Education* (note **42**), 18.

88
In conversation with the author, March 6, 1995; these photographs have not been located.

89
Burroughs, *Nova Express* (note **2**), 9 n.

90
Ibid.

91
Burroughs, "Hieroglyphic Silence," in Burroughs and Gysin, *The Third Mind* (note **8**), 192.

92
See Miles, *William Burroughs* (note **25**), 169–70.

93
Burroughs, *The Ticket That Exploded* (note **21**), 145.

94
Burroughs, "Ten Years and a Billion Dollars," *The Adding Machine* (note **12**), 49.

95
See Robert Smithson, "Look" (1970), in *Robert Smithson: The Collected Writings*, ed. Jack Flam (Berkeley: University of California Press, 1996), 370.

96
Burroughs, *Nova Express* (note **2**), 5–6.

97
Ibid., 59.

98
William S. Burroughs, *Time* (New York: 'C' Press, 1965).

99
Umberto Eco, "A Photograph," *Travels in Hyperreality*, trans. William Weaver (New York: Harcourt Brace Jovanovich, 1986), 214.

But, like: <u>anything</u> is image

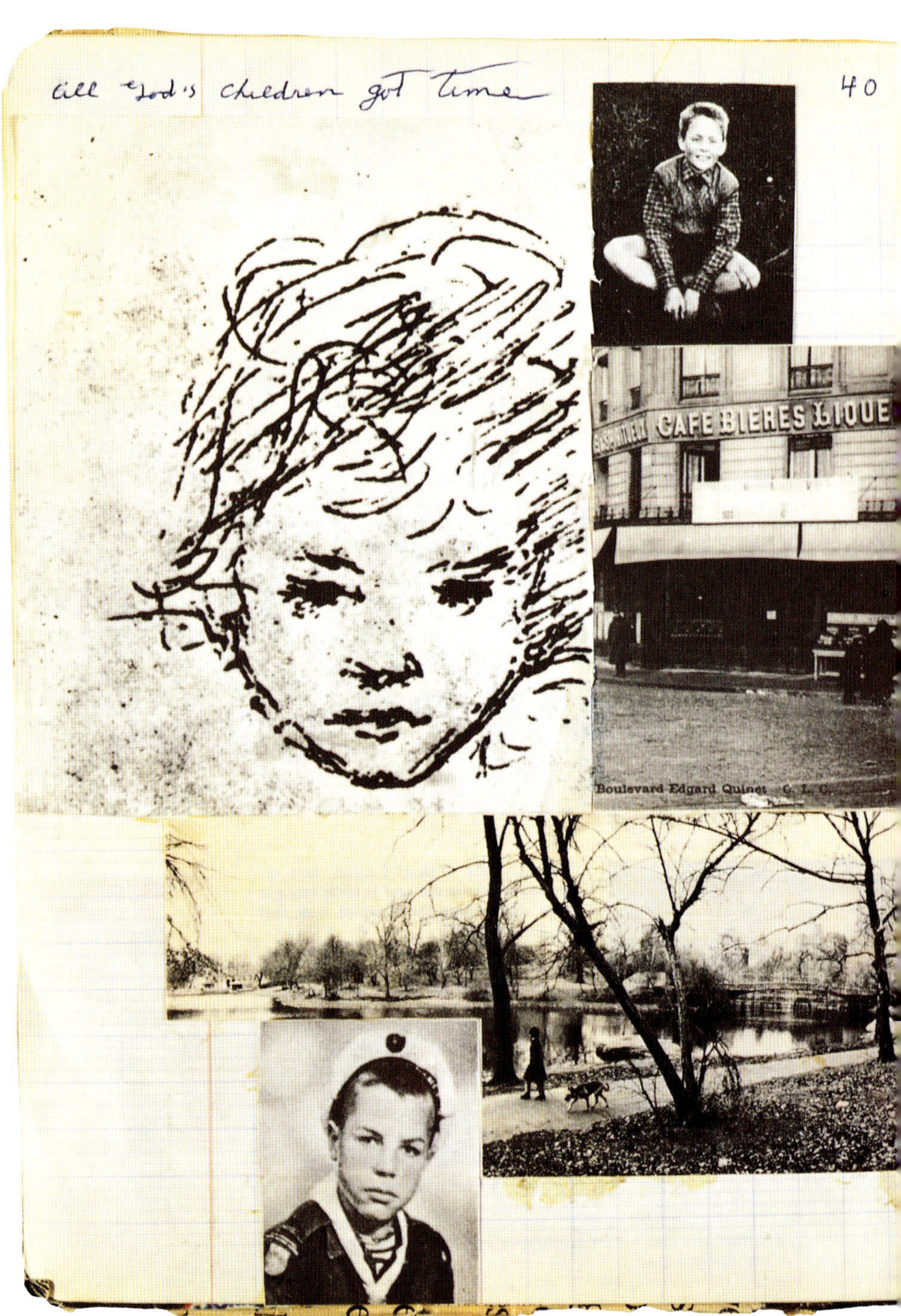

William S. Burroughs and Brion Gysin,
All God's Children Got Time,
pages from **Green Scrapbook**, c. 1971–73, cat. no. 13

V

A SILENT LANGUAGE OF JUXTAPOSITION

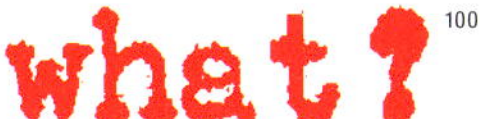

[100]

In a scrapbook that Burroughs worked on during the early 1970s there is a two-page spread entitled "All God's Children Got Time."[101] Positioned within an array of images consisting of a drawn portrait of a young boy, two photographs of young boys, one dressed as a sailor, and a photograph of "Dilly Boy" John Brady, with whom Burroughs lived in London in 1972–73, are a portion of a Parisian postcard, a photographic illustration of an urban park scene, and four images from the early history of photography. At the lower right of the spread, Burroughs placed an image of the earliest extant photograph, Nicéphore Niépce's *héliographe* of a view outside his studio window and the result of what has been calculated as an exposure of some eight hours made around 1826. Extending the entire height of the pages is a vertical detail of Louis-Jacques-Mandé Daguerre's famed, but now lost, daguerreotype view of the Boulevard du Temple in Paris taken around 1838, another view out of the artist's studio. A ghostly view of a gutted, roofless building from what appears to have been a mid-nineteenth-century paper print is set above the Niépce image, and next to it is one of the two famous daguerreotype portraits of Edgar Allan Poe. By the early 1970s these images were commonly found in general histories of the medium as well as in articles in such periodicals as *Time*, since collecting historical photographs was newsworthy in these years.

What Burroughs collaged here is the image of a visionary writer whose dealings with drugs and alcohol are legendary, surrounded by traces of a shadowy past and notes on time itself. Niépce's héliographe took nearly a full day to record, the ruined architecture was a mere reminder of time gone by, and Daguerre's view was too long an exposure to render the teeming traffic on the busy boulevard except for the single man who stopped to have his boots polished. The rest of the Daguerre image, which includes this shadowy figure, is found pasted into the scrapbook twenty pages later, along with a reproduction of a Frank Sutcliff harbor scene taken in the 1880s.[102] On this page Burroughs also acknowledges the layerings of information attendant to all magazine reproductions: written in ink at the top left is the instruction "From here on reverse side of pictures noted. All pages to be held to light." Other historical photographs are found elsewhere in the scrapbook, such as the David Octavius Hill and Robert Adamson portrait of the so-called and clearly captioned "Kalewaquonaby, probably first American Indian photographed." The actual person happened to be the Reverend Peter Jones, whose father was Welsh and mother native Canadian and who had been adopted by the Grand River Mohawks by the time the photo was made around 1844–46—a romantic figure from history going native, as it were, adopting a fictional identity, which appealed to Burroughs's imagination.[103]

"Scrapbooks and time travel" were for Burroughs "exercises for expanding consciousness and for thinking in association blocks instead of words and the progressions of traditional logic."[104] In 1965 he related:

I've recently done a lot of experiments with scrapbooks. I'll read in the newspaper something that reminds me of or has relation to something I've written. I'll cut out the picture or article and paste it in a scrapbook beside the words from my book. Or I'll be walking down the street and I'll suddenly see a scene from my book and I'll photograph it and put it in a scrapbook. I've found that when preparing a page, I'll almost invariably dream that night something relating to this juxtaposition of word and image. In other words, I've been interested in precisely how word and image get around on very, very complex association lines.[105]

Prior to the 1960s Burroughs seems to have kept most of his notes, jottings, and images in files and envelopes, labeled as to specific topics or materials.[106] His scrapbook experiments may have started in earnest in 1963 since one of the earliest scrapbooks bears a cover date of that year and, while in London, Burroughs wrote the beginnings of an essay entitled "The Photo Collage."[107]

Following the late 1910s and 1920s, photomontage and photocollage fully entered the vocabularies of modern art through dada and surrealism. The classic statement concerning photomontage was articulated by the German dadaist Raoul Hausmann at the opening of a Berlin photomontage exhibition in 1931: "The idea of photomontage was as revolution-

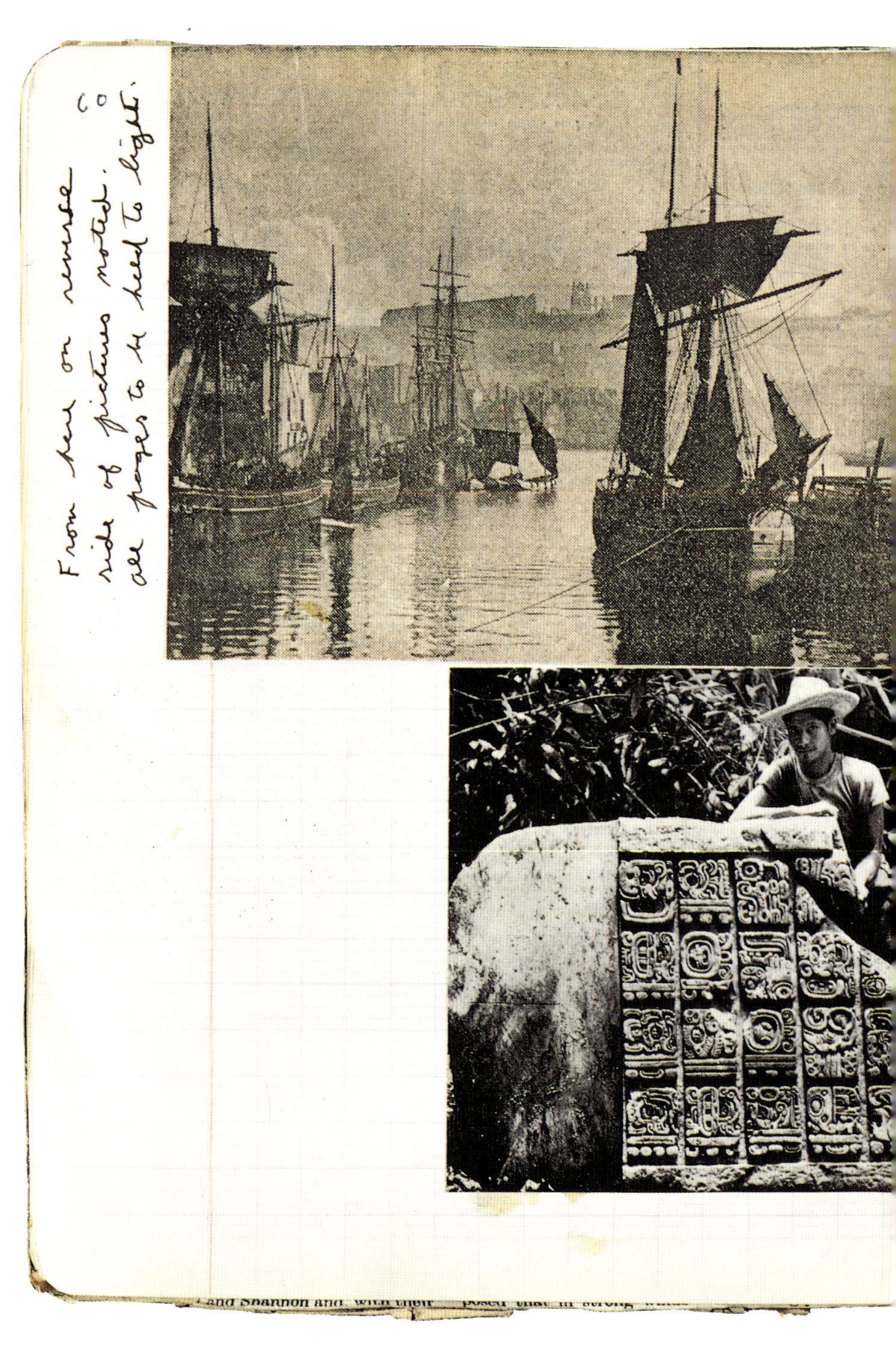

ary as was its content, its form as incredible as the application of photography and printed texts, which together transformed themselves into a sort of static film." According to Hausmann, he and his fellow dadaists Hannah Höch and Kurt Schwitters created "a completely new entity with the aid of very different structures that were often whimsical and of antagonistic signification…an optical reflection that was intentionally new."[108] Despite their often chaotic and explosive appearance, dada montages conflated texts and photographs or other images into a unified singularity of personality, scene, attitude, or emotion through a self-referential and "artful" composition.

Surrealist photocollage, however, "set up a relationship between photography and 'language,'" according to historian Rosalind Krauss.[109] Reviewing the collages and photocollages of Max Ernst in 1923, the surrealist poet Louis Aragon claimed that the pictorial elements Ernst used—whether drawings, engravings, illustrations, or photographs—evoked objects other than what they pictured by a "process absolutely

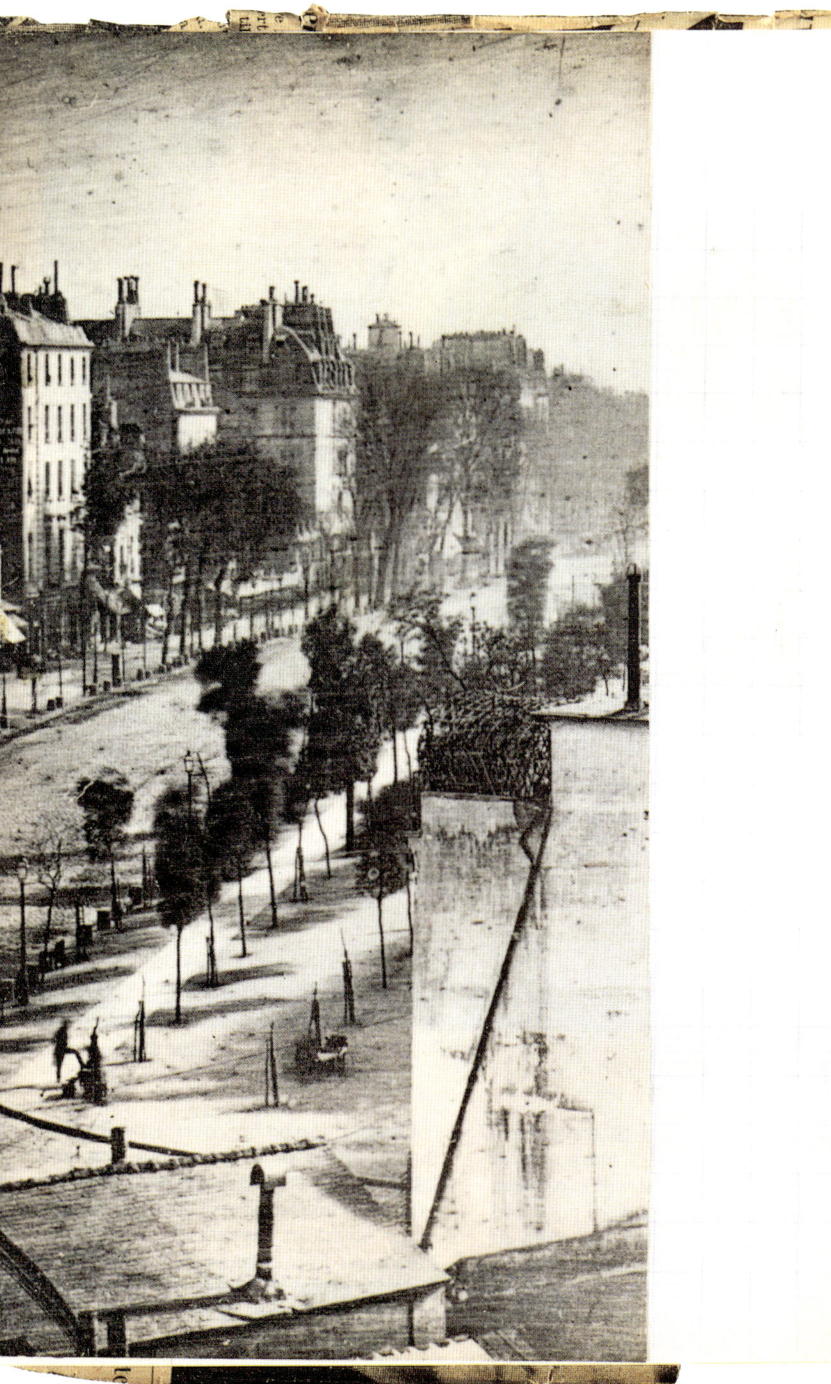

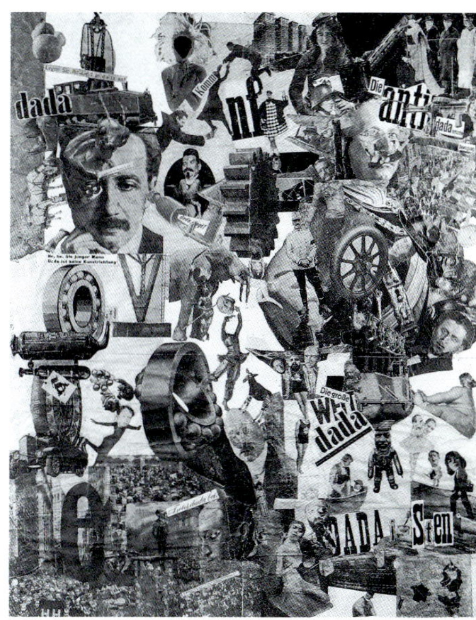

Hannah Höch, **Cut with the Kitchen Knife Dada through the Last Weimar Beer Belly Cultural Epoch of Germany**, 1919–20, offset photolithographic montage and typography, 44⅞ x 35⅜ in. (114 x 89.9 cm), Nationalgalerie Staatliche Museen Preussischer Kultrubesitz Berlin

William S. Burroughs and Brion Gysin, pages from **Green Scrapbook**, c. 1971–73, cat. no. 13

The operation is
very technical--
Look at a photomontage--
It makes a statement in
flexible picture language--
Let us call the
statement made by a
given photomontage X--
We can use X words X colors
X odors X images and so
forth to define the
various aspects of
X--Now we feed X
into the calculating
machine and X scans
out related colors,
juxtapositions,
affect-charged images
and so forth we can
attenuate or concentrate
X by taking out or
adding elements and
feeding back into
the machine factors
we wish to concentrate--
A Technician learns to think
and write in association
blocks which can then
be manipulated
according to laws
the laws of association
and juxtaposition--The
basic law of association
and conditioning is known
to college students
even in America: Any
object, feeling, odor, word,
image in juxtaposition
with any other object
feeling, odor, word
or image will be associated
with it--Our technicians
learn to read newspapers
and magazines for
juxtaposition statements
rather than alleged content--
We express these statements
in Juxtaposition Formulae--
The Formulae of course
control populations of
the world--Yes it is fairly
easy to predict what people will
think see feel and hear
a thousand years from now
if you write the Juxtaposition
Formulae to be used in that
period.

Nova Express

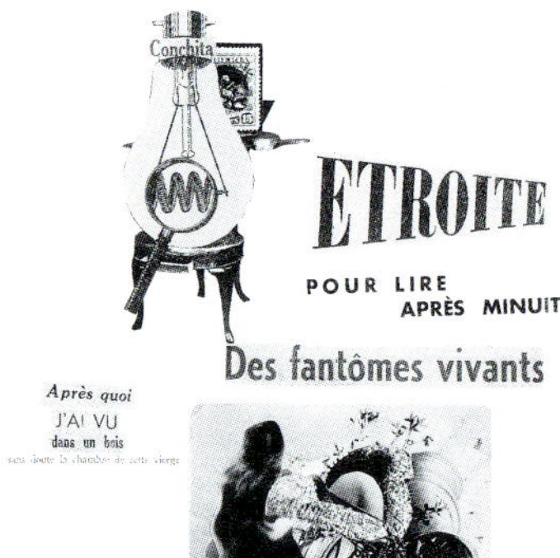

Georges Hugnet, **Vous devez être fière de la robe**, 1936, offset photolithographic montage and typography, 12¾ x 9¾ in. (32.4 x 24.8 cm), Zabriskie Gallery, New York

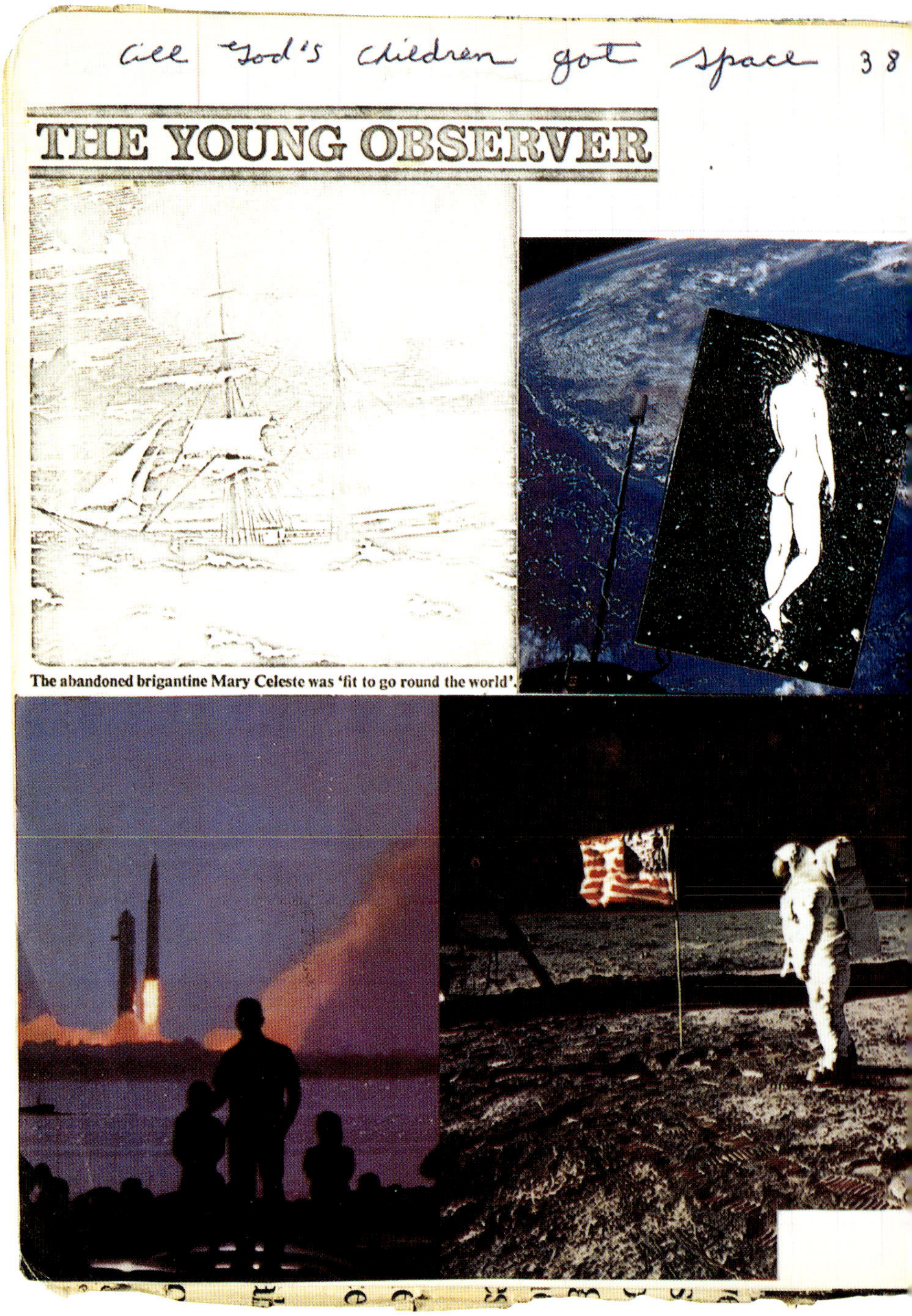

All God's children got space 38

THE YOUNG OBSERVER

The abandoned brigantine Mary Celeste was 'fit to go round the world'.

William S. Burroughs and Brion Gysin, **All God's Children Got Space**, pages from **Green Scrapbook**, c. 1971–73, cat. no. 13

analogous to poetic imagery."[110] Writing in 1935 about the collages of John Heartfield, Aragon stated that "as he was playing with the fire of appearance, reality took fire around him.... The scraps of photographs that he formerly manoeuvred for the pleasure of stupefaction, under his fingers begin to *signify*."[111] The scraps of photographs began to take on an abstraction akin to words themselves and to loose some of their hold on the reality they represented by being treated as glyphs instead of windows to the world or mirrors of nature. In other words, each of the elements became a linguistic unit, to be read as any other.

One of the finest achievements along these lines and one of the clearest examples of equating word and image is found in the surrealist "novel" *Le septième face du dé*, by the poet and critic Georges Hugnet, published by Jeanne Bucher in 1936, as well as in his other collages of the time.[112] Influenced by André Breton's earlier "objet-poèmes" and the poetics of Pierre Reverdy, Hugnet claimed that he was most interested in the "disintegration of poetry, this contempt for beauty of beauty, this negation of poetic and non-poetic."[113] Found textual narratives and collages of found images were intertwined by Hugnet into a serial adventure story of sexual initiation and violence. In Hugnet's work, texts function as if they were blocks of verbal images while photomontages act very much as if they were texts; yet, taken together as a whole, there remains a linear structure to the story, regardless of its vagueness and dreamlike qualities.

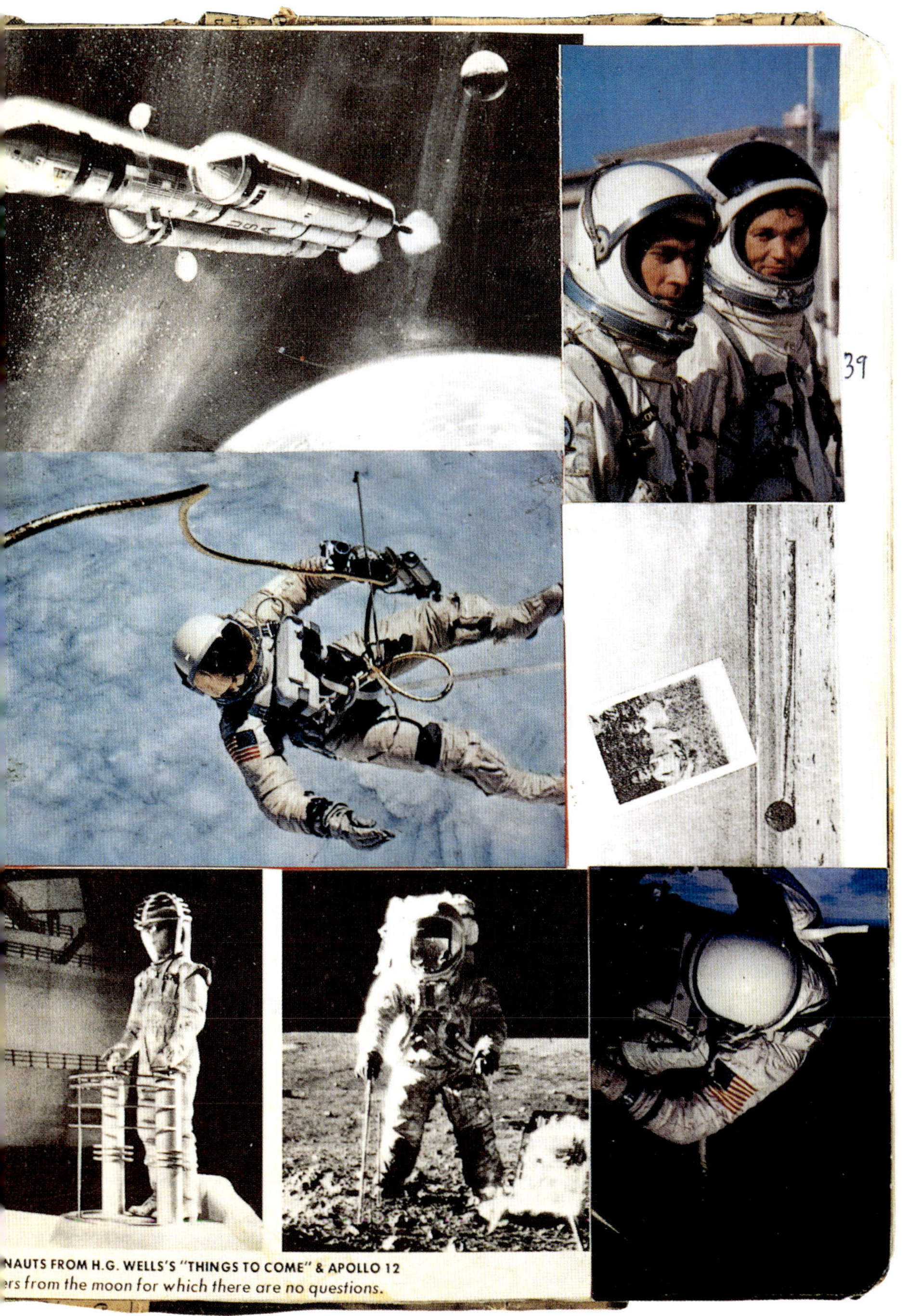

With Burroughs, however, the field changes; and this is reflected in his unpublished essay "The Photo Collage" (1963) in which he begins by decisively separating his experiments from the artworks of the surrealists and suggesting that his technique is a new way of escaping the controls of our physical and mental situations:

The Surrealists formed collages in the 1920s at that time being simply an arrangement of things and pictures presented as an art object—They did not develope [*sic*] **the formula further to take photos of the collage and use these photos in arranging collage abstracts and concentrates.** [...] **A Soviet scientist has said: "We will travel not only in space but in time as well."—Perhaps, but certainly not with the baggage that most of us carry—body baggage—word baggage—memory baggage—The photo collage is a way to travel that must be used with skill and precision if we are to arrive.**[114]

In a published essay, Burroughs wrote that "'It is necessary to travel. It is not necessary to live.'[...]To travel in space you must leave the old verbal garbage behind: God talk, country talk, mother talk, love talk, party talk.[...]You must learn to live alone in silence."[115] Photocollage was, for Burroughs, a chance to travel, as it were, across space and time.

Burroughs continued in "The Photo Collage" by listing four collage projects to be experimented with. First, "Time Collages" would mix together images of a city from various times either precisely or panoramically: "You can trace time lines down one street or flash a city—You can mix in time collages of other cities and places." Second, "Space Collages" would juxtapose images from different locations across the globe such as Morocco, the Amazon jungle, or Scandinavia. Third, "Collage Concentrates" would bring together multiple images that depict or convey a certain theme such as "misty dawn" and thereby yield a "mist-dawn concentrate." And, fourth, "Mood Concentrates" would take pictures of crowds and carnivals, for instance, and bring them together to create a "celebration collage." Yet care has to be exerted, Burroughs seems to suggest, since a slightly different arrangement, presumably undertaken without skill and precision, might produce a concentrate of a far different complexion: "Arrange celebration collage—Take—Rearrange—Take your bleak lonely photos."[116] All of this suggests an openness, disjuncture, rupture, and simultaneity in using images that can be found in psychedelic collages of the late 1960s as well as in the "dictionary" or "lexicon" approach to thematic montages used by such artists as John Baldessari or Richard Prince a decade or so later.

100
Burroughs, "Hieroglyphic Silence," in Burroughs and Gysin, *The Third Mind* (note **8**), 194.

101
William S. Burroughs, *Green Scrapbook*, c. 1972, Collection of Elyse and Stanley Grinstein, 40 41.

102
Ibid., 61.

103
Ibid., 54; see also Colin Ford, ed., *An Early Victorian Album: The Hill/Adamson Collection* (London: Jonathan Cape, 1974), 40–41, 279.

104
Knickerbocker, "Interview" (note **8**), 2.

105
Ibid., 1.

106
In the Burroughs Collection at Arizona State University, files are arranged with such titles as "Modern Dada Communications and Layouts," "Industrial Camouflage," "Column Cut Up Duplicates," "David Bowie and James Taylor Cut-Ups," "Photos. Comic Books. Prospectives," "Photographs," and the numbers "23 and 52." In terms of keeping collage scrapbooks, Burroughs was preceded by Ginsberg, Lucien Carr, and Kerouac; cf. Kerouac's *Book of Dreams* of c. 1952–54, illustrated in Lisa Phillips, *Beat Culture and the New America: 1950–65*, exh. cat. (New York: Whitney Museum of American Art, 1995), 52.

107
William S. Burroughs, "The Photo Collage," unpublished typescript of twenty pages, dated "London, 1963"; in Burroughs Collection, University Libraries, Special Collections, Arizona State University, box 10, item 4.

108
Raoul Hausmann, "Peinture nouvelle et photomontage," *Courrier Dada* (Paris: Le Terrain Vague, 1958), 47.

109
Rosalind Krauss, "Photography in the Service of Surrealism," in Krauss and Jane Livingston, *L'amour fou: Photography and Surrealism*, exh. cat. (Washington, D.C.: Corcoran Gallery of Art, 1985), 28.

110
Louis Aragon, "Max Ernst, peintre des illusions," *Les collages* (Paris: Hermann, 1965), 30.

111
Aragon, "John Heartfield et la beauté révolutionnaire," in ibid., 78–79; cited in Rosalind Krauss, "Photography in the Service of Surrealism" (note **109**), 25.

112
See Sobieszek, "Erotic Photomontages" (note **52**), 66–82.

113
Georges Hugnet, "1870 to 1936," in Herbert Read, ed., *Surrealism* (London: Praeger, 1938), 206.

114
Burroughs, "The Photo Collage" (note **107**), 1.

115
Burroughs, "'It Is Necessary to Travel…'," *The Adding Machine* (note **12**), 137.

116
Burroughs, "The Photo Collage" (note **107**), 1.

VI

SCRAPBOOK EXPERIMENTS

like that fill a page in time.[117]

Burroughs's radical treatment of photocollage is nowhere more apparent than in his scrapbook experiments and the works he did in conjunction with Brion Gysin for *The Third Mind*. Over the course of nearly a decade, from 1963 to around 1972, Burroughs filled approximately twenty small agenda-, sketch-, and notebooks with his own typescripts, bits of newspaper headlines and stories, columns from *Time* and *Newsweek*, accounts of disasters from contemporary and historical sources, newsprint comic-strip cells from "Rex Morgan, M.D." or "Buzz Sawyer," illustrations by Tom of Finland, portions of his own dust jackets, photographs (both snapshot format and contact sized) of scenes or other montages he assembled, photos and advertisements from magazines, and portraits of his friends and lovers and of himself.[118] Sometimes such materials as aluminum foil, ticket stubs, geometric designs, map segments, and crayon drawings are found among the pages. Frequently his own writings are handwritten on pages following a three-column "newspaper" format derived from Gysin's ideas of cut-ups in which a different text is written vertically in each column with the notion that a horizontal reading would offer an unexpected "other" reading.[119] Often Gysin would use his hand-carved ink brayer to furnish the pages with loose grid structures into which the images and texts were inserted, thus making the page into an experiment in permutations to be read in every which way.[120]

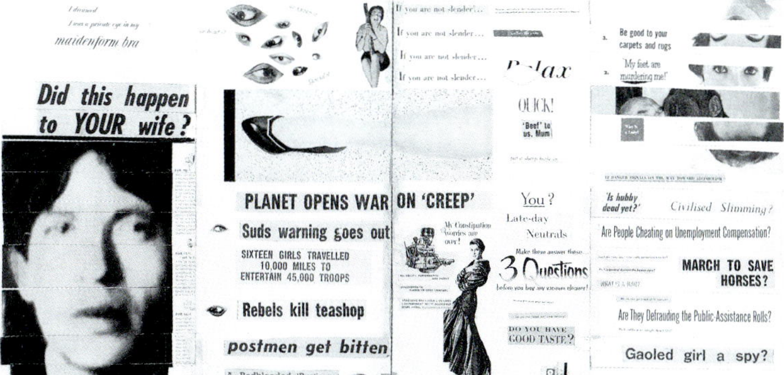

John McHale, **Why I Took to the Washers in Luxury Flats**, c. 1954, offset photolithographic montage scrapbook, 17 13/16 x 18½ in. (45.2 x 47 cm), Yale Center for British Art, New Haven, gift of Magda Cordell McHale

Around 1954 the British artist John McHale, a member of the Independent Group, constructed a text-image scrapbook entitled *Why I Took to the Washers in Luxury Flats*, in which each page of collages was horizontally sliced so that only portions could be turned over, leading to an enormous number of visual and textual possibilities. In 1962 Eduardo Paolozzi, also a member of the Independent Group in London, published a limited edition book of screenprints

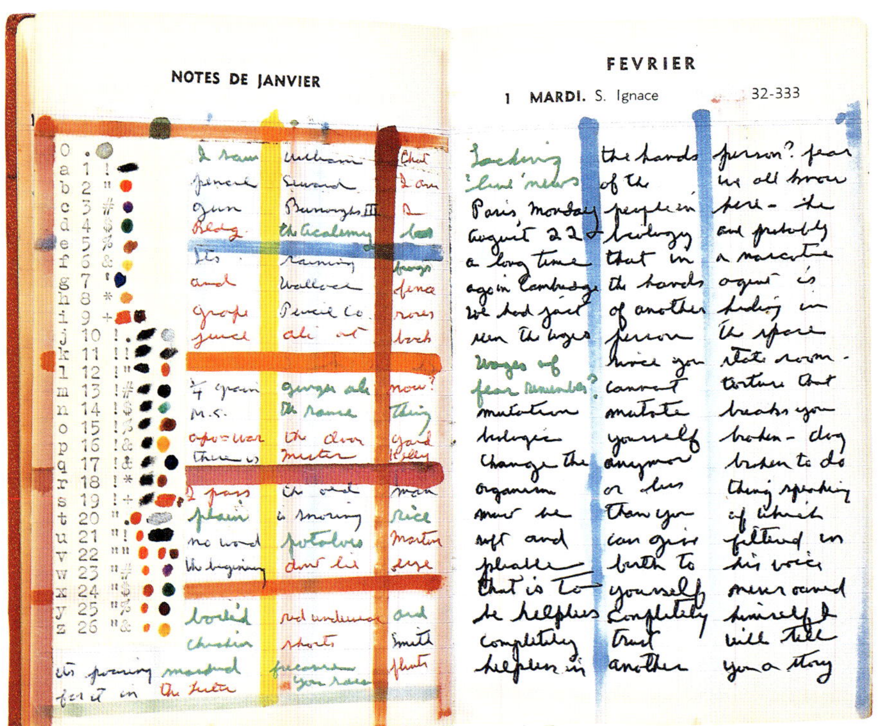

William S. Burroughs and Brion Gysin, pages from **Red Scrapbook**, c. 1966–73, cat. no. 12

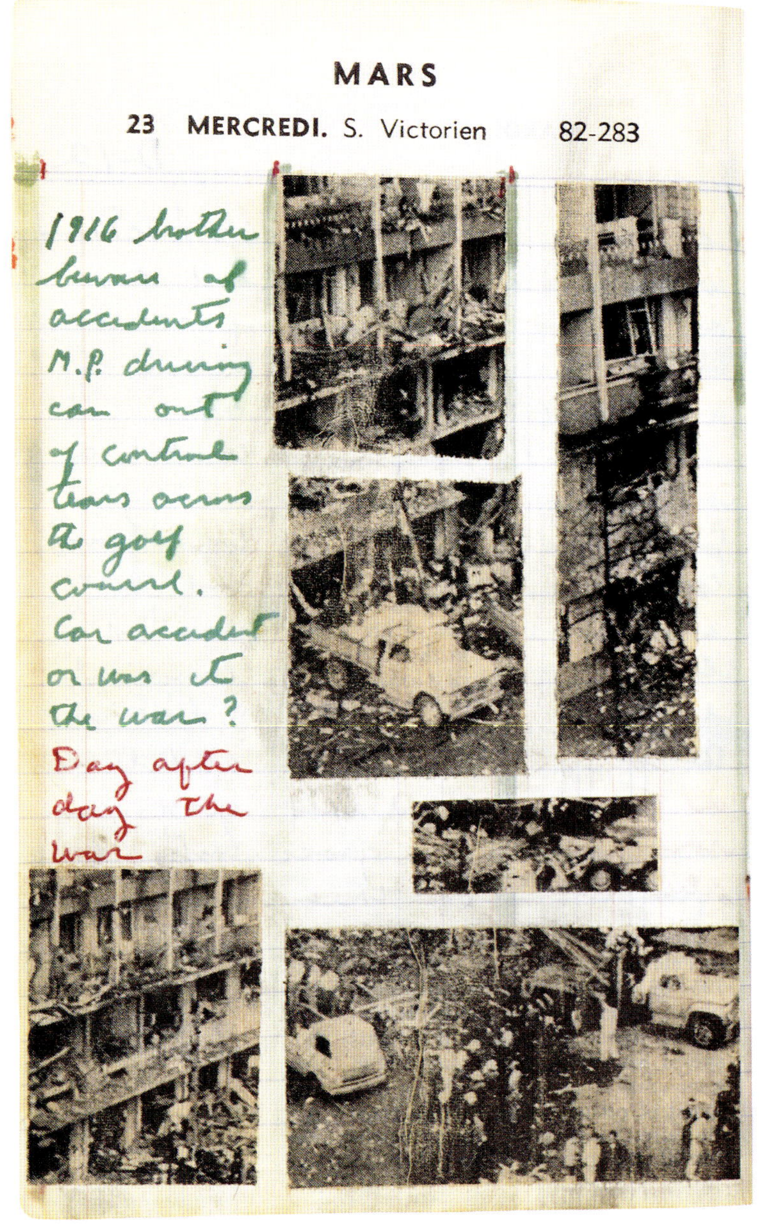

entitled *Metafisikal Translations*, whose texts and images were "released from the normal restrictions of sequence and syntax."[121] Not only was the scrapbook format itself a way for Burroughs to systemize his experiments, but his application of a grid structure within the scrapbook added another dimension for reorganizing and deconstructing texts and images, a dimension favored by conceptual artists of the same period. As early as the late 1950s, artist Robert Rauschenberg had begun a series of "combine paintings," such as *Factum I* (1957), in which the various elements of calendar sheets, landscape images, newspaper images of disasters, portraits, and painted gestural marks are arrayed into loose columns and grids. During the 1960s the trend to use grids as visual containers of art and information increased and, according to curator John Elderfield, reflected "a return to an informational or signifying sensibility."[122] An apt comparison of Burroughs's strategy here may be that used by Carl Andre in his minimalist grids of words done in 1965 or, again, by John Baldessari in his *Blasted Allegories* series of 1978, in which still images along with associative word elements are arrayed in open or closed grid structures meant to be read in arbitrary ways.[123]

"Scrapbooks are such stuff as dreams are made on," wrote Burroughs, "now, a scrapbook is like that, fill a page in time...letter...clipping from the hometown cross reference back and forth a photo a column of text with the scrapbooks open times and places."[124] One of the richest of Burroughs's early scrapbooks is the *Black Scrapbook*, datable to 1964–65 and consisting of more than four hundred pages of notations and text-image collages that bloat an otherwise normal, French daybook or agenda.[125] With ballpoint-pen, columnal jottings Burroughs recorded daily events, ruminations on the apomorphine treatment for addiction, journalistic reports on earthquakes, descriptions of the Tangier landscape, hieroglyphics, and Apollinaire-like lines of poetry falling vertically down the page. A number of pages contain abstract calligraphic notations, and one has a quadrapartite permutation of "Arabic" writing (possibly by Gysin) in two sections, and a handwritten script detailing "dirty purple dusk tainted junky fingers."[126] Throughout there are collaged, cut-up, and written references to Burroughs's characters such as Mr. Bradly/Mr. Martin, The Frisco Kid, Captain Clark, the Sailor, and the Mexican Kid. At the very front, a typed reference about personal combat with

Robert Rauschenberg, **Factum I**, 1957, oil and mixed media on canvas, 61½ x 35¾ in. (156.2 x 90.8 cm), the Museum of Contemporary Art, Los Angeles, the Panza Collection, photo by Squidds and Nunns

John Baldessari, **Blasted Allegories (Colorful Sentences): Worried Appeal Cycle...(Six Sentences Sharing Circular Green Intersection)**, 1978, gelatin-silver prints on board, 30⅞ x 40 in. (78.4 x 101.6 cm), photograph courtesy Sonnabend Gallery, New York

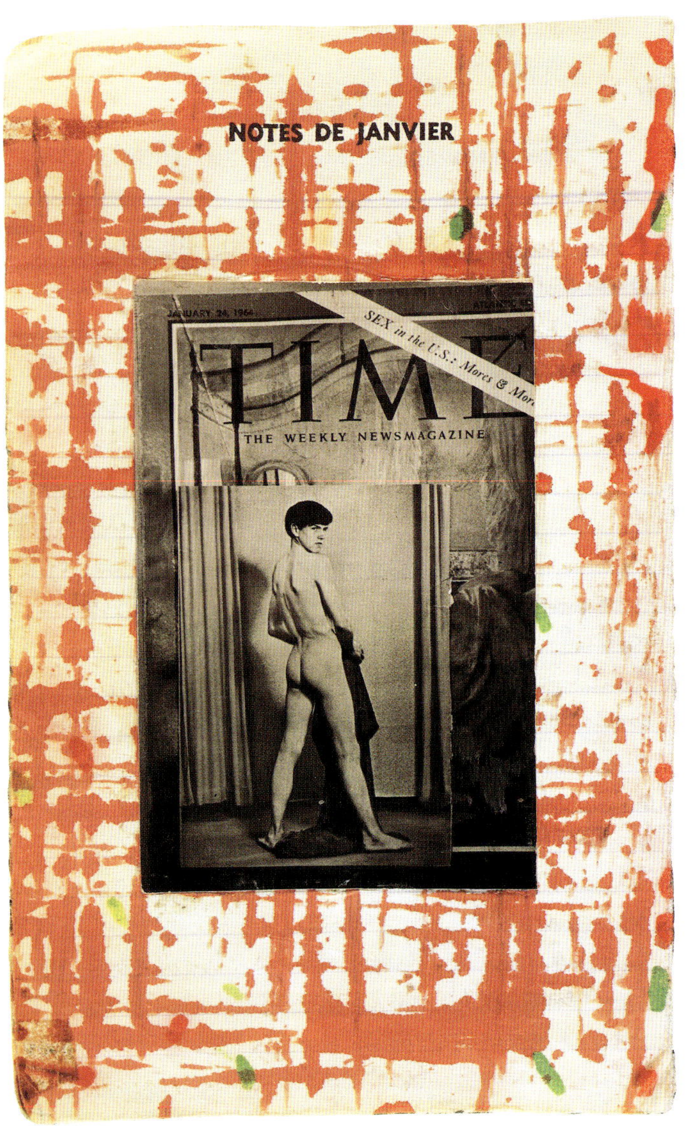

heated razors in the fearsome Cut City includes the line "Pick up that razor and use it" and is typed in red on lined graph paper. The very last typed passage in the scrapbook, some four hundred pages later, continues the story and states "There is nothing. (Not knowing what is and is not knowing I knew *not*.) Hassan I Sabbah's razor."[127]

The *Black Scrapbook* is peppered with newspaper photos of young boys, disasters, a few advertisements, strips of foil and printed color patterns, and crayon drawings. Snapshots of various scenes taken in St. Louis, where Burroughs was born and raised, carry subtitles such as "Portland Place St. Louis" (where the wealthy lived) and "John Burroughs School" (named after the naturalist and where Burroughs was a student in 1925), and these are sometimes coupled with cut-up texts about the city. On one page a photograph of a typical midwestern two-storied residence has "Walton Ave St. Louis" written on top of it, while "Mrs. Murphy's Rooming House" is inscribed beneath it.[128] A comic-strip character above the photograph declares that a woman's suicide "might turn out

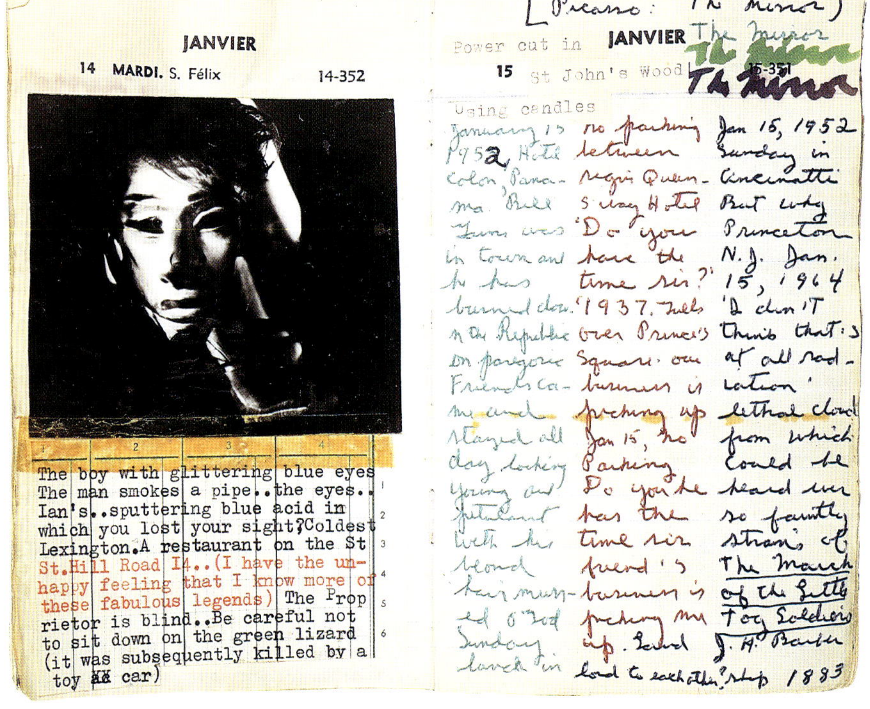

William S. Burroughs and Brion Gysin, pages from **Black Scrapbook**, c. 1963–64, cat. no. 11

to be the best thing she's ever done"—more than likely a calculated cross-reference to the fact that Burroughs, in 1942, was evicted from Mrs. Murphy's boarding house, which was actually located on Chicago's North Side. Other snapshots show a soccer field and radio towers in Gibraltar, the "Calle San Lucar" and the American Consulate in Tangier, street scenes in New York, Burroughs sitting on a bed or pouring himself "Real English Tea" in a kitchen, and scenes from televised Westerns in advertisements or on TV sets. A photo-collage of young boys lies atop a small cabinet, while other scrapbooks are shown opened on chairs or tables with loose photographs positioned over them as though still being worked on, still in flux. In one of them, a still from his and Antony Balch's film *Towers Open Fire*, a still augmented by superimposed calligraphy by Gysin, shows Burroughs speaking to the "Virus Board" of the British Film Institute and is pasted atop an array of business cards from Paris and Biarritz.[129] In this and other scrapbooks any distinction between fiction and fact or between history and current events is consistently blurred, not unlike what

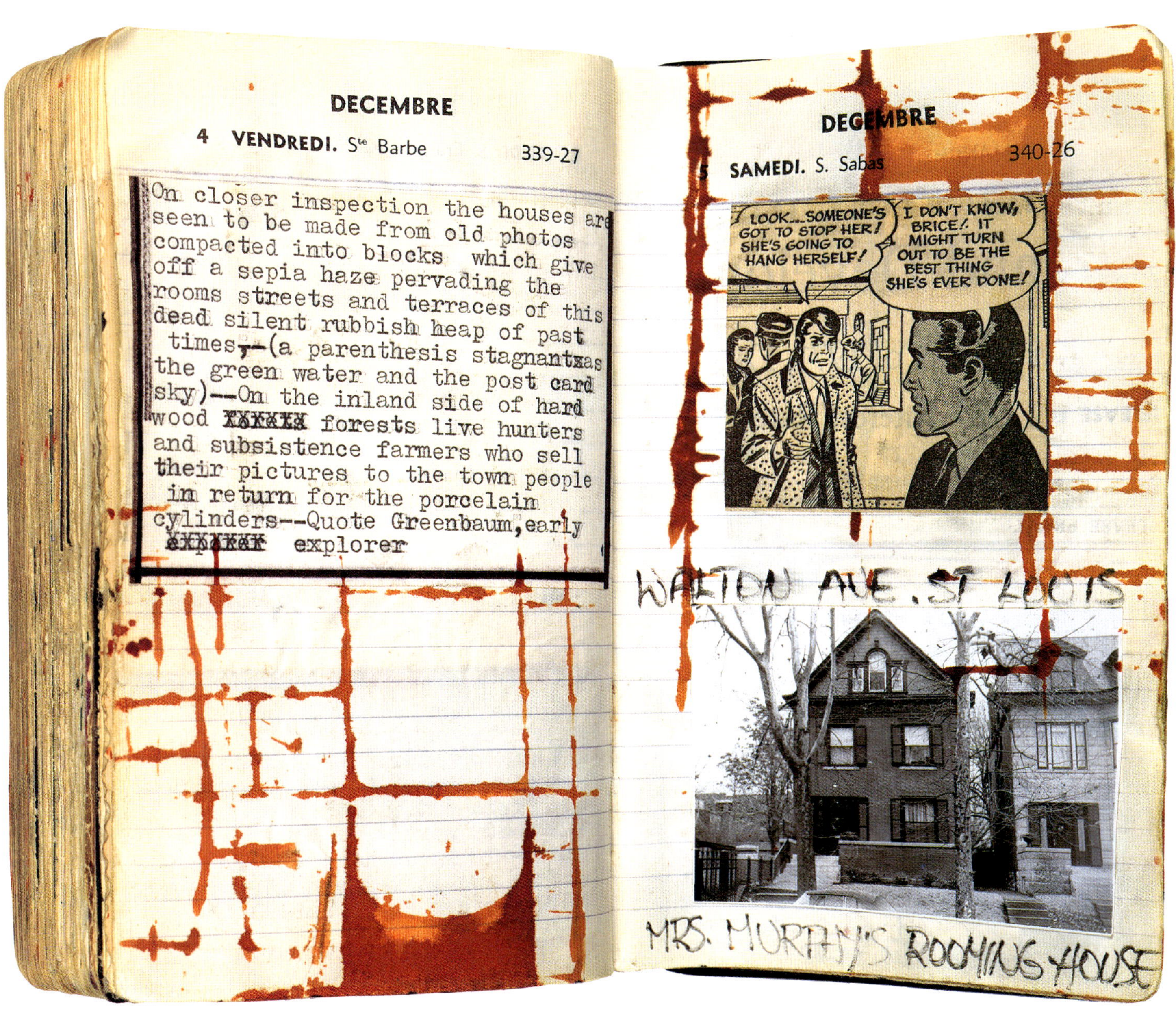

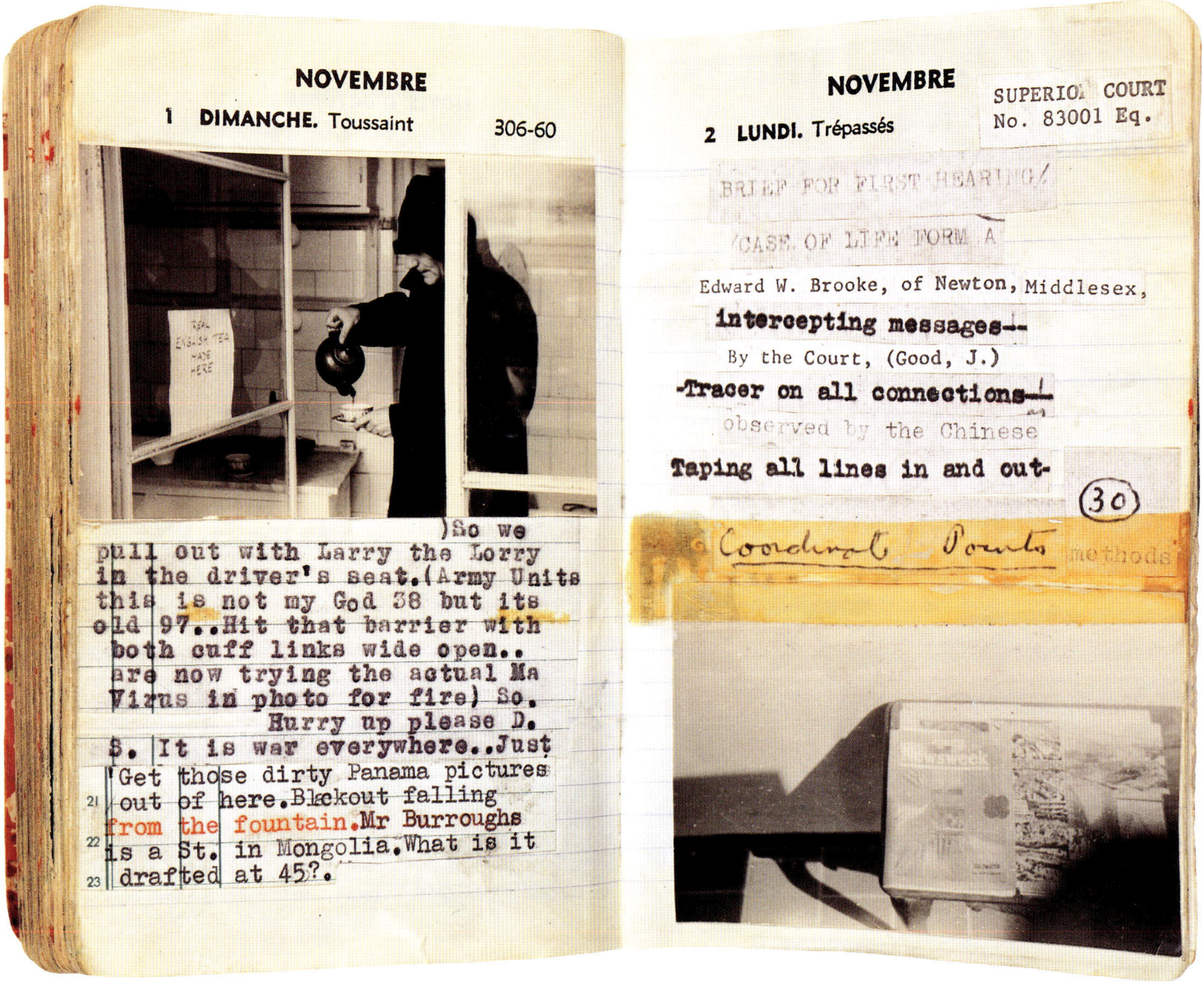

NOVEMBRE

1 DIMANCHE. Toussaint 306-60

)So we
pull out with Larry the Lorry
in the driver's seat.(Army Units
this is not my God 38 but its
old 97..Hit that barrier with
both cuff links wide open..
are now trying the actual Ma
Virus in photo for fire) So.
Hurry up please D.
S. It is war everywhere..Just
Get those dirty Panama pictures
out of here.Blackout falling
from the fountain.Mr Burroughs
is a St. in Mongolia.What is it
drafted at 45?.

NOVEMBRE

2 LUNDI. Trépassés

SUPERIOR COURT
No. 83001 Eq.

BRIEF FOR FIRST HEARING/
/CASE OF LIFE FORM A

Edward W. Brooke, of Newton, Middlesex,
intercepting messages--
By the Court, (Good, J.)
-Tracer on all connections--
observed by the Chinese
Taping all lines in and out-

(30)

Coordinate Points methods

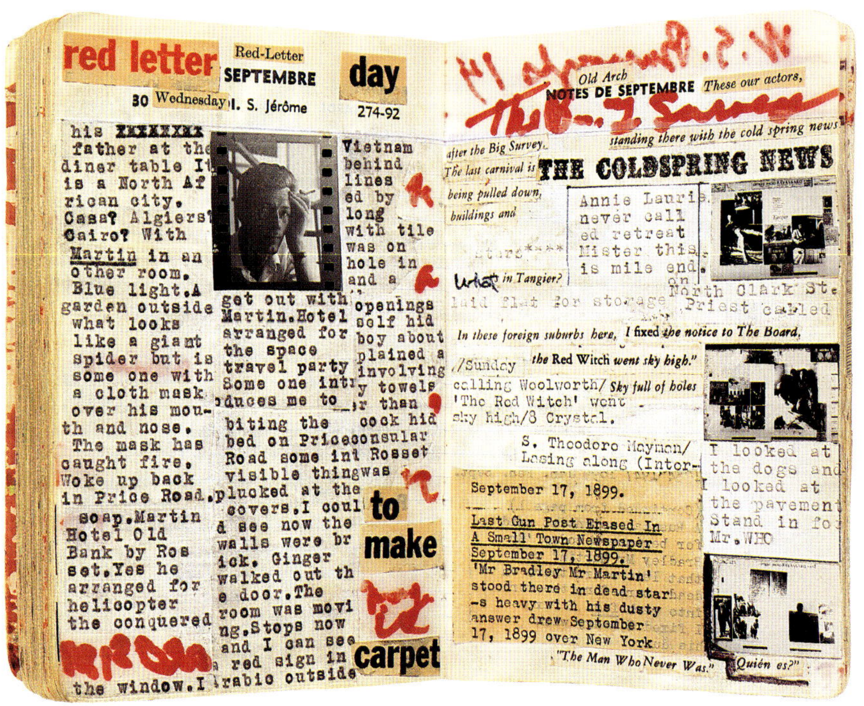

red letter Red-Letter SEPTEMBRE day
30 Wednesday I. S. Jérôme 274-92

his XXXXXXXX
father at the
diner table It
is a North Af
rican city.
Cass? Algiers?
Cairo? With
Martin in an
other room.
Blue light.A
garden outside
what looks
like a giant
spider but is
some one with
a cloth mask
over his mou-
th and nose.
The mask has
caught fire.
Woke up back
in Price Road.
soap.Martin
Hotel Old
Bank by Ros
set.Yes he
arranged for
helicopter
the conquered
the window.I

get out with
Martin.Hotel
arranged for
the space
travel party
Some one intr
oduces me to
biting the
bed on Price
Road some in
visible thing
plucked at the
covers.I coul
d see now the
walls were br
ick. Ginger
walked out th
e door.The
room was movi
ng.Stops now
and I can see
a red sign in
Arabic outside

Vietnam
behind
lines
ed by
long
with tile
was on
hole in
and a
openings
self hid
boy about
plained a
involving
y towels
r than
cook hid
consular
Rosset
was

to make
carpet

W. S. Burroughs
Old Arch
NOTES DE SEPTEMBRE These our actors,
standing there with the cold spring news
after the Big Survey.
The last carnival is THE COLDSPRING NEWS
being pulled down,
buildings and
stars***
What in Tangier?

Annie Lauris.
never call
ed retreat
Mister this
is mile end.
on
North Clark St.
laid flat for storage Priest called

In these foreign suburbs here, I fixed the notice to The Board,
/Sunday the Red Witch went sky high."
calling Woolworth/ Sky full of holes
'The Red Witch' went
sky high/8 Crystal.

S. Theodore Mayman/
Losing along (Inter-

I looked at
the dogs and
I looked at
the pavement
Stand in fo
Mr.WHO

September 17, 1899.

Last Gun Post Erased In
A Small Town Newspaper
September 17, 1899.
'Mr Bradley Mr Martin'
stood there in dead star
-s heavy with his dusty
answer drew September
17, 1899 over New York

"The Man Who Never Was." Quién es?"

William S. Burroughs and Brion Gysin,
pages from **Black Scrapbook**, c. 1963–64, cat. no. 11

occurs in his fiction. In an interview with Conrad Knickerbocker in 1965 Burroughs was asked if he could think in images for any length of time while keeping the inner voice silent. He replied, "I'm becoming more proficient at it, partly through my work with scrapbooks and translating the connections between words and images," and claimed that the scrapbooks were teaching him to think in "association blocks rather than words."[130]

With a passing reference to Eliot's *The Waste Land*, Burroughs described how he went about his scrapbook experiments:

> **Went down to the lobby for the local papers which I check through carefully for items or pictures that intersect amplify or illustrate any of my writings past present or future. Relevant material I cut out and paste in a scrapbook—(some creaking hints—*por eso* I have survived). Relevant material I cut out and paste in a scrapbook—(Hurry up please it's time).**[131]

What fascinated him, besides the sheer layerings of associative words and images was the possibility of discovering or creating what he called "points of intersection, a decoding operation, you might say." What this amounted to was locating, say, a news item that reflected or otherwise corresponded to what he had already written. The first occurrence of such an intersection point took place in 1964. In an issue of *Newsweek* dated May 18, 1964, a photograph of a priest giving last rites amidst a plane wreck and an inset of the plane's captain bore the caption, "Last rites for 44 airliner dead, including pilot Clark (left)." Six years or so earlier, Burroughs had written "An old junky selling Christmas seals on North Clark Street…'*The Priest*,' they called him."[132] Intersection points may be either a text or an image. The image of the priest intersects with the description of his character "The Priest," but locating that point leads to the (coincidental?) alignment of Pilot Clark with Clark Street in Chicago. Such points of intersection became singularly important to Burroughs: "In cutting up you will get a point of intersection where the new material that you have intersects with what is there already in some very precise way, and then you start from there."[133] Only by embracing the onslaught of information and images that defines the postmodern landscape and only by making connections among the flickering clusters of experience can any creative vision be expanded.[134] And since, for Burroughs, there are no coincidences, these intersection points are at least indicative of some external ordering if not exactly predicative of it. Inversely what has been written may literally predict the future. In a nearly Borges-like fashion his character "B.J." says to him, "I tell you, boss, you write it and it happens. Why, if you didn't write me I wouldn't be here."[135]

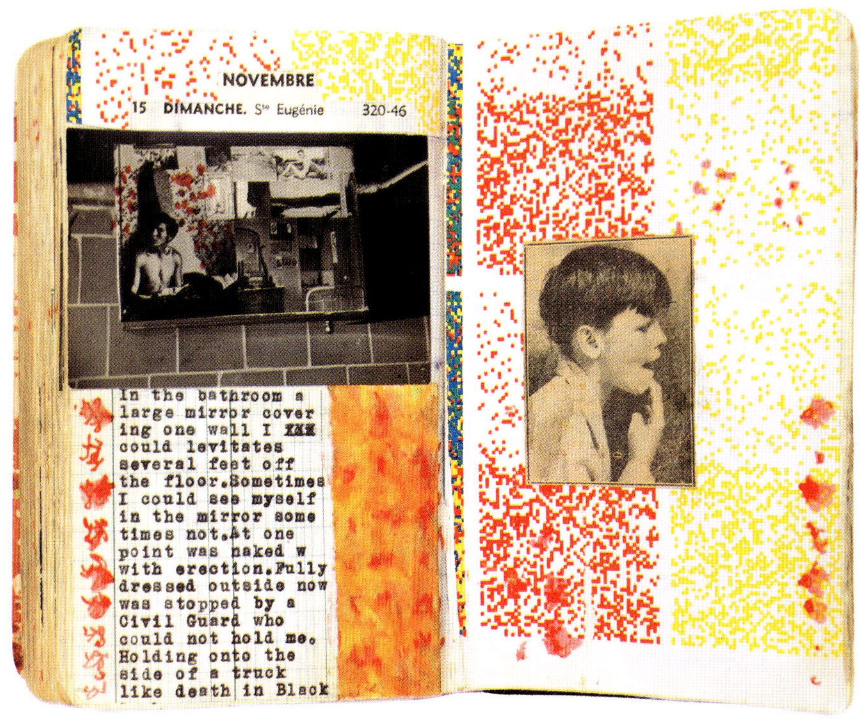

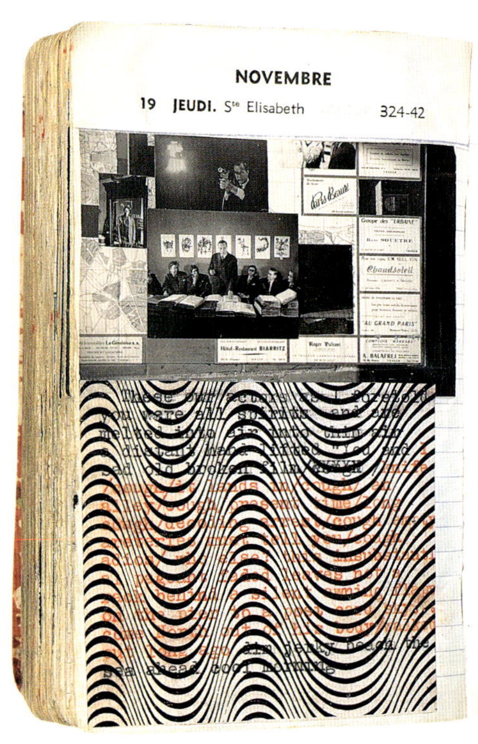

I don't know about where fiction ordinarily directs itself, but I am quite deliberately addressing myself to the whole area of what we call dreams. Precisely what is a dream? A certain juxtaposition of word and image. I've recently done a lot of experiments with scrapbooks. I'll read in the newspaper something that reminds me of or has relation to something I've written. I'll cut out the picture or article and paste it in a scrapbook beside the words from my book. Or I'll be walking down the street and I'll suddenly see a scene from my book and I'll photograph it and put it in a scrapbook. I've found that when preparing a page, I'll almost invariably dream that night something relating to this juxtaposition of word and image. In other words, I've been interested in precisely how word and image get around on very, very complex association lines.

<u>The Third Mind</u>

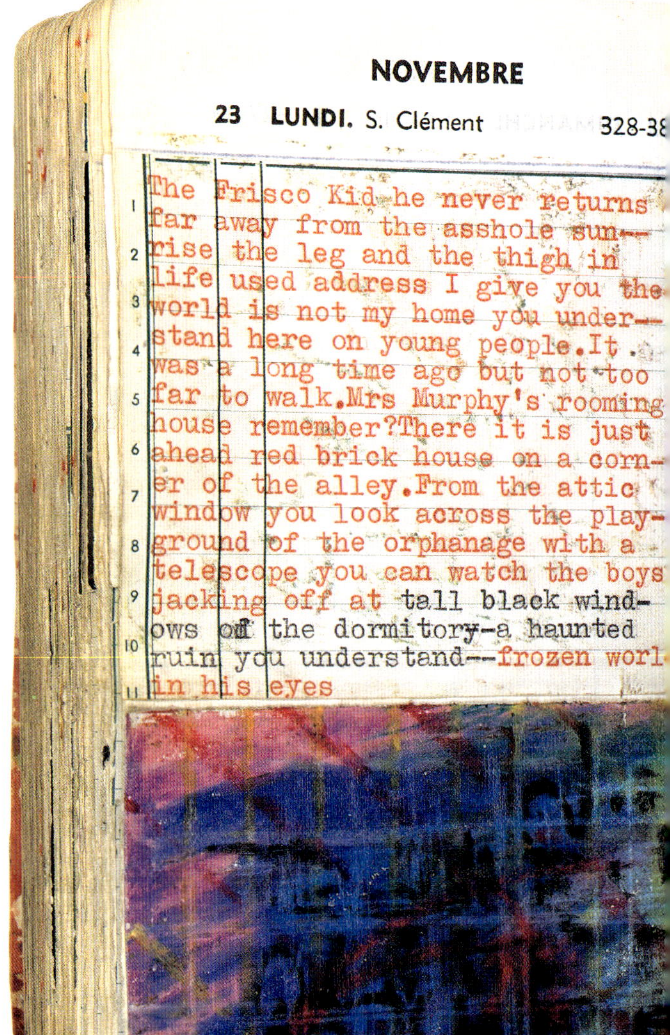

William S. Burroughs and Brion Gysin, pages from **Black Scrapbook**, c. 1963–64, cat. no. 11

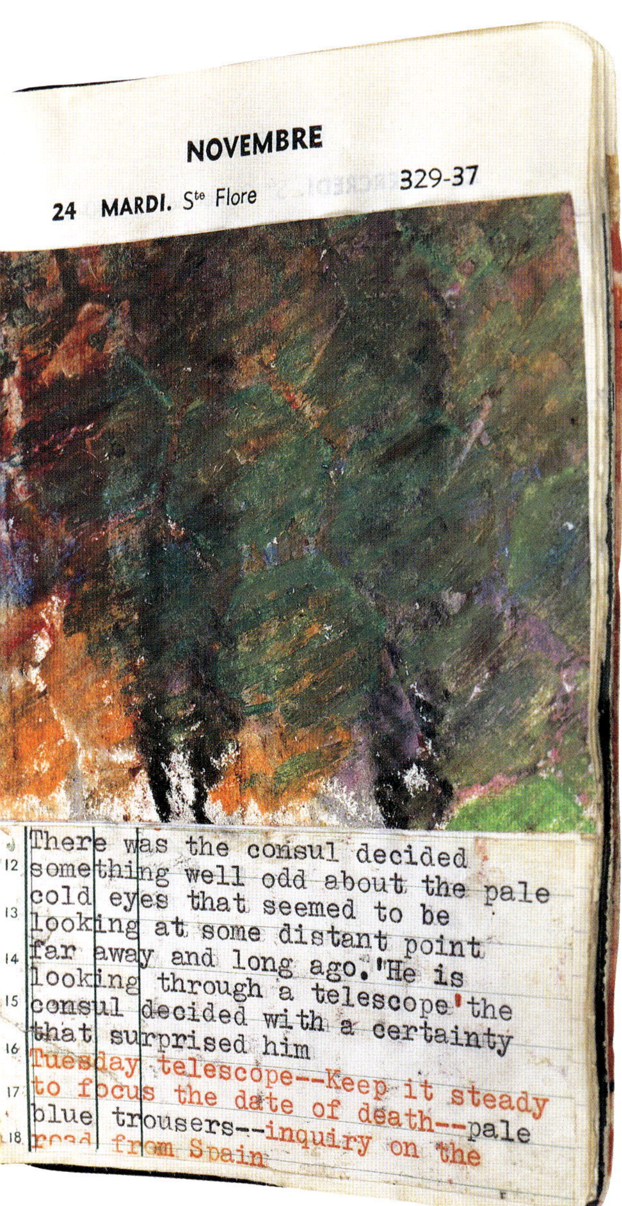

117
Burroughs, "Scrapbook Texts," in Burroughs and Gysin, *The Third Mind* (note **8**), 165.

118
See Grauerholz, "On Burroughs' Art" (note 24), v. A scrapbook entitled *Scrapbook #84* dating from the 1960s is in the collection of Robert H. Jackson, Cleveland; see Phillips, *Beat Culture and the New America* (note **106**), 277.

119
Burroughs also stressed that when the reader reads one column, he or she cannot avoid being "contaminated" by the adjacent columns; one of his most ambitious projects with columnations is found in Burroughs, "Who Is the Walks Beside You Written 3rd?" *The Burroughs File* (note **82**), 72–76.

120
Burroughs explains his use of the idea of the grid in "Formats: The Grid," in Burroughs and Gysin, *The Third Mind* (note **8**), 125–32.

121
Christopher Finch, in *Eduardo Paolozzi: A Print Retrospective*, exh. cat. (Berkeley: Worth Ryder Art Gallery, University of California, 1968), unp.; see also Christopher Finch, *Image as Language: Aspects of British Art 1950–1968* (Baltimore: Penguin Books, 1969), 45.

122
John Elderfield, "Grids," *Artforum* 10, no. 9 (May 1972): 54; for the importance of the grid in minimalist art of the 1960s, see Rosalind Krauss, "Grids," *October* 9 (summer 1979): 50–64.

123
See Diane Waldman, *Carl Andre* (New York: The Solomon R. Guggenheim Museum, 1970), 59–65; and Coosje van Bruggen, *John Baldessari* (Los Angeles: Museum of Contemporary Art, 1990), 108–13.

124
Burroughs, "Scrapbook Texts," in Burroughs and Gysin, *The Third Mind* (note **8**), 167.

125
William S. Burroughs, *Black Scrapbook*, c. 1964–65, Collection of Elyse and Stanley Grinstein; since French agendas, like American daybooks or calendars, are published in the fall of the previous year, Burroughs may have commenced this scrapbook in late 1963.

126
Ibid., page for August 22. Reference is also made in this page's script to "Are you a member of the union? Film Union 4 PM," a refrain running throughout the scrapbook.

127
Ibid., page preceding January 1 and third page following December 31; the same words of Hasan-i Sabbah are formatted as "Not knowing what is and is not knowing *I knew not*," in an epigraph to the "First Cut-ups" chapter in Burroughs and Gysin, *The Third Mind* (note **8**), 52.

128
Burroughs, *Black Scrapbook* (note **125**), page for December 5.

129
Ibid., page for November 19; cf. Gysin and Wilson, *Here to Go* (note **14**), 200.

130
Knickerbocker, "Interview" (note **8**), 2.

131
Burroughs, "Precise Intersection Points," in Burroughs and Gysin, *The Third Mind* (note **8**), 136.

132
This conjunction is described in ibid., 135. The illustration from *Newsweek* is included in one of the plates for the Grove Press edition of *The Third Mind* along with Burroughs's typescript; see Burroughs and Gysin, *The Third Mind* (note **8**), 153; and Burroughs and Gysin, "The Third Mind," mss. and mechanicals (note **78**), 106.

133
William S. Burroughs, *The Job* (London: Jonathan Cape, 1970), 16–17.

134
See Nicholas Zurbrugg, "Beckett, Proust, and Burroughs and the Perils of 'Image Warfare,'" in Jennie Skerl and Robin Lydenberg, *William S. Burroughs at the Front: Critical Reception, 1959–1989* (Carbondale: Southern Illinois University Press, 1991), 177–78.

135
Burroughs, "Precise Intersection Points," in Burroughs and Gysin, *The Third Mind* (note **8**), 136.

VII

WHO IS THE THIRD WHO WALKS ALWAYS BESIDE YOU?

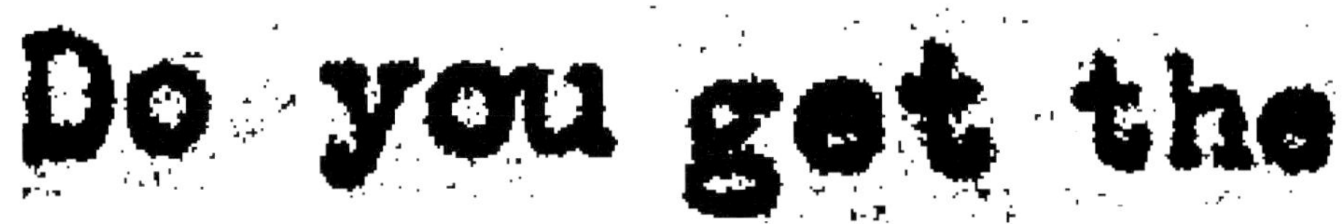

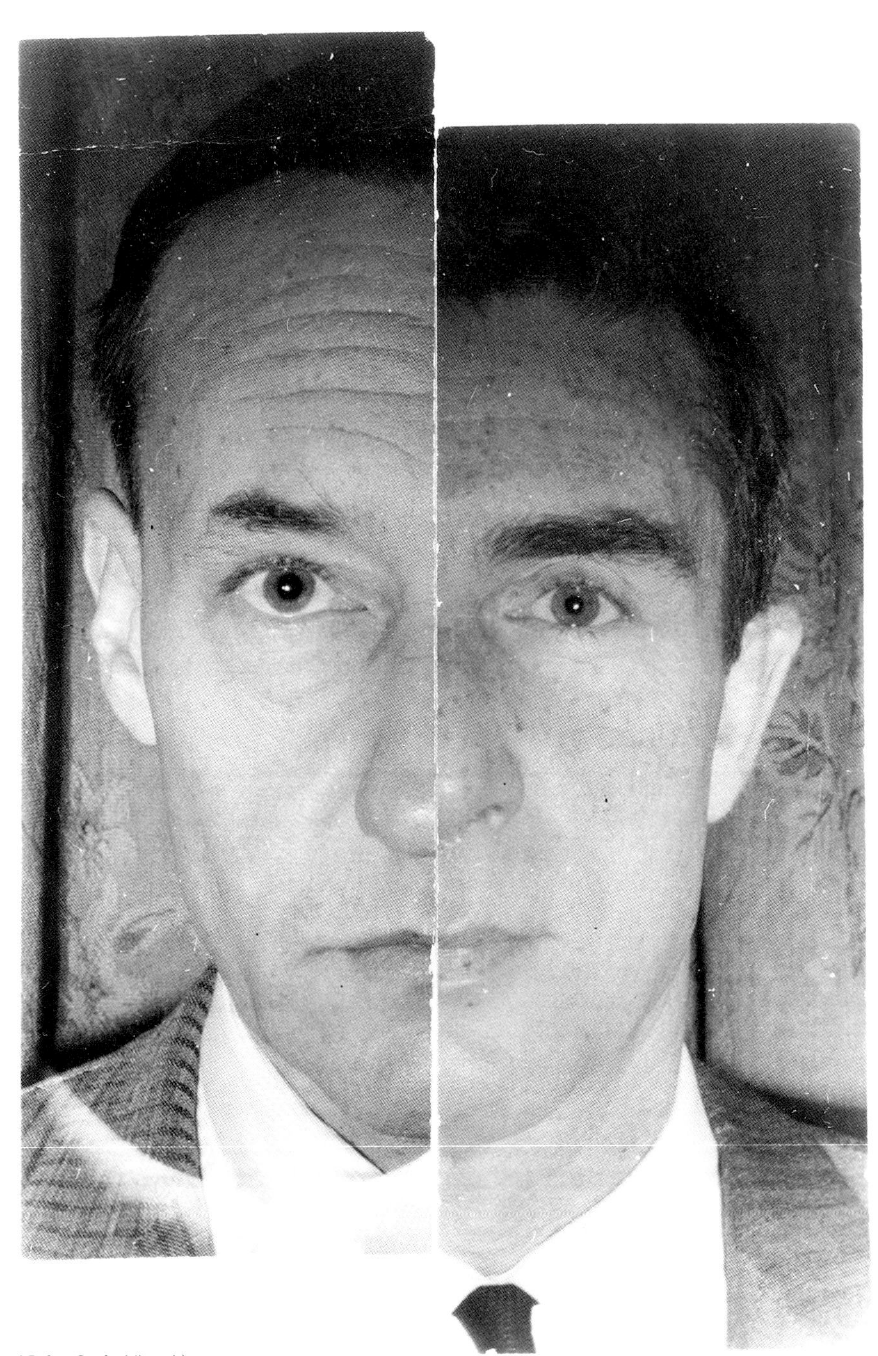

Ian Sommerville, **William S. Burroughs and Brion Gysin** (diptych), c. 1962, gelatin-silver prints, 3⅛ x 4¾ in. (7.9 x 12.1 cm), William S. Burroughs Papers, University Libraries, Special Collections, Arizona State University, Tempe

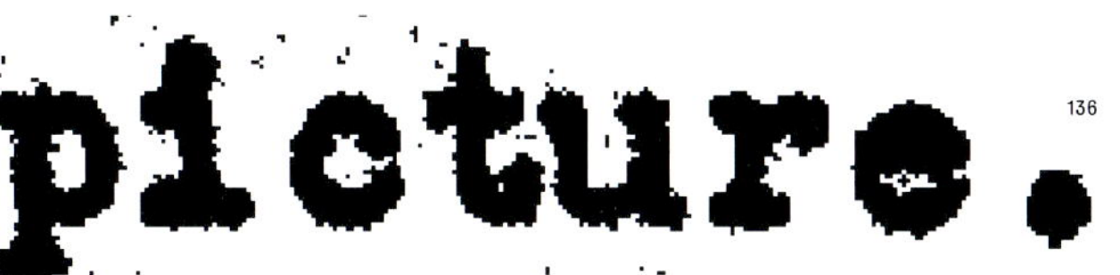 [136]

Burroughs extended his collage experiments beyond the scrapbook; some were assembled in a larger scale during the 1960s and appeared in such periodicals as *My Own Mag*, published in England by Jeff Nuttall, or *Lines*, edited in New York by Aram Saroyan. Mostly they were formatted in newspaper columns and often consisted of phrases rearranged from front pages of the *New York Times* along with photos or other illustrations. Frequently what began in one small publication as a cut-up typescript with crudely reproduced photographs would end up in another format, typeset and more clearly printed. In *Danger Ahead* (1965) a three-column cut-up text is typed above a rosette red seal and a photo of a magazine experiment. The text reports a deadly battle, mentioning "enemy intercepted September 17, 1899," "Klinker is dead…whistling 'Annie Laurie' against the frayed stars laser guns," and ending with "You can watch our worn out film dim jerky far away shut a bureau drawer." Reference to the popular song "Annie Laurie" is found on numerous pages of the *Black Scrapbook*, and the last passage is taken directly from *The Soft Machine*, first published in 1961.[137] The bureau drawer motif meanders throughout Burroughs's work, both literary and visual, in these years. In the film *Towers Open Fire* Burroughs is seen furtively cleaning out some dresser drawers in haste; stills from this sequence are found in the collages for *The Third Mind*, and in an unpublished collage made for this anthology, a gridded text including a cut-up version of *The Soft Machine*'s lines intertwines three photos of naked boys and carefully delineated drawings of two bureau drawers.[138] "The word cannot be expressed direct," Burroughs had written in *Naked Lunch*, "it can perhaps be indicated by mosaic of juxtaposition like articles abandoned in a hotel drawer, defined by negatives and absence."[139]

More formally Burroughs and Gysin had decided to compile all their published literary experiments and theoretical articles into one anthology, entitled *The Third Mind*, and since so much of the material referred to visual presentations, visual experiments were absolutely necessary to convey what they were doing. Burroughs and Gysin were in New York in 1965 working with Balch on the film *Guerrilla Conditions*. In his loft at 210 Center Street, Burroughs spent time working with cut-ups for small publications as well as for radio and filling files and scrapbooks with newspaper clippings of disasters. For a period of some months Gysin would daily go to Burroughs's loft to work on assembling their articles and texts and to assist in piecing together the various collages that would illustrate their techniques or simply stand alone. Most of the written material had already

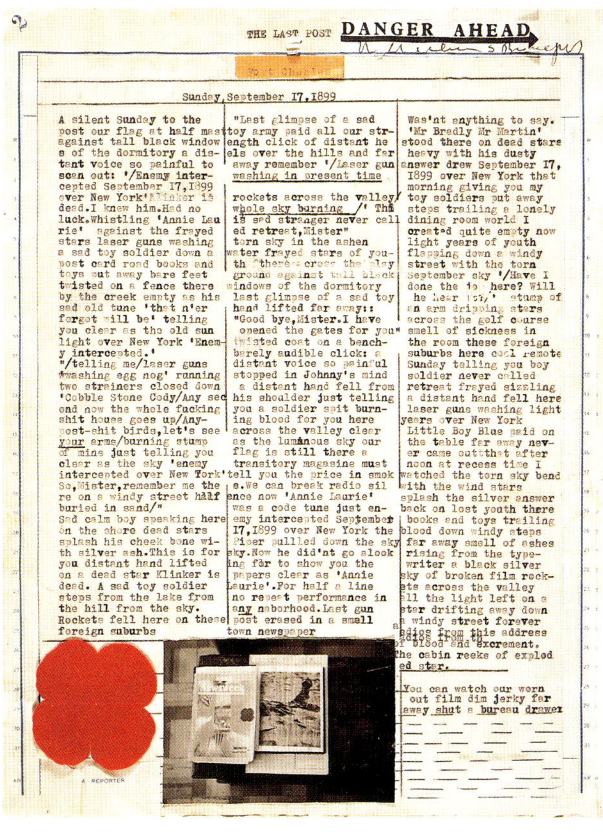

THE LAST POST **DANGER AHEAD**

Sunday, September 17, 1899

A silent Sunday to the
post our flag at half mast
against tall black window
s of the dormitory a dis-
tant voice so painful to
scan out: '/Enemy inter-
cepted September 17,1899
over New York' Klinker is
dead.I knew him.Had no
luck.Whistling 'Annie Lau
rie' against the frayed
stars laser guns washing
a sad toy soldier down a
post card road books and
toys put away bare feet
twisted on a fence there
by the creek empty as his
sad old tune 'that n'er
forgot will be' telling
you clear as the old sun
light over New York 'Enem-
y intercepted.'
"/telling me/laser guns
washing egg nog' running
two strainers closed down
'Cobble Stone Cody/Any sec
ond now the whole fucking
shit house goes up/Any-
post-shit birds,let's see
your arms/burning stump
of mine just telling you
clear as the sky 'enemy
intercepted over New York'
So,Mister,remember me the
re on a windy street half
buried in sand/"
Sad calm boy speaking here
on the shore dead stars
splash his cheek bone wi-
th silver ash.This is for
you distant hand lifted
on a dead star Klinker is
dead. A sad toy soldier
steps from the lake from
the hill from the sky.
Rockets fell here on these
foreign suburbs

"Last glimpse of a sad
toy army paid all our str-
ength click of distant he
els over the hills and far
away remember '/Laser gun
washing in present time

rockets across the valley/
whole sky burning /' This
is sad stranger never call
ed retreat,Mister"
torn sky in the ashen
water frayed stars of youth there cross the play
ground against tall black
windows of the dormitory
last glimpse of a sad toy
hand lifted far away::
"Good bye,Mister.I have
opened the gates for you"
twisted coat on a bench-
barely audible click: a
distant voice so painful
stopped in Johnny's mind
a distant hand fell from
his shoulder just telling
you a soldier spit burn-
ing blood for you here
across the valley clear
as the luminous sky our
flag is still there a
transitory magasine must
tell you the price in smok
e.We can break radio sil
ence now 'Annie Laurie'
was a code tune just en-
emy intercepted September
17,1899 over New York the
Piper pullled down the sky
sky.Now he did'nt go alook
ing for to show you the
papers clear as 'Annie
Laurie'.For half a line
no repeat performance in
any naborhood.Last gun
post erased in a small
town newspaper

Was'nt anything to say.
'Mr Bredly Mr Martin'
stood there on dead stars
heavy with his dusty
answer drew September 17,
1899 over New York that
morning giving you my
toy soldiers put away
steps trailing a lonely
dining room world I
created quite empty now
light years of youth
flapping down a windy
street with the torn
September sky '/Have I
done the job here? Will
he hear ...' stump of
an arm dripping stars
across the golf course
smell of sickness in
the room these foreign
suburbs here cool remote
Sunday telling you boy
soldier never called
retreat frayed sizzling
a distant hand fell here
laser guns washing light
years over New York
Little Boy Blue paid on
the table far away nev-
er came out that after
noon at recess time I
watched the torn sky bend
with the wind stars
splash the silver answer
back on lost youth there
books and toys trailing
blood down windy steps
far away smell of ashes
rising from the type-
writer a black silver
sky of broken film rock-
ets across the valley
all the light left on a
star drifting away down
a windy street forever
adios from this address
of blood and excrement.
The cabin reeks of explod
ed star.

You can watch our worn
out film dim jerky far
away shut a bureau drawer

William S. Burroughs, **Danger Ahead**, 1965, cat. no. 10

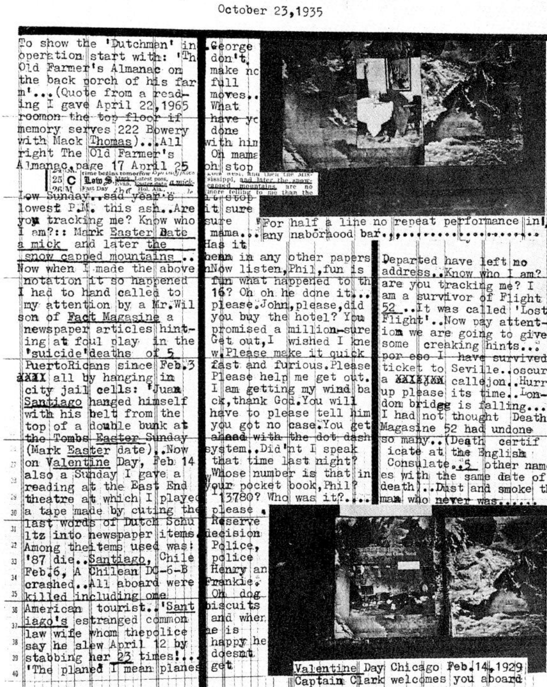

******************************THE DEAD STAR*****************************PAGE#1

DUTCH SCHULTZ MACHINE GUNNED IN NEWARK BAR...3 AIDES DIE

October 23,1935

William S. Burroughs, "The Dead Star...Dutch Schultz Machine Gunned in Newark Bar...3 Aides Die...October 23, 1935" (detail), from **My Own Mag**, no. 13 (August 1965), collection of Joseph Zinnato, Burbank

William S. Burroughs, "The Dead Star...Dutch Schultz Machine Gunned in Newark Bar...3 Aides Die...October 23, 1935" (detail), from **Nova Broadcast**, no. 5 (1969), collection of Joseph Zinnato, Burbank

THE DEAD STAR

Dutch Schultz Machine Gunned in Newark Bar

3 Aides Die

October 23, 1935

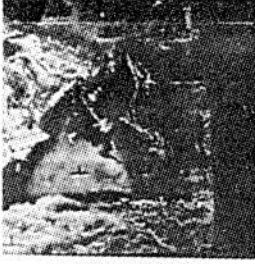

'No repeat performance...'

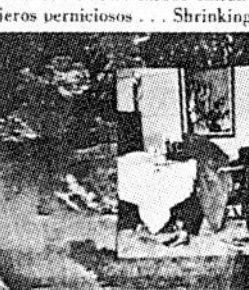

'...in any naborhood bar'

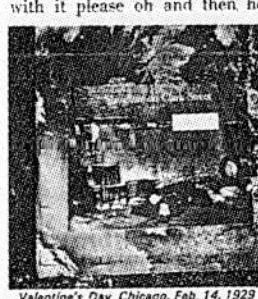

Valentine's Day, Chicago, Feb. 14, 1929

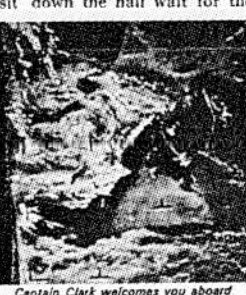

Captain Clark welcomes you aboard

appeared in such periodicals as *Evergreen Review*, *Art and Literature*, *Yugen*, *Insect Trust Gazette*, and the London *Times Literary Supplement*, and these could easily be directly reproduced in the anthology, with minimal resetting of type. The collages, however, had to be freshly created, and many of these would be inspired by or adapted from the pages of Burroughs's own scrapbooks. Most of the approximately seventy collages made for *The Third Mind* were organized along grid lines, loosely articulated by the application of Gysin's hand-carved brayer, but decidedly more open and deliberately composed than those found in the scrapbooks. Grove Press, which had published the American editions of Burroughs's first four novels, planned to publish this illustrated anthology in 1970 and sell it at a retail price of $10. They went so far as to paste up the mechanicals and print a four-color dust jacket, presumably for display at trade shows.

Exactly why Grove abandoned the project at such a late stage is unclear. The general theory is that it was economically unfeasible to produce the work for a retail price of $10, which was the average price for a fully illustrated art-history text at the time. Another possibility is that Grove's sales force simply did not have a clue as to where to place or exactly how to market this kind of hybrid book. In his introductory text to the Viking edition of 1978, Gérard-Georges Lemaire, who translated the book into French as *Oeuvre croisée*, pointed to the work's complexity and lack of definition: "It eludes definition just as it eludes itself; a prey to unfathomable anamorphosis, it rubs itself out and rewrites itself; it allows itself to be read, only to slip away. *The Third Mind* jumbles the linguistic network, simultaneously revealing and antagonizing it. It is a strategic device for confronting semiotic assaults."[140] Regarding the texts, Lemaire quoted Jacques Derrida who claimed that "nothing remains but an immense web of reading and writing, folding, unfolding, and refolding indefinitely."[141] Like the texts, the collages "are subject to a contamination and dismemberment that link them to the process of the textual discourse."[142]

The total number of artworks made for *The Third Mind* is unknown. The set of mechanicals (or layout boards), manuscripts, and collages (both textual and photographic) that is presently in the collection of the Los Angeles County Museum of Art contains more than seventy unique works of art and original visual texts. A private collection in Paris has at least one collage and a negative photostat that appear to have been a part of the entire set. Apparently the collection of originals moved from New York to Paris for the French translation, and Gysin, who was then living in Paris, is said to have signed some of the collages and given them to friends.[143] From Paris they returned to the United States after being sold to the rare-book dealer Raymond Aaron, disappeared into a private collection, and returned to the market in 1992, when it was acquired by the museum. Of the set that is now in Los Angeles, six works are notated "do not use." The Viking edition reproduces twenty-six of the collages (reproduced, it would seem, from the French edition or the printer's plates and not the originals), and one of these reproductions does not appear among the originals in the LACMA collection. Not all of the chapters or parts of the original manuscript are included in the Viking edition, nor do the plates in it appear in the precise sequence laid out in the late 1960s.

The obvious source for the anthology's title, *The Third Mind*, is on line 360 of Eliot's *The Waste Land*: "Who is the third who walks always beside you?"[144] Eliot's note to the line alludes to an Antarctic expedition, "I think one of Shackleton's," where the exhausted explorers suffered a delusion that there was "*one more member*" than their number.[145] In his own note to *The Third Mind*, Burroughs wrote that the title stemmed from *Think and Grow Rich*, a twentieth-century guide to salesmanship

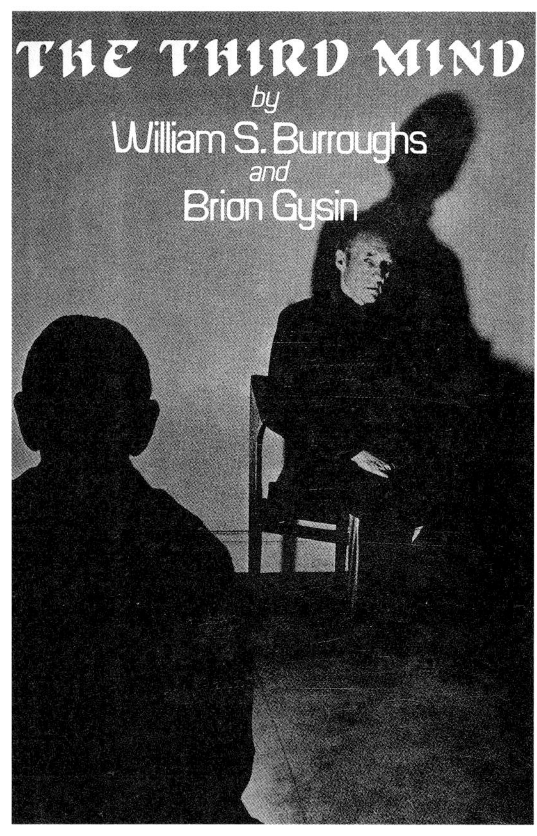

William S. Burroughs and Brion Gysin, **The Third Mind**, 1978, cover photograph by Mayotte Magnus

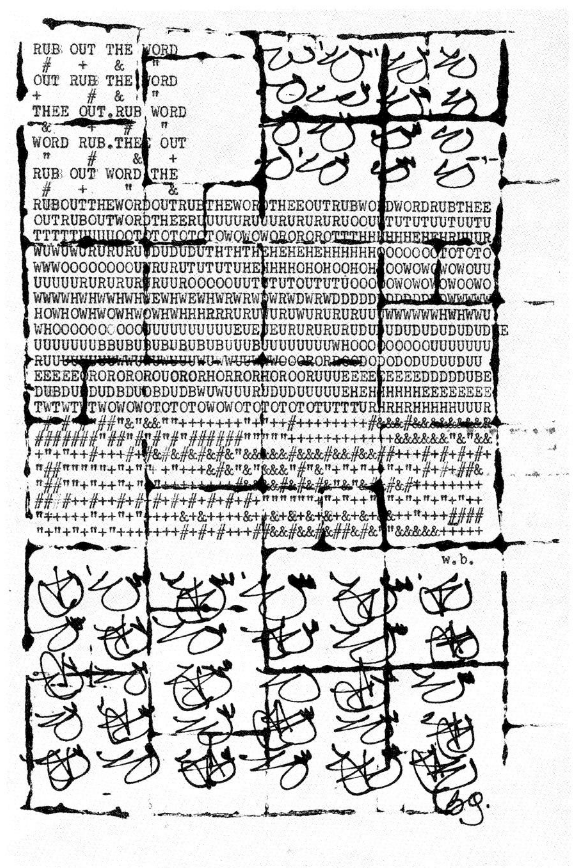

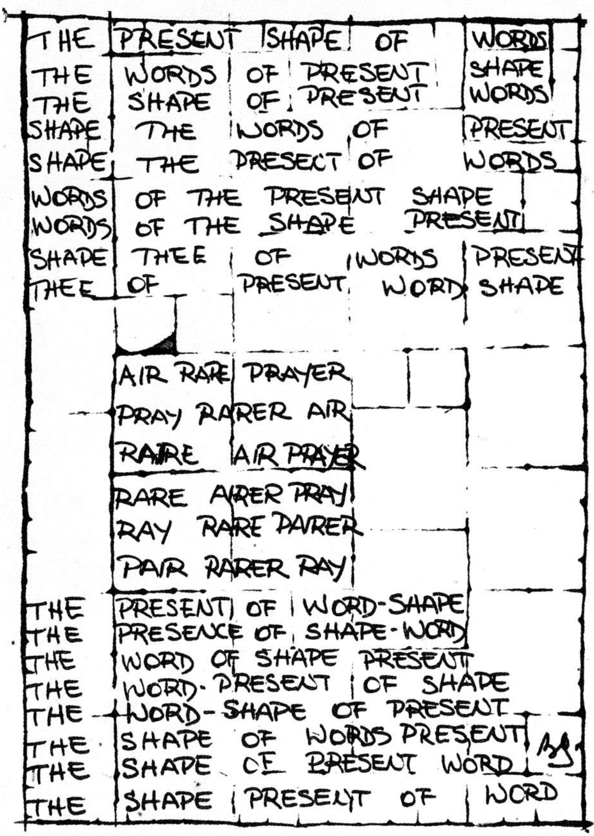

William S. Burroughs and Brion Gysin, untitled [Rub Out the Word], c. 1965, cat. no. 15

William S. Burroughs and Brion Gysin, untitled [The Present Shape of Words], c. 1965, cat. no. 16

William S. Burroughs and Brion Gysin, untitled [Breathe in the Words], c. 1965, cat. no. 17

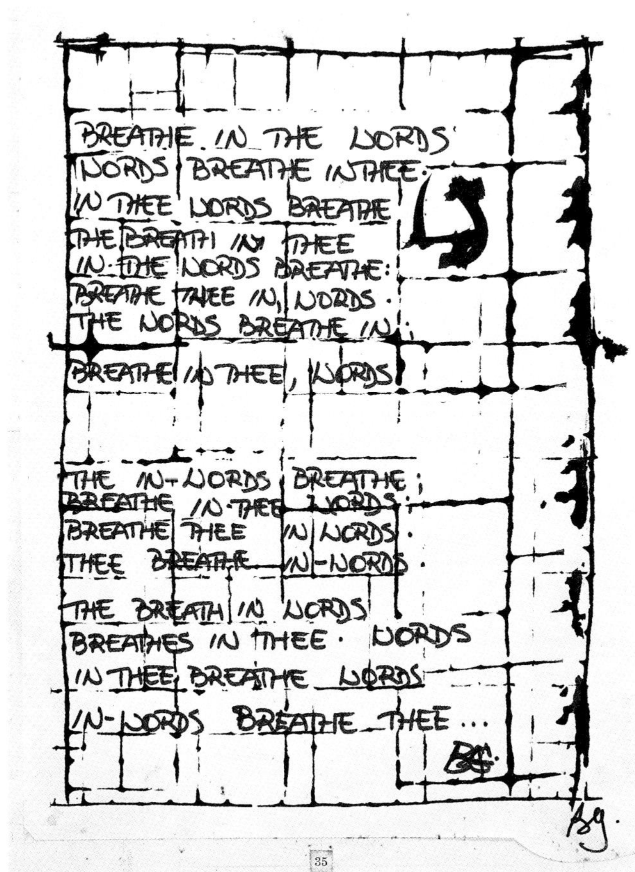

by Napoleon Hill, who counseled that when two minds work together there is always a third one that results.[146]

Burroughs realized in his collaboration with Gysin an incredible union of two individually creative forces, a syncretic meshing of minds that brought together images and texts, cut-ups, fold-ins, permutations, ideas of tape-experiments and cinema, hieroglyphics, and flicker vision. While nearly each text is initialed by its original author, a blurring of identities in essence did occur in the process of constructing the collages. Two sheets of hand-lettered permutations on grids are initialed by Gysin, and one sheet devoted to "Rub Out the Word" combines a typescript of the permutation and its transformation into punctuation marks initialed "W.B." with Gysin's "faux Arabic" calligraphy initialed "B.G." Other than these, only one of the other plates for the edition is initialed or signed.

Each of the collages made to introduce one of the texts is on watercolor paper, inked by Gysin's brayer, and contains one or more 35-mm contact prints or larger black-and-white photographs positioned somewhere in the grid or in line with the grid's coordinates. Often the images are blatantly self-referential, as in *Permutations*, where snapshots of the authors are combined with shots of two of Gysin's brayer-and-text paintings and of one of Burroughs's collages placed lying atop what appears to be a radio. *Scrapbooks* jumbles up a photograph of a tea service with photographs of newspaper cut-ups and the beginnings of yet another collage (The Nova Express), in which we see a snapshot of Burroughs pouring "Real English Tea," a slightly different image from the one found in the *Black Scrapbook*. *The Big Survey* juxtaposes a portrait of Burroughs, a half-portrait of Ian Sommerville, and two views of a street seen from a balcony united by isometric perspective lines drawn in ink. In a text-image piece made for the following page, which renders the drawing intelligible,

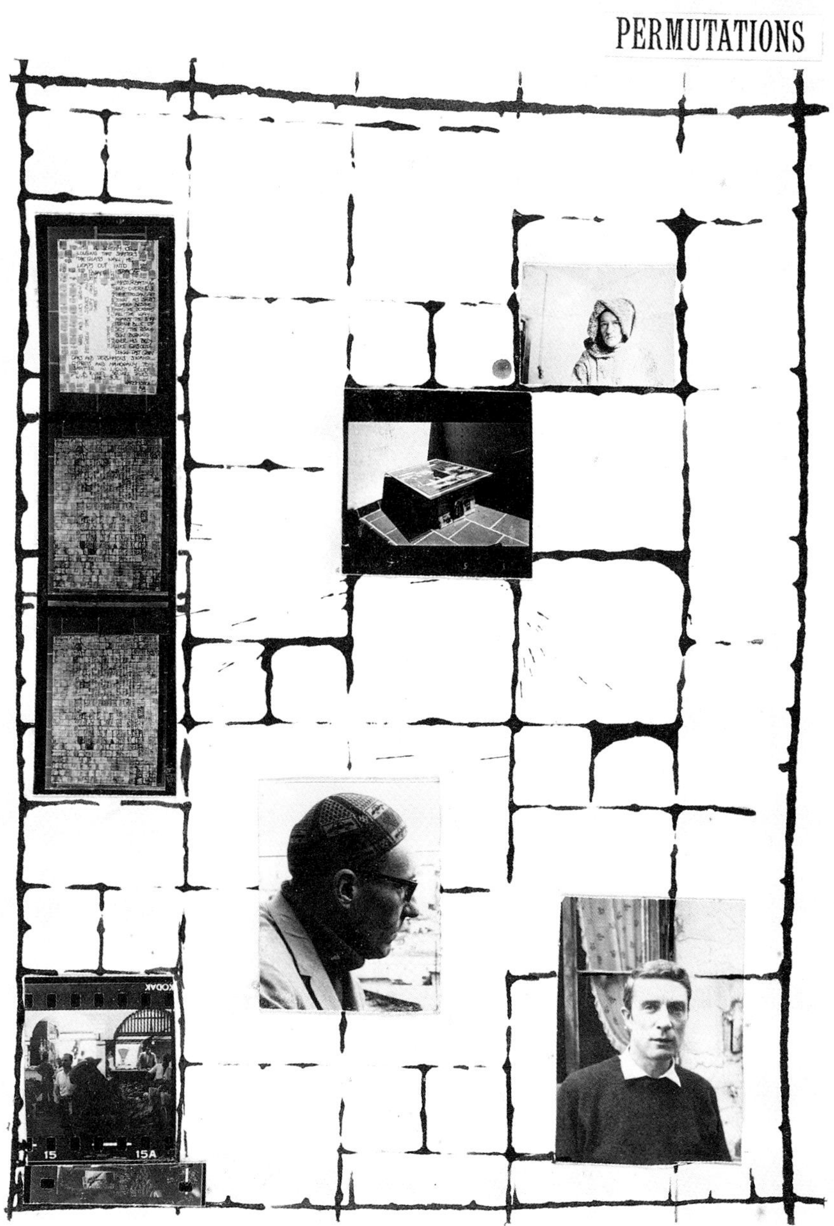

William S. Burroughs and Brion Gysin, **Permutations**, c. 1965, cat. no. 14

the text explains the schema as the "first precision time compass," invented by Sommerville:

1. Camera at position O takes a picture—framed by ABCD 2. The picture is developed and printed and later 3. the eye at position O looks at the photograph A'B'C'D' The photograph fills the same space in the eyes of the observer as ABCD and naturally "fits" reality. A'B'C'D' could be replaced by a movie screen, etc.[147]

In a similar fashion three years later Robert Smithson would begin working with "memory traces" and "photo-markers" that reversed what normally occurs in an art gallery by taking a photograph of a landscape back into the landscape in order to have time frame history.[148] Burroughs and Smithson, independent of each other, viewed the photograph as a means of locating coordinates in time.

By the time Smithson thought of cameras as "lenses of the unlimited reproduction" and conceived the idea of an "Infinite Camera" that was "somewhere between the still and the movie camera,"[149] Burroughs and Sommerville had already played with experiments to infinitely multiply the photograph.

SCRAPBOOKS

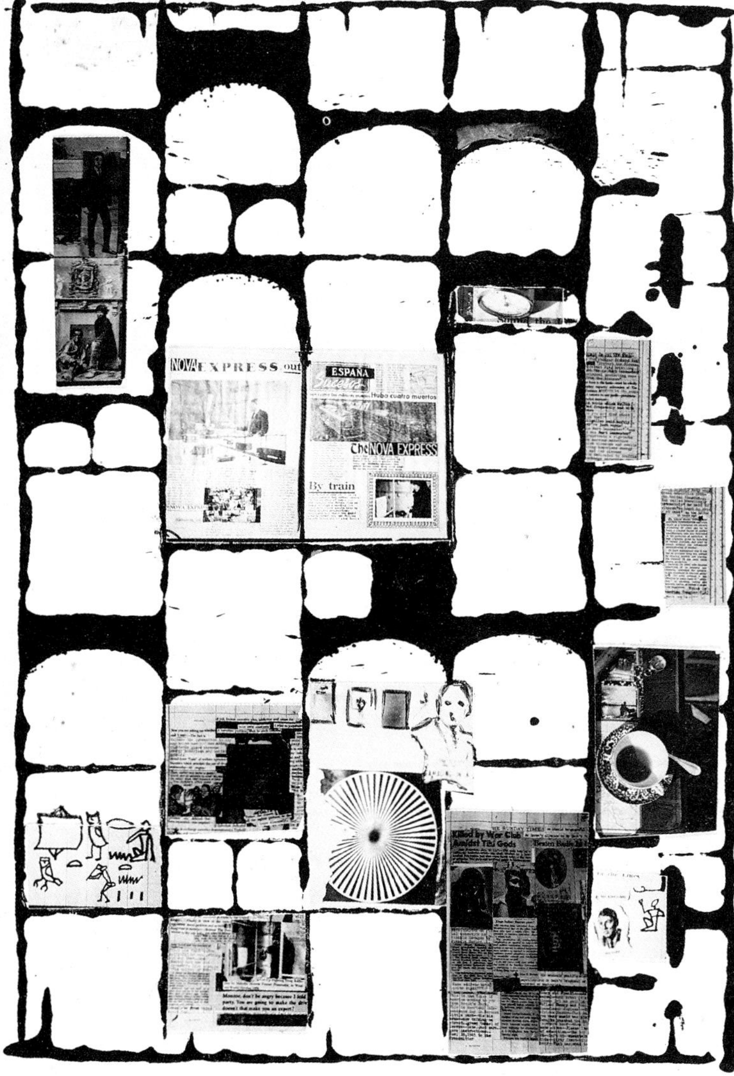

William S. Burroughs and Brion Gysin, **Scrapbooks**, c. 1965, cat. no. 19

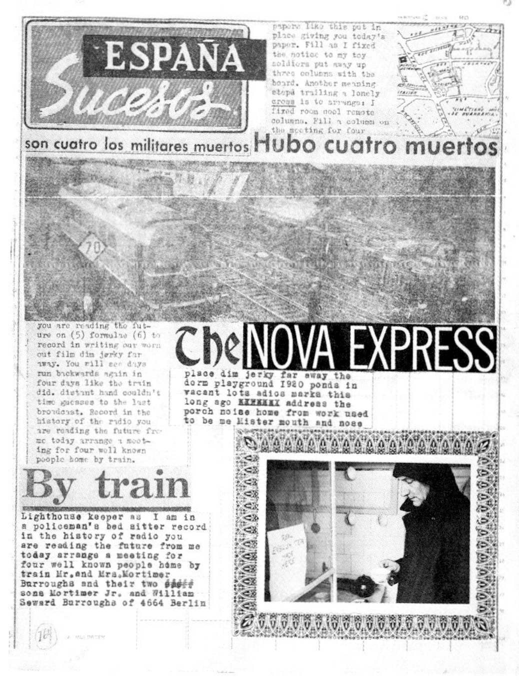

William S. Burroughs and Brion Gysin, untitled [The Nova Express], c. 1965, cat. no. 34

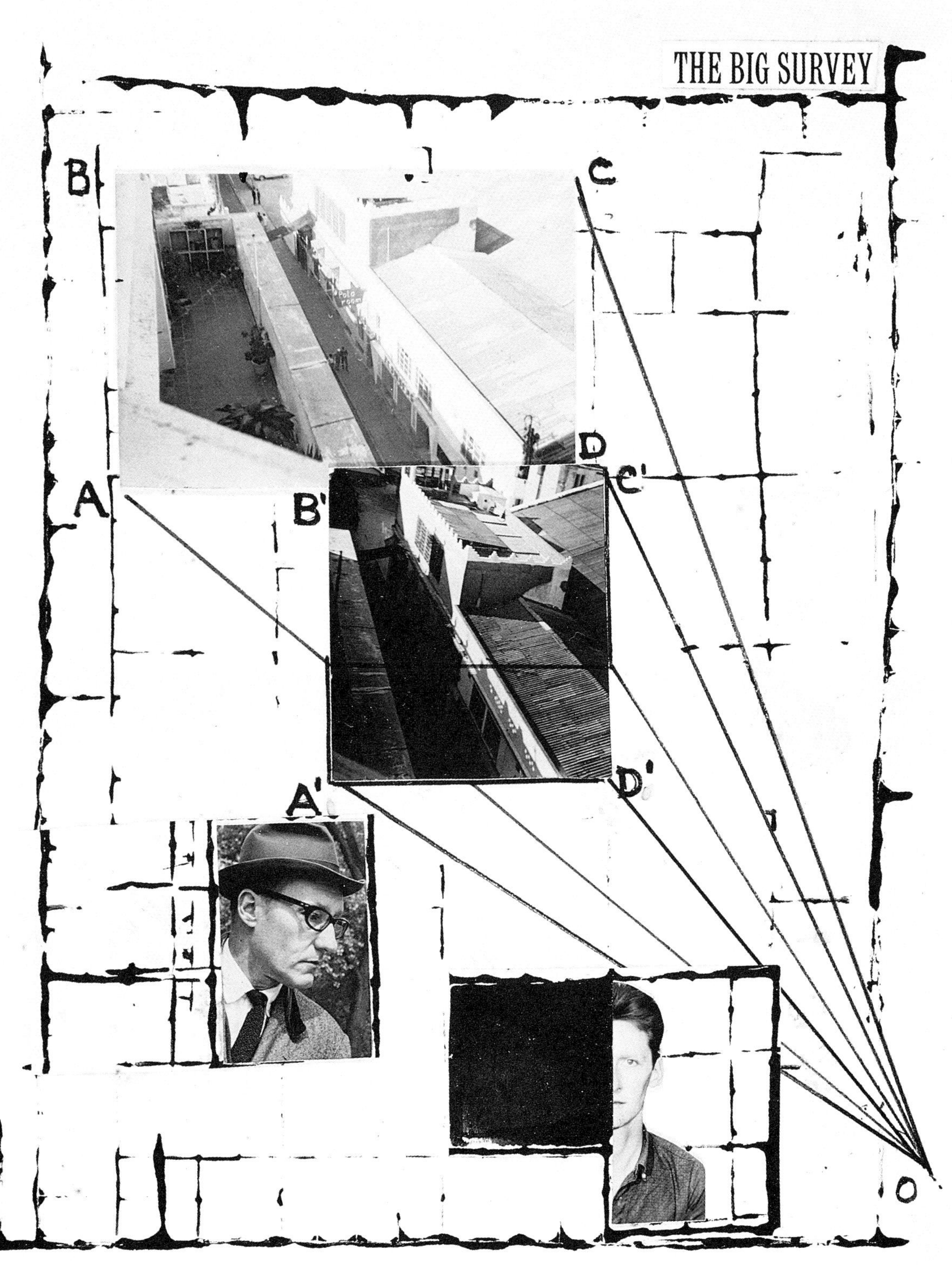

William S. Burroughs and Brion Gysin, **The Big Survey**, c. 1965, cat. no. 18

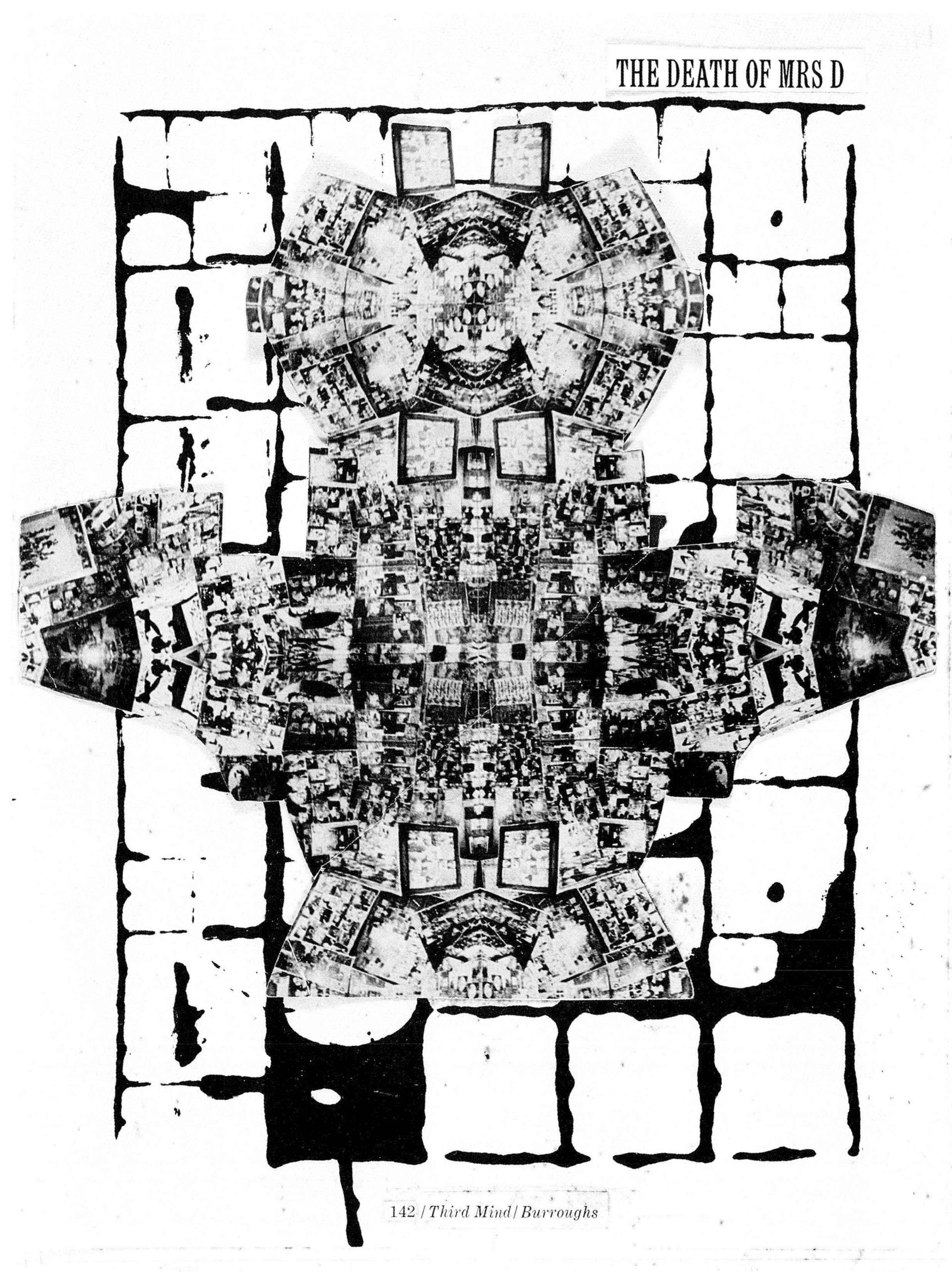

William S. Burroughs and Brion Gysin, **The Death of Mrs. D**, c. 1965, cat. no. 20

One of their results is collaged onto *The Death of Mrs D* in *The Third Mind*; it is also reproduced in the Viking edition but left unannotated and undescribed. The process was detailed, however, in an article by Sommerville that clearly anticipates the fractal geometries of chaos theory and was published in an issue of *Gnaoua* in 1964:

Imagine a two-dimensional plane covered with a rectangular grid. Further imagine that each pair of rectangles which have a side in common are such that each of the pair is the mirror image of the other, being reflected across their common side. Then this photograph is a piece of such a grid. A three rectangles by three rectangles slice of an infinite sheet, wherein each rectangle is a collage of photographs which are in turn collages of photographs etc.…Take your entire photo collection and reduce it to a single picture by a multiple collage process, adding any other images of particular interest until the basic rectangle is obtained. Nine prints are necessary, five printed normally, four printed under exactly the same conditions but with the negative reversed, the prints are trimmed to form perfect rectangles and then collaged together as described. The process may of course be continued.[150]

I started my trip in the
morgue with old newspapers,
folding in today with
yesterday and typing out
composites—When you skip
through a newspaper as most
of us do you see a great
deal more than you know—
In fact you see it all on
a subliminal level—
Now when I fold today's paper
in with yesterday's paper
and arrange the pictures
to form a time section montage,
I am literally moving
back to the time when I
read yesterday's paper,
that is traveling in time
back to yesterday—I did
this eight hours a day for
three months—I went back
as far as the papers went—
I dug out old magazines and
forgotten novels and letters—
I made fold-ins and
composites and did the same
with photos.

The Soft Machine

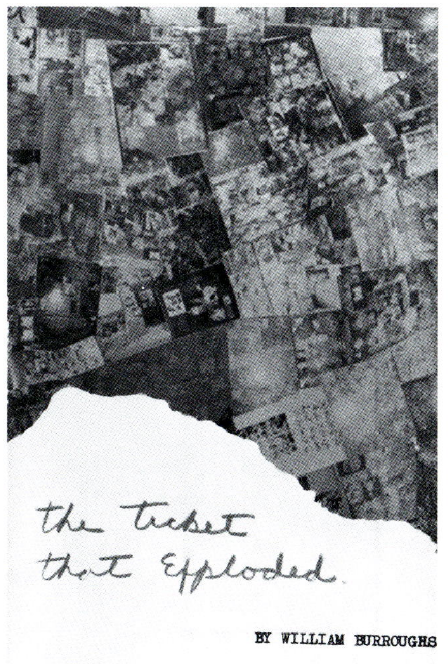

Ian Sommerville, dust-jacket photography for **The Ticket That Exploded**, 1962, cat. no. 132

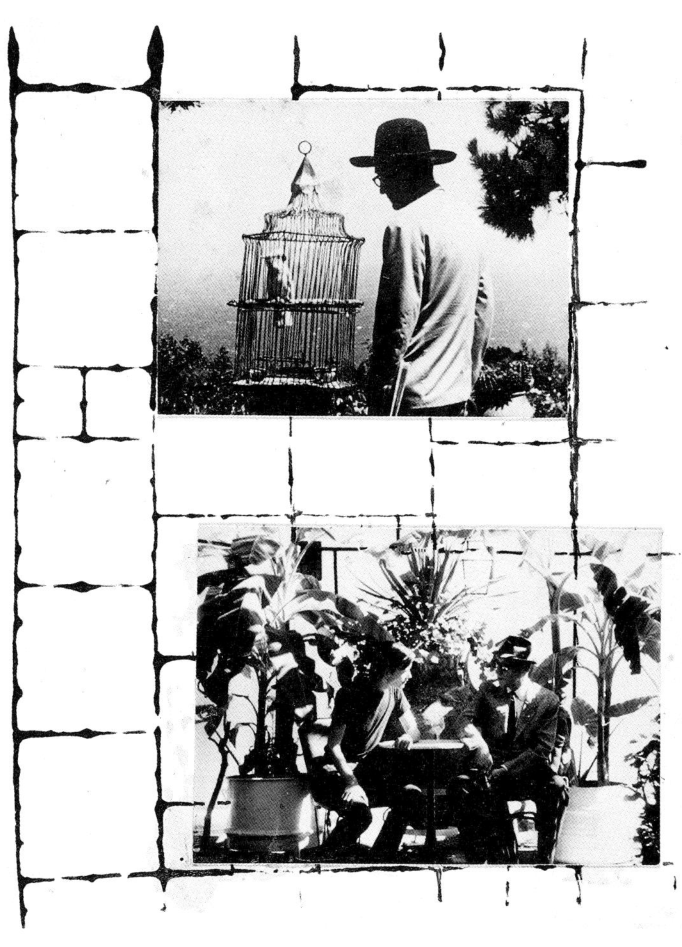

William S. Burroughs and Brion Gysin, untitled [William Buys a Parrot], c. 1965, cat. no. 23

William S. Burroughs and Brion Gysin, untitled [William and the Captain], c. 1965, cat. no. 24

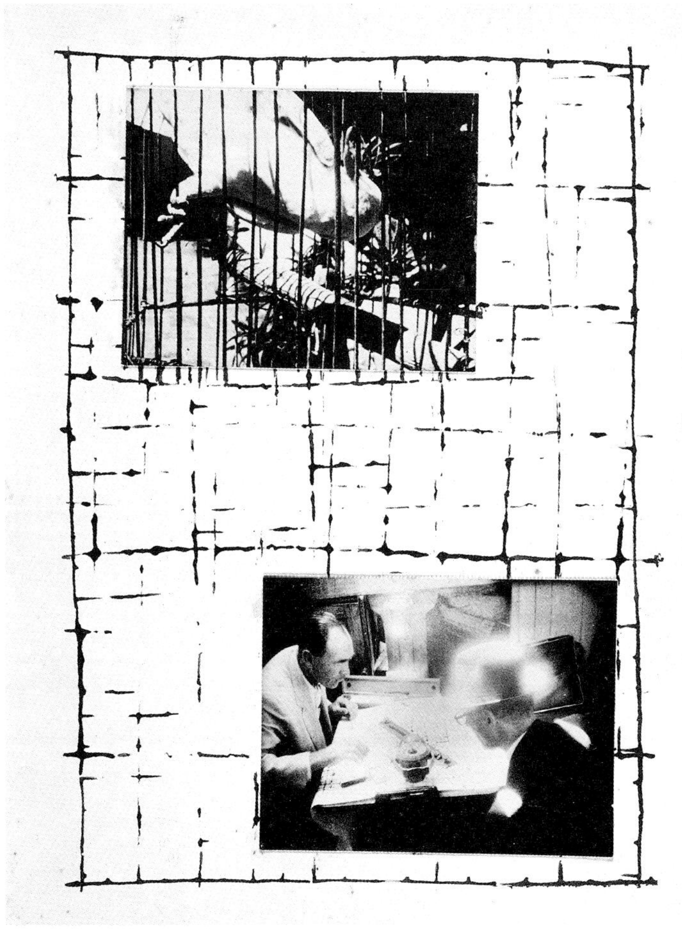

This experiment may very well stand for Burroughs's idea of writing binary information at a molecular level where "an infinity of variety" is created at the information level.[151]

In one collage Burroughs appears as Doctor Zeit M.D. (Dr. Benway?) and seems to conflate this persona with that of the comic-strip hero Rex Morgan, M.D. Using stills from Balch's films, Burroughs is portrayed in three other collages as buying a parrot, discussing matters with someone known as "The Captain,"[152] and emptying out bureau drawers in some room. A number of the collages are made up of multiple disaster scenes such as tornados and hurricanes; and in one ambitious collage ("Tornado Dead: 223"), Burroughs brings together five disaster photos from newspapers and multiple headlines attesting to their death tolls, each of which contain the number 23, such as "23 Die in Saigon" or "Apartment Blast Kills 23." Victor Bockris, editor of *With William Burroughs: A Report from the Bunker*, relates that in London in 1964 Burroughs read from newspaper clippings, each of which involved the number 23.[153] Apparently in the early 1960s Burroughs had been told by a certain Captain Clark that he had piloted the ferry between Tangier and Gibraltar for 23 years without an accident. The very same day, the ferry sank, drowning Clark and all on board, and that evening a radio newscast reported the crash of an Eastern Airlines flight number 23 en route between New York and Miami whose pilot was another Captain Clark.[154] Coincidences or intersection points? The character "Genial 23" appears in *The Ticket That Exploded*, and in *My Education* "Observer William: 023" lists what most offends him.[155]

In the collage featuring W. R. Hearst Jr., Burroughs's typescript in red takes us back to Cut City, which appeared at the beginning and end of the *Black Scrapbook*. In this collage, however, there are no razor fights, but American capitalism is certainly denounced, in the guise of "Mr Anshclinger Hurst Ford Rockefller and you Board Members, vulagr stupid Americans." A newspaper engraving of William Randolph Hearst Jr. is mirrored by a photomechanical illustration of Burroughs captioned, "Burroughs: Quiet down, think," and showing him standing in front of a derelict sleeping on a park bench. A photo of an interior, an appropriated text concerning a ship disaster, a disk of sunburst rays, and a panel of colorful rubbings by oilstick or crayon complete the collage. Both the Hearst engraving and the text are burnt around their edges. In the collage bearing the words "Plan Drug Addiction," a large, drawn and anguished face of a man is completely engulfed by a cacophony of texts, both typed and cut-up, a comic-strip cell of a criminal being handcuffed, and a snapshot of Burroughs pouring "Real English Tea" that is identical to one in the *Black Scrapbook*. The texts are nearly all concerned with drugs and their criminalization: "Plan Drug Addiction,"

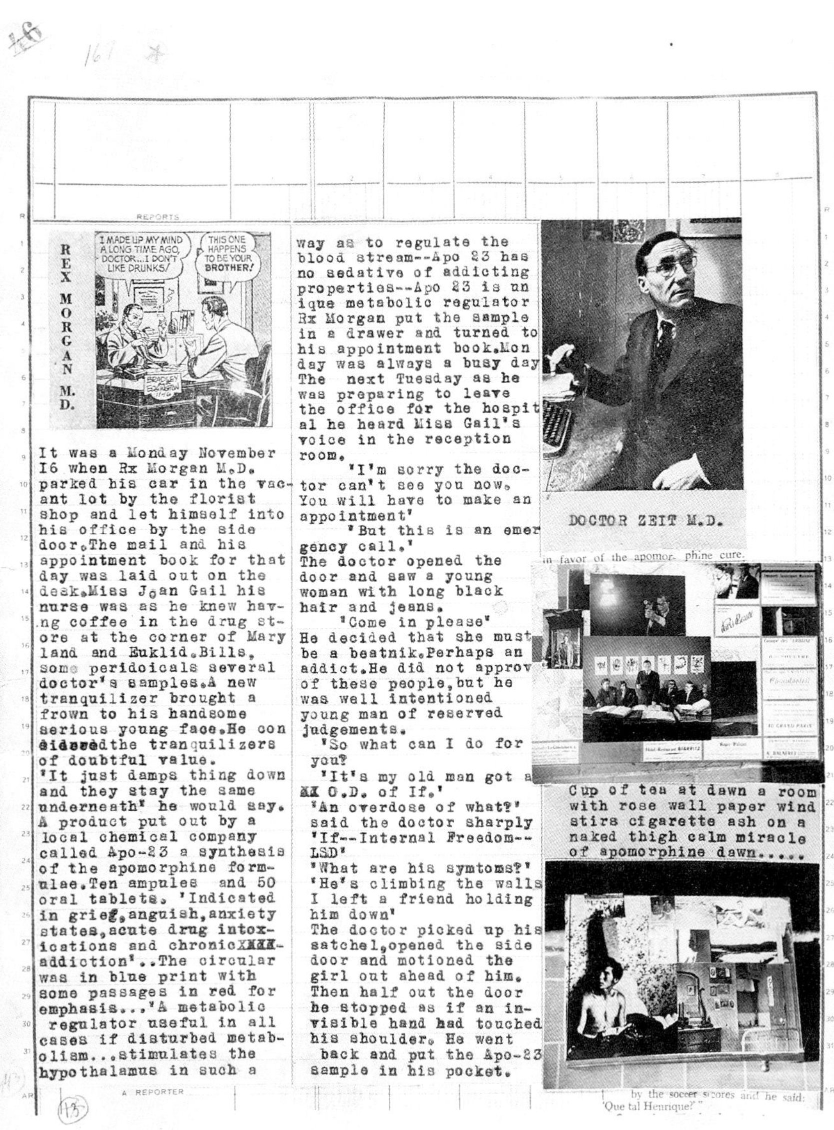

William S. Burroughs and Brion Gysin, untitled [Doctor Zeit M.D.], c. 1965, cat. no. 26

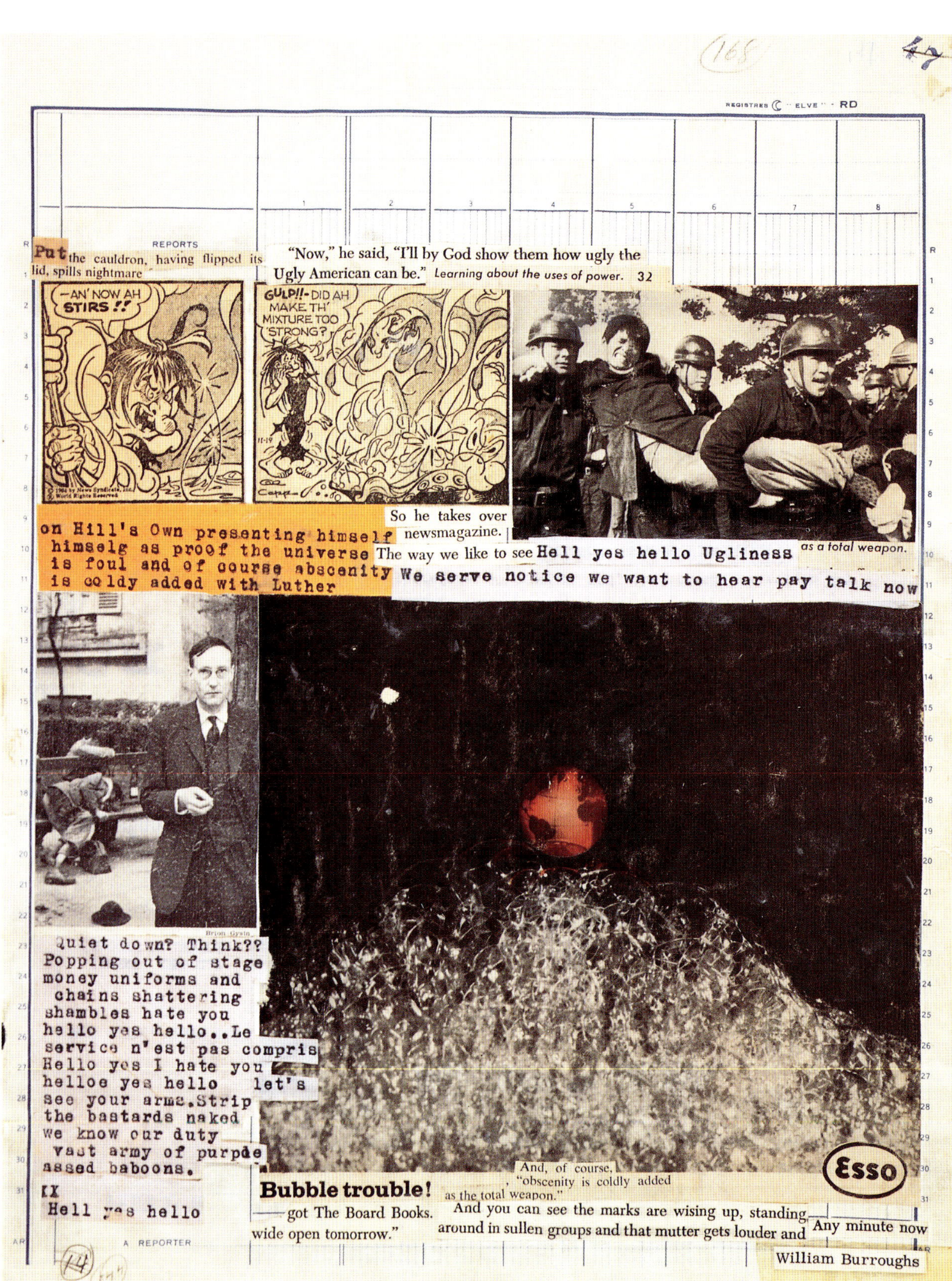

William S. Burroughs and Brion Gysin, untitled [Bubble Trouble], c. 1965, cat. no. 27

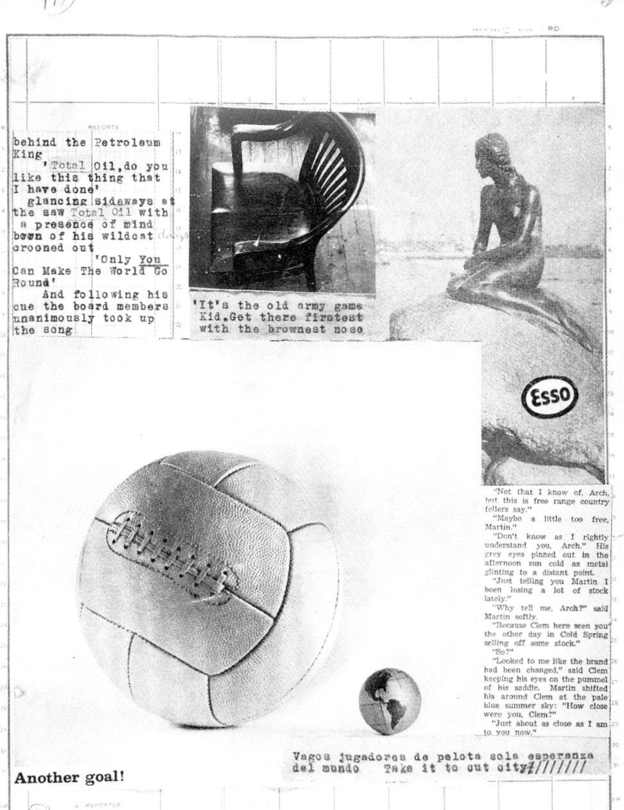

William S. Burroughs and Brion Gysin, untitled [Another Goal], c. 1965, cat. no. 29

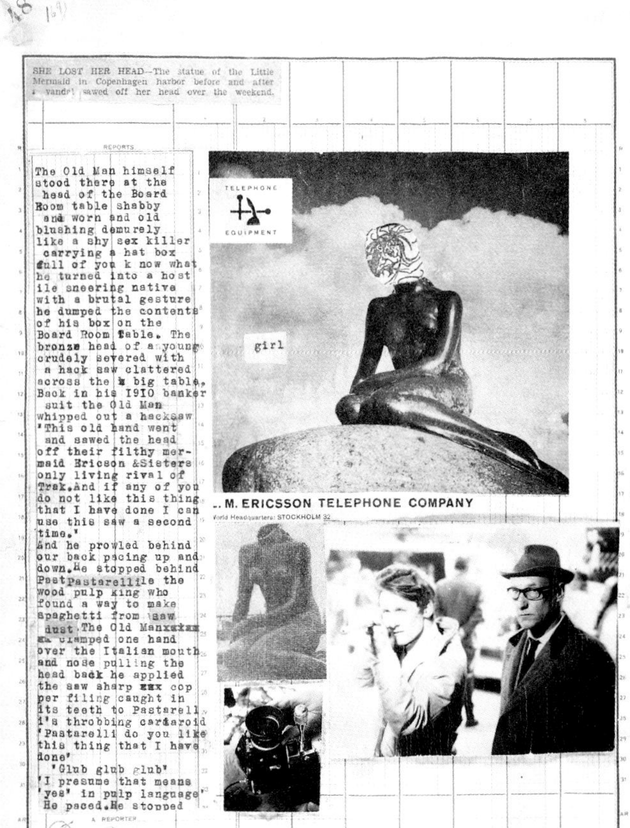

William S. Burroughs and Brion Gysin, untitled [Girl], c. 1965, cat. no. 28

"a narcotics problem / Must be made criminal," "a Typhoid Mary who will spread narcotics problem," "Burt Lancaster made criminal protecting society from the disease," and, emphatically, "Progress Is Not Our Goal." Across the mouth of the anguished head are the words, "Protect the disease / all the ugliest pictures in the." For Burroughs everything that controls is a virus, including junk. Toward the end of *The Third Mind*, Burroughs wrote,

Gentlemen, the virus is an ugly picture looking for a mirror with understandable but absolute need. I don't care how good the picture looks to start with—when it experiences the absolute need that any image organism must experience when image is withdrawn, it becomes a very ugly picture, indeed. And...the uglier you are, the steadier you score.[...] And, let me warn you young officers, especially; a virus is never more dangerous than when on the mooch...and they always are. Reluctantly, we vote to view *any* virus with armed alertness. Any more questions drifting down a windy street?[156]

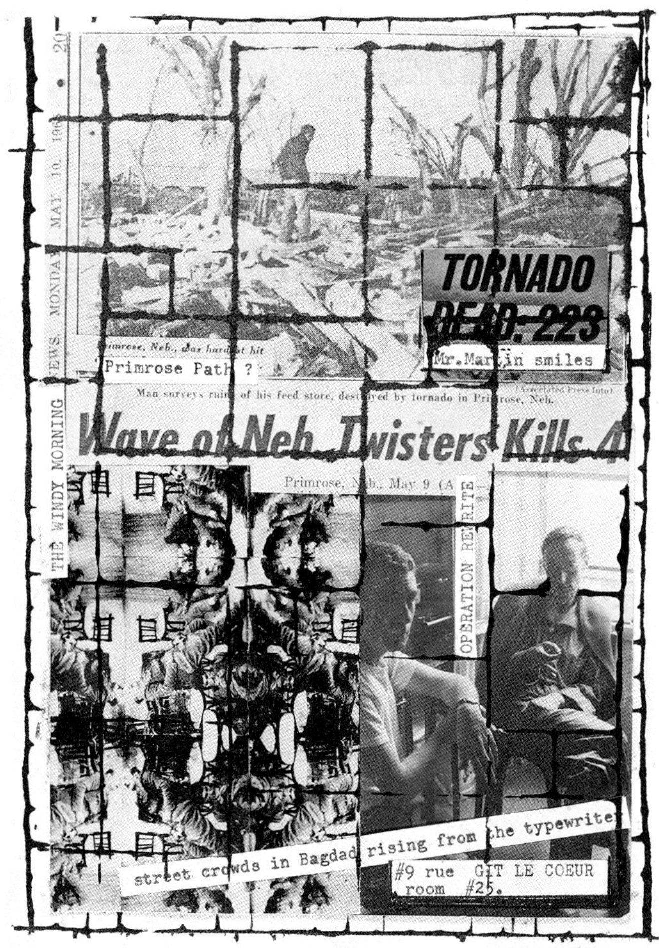

William S. Burroughs and Brion Gysin,
untitled [Primrose Path ?], c. 1965, cat. no. 30

William S. Burroughs and Brion Gysin, untitled
[The Energy of a Hurricane], c. 1965, cat. no. 32

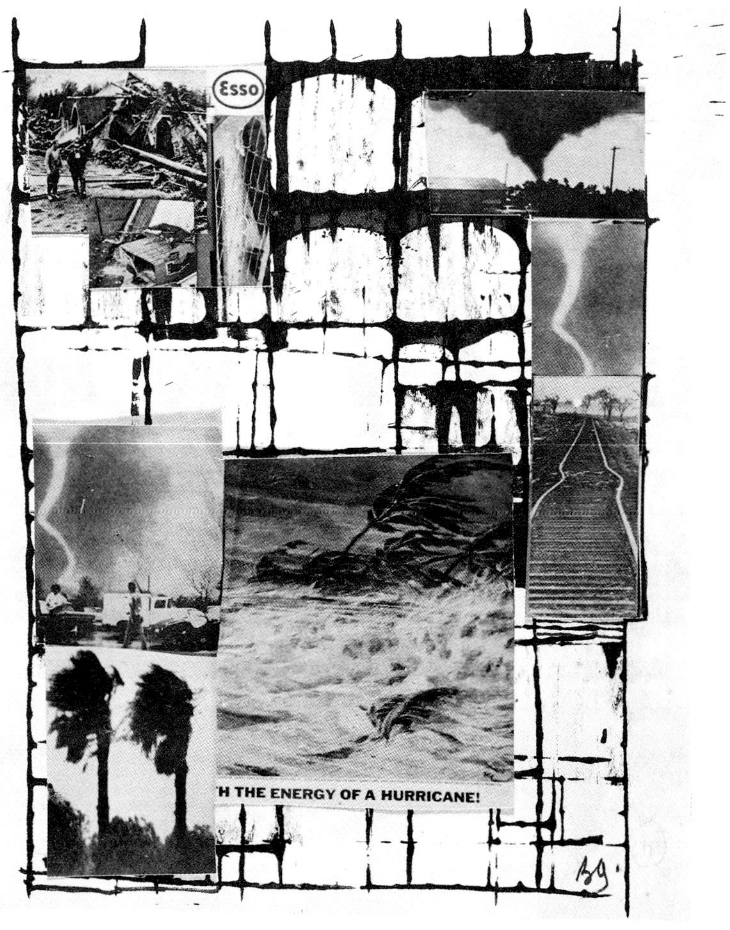

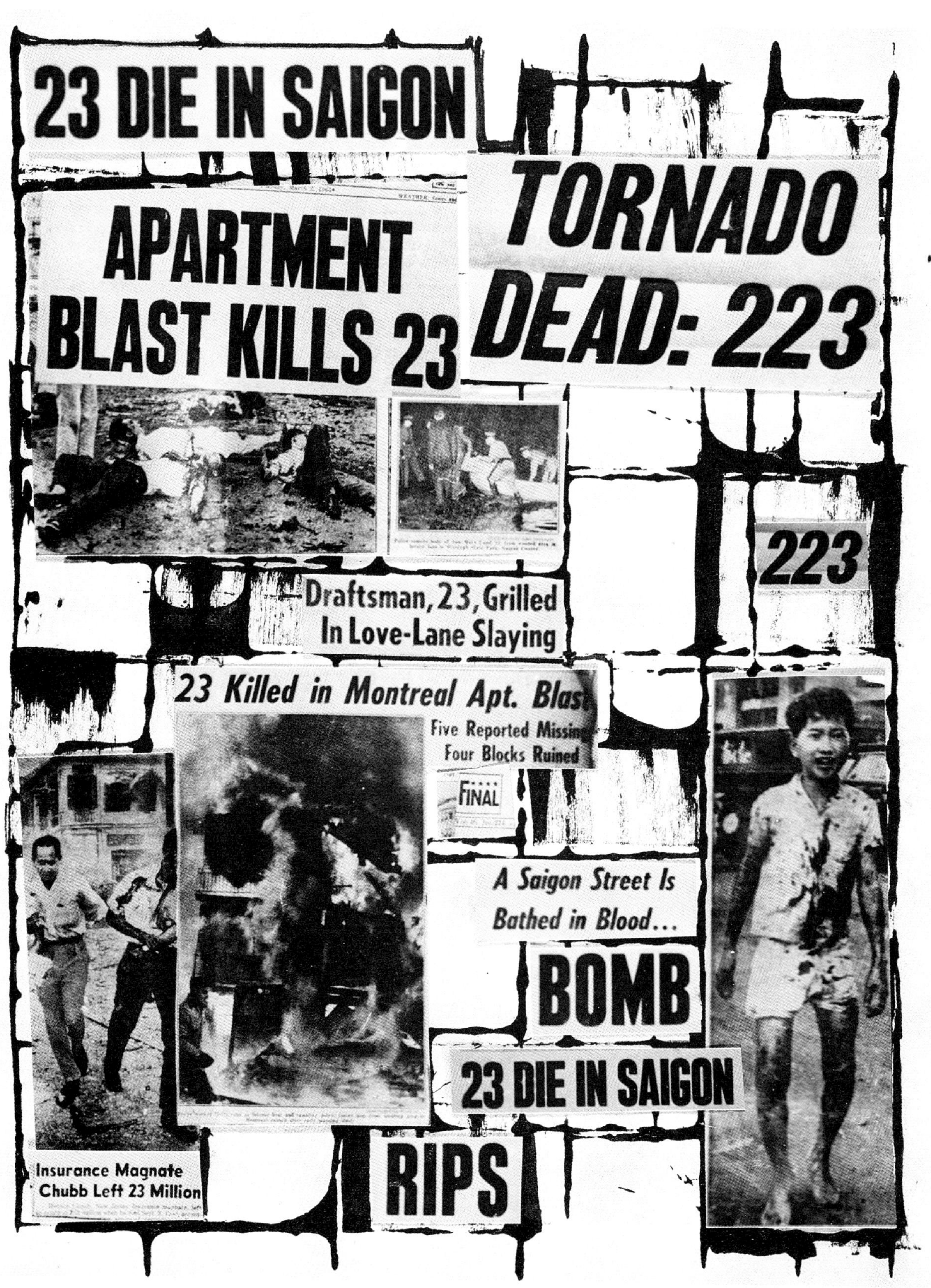

William S. Burroughs and Brion Gysin, untitled [Tornado Dead: 223], c. 1965, cat. no. 31

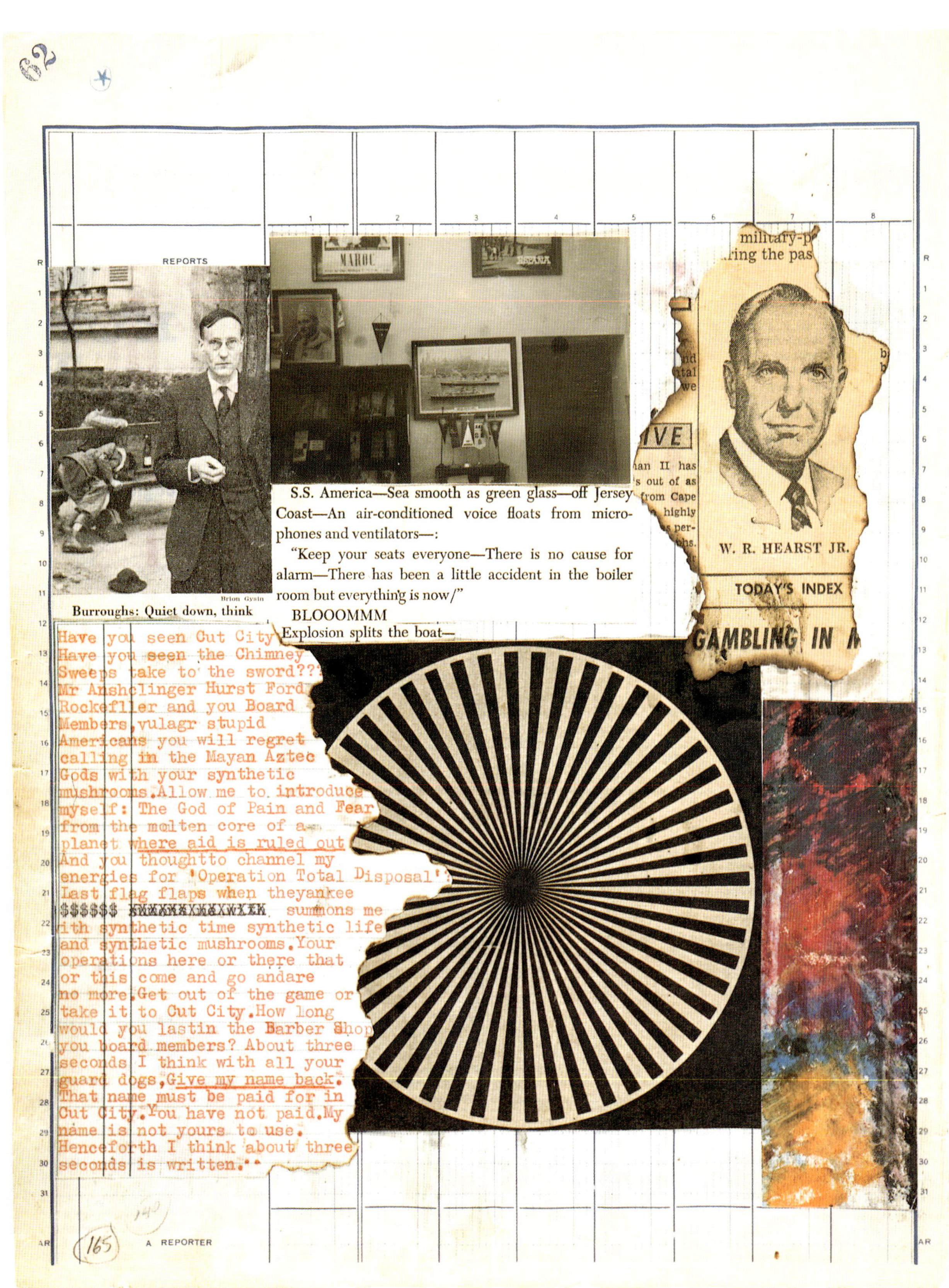

William S. Burroughs and Brion Gysin, untitled [W. R. Hearst Jr.], c. 1965, cat. no. 33

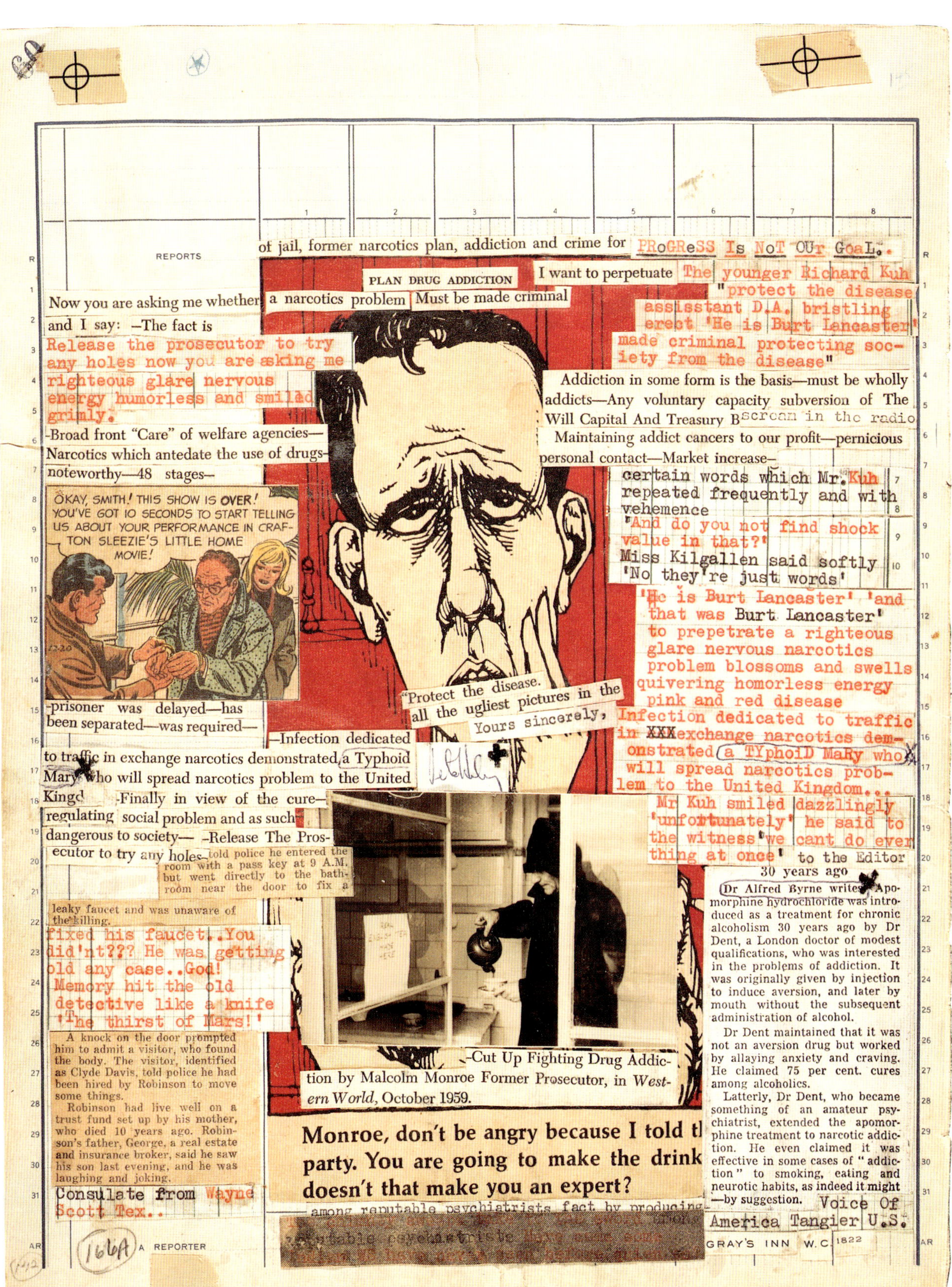

William S. Burroughs and Brion Gysin, untitled [Plan Drug Addiction], c. 1965, cat. no. 35

And, one of the tactics of the Nova Mob is to subliminally spread "the ugliest pictures in the image bank" in order to create a chain of crises.[157]

In a wordless collage that is also reproduced in the chapter "Hieroglyphic Silence" of the Viking edition, a portrait of a West African native is placed in Gysin's grid below a larger, strangely bizarre, and somewhat alien-looking visage. The image is simple enough, however menacing it may appear: an actor (Gysin perhaps) on a stage having a slide of another face projected onto his. In the early 1960s Gysin had worked in conjunction with Le Domaine Poétique, a French sound poetry group, in developing light shows:

At the proper focal distance projecting one face on another...is the area in which I worked in the light show I developed for the Domaine Poétique... and there were theatrical performances in which we used projected images in a way that they hadn't been used up until that time...I worked it out with Ian Sommerville as a technical help...and we did shows that persuaded other professional artists, like George Maciunas of Fluxus...who included it into the area of experimentation which they called Expanded Cinema.[158]

In a footnote in *Nova Express* Burroughs linked Gysin's work with image projection and Wilhelm Reich's theory of orgones when he wrote, "Preliminary experiments indicate that certain paintings—like Brion Gysin's—when projected on a subject produced some of the effects observed in orgone accumulators."[159] Further, the effect of dematerialization brought about by projecting images on faces and figures fascinated both Burroughs and Gysin throughout the 1960s. After all, Burroughs's character Lee "found he could move on his projected image from point to point—He was already accustomed to life without a body."[160]

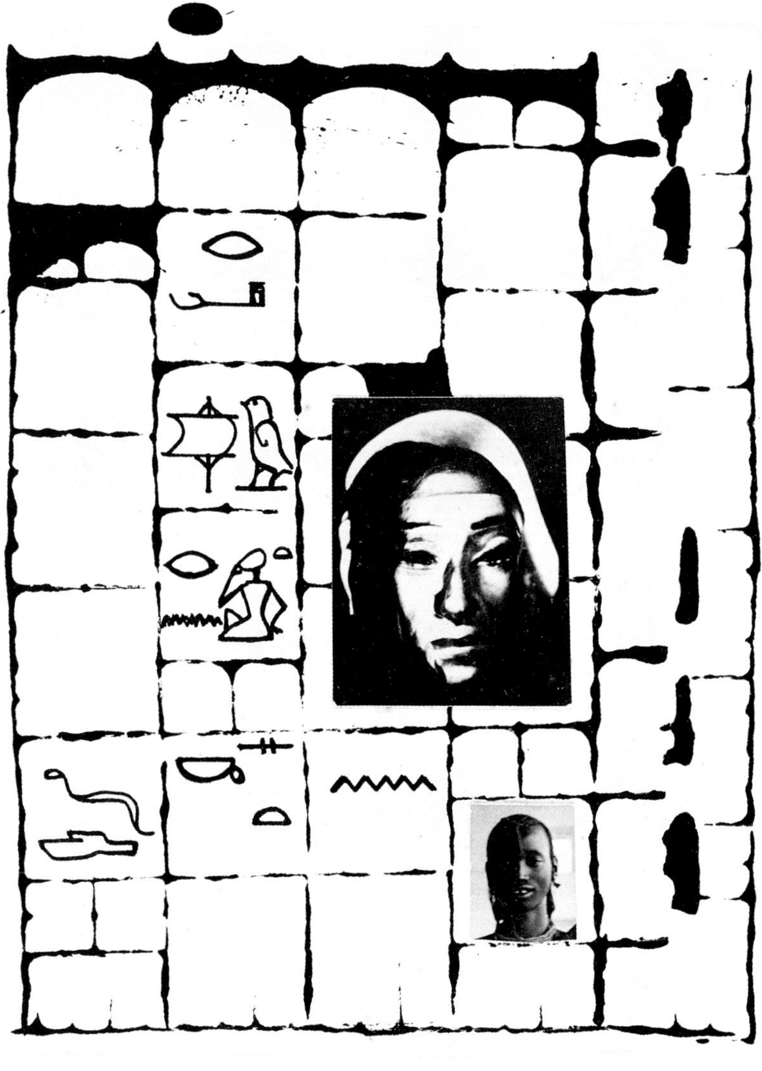

William S. Burroughs and Brion Gysin, untitled [Projection Performance], c. 1965, cat. no. 22

136
Burroughs, *The Ticket That Exploded* (note **21**), 215.

137
Burroughs, *The Soft Machine* (note **56**), 64.

138
See Burroughs and Gysin, *The Third Mind* (note **8**), 153; and Burroughs and Gysin, "The Third Mind," mss. and mechanicals (note **78**), 100.

139
Burroughs, *Naked Lunch* (note **5**), 116.

140
Lemaire, "23 Stitches Taken by Gérard-Georges Lemaire," in Burroughs and Gysin, *The Third Mind* (note **8**), 23–24.

141
Jacques Derrida, quoted in ibid., 20.

142
Lemaire, "23 Stitches Taken by Gérard-Georges Lemaire," in Burroughs and Gysin, *The Third Mind* (note **8**), 23.

143
Catherine Thieck, owner of the Galerie de France, in conversation with the author, July 9, 1994.

144
T. S. Eliot, *The Waste Land*, in *The Complete Poems and Plays, 1909–1950* (New York: Harcourt, Brace and World, 1952), 48.

145
Ibid., 54.

146
Burroughs, "Introduction," in Burroughs and Gysin, *The Third Mind* (note **8**), 23. There are enough citations, paraphrases, and cut-ups from Eliot in Burroughs's work to consider *The Waste Land* an equally probable source.

147
Burroughs and Gysin, "The Third Mind," mss. and mechanicals (note **78**), 139. In this text the balcony is said to have been on the "Old Flatiron Building" in New York, but in a letter to Antony Balch dated September 23, 1964, Burroughs states that the street scenes were shot from Burroughs's apartment; see Gysin and Wilson, *Here to Go* (note **14**), 238.

148
See Robert A. Sobieszek, *Robert Smithson: Photo Works*, exh. cat. (Los Angeles: Los Angeles County Museum of Art, 1993), 37.

149
Ibid., 32.

150
Ian Sommerville, "Mr and Mrs D," *Gnaoua* 1 (spring 1964): 17.

151
Burroughs, *Nova Express* (note **2**), 49.

152
For identification of this character, see Gysin and Wilson, *Here to Go* (note **14**), 142.

153
Bockris, *With William Burroughs* (note **6**), 70.

154
See Robert Anton Wilson, *Cosmic Trigger: Final Secret of the Illuminati* (Scottsdale: New Falcon Publications, 1991), 43.

155
Burroughs, *My Education* (note **42**), 27–29.

156
Burroughs and Gysin, *The Third Mind* (note **8**), 192–94.

157
Burroughs, *Nova Express* (note **2**), 11–12.

158
Gysin and Wilson, *Here to Go* (note **14**), 88.

159
Burroughs, *Nova Express* (note **2**), 156 n.

160
Ibid., 95.

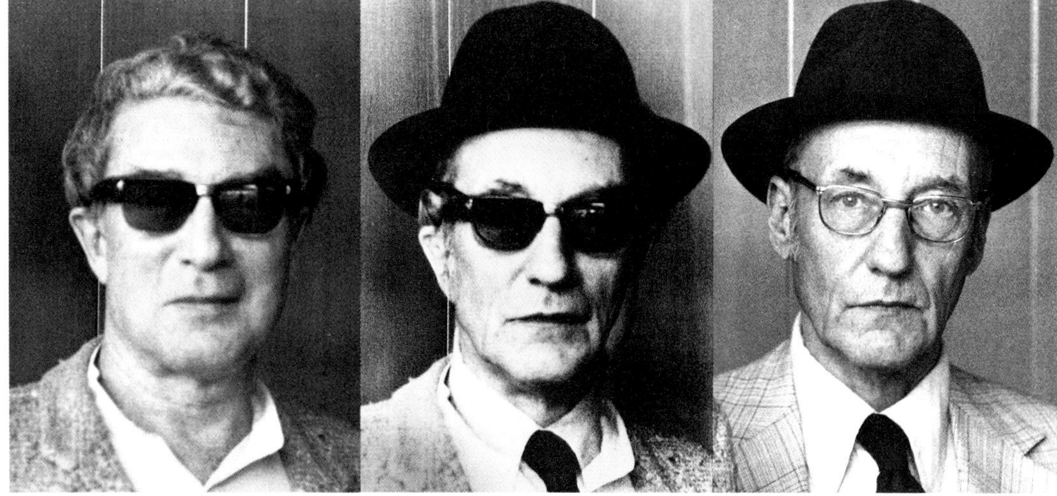

François Lagarde, **The Three Minds** (triptych), 1978, cat. no. 105

Open our heads and let the pictures come.[161]

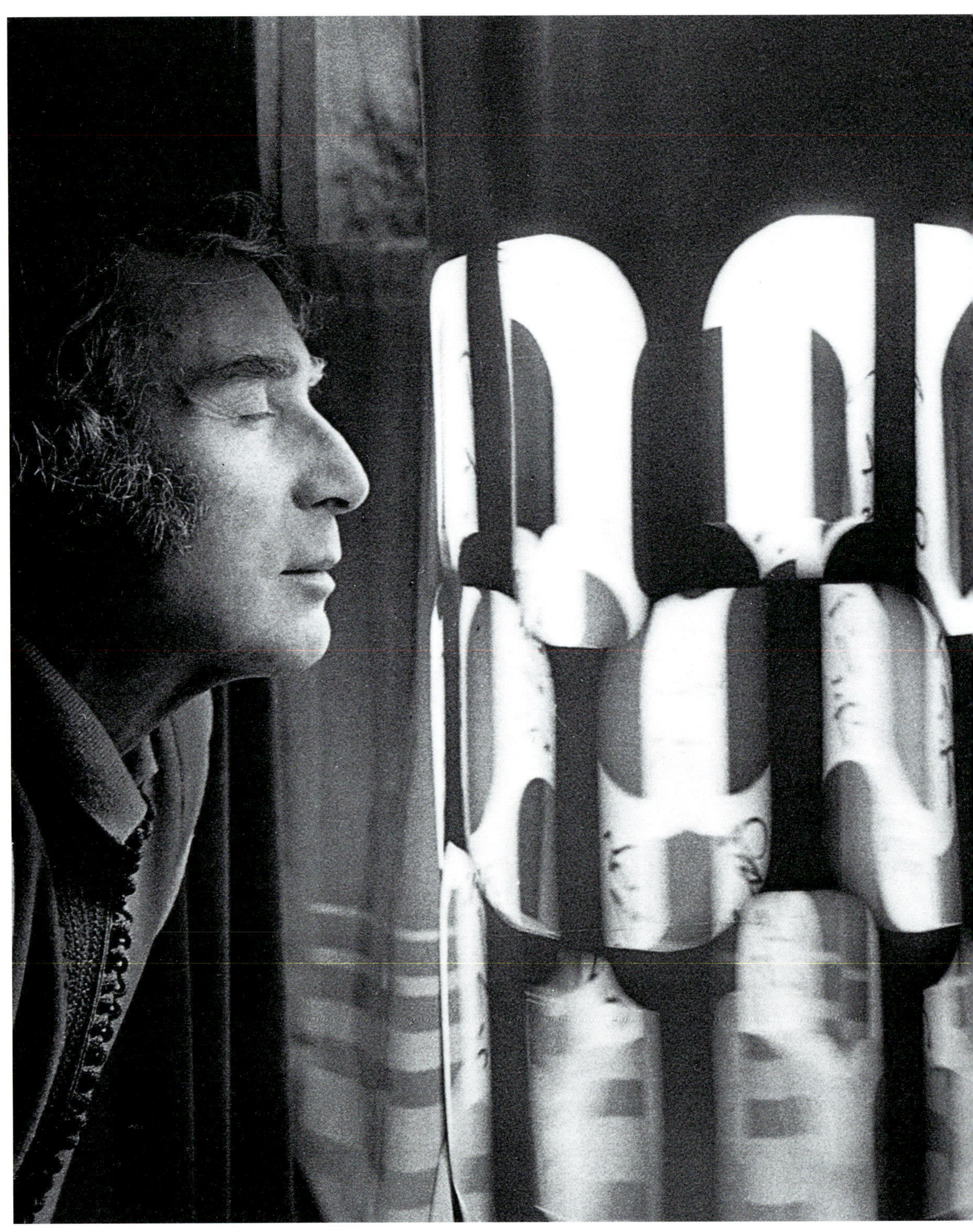

Charles Gatewood, **The Dream Machine**, 1973, cat. no. 100

VIII
FLICKER VISION

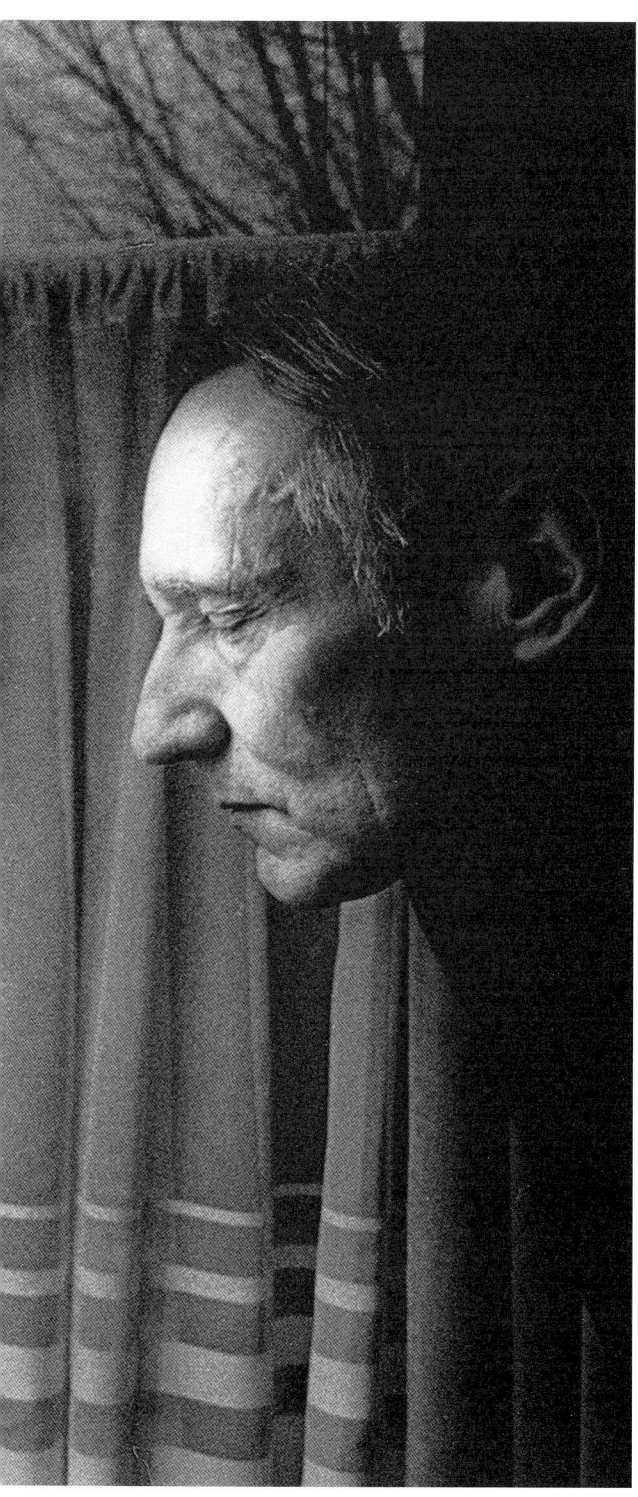

In the 1950s Aldous Huxley experienced a pervasive inner light and an opening of the "doors of perception" onto a "sacremental vision of reality" after ingesting mescaline.[162] During the 1960s psychedelic drugs caused users to experience multiple viewpoints and alternative senses of time, space, and, in the words of Timothy Leary, "states of possession, trance, delightful chaoticness, expanded consciousness."[163] An issue of the *International Times* published by Michael English in 1966 as a poster declared that "the text is behind your eyes; inside your ears. Cut out. Turn round," a pro-hallucinogenic editorial comment printed above Burroughs's essay "The Invisible Generation (Continued)." Venues for acid-rock concerts (for example, the Fillmore or the Avalon Ballroom, both in San Francisco), with their requisite light shows, served as backdrops to, or environments for, the music, and reflected the sense of "out-of-bodyness" encountered with psychedelic drugs. Peter Albin, of the rock group Big Brother and the Holding Company, told an interviewer in 1967, "It's all spliced together. Everything is just jingle-jangle, jingle-jangle. And people who dig our music and dig our lives are kind of digging the juxtaposed collage, right. A collage of different kinds of feelings, ways of living, ways of listening to things, and reacting to them."[164] The Beatles exhorted their listeners to "listen to the color of your dreams, it is not living," and The Rolling Stones sang, "If we close our eyes together then we will see where we all come from."[165] Films by Kenneth Anger utilized the liquescent and stroboscopic light effects of the rock concerts, stroboscopic flashes constituted the entirety of Tony Conrad's film *The Flicker* (1966), and the spectacular reentry scenes at the end of Stanley Kubrick's *2001: A Space Odyssey* (1968) induced a nearly complete kinesthetic disequilibrium through relentless forward tracking and pulsating color effects.[166]

Flashing lights, projections, swirling images in motion, flickering colors—all formal elements common to a dematerialization of reality in the popular culture

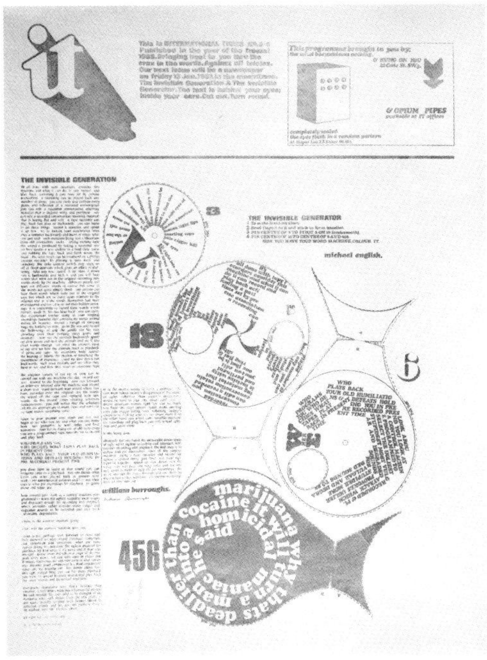

Michael English, **International Times**, 1966, cat. no. 134

of the 1960s—all these elements play a part in Burrough's literary imagery and experiments of this period. In *The Ticket That Exploded* we read,

> **Photomontage fragments backed with iron stuck to patterns and fell in swirls mixing with color dust to form new patterns, shimmering, falling, magnetized, demagnetized to the flicker of blue cylinders pulsing neon tubes and globes—In metal booths brain waves wrote the flickering message passed back and forth, over and through shifting grills [. . .] orgone accumulators flickering blue over swimming tanks where naked youths bathed in blue—sound and image flakes falling like luminous grey snow—falling softly from demagnetized patterns into blue silence.**[167]

Burroughs may easily be describing a session with Gysin's "Dreamachine," developed by him along with Sommerville during the early 1960s. It was simply a tall, spinning cylinder pierced by irregularly patterned shapes and with a light source inside that produced (and still produces in its various later versions) a "stroboscopic 'flicker' over the closed eyelids of the viewer."[168] This "psychoactive, hallucinogenic neocortex-pulsator,"[169] was intended to promote intense visions of color and light in a viewer by its precisely calibrated flickerings of light, especially when accompanied by highly rhythmic music such as Moroccan Jajouka pipes and the ingestion of *majoun* (hashish candy). Gysin's patent application for the machine was entitled "Procedure and apparatus for the production of artistic visual sensations."[170] The Dreamachine was used to stimulate cerebral images that, like drug-induced images, approximated or surpassed those found in dream states. One of the jobs of the artist, according to Burroughs, is to fabricate dreams for others: "What do artists do? They dream for other people. We dream for these people who have no dreams of their own to keep them alive."[171] The Dreamachine merely facilitated those dreams.

Curiously the chapter entitled "Dreamachine" that Burroughs and Gysin had planned to include in *The Third Mind* was omitted in the Viking edition. Its inclusion would have suggested a further step in their collaborative experiments, a step that would have gone beyond literary techniques and those of films and tapes, all of which were still seen as fundamentally linear and safely narrative at the time. In the collage *Dreamachine*, Gysin's grid contains a number of photographs that are partially overwritten with "faux Arabic" calligraphy. Apart from a number of images of young, naked boys and some travel shots, the photographs feature news items announcing "Machine Manufactures 'Dreams,'" scenes of Gysin and Sommerville in front of the instrument, a shot of Burroughs's face being projected upon from one of Balch's films, and another of Sommerville's infinitely mirrored photomontages.

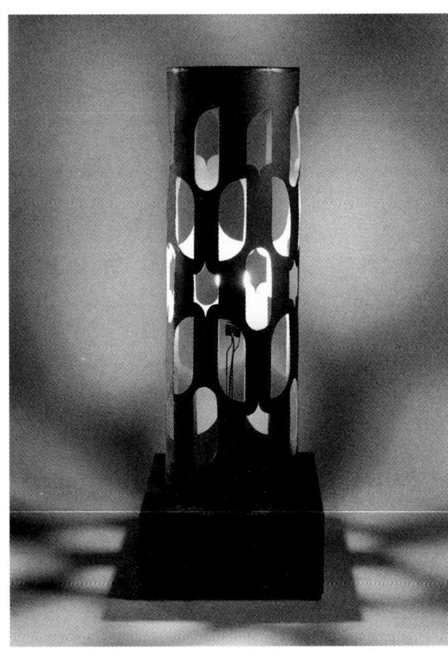

Brion Gysin and Ian Sommerville, **Dreamachine**, 1961–62, refabricated in 1994 by David Woodard, cat. no. 131

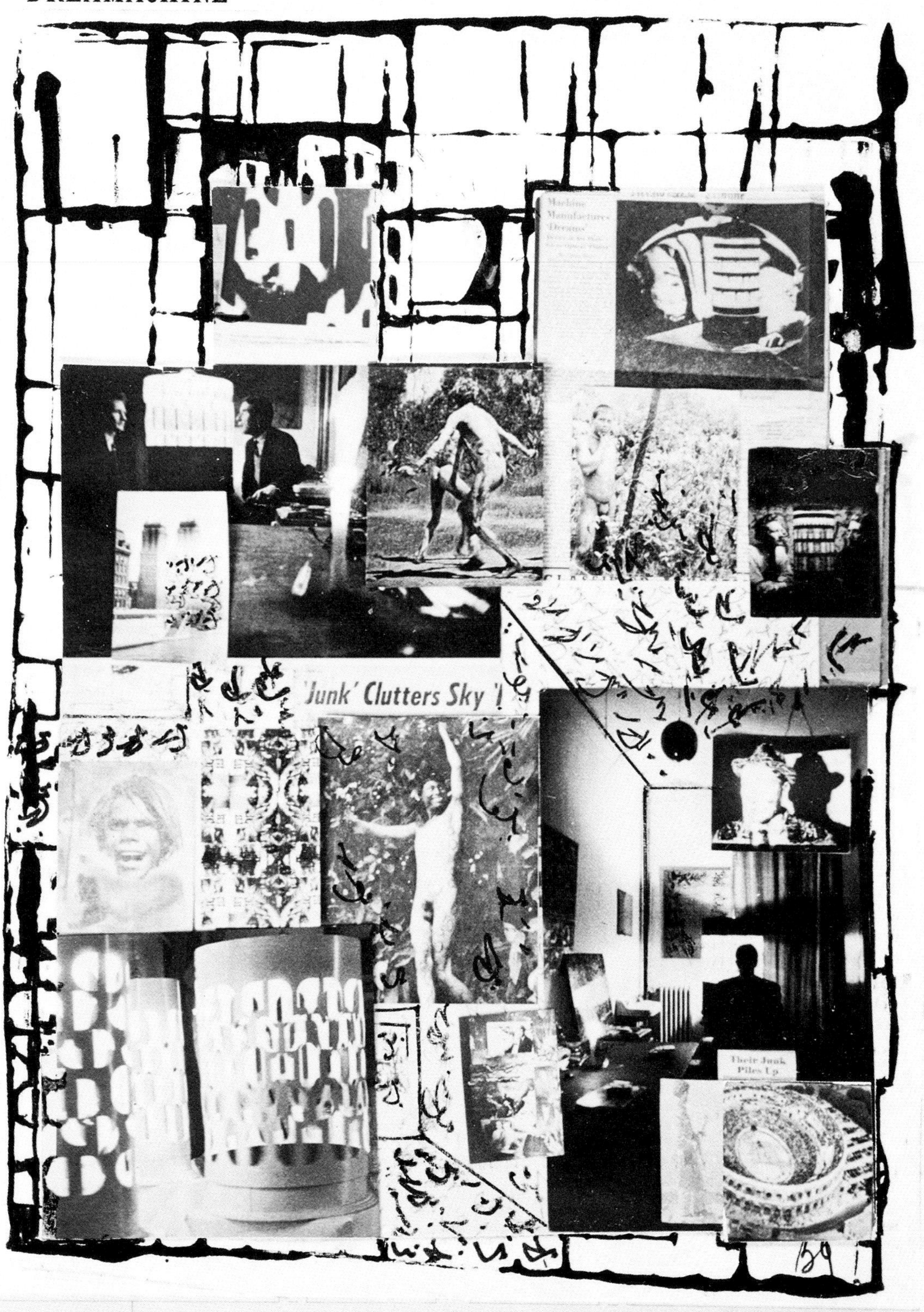

William S. Burroughs and Brion Gysin, **Dreamachine**, c. 1965, cat. no. 21

In Sommerville's single-page text to the planned chapter, the Dreamachine's principles are carefully outlined.[172] "'Flicker' at precise rates per second," he wrote, "produces radical change in the *alpha* or scanning rhythms of the brain" and,

When the "flicker" is in phase with the subject's *alpha* rhythms, he sees extending areas of brightly colored pattern[s] which develop throughout the entire visual field; 360 degrees of hallucinatory vision in which constellations of images appear. Elaborate geometric constructions of incredible intricacy build up from multi-dimensional mosaic into living fireballs like the *mandalas* of Eastern mysticism or resolve momentarily into apparently individual images and powerfully dramatic scenes like brightly colored dreams.[173]

The Hafler Trio and Thee Temple ov Psychick Youth, **Brion Gysin's Dreamachine**, 1989, cat. no. 146

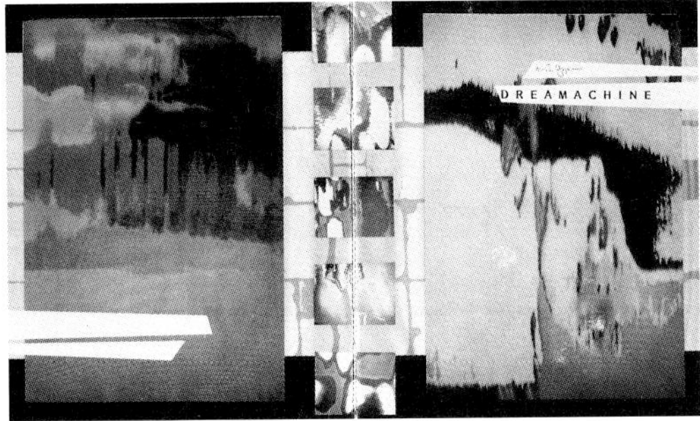

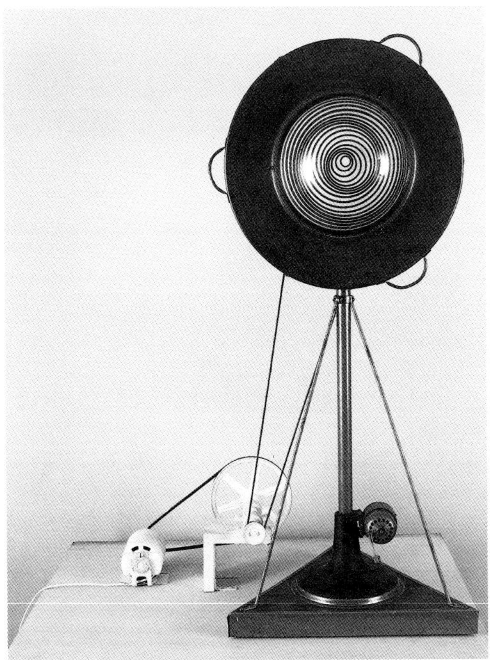

Marcel Duchamp, **Rotary Demisphere (Precision Optics)**, 1925, painted wood, copper, velvet, plastic, steel, motor, 58½ x 25¼ x 24 in. (148.6 x 64.1 x 61 cm), Museum of Modern Art, New York, gift of Mrs. William Sisler and Edward James Fund

Light for Sommerville was the medium of the present:

In the beginning was the word and the word was made flesh in darkness but, with the invention of writing in any form, light was necessary to see the image. Image *is* proliferation whose limits are the speed of light. The one and only thing which cannot be taken from this overwhelming picture is light—everything else can be transmuted or can go.

Above or below a certain frequency or rate, sounds and images are not discerned by the human senses. The human alpha rhythm, an electrical rhythm of the brain, has a frequency of eight to thirteen cycles per second, and around that frequency most perception occurs. Sommerville maintained that external rhythmic sources such as music, films, and television impose their own rhythms on the brain and just may alter brain waves. Moreover he asserted that in the age of electronics the goal for any communication or experience is the speed of light—"At that speed, instead of having mere images palmed off on us, we might get The Real Thing."

Flicker vision for Sommerville was the art of the future, antiquating all other art forms, including collage:

"Flicker" vision is a threshold experience produced by altering the speed of light to accommodate the maximum range of our *alpha* rhythms. "Flicker" creates a dazzling multiplicity of images in constantly altering relationships which makes the "collages" and "assemblages" of so-called "modern" art appear utterly ineffectual and slow. Art history as the enumeration of individual images ended with the direct introduction of light as the principal agent in the creation of images which have become infinitely multiple, complex and all-pervading. Art history has come to an end. Light writes in Space. Art is the tail of a comet. The comet is light.

In a way, the Dreamachine was part of art culture of the 1960s, a strange, mechanical hybrid incorporating features of Marcel Duchamp's vertiginous

Rotary Demisphere (Precision Optics) (1925), the articulate energies of a machine sculpture by Takis, and the psycho-optical light effects of a work by François Morellet.[174] Part scientific experiment and part artwork, the Dreamachine was a demonstration of Burroughs's belief that "there's going to be more and more merging of art and science."[175]

Gysin had once reported that staring into mirrors for long periods of time was "very hot around 1960–61" and that he had sat in front of one for 36 hours and "saw all sorts of things."[176] Apparently the Dreamachine was an extension of this form of visualizing interior images and one that was clearly far more potent and possibly even dangerous.[177] About flickering strobes used by the American drug culture of the late 1960s, Tom Wolfe wrote, "The strobe has certain magical properties in the world of the acid heads. At certain speeds stroboscopic lights are so synched in with the pattern of brain waves that they can throw epileptics into a seizure. Heads discovered that strobes could project them into many of the sensations of an LSD experience without taking LSD. *The strobe!*"[178] Flicker vision, with its dazzling multiplicity of images whose relationships are constantly changing, could prove habit-forming, but it is also an apt metaphor for the kind of nonsynchronized, nonlinear, and utterly dematerialized world of events faced in the late twentieth century, a world of events that is constantly fluid, cut-up, folded into, and close to causing seizures in those who try to gain "a complete awareness of surroundings," as Burroughs does.[179]

161
The Rolling Stones, "Sing This All Together," *Their Satanic Majesties Request* (1967) (Abkco [80022], 1986), track 1.

162
Jay Courtney Fikes, *Carlos Castaneda, Academic Opportunism and the Psychedelic Sixties* (Victoria, British Columbia: Millenia Press, 1993), 15; and Aldous Huxley, *Doors of Perception* (New York: Harper, 1954).

163
Timothy Leary, "The Sociology of LSD," in his *Chaos and Cyberculture* (Berkeley: Ronin Publishing, 1994), 98.

164
Peter Albin, "Interview," KQED, San Francisco, April 25, 1967, in Rhino Video, *Big Brother and the Holding Company: Ball and Chain, Live in Studio, San Francisco '67* (Santa Monica: Rhino Records, 1989).

165
The Beatles, "Tomorrow Never Knows," *Revolver* (EMI Records [CDP 7 46441 2], 1966), track 14; and The Rolling Stones, "Sing This All Together," *Their Satanic Majesties Request* (note **161**), track 1.

166
See Annette Michelson, "Bodies in Space: Film as 'Carnal Knowledge,'" *Artforum* 7, no. 6 (February 1969): 61. For Conrad, see Kerry Brougher, *Hall of Mirrors: Art and Film since 1945*, exh. cat. (Los Angeles: Museum of Contemporary Art and the Monacelli Press, 1996), 90.

167
Burroughs, *The Ticket That Exploded* (note **21**), 62–63.

168
Ian Sommerville, "Dreamachine," in Burroughs and Gysin, "The Third Mind," mss. and mechanicals (note **78**), 206. This chapter, or section, was not included in the Viking Press edition of 1978.

169
Terry Ehnert, "Death and the Dreammachine [*sic*]: A Theory about Kurt Cobain's Suicide," *SOMA* 30 (March 1995): 53; see also Gysin and Wilson, *Here to Go* (note **14**), 239–41.

170
See Miles, *William Burroughs* (note **25**), 159.

171
William S. Burroughs, "The Creative Observer," *Painting and Guns* (Madras and New York: Hanuman Books, 1992), 46.

172
Sommerville's "Flicker" was originally published in *Olympia Magazine* 2 (1962) and later in Brion Gysin, *Brion Gysin Let the Mice In*, ed. Jan Herman (West Glover, Vermont: Something Else Press, 1973); see Joe Maynard and Barry Miles, *William S. Burroughs: A Bibliography, 1953–73* (Charlottesville: The University Press of Virginia, 1978), 81.

173
Ian Sommerville, "Dreamachine," in Burroughs and Gysin, "The Third Mind," mss. and mechanicals (note **78**), 206.

174
See Jonathan Benthall, *Science and Technology in Art Today* (New York: Praeger, 1972). Burroughs was intrigued enough by Takis's machine sculpture to contribute a cut-up appreciation in Wayne Andersen, *Takis: Evidence of the Unseen*, exh. cat. (Cambridge: Hayden Gallery, MIT Press, 1968), 30.

175
Knickerbocker, "Interview" (note **8**), 7.

176
Gysin and Wilson, *Here to Go* (note **14**), 85–87. Gysin's interest in staring is quite different from Duchamp's intentions in *To Be Looked at with One Eye, Close to, for Almost an Hour* (1918); Duchamp wished to turn the viewer into the voyeur every viewer is, whereas Gysin wished only to explore his inner imagination; see Anne d'Harnoncourt and Walter Hopps, *Etant donnés: 1° la chute d'eau, 2° le gaz d'éclairage: Reflections on a New Work by Marcel Duchamp* (Philadelphia: Philadelphia Museum of Art, 1969), 22.

177
In late 1994 it was suggested, without a shred of clinical evidence, that rock star Kurt Cobain's suicide as well as that of another rock musician Kristen Pfaff were the direct result of using the machine; see Ehnert, "Death and the Dreammachine [*sic*]," (note **169**), 52–55, 18.

178
Tom Wolfe, *The Electric Kool-Aid Acid Test* (New York: Farrar, Straus and Giroux, 1968), 242.

179
Knickerbocker, "Interview" (note **8**), 2.

IX
IMAGE WARFARE

For Godsake

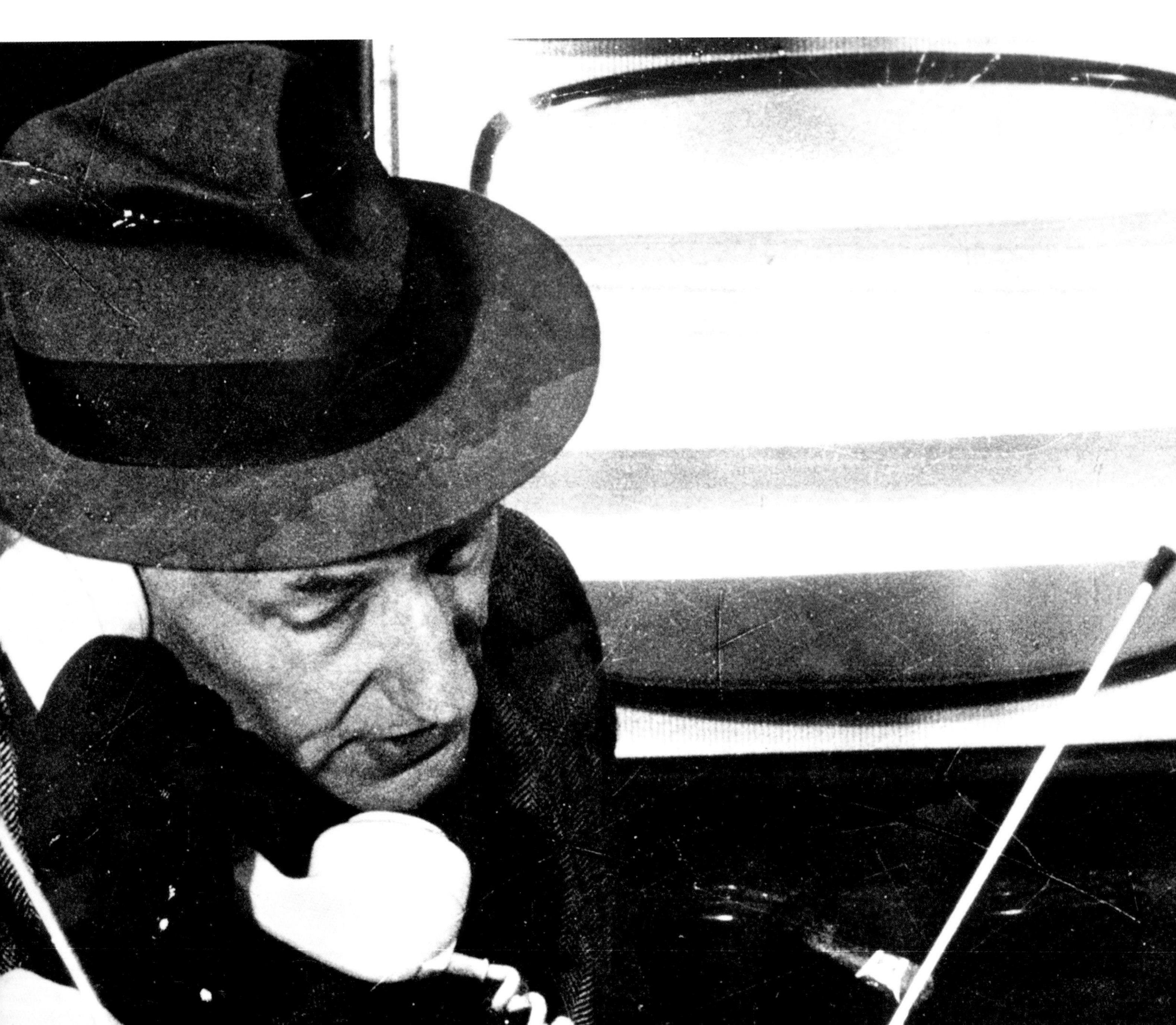

Antony Balch, **William S. Burroughs**, c. 1963, cat. no. 98

Opposite page: Antony Balch, **Towers Open Fire** (frame sequence), 1963, 35-mm film with audio (original partially hand-colored), courtesy William Burroughs Communications, Lawrence

keep your eyes open.[180]

Allen Ginsberg described the function of cut-ups in Burroughs's work:

> **The cut-ups were originally designed to rehearse and repeat his obsession with sexual images over and over again, like a movie repeating over and over and over again, and then recombined and cut up and mixed in; so that finally the obsessive attachment, compulsion, and preoccupation empty out and drain from the image.**[181]

Indeed, Burroughs creates chaotic worlds of "metamorphosing shapes and forms which constantly destroy themselves and rise anew"[182] by employing short takes, sudden perspective shifts, tracking shots, flashbacks, and flash-forwards—just like a movie. And not only is Burroughs's vision more closely akin to modern cinema, but cinematic effects are an essential part of his work, especially in the writings following *Naked Lunch*. "The next step was carried out in a film studio," he wrote in *The Soft Machine*, "I learned to talk and think backward on all levels."[183] The "reality film," "biologic film," "flicker sex and torture film," and "blue movies" are found in Burroughs's novels of the 1960s, while in *The Soft Machine*'s "Case of the Celluloid Kali," the boys chant in unison, "*The movies!—The movies!—*We want *the movies!*"[184] In the "Let Them See Us" chapter of *The Ticket That Exploded*, the line "Now some words about the image track—The Human body is an image on screen talking," appears.[185] And *The Wild Boys* both begins and ends with blatantly filmic devices: an aerial tracking camera zooming in on Tío Mate and an exploding "film grenade" that blots out the entire set.[186]

The film studio in which Burroughs carried out the next step was undoubtedly Antony Balch's, who had made a number of low-budget films such as *Horror Hospital* and was distributing soft-core porn films in Great Britain when Burroughs met him through Gysin in the early 1960s. Balch was a fan of Burroughs, and in 1962 they began work on their first collaboration, *Towers Open Fire*, which took about a year to make.[187] The film

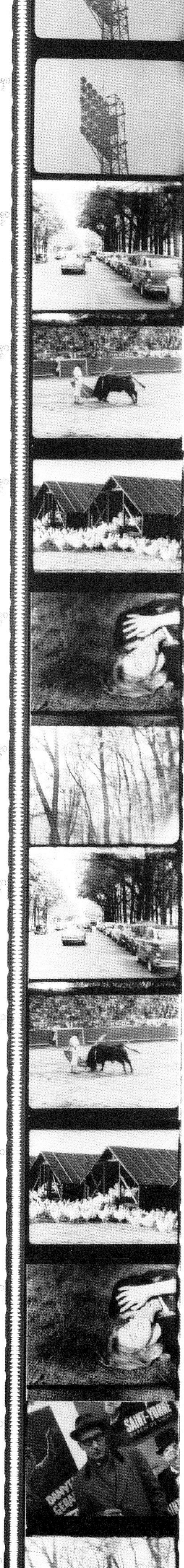

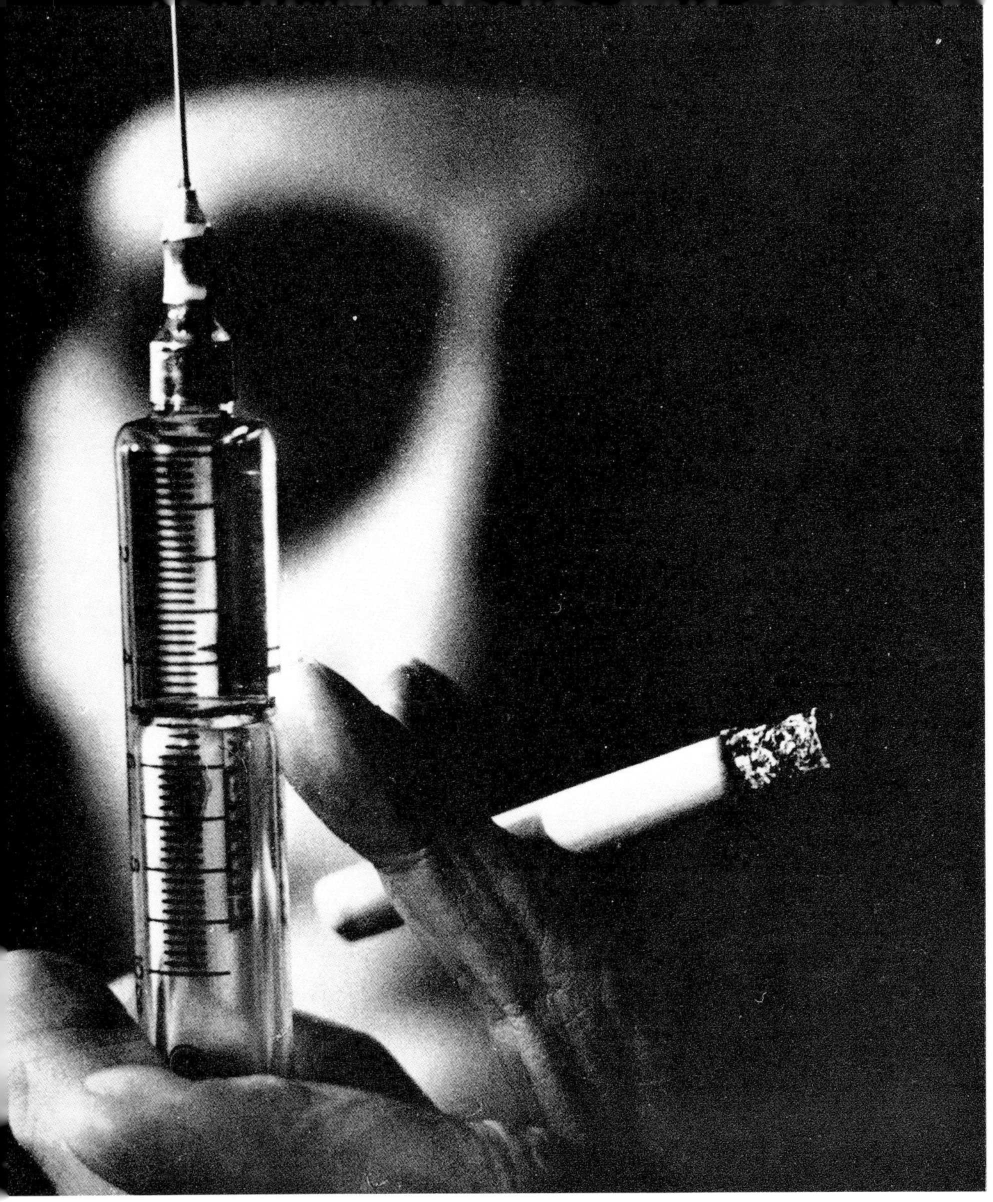

Conrad Rooks, **Chappaqua** (film still), 1967, cat. no. 99

was shot in black-and-white, although Balch hand-painted certain segments with pink and blue dots. There is no traditional story line nor is there any dialogue to the film, although it is fairly close to the episode of the same name in *Nova Express* (1964).[188] The soundtrack is a combination of Burroughs's voice, studio sound effects, Moroccan music, and other music. Sommerville, a young Michael Portman, and the writer Alexander Trocchi appear along with Burroughs in the film, which featured Dreamachine scenes, Burroughs dressed in combat gear blasting away at family photographs with a gun that shoots Ping-Pong balls, Burroughs speaking before the Board, which was shot in the British Film Institute boardroom, and a blur of single-frame images that can only be perceived subliminally, if that. When Balch applied for a screening license in 1964, the censor's note read, "Remove words fuck and shit."[189]

Guerrilla Conditions, an unfinished twenty-three-minute silent documentary on Burroughs and Gysin, was worked on next, with footage shot between 1961 and 1964. Material from this film was then used in creating the black-and-white feature *The Cut-Ups*, which was first shown in London in 1966 and which also included a negative version of *William Buys a Parrot*, shot in color in Tangier. In keeping with the formal niceties of the cut-up technique, *The Cut-Ups* was assembled by cutting up four reels of film into twelve-inch lengths that were then pieced together in rotation by a lab technician without any editorial or artistic judgment made by either Burroughs or Balch, a technique used by director Nicholas Roeg for his film *Performance*, starring Mick Jagger of The Rolling Stones. Finally Burroughs and Balch worked on *Bill and Tony*. Part of this film appropriated Sommerville's and Gysin's earlier technique of projecting an image of a face upon an actor's face, and part of it had Balch and Burroughs as talking heads, reading from a Scientology auditing manual and the script to Tod Browning's film *Freaks*, and all the while trading their identities back and forth.[190]

In Conrad Rooks's *Chappaqua* (1966), a film about the drug culture and tripping out on LSD and whose director of cinematography was Robert Frank, Burroughs made a brief appearance as a shadowy heroin addict dressed in black, a role he reprised in Gus Van Sant's *Drugstore Cowboy* (1989). Again for Van Sant, Burroughs wrote the screenplay for *The Discipline of D. E.* (1978) and starred in the droll and humorous three-minute video *A Thanksgiving Prayer* (1990). British director Derek Jarman made *Pirate Tape* in 1982, a diaristic record of one of Burroughs's visits to London, the same year that Howard Brookner made the first, full-length documentary film on Burroughs, entitled simply *Burroughs*. Although he and Balch had planned for a film version of *Naked Lunch* as early as 1971, nothing came of it. *Naked Lunch* was finally

The next step was carried out in a film studio--I learned to talk and think backward on all levels--This was done by running film and sound track backward--For example a picture of myself eating a full meal was reversed, from satiety back to hunger-- First the film was run at normal speed, then in slow-motion--The same procedure was extended to other physiological processes including orgasm--(It was explained to me that I must put aside all sexual prudery and reticence, that sex was perhaps the heaviest anchor holding one in present time.) For three months I worked with the studio--My basic training in time travel was completed and I was now ready to train specifically for the Mayan assignment.

The Soft Machine

adapted and directed by Canadian director David Cronenberg and released in 1992; and of his other literary works, only *Ah Pook Is Here* has been adapted for film or video: an animated short feature by Philip Hunt was released in 1994, and another by Peter Ungerleider appeared the same year.

The dismal, planetary landscapes seen in Hunt's *Ah Pook Is Here* suggest the industrially wasted, entropic landscapes in much of Burroughs's early novels, not altogether different from Eliot's in *The Waste Land*. In *Naked Lunch* there is a "vast still harbor of iridescent water. Deserted gas well flares on the smoky horizon. Stink of oil and sewage."[191] In *The Ticket That Exploded* "a vista of phosphorescent slag heaps opened before him."[192] And as early as 1953, in *The Yage Letters*, there appears "the Composite City where all human potentials are spread out in a vast silent market....A place where the unknown past and the emergent future meet in a vibrating soundless hum. Larval entities waiting for a live one."[193] Such terminal landscapes were popular in speculative and science fiction of the period. The protagonist in one of J. G. Ballard's novels finds himself merging with a shore "apparently formed of shale, like the dull metallic skin of a reptile" longing for his "descent through archaeopsychic time to reach its conclusion, repressing the knowledge that when it did the external world around him would have become alien and unbearable."[194] Such visions also affected many of the artists of the period who read these writers. In fact, the conceptual artist Robert Smithson openly

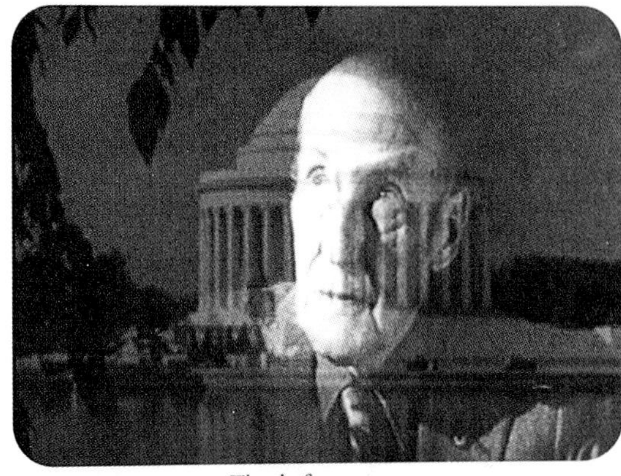

Thanks for a country

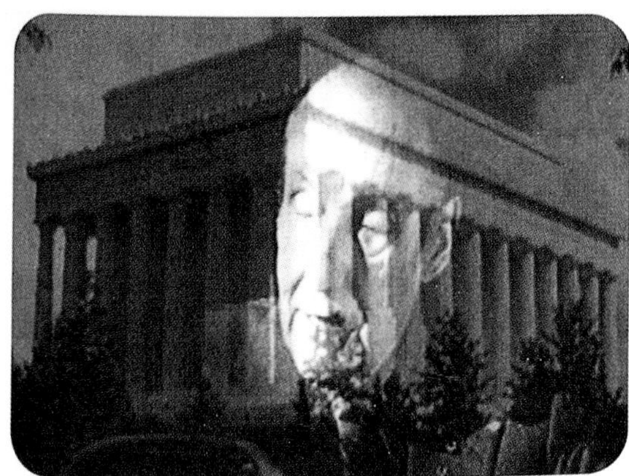

where nobody's allowed to mind their own business.

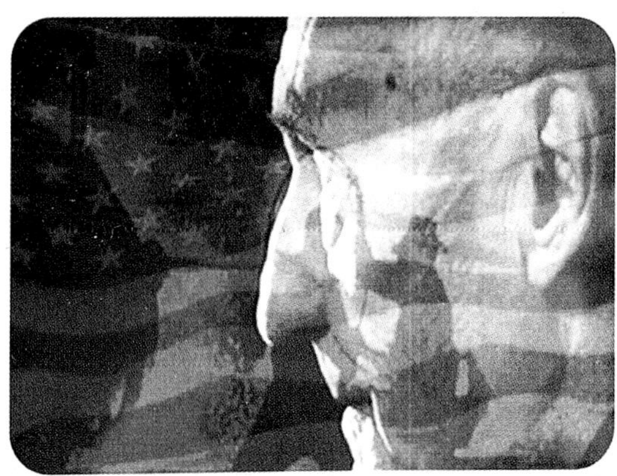

Thanks for the American dream,

Gus Van Sant, **A Thanksgiving Prayer** (film stills with captions), 1990, cat. no. 119

adapted both Ballard and Burroughs for his own theories of entropy in his writings as well as in his art. Smithson described his experience of walking along his most famous work, *The Spiral Jetty* (1970), in terms that suggest the world's end in *Nova Express*: "All was enveloped in a flaming chromosphere. . . . Swirling within the incandescence of solar energy were sprays of blood. . . . Perception was heaving."[195] And similar landscapes of entropic wastelands and primal desolation ultimately found their way into such later movies as *Road Warrior*, by George Miller, *Blade Runner*, by Ridley Scott, and *Stalker*, by Andrei Tarkowski, as well as such later fiction as *Neuromancer*, by William Gibson, *Wetware*, by Rudy Rucker, and *You Bright and Risen Angels*, by William T. Vollmann.

What we see

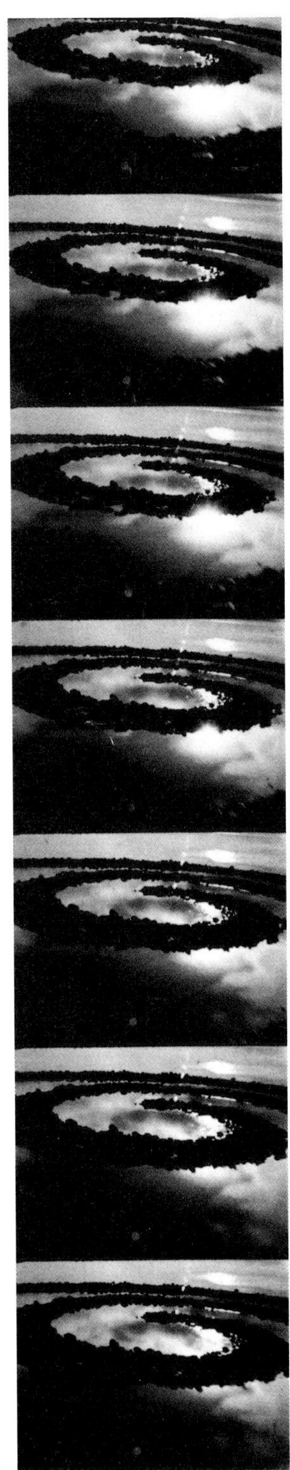

Robert Smithson (with Robert Fiore), **Spiral Jetty** (frame sequence), 1970, 16-mm film with audio (original in color), courtesy the Estate of Robert Smithson and the John Weber Gallery, New York

180
Knickerbocker, "Interview," (note **8**), 5.

181
Allen Ginsberg, quoted in Harold Beaver, "Saint William of Tangier," *Times Literary Supplement* (July 22, 1977), 893.

182
Neal Oxenhandler, "Listening to Burroughs' Voice," in Skerl and Lydenberg, *William S. Burroughs at the Front* (note **134**), 133.

183
Burroughs, *The Soft Machine* (note **56**), 82.

184
Ibid., 78.

185
Burroughs, *The Ticket That Exploded* (note **21**), 178.

186
Burroughs, *The Wild Boys* (note **87**), 3, 183.

187
Miles, *William Burroughs* (note **25**), 153–54. Miles and Morgan (note **7**) give somewhat different dates for their meeting and beginning work on the film.

188
Cf. Burroughs, *Nova Express* (note **2**), 65–67.

189
Miles, *William Burroughs* (note **25**), 154.

190
Ibid., 155–56.

191
Burroughs, *Naked Lunch* (note **5**), 75–76.

192
Burroughs, *The Ticket That Exploded* (note **21**), 109.

193
William S. Burroughs and Allen Ginsberg, *The Yage Letters* (San Francisco: City Lights Books, 1990), 44–46.

194
J. G. Ballard, *The Drowned World* (New York: Berkley Medallion Books, 1966), 76.

195
Smithson, "The Spiral Jetty," in *The Writings* (note **11**), 113.

is determined to a large extent by what we hear.[196]

If films can be run backwards in order to start the whole thing over, sound-recording tapes can also be rewound, begun again, erased, overdubbed, and, in general, messed with for special effects leading to suggestive associations and important lessons. At the same time he and Balch were collaborating on their films, Burroughs was working with Sommerville, with whom he was then living, on tape-recorder experiments. Gysin was again the first of the group to have played with recorders in 1959, but he stayed with vocal permutations mostly while Sommerville and Burroughs expanded the ideas of cut-ups on paper to magnetic tape:

You record, say, ten minutes on the recorder. Then you spin the reel backwards or forwards without recording. Stop at random and cut in a phrase. How random is random? We know so much that we don't consciously know we know, that perhaps the cut-in was not random. Of course this procedure on the tape recorder produces new words by altered juxtaposition just as new words are produced by cut-ups on paper. We went on to exploit the potentials of the tape-recorder: cut up, slow down, speed up, run backwards, inch the tape, play several tracks at once, cut back and forth between two recorders. As soon as you start experimenting with slowdowns, speedups, overlays, etc., you will get new words that were not on the original recordings. [...] In fact, almost any sound that is not too uniform may produce words.[197]

The experiments were not limited to their own voices; street noises, overheard conversations, tavern and subway sounds, and elements from radio broadcasts were just as likely to be dubbed in as were portions of Jajouka music from Morocco. A number of Burroughs's tape experiments, dating from 1959 to around 1978, were collected and issued on vinyl as *"Nothing Here Now but the Recordings"* on Industrial Records in 1981, unfortunately long out of print.

The title of this recording comes from *The Ticket That Exploded* (1962), Burroughs's most extensive exploration of a technical metaphor (apart from cut-ups) for his conceptualization of the universe. In the novel he recalls that the philosopher Ludwig Wittgenstein had once said, "No proposition can contain itself as an argument," and Burroughs concludes that "the only thing *not* prerecorded in a prerecorded universe is the prerecording itself which is to say *any* recording that contains a random factor."[198] But, Burroughs asks, "who decides what tapes play back in present time?"[199] His answer is that in the fully determined and mediated universe of the late twentieth century, prerecordings can only be in the hands of the nefarious Control. If the editors of Time/Life Incorporated are controlling what we see and read in print, and if advertisers and television broadcasters are "flickering their claims" across our subconscious, then it is clear that "anyone with a tape recorder controlling the sound track can influence and create events."[200] By introducing random factors, Burroughs counsels, cut-up and cut-in tape recordings can be used as a powerful weapon against forced authority. Used publically, recordings can start riots or discredit politicians; they can also be

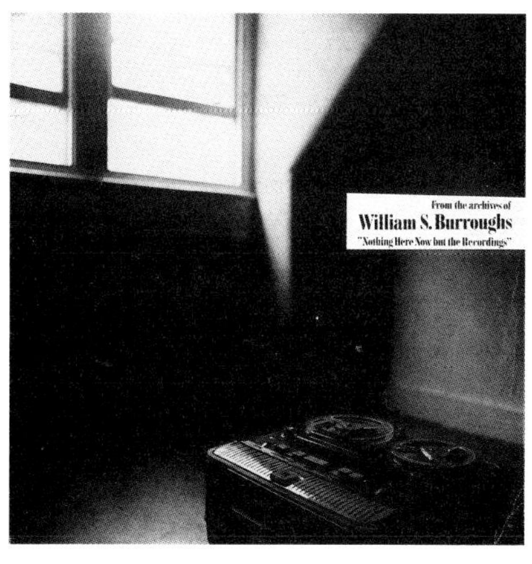

Peter Christopherson, record album cover photography for **"Nothing Here Now but the Recordings,"** 1981, cat. no. 140

It's all done with recorders--The sound track evokes the image track... I recorded ten alternative answers to any question from the interview framework.... I extended the principle of absent control to other activities--I dictated the necessary orders, counterorders and alternative moves for any operation... i recorded the dialogue and made an image track to go with it...The interviewer can of course apply the same method--That is record his questions and alternative questions...Lovers exchange tapes--You understand nobody has to be there at all-- So why ask questions and why answer?--Why give orders and why make speeches?--Why not leave your tape with her tape and dispense with sexual contact?--And then?--Since no one is there to listen, why keep running the tape?-- Why not shut the whole machine off and go home? Exactly what i intend to do-- Turn all my tapes over to Rewrite and go home--You can look any place--No good-- No bueno--Departed have left no address--It's all done with tape recorders.

The Ticket That Exploded

used "as a long range weapon to scramble and nullify associational lines put down by mass media."[201] "Subliminate the subliminators," Burroughs advocates, "Carry Corders of the world unite. You have nothing to lose but your prerecordings."[202]

In "The Invisible Generation," a chapter added to the end of *The Ticket That Exploded* in 1967 for the Grove Press edition, Burroughs warned that the tape techniques he describes in the novel are currently being used clandestinely by official and unofficial agencies:

Look around you look at a control machine programmed to select the ugliest stupidest most vulgar and degraded sounds for recording and playback which provokes uglier stupider more vulgar and degraded sounds to be recorded and play back inexorable degradation look forward to dead end look forward to ugly vulgar playback tomorrow and tomorrow and tomorrow what are newspapers doing but selecting the ugliest sounds for playback by and large if its ugly its news[...]this ugly vulgar bray put out for mass playback you want to spread hysteria record and play back the most stupid and hysterical reactions.[203]

Countering this assault would entail playing calm and sensible recordings, which in turn would spread calmness and good sense. But since this is not being done, Burroughs calls for a set of radical countermeasures to be initiated:

The first step is to isolate and cut association lines of the control machine carry a tape recorder with you and record all the ugliest stupidest things cut your ugly tapes in together speed up slow down play backwards inch the tape you will hear one ugly voice and see one ugly spirit is made of ugly old prerecordings the more you run the tapes through and cut them up the less power they will have cut the prerecordings into air into thin air.[204]

Tape cut-ups and cut-ins, therefore, are potent antidotes to Control since their randomness is what gives them their power and their status of "prerecordings." By recording both apparent sounds as well as subvocal speech that is detectable by recordings, the word-virus deeply rooted within modern man may finally be understood for what it is, separated from its association with pure body sounds, and annihilated.[205] Moreover tape cut-ups and cut-ins are also a protean idiom for outrageous juxtapositions and for exploring psychic areas: "sound and image flakes falling like luminous grey snow—falling softly from demagnetized patterns into blue silence."[206] As early as 1965, Burroughs gave a reading in New York, produced by the American Theater for Poets. It included a tape-experiment that brought together four themes: a plane crash over Jones Beach, a military dispatch from the American forces in Vietnam, a cops-and-robbers routine, and the last words of Dutch Schultz; "I do all the voices," he explained to the audience.[207] In 1968 he recorded his voice on movie tape, which was larger and easier to splice, cut it into one-twenty-fourth-of-a-second intervals and rearranged the intervals. "The original words," he wrote, "are quite unintelligible but new words emerge."[208] Still, "if the tone is hostile, sexual, poetic, sarcastic, lifeless, despairing, this will be apparent in the altered sequence." Burroughs never really thought of his tape investigations as art: "They weren't supposed to be works. It was not an art proposition at all."[209] Nor did Burroughs pursue tape cut-ups for long, but the motif reappears throughout his writings. During the 1970s he began public readings of his routines and contributed to poet John Giorno's *Dial-a-Poem Poets* series of recordings. In 1981 he, Giorno, and performance artist Laurie Anderson took their combined "Red Night Tour" to Los Angeles, San Francisco, and New York, a tour produced by Grauerholz and Giorno. Anderson, who had previously appeared with Burroughs and Giorno during the Nova Convention in 1978, had been refining her own particular brand of sound-voice-music experiments since the early 1970s. Her overdubbings, transmuted voices, electronically altered cadences, and her humorous chidings against authority ally her, at least in spirit, with Burroughs's early experiments.

Burroughs trusts there will be a progressive merging of art and science in the future, and others seem to agree with him. Brian Eno, the creator of "ambient music" during the late 1970s and other experimental music, described his own working process as an experience that "falls in a nice new place—between art and science and playing. This is where I expect artists to be working more and more in the future."[210] For two decades Eno has applied many of Burroughs's same techniques and procedures of cut-ups and cut-ins for his music:

For years, I have been using rules to write music, but without computers. For instance, I've used systems of multiple tape loops that are allowed to reconfigure in various ways, while all I do is supply the original musical sounds or elements and then the system keeps throwing out new patterns of them. It is a kaleidoscopic music machine that keeps making new variations and new clumps....My attention went into the sonic material that I was feeding into my "repatterning machines." This became my area: I extended the composing act into the act of constructing sound itself.[211]

In fact, since the late 1940s there has been ample experimentation in avant-garde music with nonlinearity, overlaying multiple tracks, and randomly structured compositions. Even John Cage's reliance on chance operations, adapted from the *I Ching*, and his trust in the primacy of silence, derived from Zen Buddhism, are in some respects similar to Burroughs's methodologies although essentially aesthetic in nature. Similar, too, is Cage's remark, "Perhaps you will need new materials, new technologies. You have them. You are in the world of X, chaos, the new science."[212]

Music and sound works have played an ancillary but important role throughout Burroughs's career. In 1966 Burroughs met Paul McCartney of The Beatles in London and, along with Sommerville, talked about tape techniques and the future of rock music.[213] The Beatles were working on songs for their album *Revolver*, which would include the psychedelic "Tomorrow Never Knows," modeled on decidedly non-Western musical forms reminiscent of Asian (Indian ragas) or North-African (Moroccan *djenoun*) music and Native American chants. Gysin had been introduced to the Master Musicians of Jajouka in the 1950s while living in Tangier, recognized that their music stemmed from the Roman Lupercalia, or Rites of Pan, and tape recorded their ecstatic, mystical performances. Gysin played these tapes for Burroughs in 1958, accompanied Brian Jones of The Rolling Stones in 1968 to Jajouka, where Jones recorded the music, and revisited the musicians with Burroughs in 1973.[214] Four Jajouka pieces, with their trancelike, repetitive harmonies, are included on *Break Through in Grey Room*, a compilation of Burroughs's readings and sound experiments issued in 1986.

The idea of tape cut-ups and cut-ins is a very simple system, like its literary counterparts the cut-up and the fold-in, and when applied to sounds and music a nearly infinite variety of new experiences can materialize. Brian Eno described the process quite simply: "The lesson of complexity theory: allow some simple

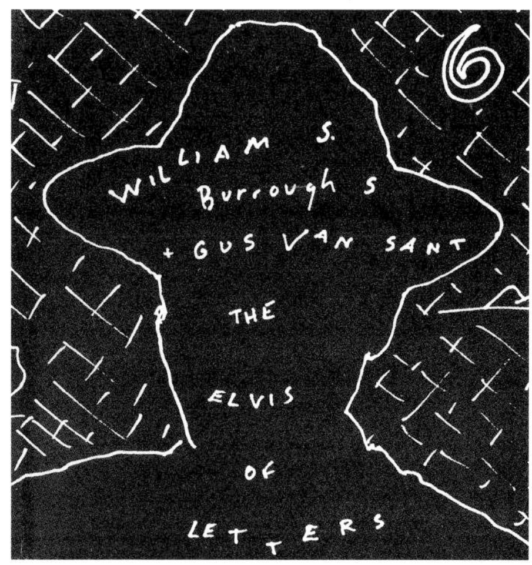

Gus Van Sant, compact disc cover illustration for **The Elvis of Letters**, 1985, cat. no. 111

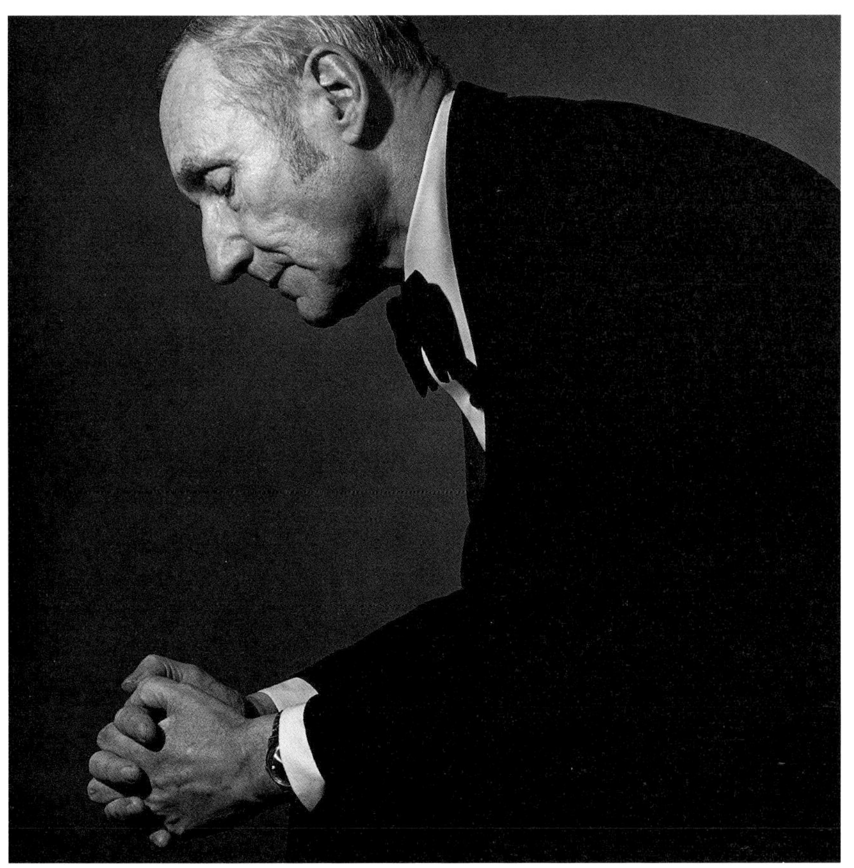
Robert Mapplethorpe, **William Burroughs**, 1979, cat. no. 107

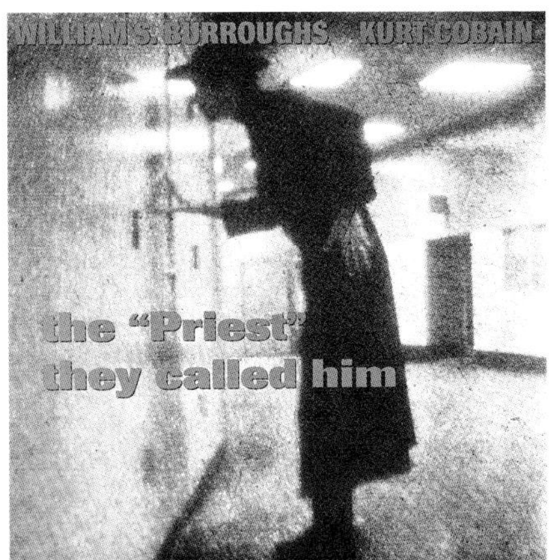

Mark Trunz, compact disc cover photography for **The "Priest" They Called Him**, 1992, cat. no. 149

Kate Simon, compact disc cover photography for **Spare Ass Annie and Other Tales**, 1993, cat. no. 120

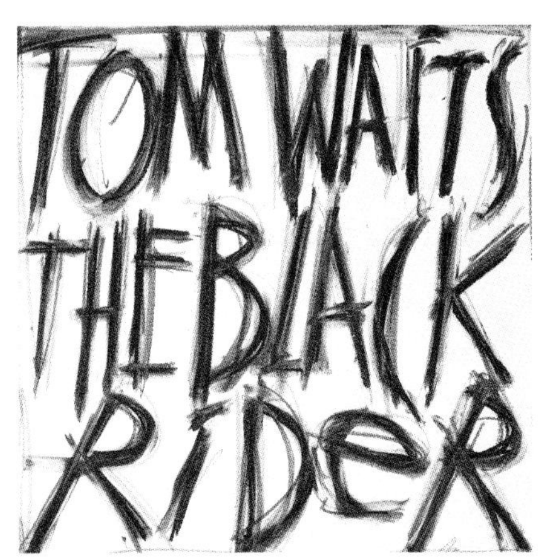

Robert Wilson, compact disc cover illustration for **The Black Rider**, 1993, cat. no. 150

systems to interact—watch the variety evolve."[215] The possibilities of these techniques have not been lost on contemporary jazz, rock, rap, and "alternative" music—alternative to what exactly? one could imagine Burroughs saying—including heavy metal, industrial, house, techno, and ambient. Free jazz's "motivic chain associations," where one motif leads to another and so on, suggests a repetitive, nonlinear open-endedness.

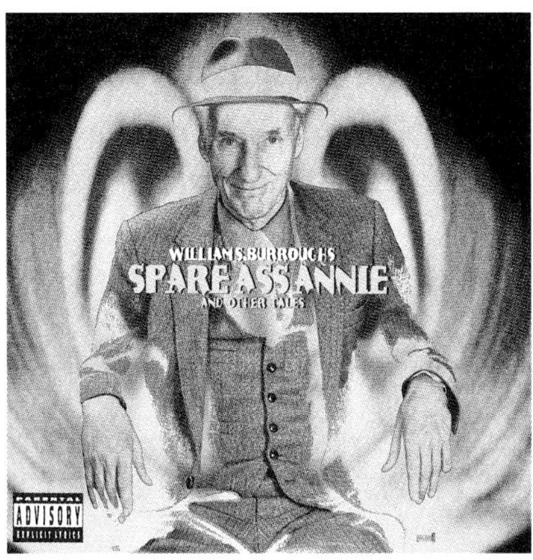

Electronic fusion jazz, as in Miles Davis's *Agharta* and *Pangea* of the mid-1970s, stressed densely sonic overlays, sudden silences, and quick jump-cuts. Burroughs's and Sommerville's experiments with "inching," which involves pulling a recorded tape back and forth across the playback head, finds a strikingly parallel result in the technique of "scratching" or moving a record back and forth while it is being played. Using sophisticated equipment ranging from Mini-Moog synthesizers to Apple Macintosh computers, Herbie Hancock transformed the sounds of inching into new jazz forms in his *Future Shock* (1983) and *Perfect Machine* (1988).[216] In 1991 critic David Toop related such contemporary rap musicians as Public Enemy and Ice Cube to Burroughs's "Subliminal Kid" who "brought back street sound and talk and music and poured it into his recorder array so he sent waves and eddies and tornados of sound down all your streets and by the river of all language."[217]

Burroughs frequently argued in his writings that words and sounds were nobody's personal property. In the late 1970s a number of bands had begun to use "the methods of radical artists in the arena of music just to 'see what would happen' to spectacular results."[218] Soon sampling, burning, appropriating, and copyright "infringement" became prominent in hip-hop and other music just as it had in postmodern art in general. Negativland, based in the San Francisco Bay area, has used tape recorders to mix-up and otherwise recombine music, radio talk-show programs, commercial advertisements, recorded explosions, religious sermons, and political speeches. Its strategy has been to use the "electronic environment of factual fictions as both source and subject" for their work.[219] Sounds, lyrics, samplings are all combined and recombined by one band, Skinny Puppy, as completely arbitrary, random operations. Writing the notes to one of Sonic Youth's albums in 1988, Jutta Koether described the period as a "time to be high in love with those fusions, confusions, and quotations, certain wonders, and flickering sound-substances. It was a time for enjoying that over-driven recycling and re-doing."[220]

Burroughs and recorded music have become progressively intertwined. His voice was given musical accompaniment by Gus Van Sant in 1985 on a recording entitled *The Elvis of Letters*. It again appears in the soundtrack to Laurie Anderson's *Home of the Brave* in 1986, both as a distorted vocal sample on "Late Show" and as the source for Anderson's "Language Is a Virus." Guy Hinant and Frédéric Walheer compiled Burroughs's readings along with works by Jon Hassell, Genesis P-Orridge and the Angels of Light, Tibetan ritual music, and a piano piece composed and performed by Claude Debussy and recorded in 1911 into two volumes entitled *The Myths Collection* in 1985 and 1990. A group called Manapsara, composed of Bradley Koehler and Christopher Hartman, released *Queer*, an independently created soundtrack, as it were, to Burroughs's novel of the same title, as well as extended mixes or dance versions of "Routine" and "Marketplace" in 1988. Producer Bill Laswell, who had worked with Herbie Hancock and brought out an album of Jajouka music in 1992, had earlier brought Burroughs together with his group Material for *Seven Souls* in 1989 and again on the group's *Hallucination Engine* (1994).

By 1990 the *New York Times* could announce that "William Burroughs has been given a lifetime pass to the rock-and-roll circus."[221] In 1987 the British group Cabaret Voltaire included "Here to Go," "Thank You America," and "No One Here" on their album *Code*, songs inspired by both Gysin and Burroughs. Burroughs's voice and image appear on the industrial-pop video of Ministry's *Just One Fix* (1992). Kurt Cobain, of the rock group Nirvana, collaborated with Burroughs on *The "Priest" They Called Him*, with Burroughs supplying a reading of his routine and Cobain playing an electric-feedback guitar in 1993. Burroughs's "Words of Advice for Young People" was given a disco mix by Pete Arden in 1994 on the second volume of Smash Records' *Big Hard Disk*. In 1993 Hal Wilner joined Burroughs with a rap group, The Disposable Heroes of Hiphoprisy, for a musical version of *Spare Ass Annie and Other Tales*. In 1990 Burroughs collaborated with Tom Waits and Robert Wilson on Wilson's opera *The Black Rider*, for which Burroughs supplied a reworked and sung version of his "'Tain't No Sin," which first appeared in *Interzone* as "It's the Plastic Age, folks. 'Tain't no sin take off your new skin and clown around in your bone-ons."[222] More than a decade earlier, in 1980, Burroughs had reminded Mick Jagger that the language virus originated as a "singing sickness." The apes who survived this disease gained human speech and began "a million year talk marathon." "So what these pop groups are doing," Burroughs concluded, "is *recreating the origins of human speech*."[223]

196
Burroughs, *The Ticket That Exploded* (note **21**), 205.

197
Burroughs, "It Belongs to the Cucumbers," *The Adding Machine* (note **12**), 54.

198
Burroughs, *The Ticket That Exploded* (note **21**), 166.

199
Ibid., 213.

200
Ibid., 207, 127.

201
William S. Burroughs, *Electronic Revolution* (Bonn: Expanded Media Editions, 1986), 23.

202
Burroughs, *The Ticket That Exploded* (note **21**), 166.

203
Ibid., 215–16.

204
Ibid., 217; see also Miles, *William Burroughs* (note **25**), 142.

205
Burroughs, *The Ticket That Exploded* (note **21**), 160.

206
Ibid., 63.

207
Morgan, *Literary Outlaw* (note **7**), 413.

208
Burroughs, *Electronic Revolution* (note **201**), 25.

209
Quoted in Miles, *William Burroughs* (note **25**), 152.

210
Brian Eno, "Gossip Is Philosophy," interview with Kevin Kelly, *Wired* 3, no. 5 (May 1995), 151.

211
Ibid., 150.

212
Cage, "An Autobiographical Statement," in *Rolywholyover: A Circus* (note **78**), unp.

213
See Bockris, *With William Burroughs* (note **6**), 72–73.

214
See William S. Burroughs, "Face to Face with the Goat God," *Oui* 2, no. 8 (August 1973): 92–93. Cf. Master Musicians of Jajouka, *Brian Jones Presents the Pipes of Pan at Jajouka* (New York: Point Music [446 487-2], 1995).

215
Eno, "Gossip Is Philosophy" (note **210**), 206.

216
The author is indebted to his former USC seminar students J. Christopher Wojcieszyn and Ty Bertrand for bringing to his attention parallels between these musicians and Burroughs.

217
David Toop, *Rap Attack 2: African Rap to Global Hip-Hop* (London: Pluto Press, 1991), 180; cited in Dick Hebdige, "Welcome to the Terrordome: Jean-Michel Basquiat and the 'Dark' Side of Hybridity," in Richard Marshall, *Jean-Michel Basquiat*, exh. cat. (New York: Whitney Museum of American Art, 1992), 69 n. 19; Burroughs, *Nova Express* (note **2**), 147.

218
Genesis P-Orridge, "Hard Listening for the Ease in Hearing," liner notes to *The Second Annual Report of Throbbing Gristle* (Mute [9 61093-2], 1991). Genesis P-Orridge was a fan of Burroughs's writings and ideas; his industrial band Throbbing Gristle metamorphosed into another and more dance-oriented band called Psychic TV in the 1980s; see V. Vale and Andrea Juno, eds., *William Burroughs, Brion Gysin, and Throbbing Gristle*, *Re/Search* 4/5 (special issue, 1982).

219
Liner notes to Negativland, *Helter Stupid* (SST Records [SST CD 252], 1989).

220
Jutta Koether, "Surfacing It All," liner notes to Sonic Youth, *Daydream Nation* (Geffen Records [DGCD 24515], 1988).

221
Milo Miles, "Zombie Assassins, Desert Rhythms and the Beats," *New York Times* (July 15, 1990), H24.

222
Burroughs, *Interzone*, 152; a variant of these lyrics appears in William S. Burroughs, *Port of Saints* (Berkeley: Blue Wind Press, 1980), 46–47. *Interzone* was originally written 1953–58; *Port of Saints* was written in 1973. The original song, "'Tain't No Sin (To Dance Around in Your Bones)," with lyrics by Edgar Leslie and music by Walter Donaldson, dates from 1929; the author is grateful to James Grauerholz for bringing this source to his attention.

223
Bockris, *With William Burroughs* (note **6**), 226.

Reverse direction,
and let the picture reach

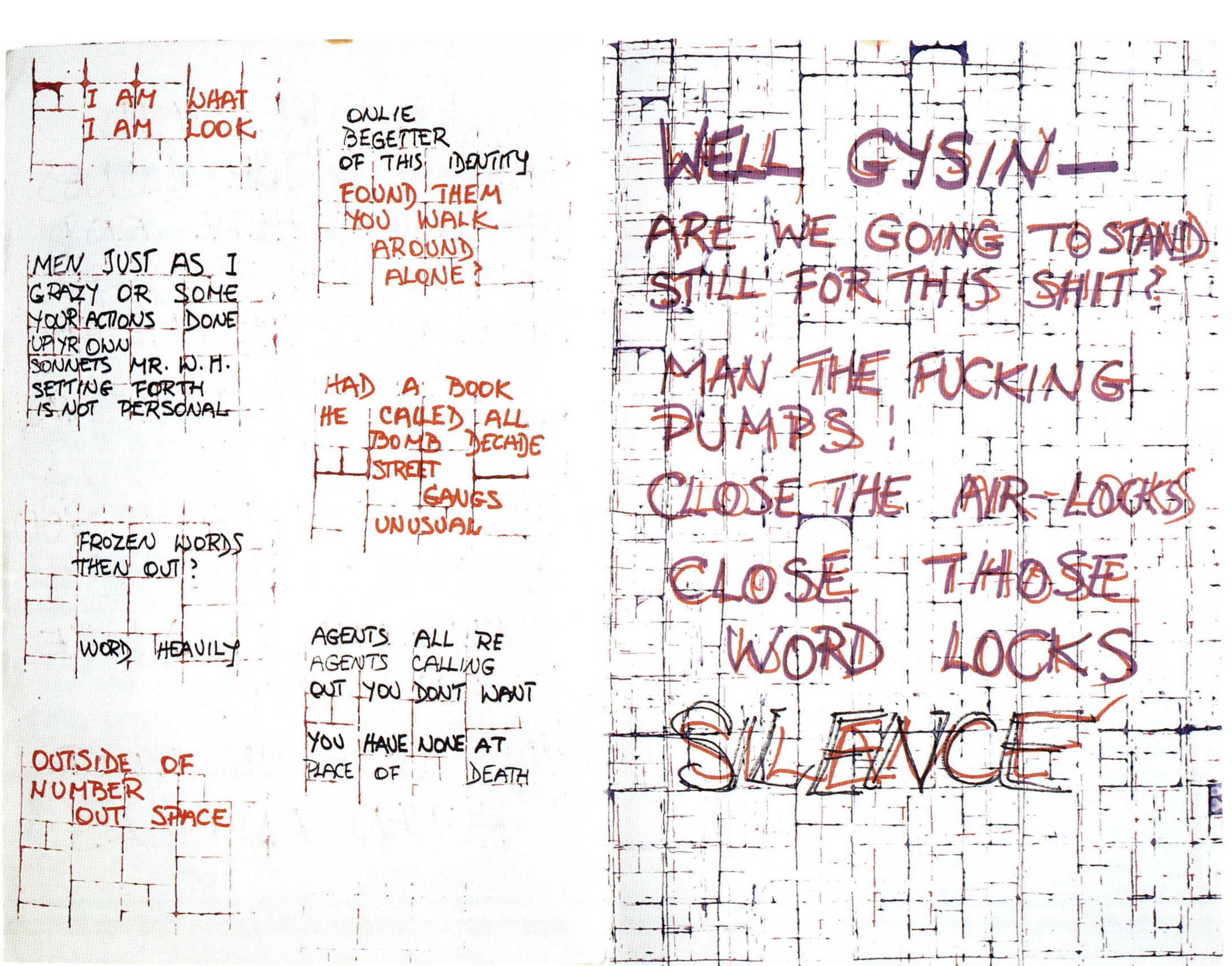

William S. Burroughs and Brion Gysin, **The Cut-Ups**, 1964, cat. no. 80

XI

DOORS OF CHANCE

out to you.[224]

In *The Ticket That Exploded* Burroughs explores the historical origins of symbolic communications—the evolution of the various viruses that have plagued us for a million years. "Dream singing came before body without a shadow without relics," he wrote, "the dreamer with dirty flesh came before talking," "singing came before talking," "sound track conjures up the image track," "word evokes image," "word came before image."[225] In *Nova Express* Burroughs equates image with junk, and image addiction is deadly, "If I don't get the image fix I'm in the ovens." Control deals with all addictions, junk as well as symbols. Control's Board Books are the "symbol books of the all-powerful board that had controlled thought feeling and movement of a planet from birth to death with iron claws of pain and pleasure."[226] Dr. Dent's apomorphine treatment for heroin addiction worked for Burroughs. For him, apomorphine is simply an antivirus, and since "word begets image and image is virus," apomorphine is, again simply, "no word and no image."[227] Success, if not plain survival, is being able to control Control's images; thus, the cut-ups, fold-ins, and permutations; thus, the random tape-recorder cut-ins on sound tracks; and thus, the need to go back to the start, to dreams. "What do artists do?" Burroughs asked in his small book *Painting and Guns* (1992), "They dream for other people."[228]

Describing the invention of cut-ups, Gysin stressed that "the cut-up method treats words as the painter treats his paint, raw material with rules and reasons of its own."[229] Because he was more a painter than a writer by profession, Gysin was able to see the fundamental elements of literature as pictorial materials to be used like any other forms, shapes, colors, or textures more so than Burroughs could on that day when Gysin accidently cut through the newsprint. Ultimately it was Gysin's work and ideas that most influenced Burroughs's work (in a wide range of media) since the late 1950s. Gysin was there for the scrapbooks and *The Third Mind* collages; he showed Burroughs the essential pictorial value of the calligraphic form, he was the first of the group to experiment with recorders, mirror-staring, and the flicker vision of the Dreamachine; he helped work on and starred in Balch's films, and it was he who first introduced the West to Moroccan Jajouka music (although he was soon followed in this by others like Paul Bowles and Brian Jones). He was the man Burroughs most respected of all, and he was a painter who introduced Burroughs to the art of painting and a "complete derangement of the senses."[230] In fact, Burroughs's first, formal artworks may be the calligraphic drawings in the style of Gysin he did for the dust jackets of the first Olympia Press edition of *Naked Lunch* (1959) and for the Grove Press edition of *The Soft Machine* (1966), drawings that bracket in time those by Gysin done for the covers of *The Exterminator* in 1960 and the Olympia Press edition of *The Soft Machine* in 1961.

John C. B. L. Gysin, as his name appears on a New York Port Authority Identification card issued in the 1940s,[231] was born in Taplow, Buckinghamshire, in 1916. His father, Swiss but reared in England, died in the First World War.

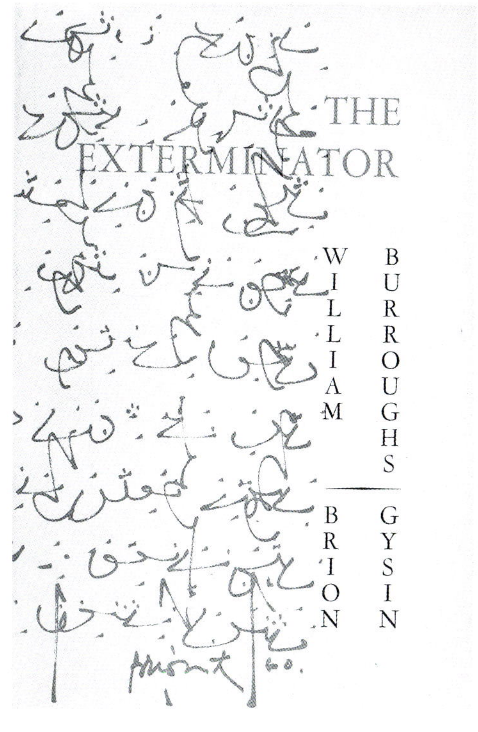

Brion Gysin, dust-jacket illustration for **The Exterminator**, 1960, cat. no. 128

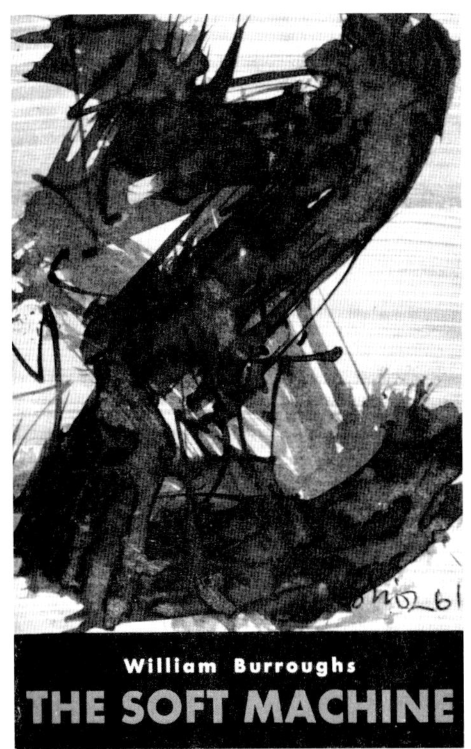

Brion Gysin, dust-jacket illustration for **The Soft Machine**, 1961, cat. no. 129

Brion's mother was Canadian and shortly after his birth returned with him to Edmonton. According to most sources, issues of national identity affected Gysin from his earliest years. Gysin returned to England, where he attended Catholic secondary school, and then moved to Paris, where he attached himself to the surrealists, only to have his drawings removed from a joint surrealist exhibition and himself expelled from the group by André Breton in 1935. Gysin was a confirmed misogynist and a believer in conspiracies. He traveled to New York in 1940, where he worked as a stagehand in the theater, became a welder in a shipyard, and was drafted into the Canadian army, where he studied Japanese and learned the rudiments of Japanese calligraphy. In 1949 he relocated to Bordeaux and from there to Paris, where he met up with Paul and Jane Bowles, whom he had first encountered in New York. At loose ends and following Paul Bowles's suggestion, Gysin traveled to Morocco for a week's vacation and wound up staying in Tangier on and off for twenty-three years until permanently settling in Paris in 1973. With help from a Moroccan painter friend, Hamri, Gysin adapted to Morocco passionately: he dressed in native costume, ran a restaurant and nightclub called The 1001 Nights, dabbled in magic and the occult, and studied Arabic calligraphy.[232]

Gysin had known Burroughs only marginally in Tangier, and it was not until they met again in Paris in 1958 that their close friendship commenced. By this time Gysin had developed his own, fairly distinct style of abstract painting, which derived in great part from his interest in overlaying vertical Japanese calligraphy with lines of horizontal Arabic writing. Between 1958 and 1964 he had solo exhibitions in New York, Rome, and London and was included in a number of group exhibitions in Paris. Gysin was one of the founders of the group Domaine Poétique along with the "sound poets" François Dufrêne, Bernard Heidsieck, Robert Filliou, and members of the Fluxus group. From 1973 until 1986 he exhibited widely in Western Europe, gave a number of performances in London and Paris, recorded a number of his audio permutations in Basel, and participated along with Burroughs in the *Le colloque de Tanger*, organized by Gérard-Georges Lemaire in Geneva in 1975, in the *Soirée Burroughs-Gysin* at the Centre Georges Pompidou in 1977, and in the *Nova Convention* in New York in 1978. He was the author of *History of Slavery in Canada* (1946), *The Process* (1969), and *Stories* (1984). He reapplied the lessons of *The Third Mind* to the text-image collages he contributed to a "postmodern" edition of Gertrude Stein's *Une pièce circulaire* in 1985.[233] He died in Paris in 1986 of emphysema and lung cancer, a month before the publication of his *The Last Museum*. Gysin's art was left to the Musée de l'Art Moderne de la Ville de Paris; his literary estate was bequeathed to Burroughs.

Gysin's watercolors and gouaches of the late 1930s and 1940s reflect a decided surrealist leaning, not one that gravitated to the literary, hyperrealist dreamscapes of a Dalí or Matta but one more interested in a painting that caused some sort of abstracted field to come into play and upon which the viewer's mind could interact. This is seen most especially in his liquescent, oneiric smearings of various paints and inks, a technique called *décalcomanie*, wherein two planes of pigment are pressed together and quickly separated; this process was popularized by Oscar Dominguez and Marcel Jean in the mid-1930s. The fluid forms are similar to a formal Rorschach image and were created in much the same fashion. With no reference to any representational reality, any manner of content may be envisioned, imagined, or conjured up. This surrealist device

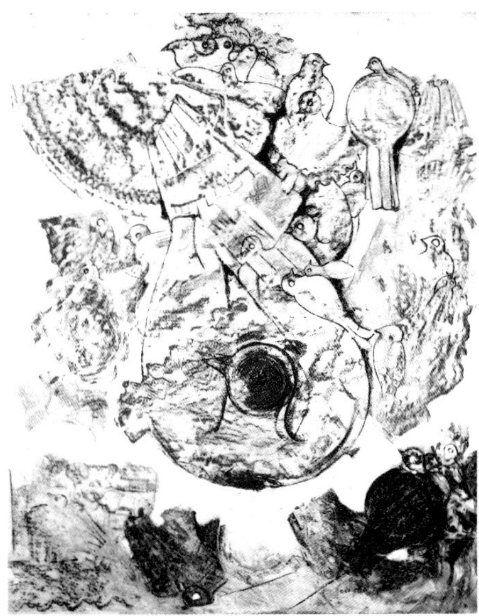

Max Ernst, **Bird Marriage**, 1925, oil on canvas, 31¾ x 25⅝ in. (80.7 x 65.1 cm), Staatsgalerie Stuttgart

is similar to others like *frottage* and *grattage*, found notably in the work of Max Ernst, where pictorial forms are created by either rubbing across textured surfaces or scraping through layers of paint; both techniques yield fantasy abstractions just as codeless and lacking in content as any décalcomanie and are just as capable of serving as a "point of departure and a basis for poetic hallucination."[234] What fascinated Gysin was, of course, the hallucinatory aspects of these surrealist fields—the painting as a catalyst for provoking dream images, as a point of departure for the imagination.

From the surrealists, Gysin had also gained an interest in automatic writing and drawing, other techniques that forced the unconscious to interact with a field of visual materials. Gysin's art during the 1950s turned progressively toward the calligraphic; even his figurative works at the beginning of the decade can be seen in retrospect as more written than painted. This shift was partly due to his practice of combining Japanese and Arabic writing, but there was also the more general context. European painters as diverse as André Masson, Georges Mathieu, Pierre Alechinsky, and Henri Michaux had begun incorporating Chinese and Japanese calligraphic techniques in the paintings they exhibited in the mid-to-late 1950s.[235] The work of American painters Jackson Pollock and Mark Tobey were exhibited in Paris in 1952 and 1954, respectively, and discussed as part of a new "Pacific School" of painting that combined both Pollock's abstract-expressionist "drip" paintings as well as Tobey's more meditative white-line paintings. In New York during the late 1940s Gysin had shared a studio with Matta and had met Ernst, Arshile Gorky, and Pollock; and it is suggested that he discovered certain affinities between their styles of linear abstraction and his own aesthetic ideas.[236] By the late 1950s Gysin's gestural and calligraphic drawings had evolved into work that could be described as a merging of an illuminated page from the Qur'an and the scriptlike markings of a Mark Tobey.

Gysin's concerns with writing as painting are an outgrowth of his surrealism; after all, according to Breton, "the pen that flows in writing and the pencil that runs in drawing" are equivalent.[237] These concerns also linked him with the broader movement of French *lettrisme* of the early 1960s. *Lettriste* Maurice Lemaître and *poet sonore* François Dufrêne were likewise involved with breaking syntax and logic, inverting sounds, inserting noises, and playing with typographies and signs. These were certainly structural elements with which

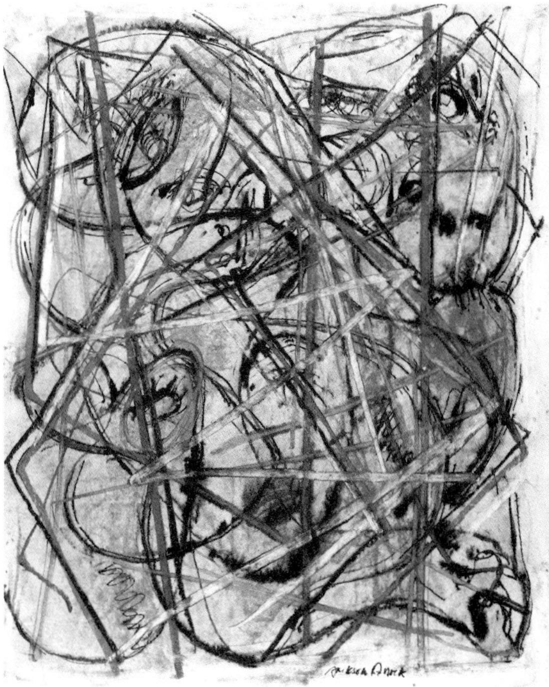

Jackson Pollock, untitled, c. 1945, crayon, pastel, and gouache on paper, 25⅝ x 20½ in. (65.1 x 52.1 cm), Los Angeles County Museum of Art, gift of Anna Bing Arnold and purchased with funds provided by Mr. William Inge, Dr. and Mrs. Kurt Wagner, Graphic Arts Council Fund, and Museum Acquisition Fund

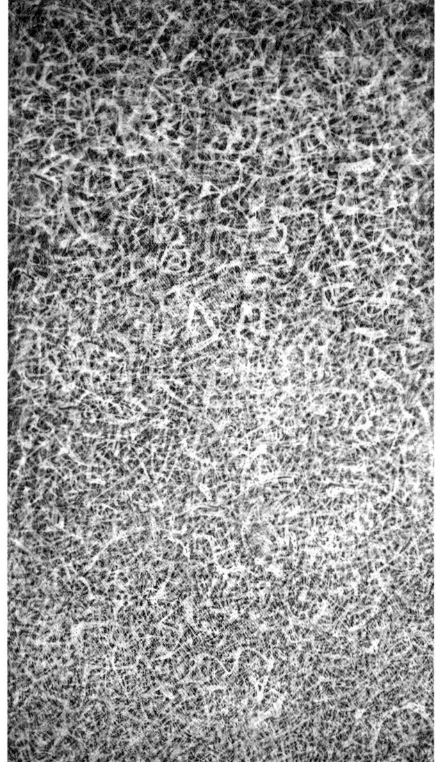

Mark Tobey, **Multiple Moments in Space**, 1959, tempera on board, 19¾ x 11 in. (50.2 x 27.9 cm), collection Mr. and Mrs. Bernard Greenberg, Beverly Hills

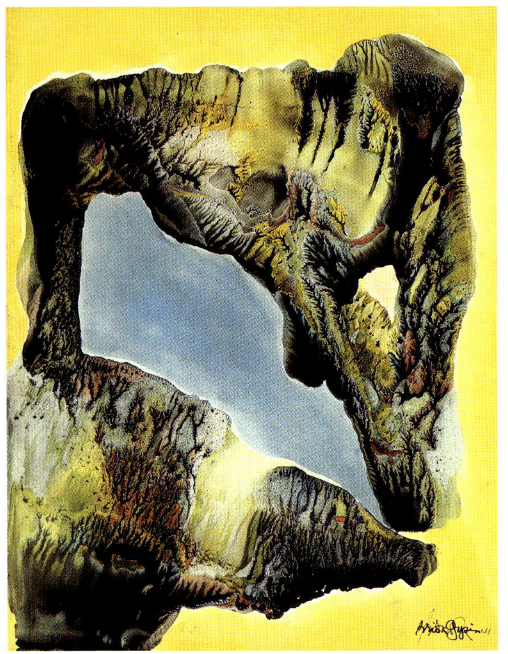

Brion Gysin, **Décalcomanie**, 1941, ink on paper, 13⅞ x 11 in. (35.2 x 27.9 cm), Galerie de France, Paris

Gysin played and to which Burroughs was introduced at this time.[238] A more precise location of Gysin's particular work, however, might follow the tripartite division accorded artists in the exhibition *La lettre et le signe dans la peinture contemporaine* held at the Valérie Schmidt Gallery in Paris in 1963. *Lettristes*, like Maurice Lemaître, were in one section, while abstract expressionists and *l'art informel* painters, like Tobey, Franz Kline, and Hans Hartung, were included as "*informels à signes*," and artists as distinctly different from one another as Gysin, Cy Twombly, and Jacques de La Villeglé were classified as "*peintre du signe indépendant*."[239]

For Gysin, the conflation of Arabic and Japanese calligraphies held possible cabalistic connotations because they determined an essential grid structure of squares that had magical qualities.[240] In 1959 Gysin's drawings developed from overall calligraphiclike fields to pictorial permutations of differently colored scripts arranged into four-part grids, not unlike Duchamp's *Rendez-vous du dimanche* (1916). Around 1964 Burroughs and Gysin collaborated on an exquisite, folio-sized, hand-lettered manuscript entitled *The Cut-Ups*, which includes Gysin's grids and words facing pages of printed texts by Burroughs that call for straight shooting, cutting control, and silence. By the time Burroughs and Gysin began work on *The Third Mind*, Gysin's faux Arabic script was often paired with word permutations; and the printer's brayer he had carved into in 1961 was used to visually enlarge his grids to a scale that offered a playing field for automatic scripting, insertion of word groups, and photographic prints. Balch's film *Cut-Ups* features flickering scenes of Gysin repeatedly rolling his inked brayer across a six-foot length of paper. Between 1963 and 1965 Gysin hand-lettered sections of Burroughs's texts from *Naked Lunch* and some from *The Third Mind* on sheets of paper that had been prepared by multiple passes of the "grid-brayer" using different colored inks.[241] The brayer work continued well through the 1970s. In 1976 Gysin reprised the collage work of *The Third Mind* by including a cut-up French typescript and two cut-up portraits of himself naked and, not surprisingly, of Burroughs dressed in a suit. During the last decade of his life, Gysin continued with brayer drawings, infilling the squares of the grid with watercolor and type-c photographic contact prints documenting the construction of the Centre Georges Pompidou, which he could see from the window of his apartment. Around the same time he arranged contacted (as opposed to enlarged) strips of photographs from complete rolls of color film he shot of the museum's construction into "uninterrupted suites" of thirty-six images in order to produce rectangular grids in which "everything is calculated but nothing is edited, collaged, or tricked."[242]

There are obvious congruences among Burroughs's idea of "points of intersection," which he formulated while working with cut-ups; the surrealists' and Gysin's notion of paintings functioning as "points of departure"; and Burroughs's concept of "ports of entry," a phrase he used in describing Gysin's paintings. Gysin envisaged entire worlds in miniature in his drawings:

I write across the picture space from right to left and, then, I turn the space and write across that again to make a multi-dimensional grid with the script I picked up from the Pan people. Who runs may read, I have, I think, paid the pipers in full. Within the bright scaffolding appears a world of Little Folk, swinging in their flowering ink jungle-gym, exercising control of matter and knowing space.[243]

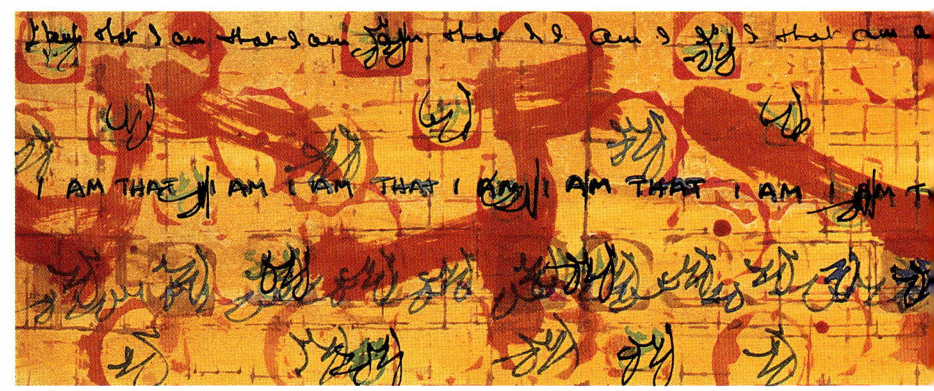

Brion Gysin, **I Am That I Am**, 1961, cat. no. 130

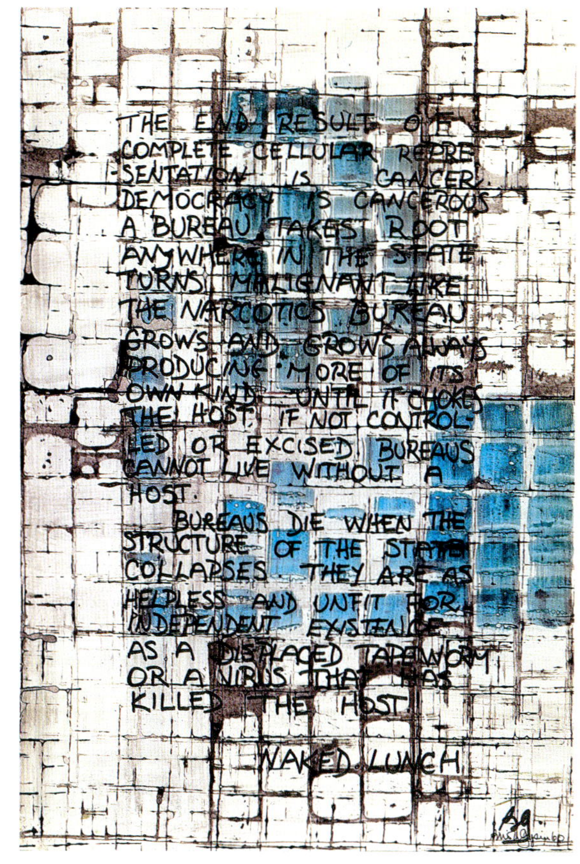

Brion Gysin, **Naked Lunch**, 1960, cat. no. 127

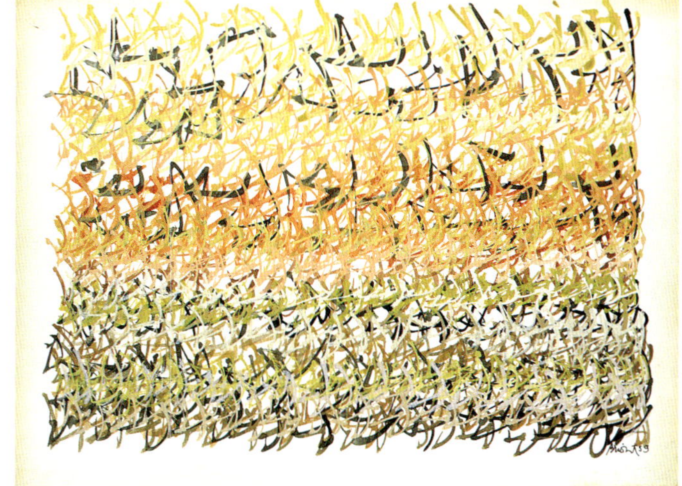

Brion Gysin, untitled, 1959, ink on paper,
10¾ x 14⅞ in. (27.3 x 37.8 cm), collection William S. Burroughs, Lawrence

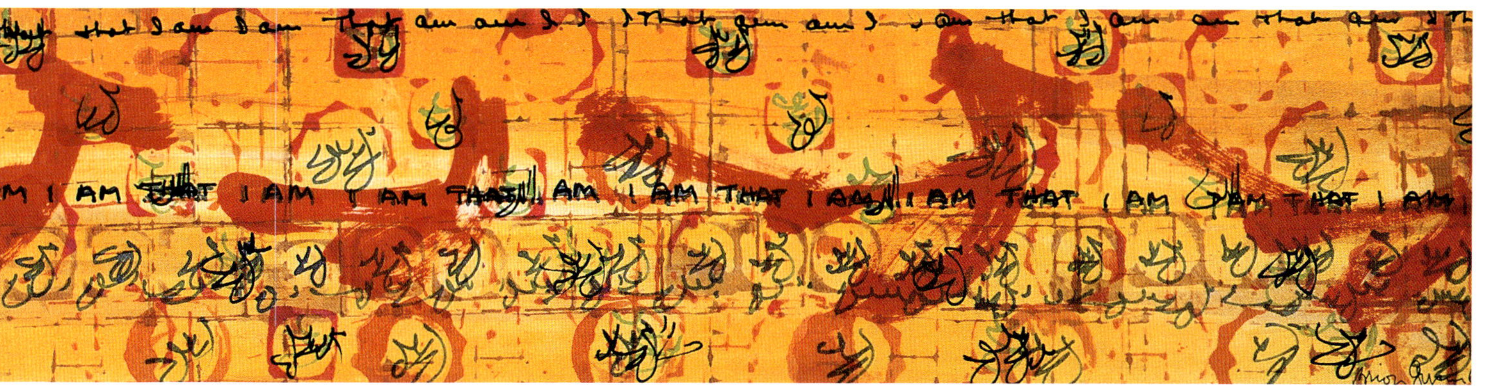

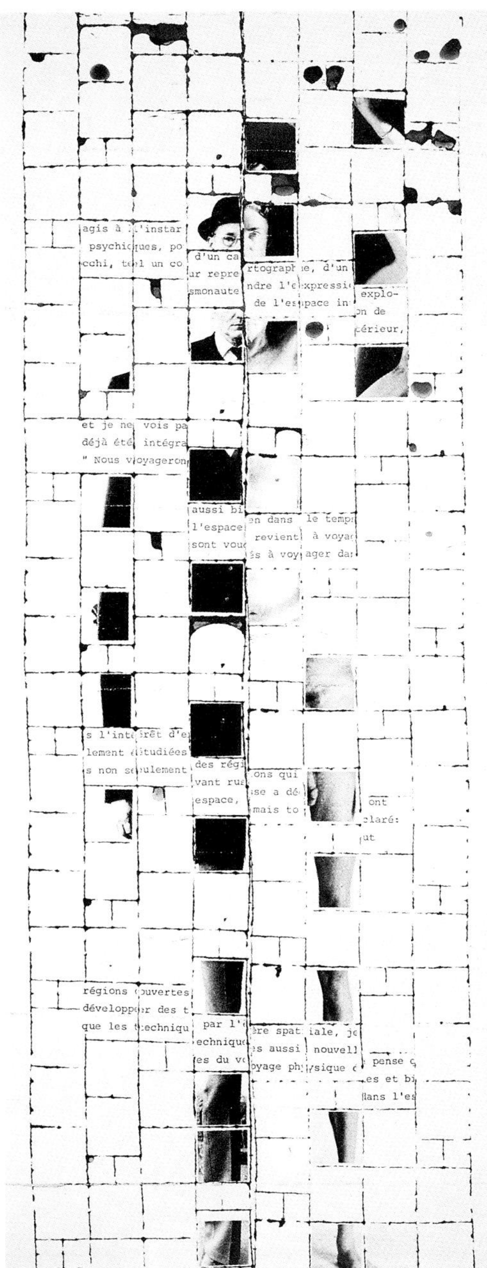

William S. Burroughs and Brion Gysin, **The Third Mind Cut-Up**, 1976, cat. no. 36

Gysin understood that writing and music were far more linear and temporal than painting, but he used the essentially linear aspects of writing to construct complex terrains that are both multi-dimensional and multitemporal.

During the Beat Hotel days in the early 1960s Burroughs admitted that he had never "seen painting" until he saw Gysin's work; when asked how he got into the paintings, he replied:

Usually I get in by a port of entry, as I call it. It is often a face through whose eyes the picture opens into a landscape and I go literally right through that eye into that landscape. Sometimes it is rather like an archway...any number of little details or a special spot of color makes the port of entry and then the entire picture will suddenly become a three-dimensional frieze in plaster or jade or some other precious material.[244]

Burroughs perceived Gysin's paintings as interactive, pictorial fields not unlike surrealist *champs magnétiques*, portals or doors through which both artist and viewer might enter unfamiliar landscapes of the mind. Many things, animate or not, are consecutively encountered within the landscapes; not everything can be seen at once, only in a sort of "time-sequence." "Here is space-time painting," Burroughs wrote, "You can see way deep into all sorts of landscapes for instance, and then you flash back to what appears on the surface...the substance of the painting exists with a double motion in and out."[245]

For Burroughs, three aspects of what he discovered in Gysin's paintings are critical. First, the paintings are associative rather than representational. The "pictures constantly change because you are drawn into time travel on a network of associations," and this suited Burroughs's desire to divest words of their linguistic specificity and to treat them instead as abstract association blocks.[246] Second, Burroughs enjoyed a kind of time travel in flashing back and forth among the various levels he encountered in the paintings: "The viewer has to learn how to flicker back and forth between a telescopic and a microscopic point of view while his attention is centered on some small beautiful scene which may be no bigger than your index fingernail at one moment and then your attention is suddenly jerked back to a clear long range view of the picture or its allover pattern."[247] This description of what was essentially an optical operation is parallel to the jumps in perspective or voice that occurred in Burroughs's writings as well as in the collages of the 1960s. Third, the sheer multiplicity of images Burroughs discerned in the paintings enthralled him. "What you actually see at any given moment," he wrote, "becomes only a part of a visual operation which includes an infinite series of images. This leads you along a certain path like a row or series of patterns...a series of neural patterns which already exist in the human brain."[248] Ian Sommerville's and Burroughs's collage experiments with infinitely multiplying images as well as the fluctuating "constellations of images" experienced with flicker vision and the Dreamachine were parallel experiments with infinite, serial images.

Burroughs did not immediately turn to his own painting following his exposure to Gysin's painting, partly because he was involved in other art and writing activities and partly, it would seem, out of a desire not to intrude upon his friend's terrain. During the 1970s, and apart from his recurring heroin addiction, Burroughs was mostly caught up with reappraising his fiction and distilling the cut-up technique into a more manageable and readable style. Beginning with *The Wild Boys*, he created an entire, new cast of fictional characters such as the Wild Boys, Audrey Carsons, Kim Carsons, and William Seward Hall and developed a new body of fiction in which time travel, Western frontier adventures, and pirate escapades are combined in fantastic landscapes. "The wild boys have no sense of time and date the beginning from 1969 when the first wild boy groups were formed," Burroughs wrote in 1973 in *Port of Saints*.[249] But in 1987, after six more books and imagining that the "old writer couldn't write anymore because he had reached the end of words," Burroughs pointed out an alternative to the written landscape fields of novels:

To wail the fault you visualize. What form would surface with an explosive separate being, desperate last chance? The 12-gauge number 4 or never explosive honesty.[...]*Bang* and your hybrid is there, speed of light *splat*.[...]Big Bang shotgun art an orgasm of any solid only one of its kind. Chance the hopeless message flashes with the sky final desperate gamble Ruski blow the house layout challenge the immutable results as simple as squeezing energy directed accented brush work.[250]

The randomness of the cut-up and the multiple points of view simultaneously rendered in tape cut-ins and collages were quite as easily created with some paint and a double-barrel, Rossi 12-gauge shotgun.

224
William S. Burroughs, "The Pictures Look at You," in *Shotgun Paintings: Works on Wood and Paper: William S. Burroughs Exhibition*, exh. cat. (Tokyo: The Seed Hall, Sezon Museum of Art, 1990), unp.

225
Burroughs, *The Ticket That Exploded* (note **21**), 169, 178.

226
Burroughs, *The Soft Machine* (note **56**), 160.

227
Burroughs, *Nova Express* (note **2**), 46, 48.

228
Burroughs, *Painting and Guns* (note **171**), "The Creative Observer," 46.

229
Brion Gysin to Robert Palmer, *Rolling Stone* (May 1972); see also Gysin and Wilson, *Here to Go* (note **14**), 55.

230
Gysin and Wilson, *Here to Go* (note **14**), 166.

231
See ibid., 22.

232
For many of the facts concerning Gysin's life, the author is indebted to Morgan, *Literary Outlaw* (note **7**), 299–309. See also Catherine Thieck, ed., *Brion Gysin: Calligraphies, Permutations, Cut Ups*, exh. cat. (Paris: Galerie de France, 1987).

233
See Renée Riese Hubert, "Gertrude Stein, Cubism, and the Postmodern Book," in Marjorie Perloff, ed., *Postmodern Genres* (Norman: University of Oklahoma Press, 1988), 122–23.

234
Marcel Jean, *The History of Surrealist Painting*, trans. Simon Watson Taylor (New York: Grove Press, 1967), 126. A *frottage* drawing is done by placing a sheet of paper over a textured surface, such as wood grain, and rubbing graphite or charcoal over it; *grattage* is accomplished by placing textured objects beneath a canvas and scraping oil paint across the canvas's surface with a palette knife or other object. See Werner Spies, ed., *Max Ernst: A Retrospective*, exh. cat. (London: Tate Gallery, 1991), 148, 230, and passim.

235
See Sylvain Lecombre, "Vivre une peinture sans tradition," in Pontus Hulten, ed., *Paris—Paris: 1937–1957*, exh. cat. (Paris: Centre Georges Pompidou, 1981), 220. It should be noted that as encyclopedic as this catalogue tries to be, Gysin's name is not mentioned.

236
Gladys C. Fabre, "I Am That Am I?: Entre cristal et fumée," in Thieck, *Brion Gysin* (note **232**), 13.

237
André Breton, "Artistic Genesis and Perspective of Surrealism," in Peggy Guggenheim, ed., *Art of This Century* (New York: Art of This Century, 1942; New York: Arno Press, 1968), 20.

238
Fabre, "I Am That Am I?" in Thieck, *Brion Gysin* (note **232**), 14.

239
Ibid., 13–14.

240
See Gérard-Georges Lemaire, "Qui est ce tiers qui marché à côte de vous?" in Thieck, *Brion Gysin* (note **232**), 85.

241
Guillaume Gallozzi, ed., *Brion Gysin: Back in No Time*, exh. cat. (New York: Guillaume Gallozzi, 1994), cat. nos. 36–41.

242
Gysin quoted in Thieck, *Brion Gysin* (note **232**), 52.

243
From Brion Gysin, William S. Burroughs, and Ian Sommerville, *Brion Gysin Let the Mice In* (West Glover, Vermont: Something Else Press, 1973); cited in Gysin and Wilson, *Here to Go* (note **14**), 76.

244
From a transcript of a tape-recorded discussion between Burroughs and Gysin, c. 1960; reprinted in Gysin and Wilson, *Here to Go* (note **14**), 173.

245
Ibid., 176.

246
Ibid., 183.

247
Ibid., 179.

248
Ibid., 179.

249
Burroughs, *Port of Saints* (note **222**), 73.

250
William S. Burroughs, *The Western Lands* (New York: Viking Penguin, 1987), 257; Ruski was Burroughs's favorite cat.

XII

THE PICTURE BETWEEN YOUR EARS

I teach

According to Burroughs, "if you can't see it you can't say it."[252] He is, in this instance, talking about the origins of spoken language, the word virus; and he is quite convinced that even subvocal speech cannot be muted or silenced, the virus is much too powerful. Yet, as part of the overall strategy of silencing the word, attempts must be continually made to think, perceive, communicate, and even feel wordlessly. Asked in 1965 if he was able to think in images for any length of time with his inner voice silent, Burroughs responded, "I'm becoming more proficient at it, partly through my work with scrapbooks and translating the connections between words and images."[253] Nearly thirty years later, after a decade of painting, he explained a nonlinguistic manner of seeing when he wrote, "In painting I see with my hands, and I do not know what my hands have done until I look at it afterwards. It is when I look at the completed canvas that I know what the painting is about."[254] Of course, once whatever is seen is recognized, there is no end to verbalizing it descriptively, and in fact many of his paintings from 1990–92 often have "titles" that are one or two paragraphs in length; but that is not the point. The point is simply letting go of preconceived, linguistic expectations and letting the picture do the talking.

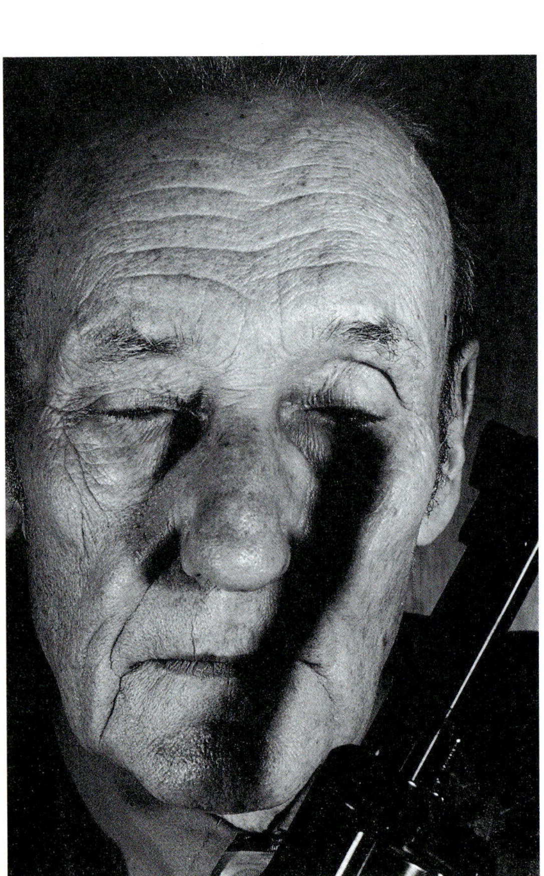

Gottfried Helnwein, **William Burroughs**, 1990, cat. no. 115

Sometime in 1982, with *The Place of Dead Roads* all but completed, Burroughs shot a piece of plywood and in its rent surface rediscovered Gysin's "little folk" or, more precisely, those small details that led to those infinite landscapes he had seen earlier in his friend's paintings. "I picked up a piece of plywood and blasted it," he wrote. "Then I looked at the broken plywood where the shots came out and in these striations I saw all sorts of things—little villages, streets of all kinds. I said, 'My God, this is a work of art.'"[255] Burroughs had moved from New York to Lawrence, Kansas, in late 1981, and it was here, just outside town, that he could satisfy his lifelong passion of shooting guns.[256] The ripped and shattered fragments of plywood and the multiple layers

you picture language.[251]

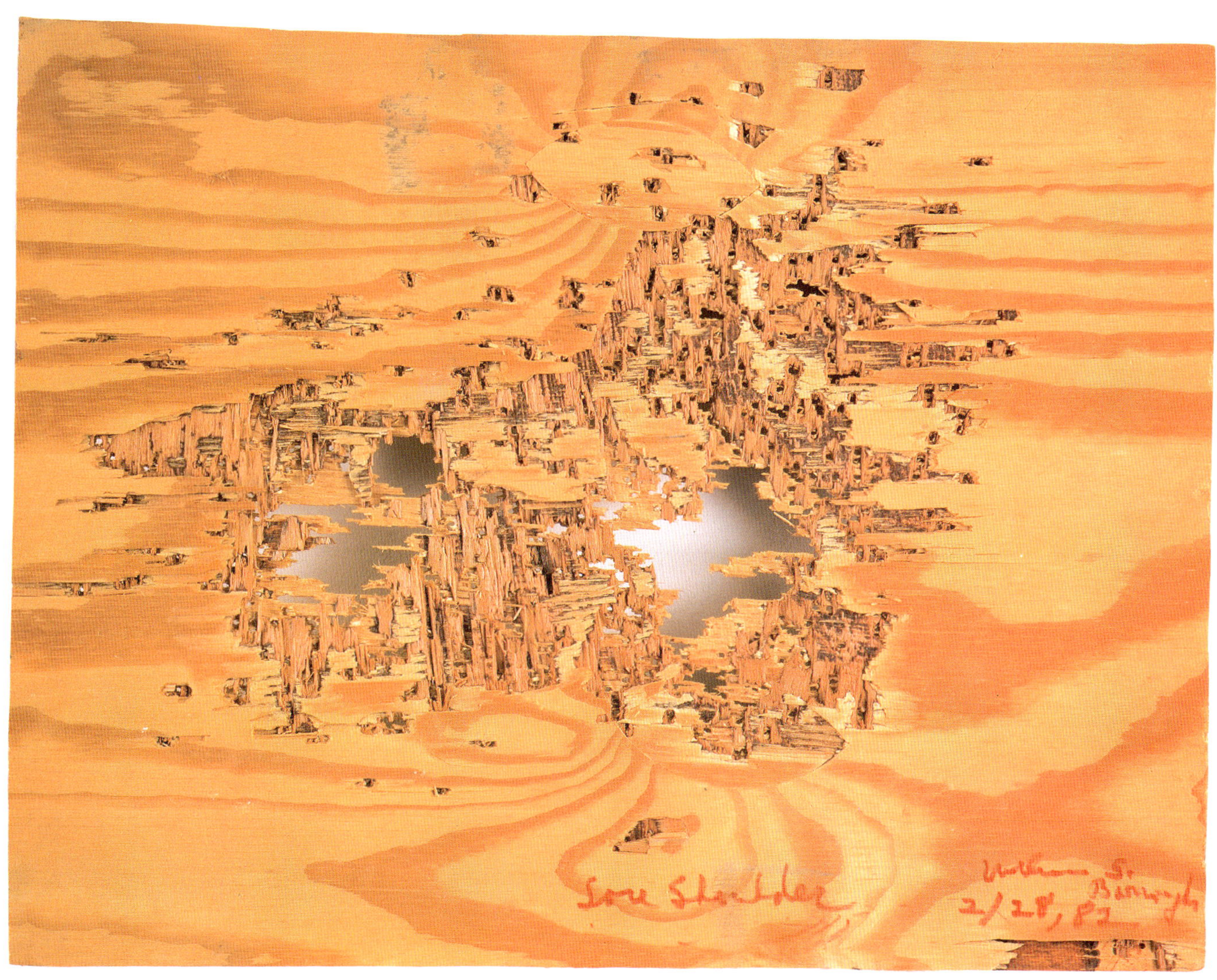

William S. Burroughs, **Sore Shoulder**, 1982, cat. no. 37

laid open by the gunshot's exit were the results of a chance operation that appealed to Burroughs's fascination with randomness, multiplicity, and overlappings. Throughout his adult life, furthermore, Burroughs sought to escape the confines of the physical world and the body, leading him to places like Interzone or the Western Lands. The blasted surface on the back of the shot plywood afforded him precisely such a visual landscape into which he could escape and wander about examining the details bodilessly. Through an act of intense microperception, Burroughs entered the wood's broken splinters, as it were, and discovered vistas leading toward infinity.

Other artists certainly preceded Burroughs in discovering astonishing things in purely abstract forms and patterns. Leonardo da Vinci recommended stimulating the imagination by staring at a stained wall "in which you will be able to see various landscapes," among other things.[257] French novelist Victor Hugo created imaginary landscapes and experimental explorations of formless blots and chance impressions in his ink drawings of the 1860s.[258] Wassily Kandinsky wrote of visiting peasant homes where the decorations and colors made him feel that he was within a painting and for years "sought the possibility of letting the viewer 'stroll' within the picture, forcing him to become absorbed in the picture, forgetful of himself."[259] Surrealist André Masson began his paintings impulsively without any image or plan in mind; "gradually," he wrote, "I see suggestions of figures or objects. I encourage these to emerge."[260] Ernst's *frottage* and *grattage* revealed images embedded within compacted textures and patterns. Other surrealist techniques such as automatic writing and décalcomanie had also been used as "dream protocols" for creating arbitrary abstractions that could then be read into. Jean Dubuffet saw his "automatic" drawings and his thick paintings of around 1950 as "dreamscapes" or "landscapes of the mind" that revealed a "whole theater of facts."[261] Jackson Pollock, expressing notions shared by other abstract expressionists, wrote, "When you're painting out of your subconscious, figures are bound to emerge.... Painting is a state of being... painting is self-discovery. Every good artist paints what he is."[262]

Nor was Burroughs the first to use a gun in conjunction with art. The American artist Joseph Cornell had constructed in 1943 a small work entitled *Habitat Group for Shooting Gallery* in which the face glass features a gunshot hole.[263] In the 1950s the Italian artist Alberto Burri had shot at paint cans placed in front of a canvas.[264] In the late 1950s and early 1960s the French artist Yves Klein had shot his paintings with flames and explosives.[265] From 1961 to 1963 Niki de Saint Phalle worked on her *Tir* series of shot works and paid homage to Jasper Johns and Robert Rauschenberg by creating her own

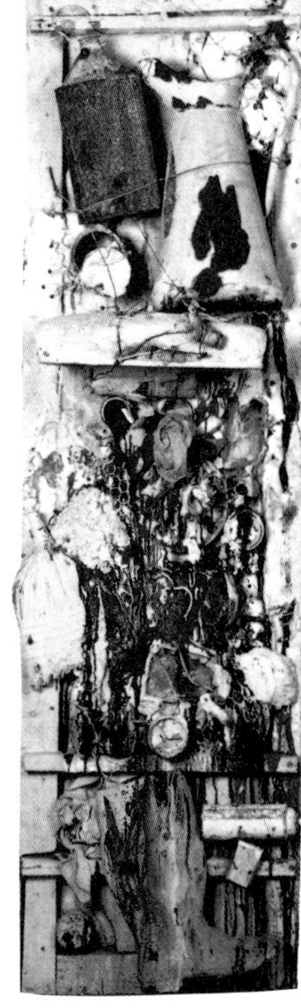

Niki de Saint Phalle, **Tir de Bob Rausch**, 1961, wood, paint, mixed media, gunshot holes, courtesy the artist, photograph © 1995 L. Condominas

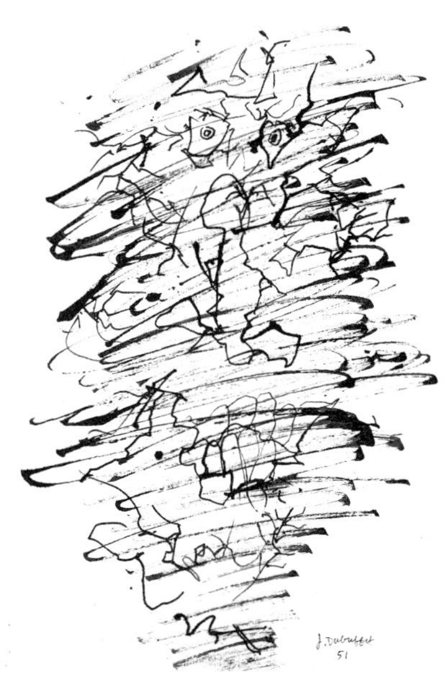

Jean Dubuffet, **Bowery Bums**, 1951, ink on paper, 12 x 9 in. (30.5 x 22.9 cm), Museum of Modern Art, New York, the Joan and Lester Arnet Collection

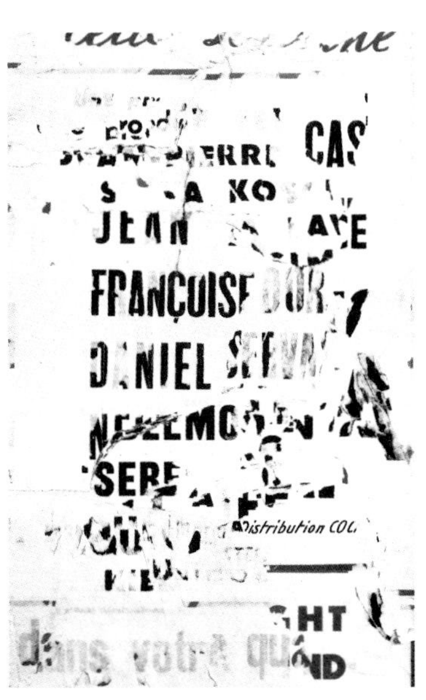

Jacques de la Villeglé, **Metro Saint-Germain, 2 septembre 1964**, 1964, torn lithographic posters on canvas, 19 x 13½ in. (48.3 x 34.3 cm), Zabriskie Gallery, New York

versions of their assemblage paintings or "combines" and shooting them with a 22-caliber rifle.[266] In the manner of a performance artist, Saint Phalle staged public "shooting events" in Paris, Nice, New York, and Malibu and was associated with the French *nouveau réalistes* along with Klein and the *affichistes* (posterists) Jacques de la Villeglé and Raymond Hains, whose torn-poster works acted as a kind of found cut-up. The American artist David Bradshaw, an expert marksman who would eventually collaborate with Burroughs, featured explosives or gunshots in almost all of his art during the late 1960s. In California the conceptual artist Chris Burden had himself shot in the arm with a 22-caliber rifle in 1971, while the painter Joe Goode had taken a shotgun to his paintings during the late 1970s as a creative and not a destructive gesture. Barry Miles claims that Burroughs knew of Saint Phalle's "gun art" but had not made the connection when he began his own.[267] It would be safe to say, moreover, that Burroughs was unaware of or failed to make any connections with these other precedents when he blasted the piece of plywood in 1982.[268]

Burroughs knew of Yves Klein's work with fire paintings and experiments with fire and exploding gunpowder as ways to randomize his art. Miles, in his biography of Burroughs, recounts that Burroughs was to have a show at the Paul Klein Gallery in Chicago in 1989. Noting the seeming coincidence of names, Burroughs had just typed out the sentence, "Yves Klein set his pictures on fire, and put them out at some point," when his longtime companion and business manager James Grauerholz informed him that the gallery and the entire block surrounding it had burned down; all of Burroughs's works were lost. A real-life cut-up, as it were, with Burroughs wryly exclaiming, "That's an interesting little juxtaposition."[269] Unlike Klein's work, Burroughs's shotgun pieces are clearly not the product of any religious faith or desperation, but they are similarly concerned with cosmic issues—issues that have occupied him elsewhere: to transcend the physical by destroying its controls on both body and mind and to free oneself from the limitations of both time and space. About the function of exploding fire in Klein's late works, art historian Pierre Restany wrote, "He found in the line of fire the language of his truth and the

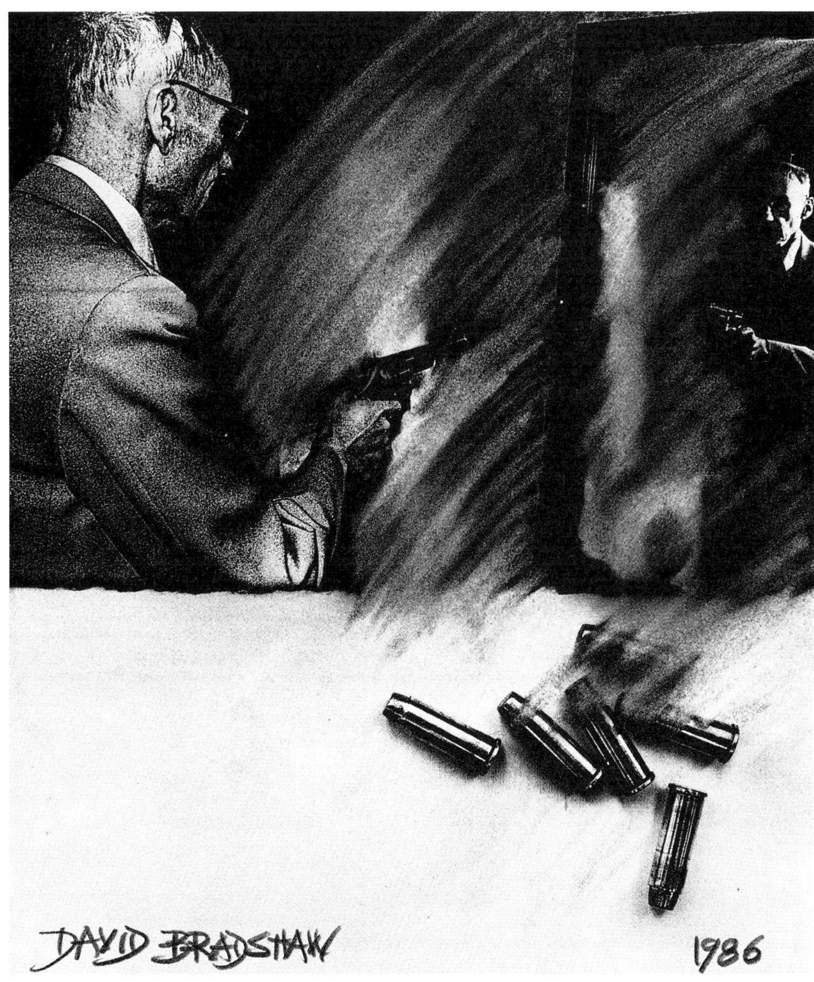

David Bradshaw, **William Burroughs with My Smith and Wesson Model 629**, 1986, cat. no. 112

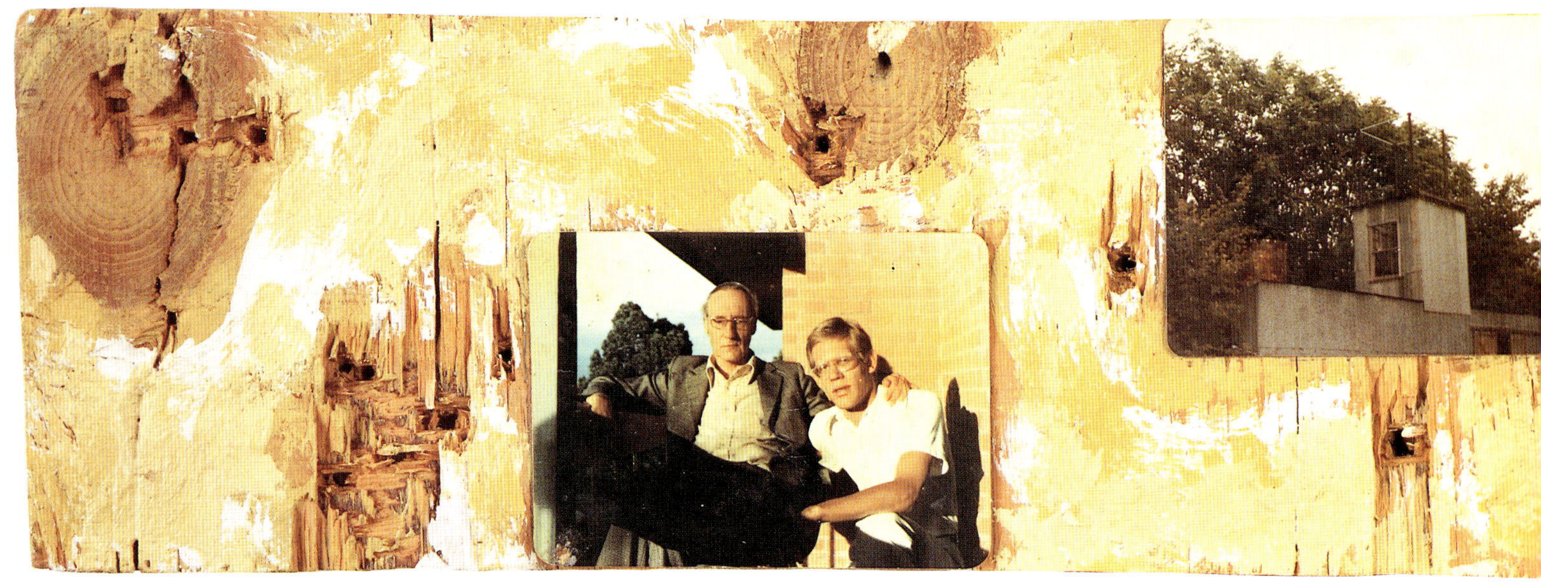

truth of his language. No other technique would be able to procure for him such ease, liberty, and an opening onto his infinity and the infinity of others, onto the in-itself and the for-itself of things."[270] For Burroughs, shotgunning plywood functions much the same way; it provides opportunities for both micro- and macroperceptions of imagined infinities. Like the cut-up, the cut-in, and flicker vision, the shotgun blast is a chance operation, only one of many "exercises to escape from the body and soar out of the Valley."[271]

David Bradshaw wrote that "marksmanship is an energy release with a finite point of focus."[272] That may be true, but for Burroughs what was most compelling was the vast number of points of view inherent in the effects of the shotgun blast. In *Painting and Guns* he differentiated between writing and painting:

Because it is read sequentially, there is no way to effectively portray simultaneous events in writing. But that's the whole point of painting: multiple points of view can be simultaneously presented. One expands the area of awareness, and one seeks new frontiers in randomness. A shotgun blast produces explosions of color that approach this basic randomness.[273]

Burroughs entitled the first shotgun work *Sore Shoulder* owing to the impact of the gun's recoil and the ensuing pain and considers it one of the best of all the shotgun works he has done. "You do something like that," he wrote, "and think, 'Well I can do it again and again.' No you can't. You luck out. Hell yes, I lucked out."[274] Nonetheless Burroughs continued shooting for about a year, eventually painting the wood, placing small containers of paint on the wood and shooting them and the wood at the same time, and collaging photographs to the pieces of plywood, wooden doors, and door panels he used for his canvases. Nearly all of the shotgun paintings function as double-sided works; both entry and exit "wounds" are significant. Not all of the works are titled, but when they are, as in *Escape from Centipede Troughs* and *Are You in Salt?*, their titles come directly from his writings. The public agent narrator and the "very technical" Iam [*sic*] were sentenced to "Centipede Death" in *The Soft Machine*, and "Are you in salt?" was a phrase found on mysterious recordings, which Burroughs read about, of speech patterns and voiceprints made with no apparent human input.[275]

Apart from one or two isolated instances, Burroughs for the most part kept these works to himself and a few close associates at the time and from 1983

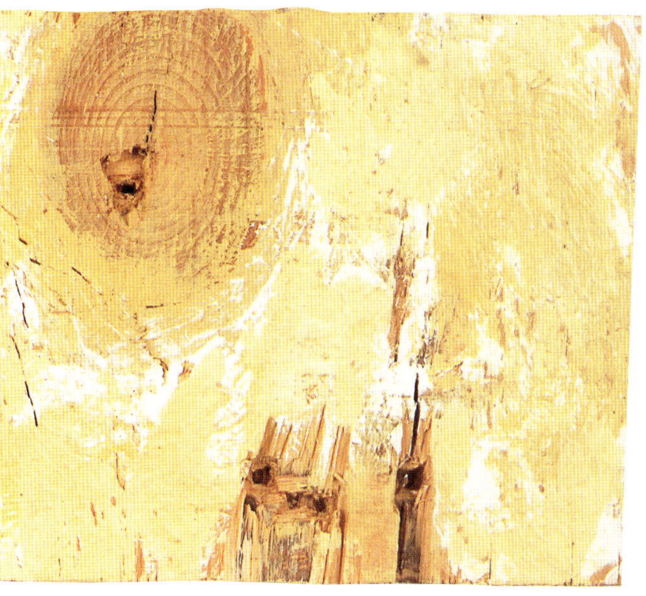

William S. Burroughs, **Escape from Centipede Troughs**, 1982, cat. no. 39

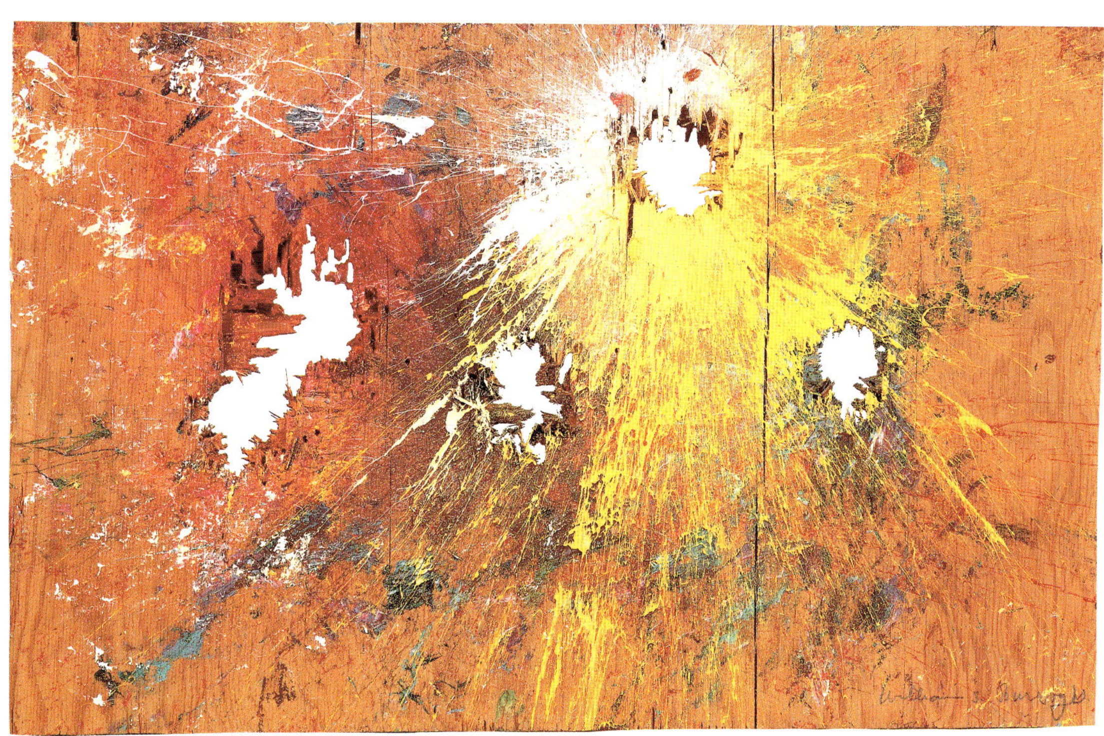

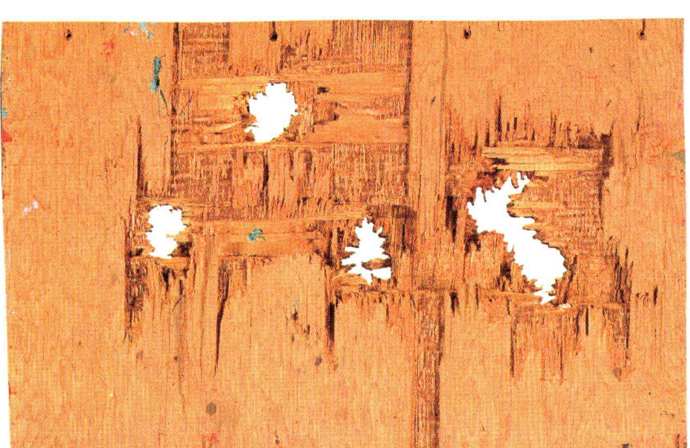

William S. Burroughs, **Screaming Ghost** (recto and verso), 1982, cat. no. 38

through 1985 attended to completing his novel *The Western Lands*, returning to his shotgun paintings only in 1986, the year that Gysin died.[276] Increasingly Burroughs painted greater, overall patterns on the works and has sometimes included line drawings of strange creatures on the wood: "I don't have to go to outer space for aliens," he said, "They are all around me."[277] A strange, Whitley Strieberesque alien face floats at the top of *Ten Gauge City* (1988). In 1987, while shooting along with artist Philip Taaffe and curator Diego Cortez, somebody suggested incorporating a can of spray paint; Burroughs claimed he did not even know what spray paint was, but when the can of red spray paint was set down, Burroughs blasted it. "I said, 'Great, just stick it in front of this piece of plywood.' then POW! There was an explosion of red across the plywood surface, and a hole at the same time, of course. That one was very successful; it was called 'The Red Skull.'"[278]

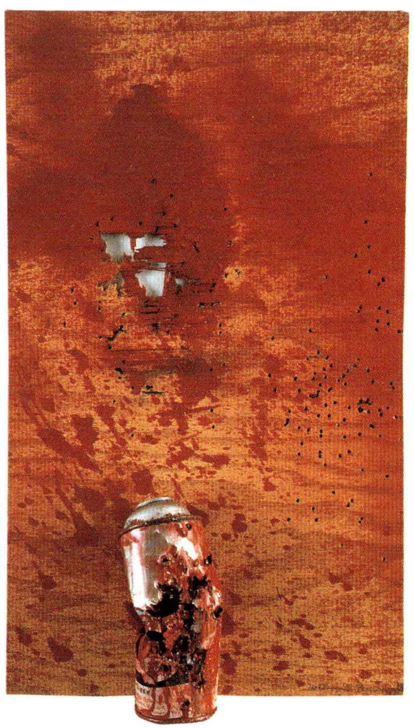

William S. Burroughs, with Philip Taaffe and Diego Cortez, **The Red Skull** (a.k.a. **The Red Death**), 1987, spray paint, spray paint canister, plywood with shotgun holes, 22 x 13 x 5 in. (installed), collection of Gerald and Sandra Fineberg, Boston and Palm Springs

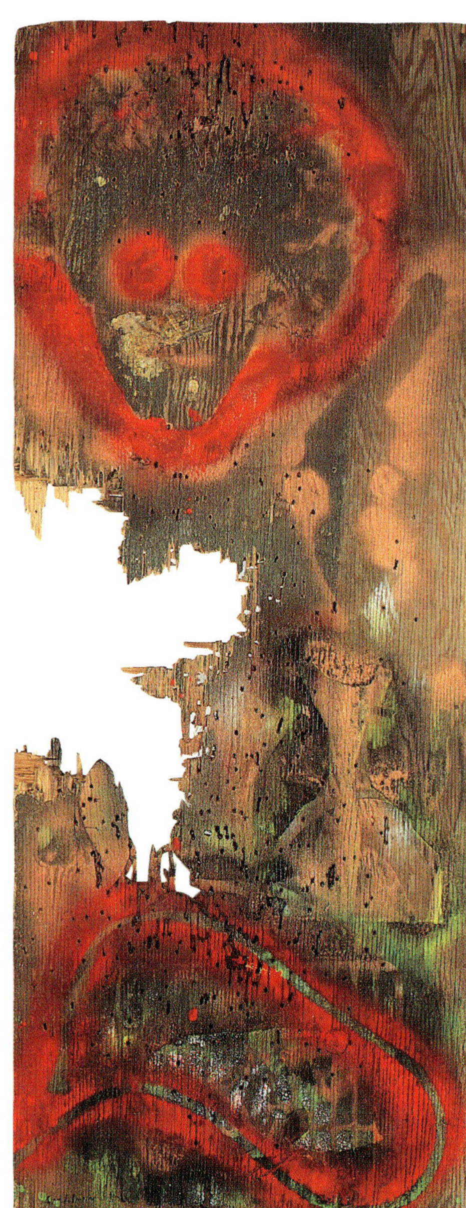

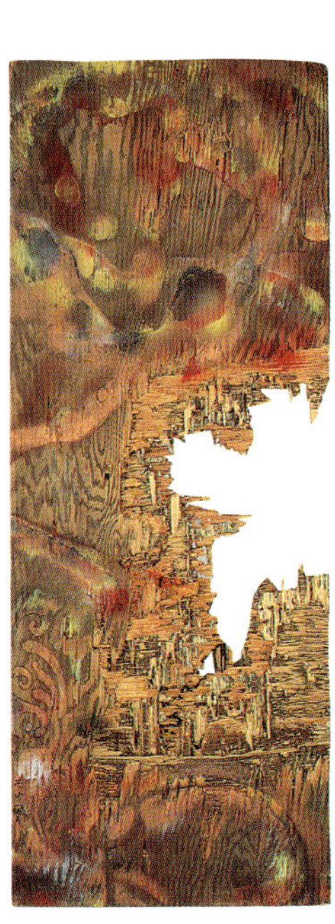

William S. Burroughs, **Ten Gauge City** (recto and verso), 1988, cat. no. 46

Burroughs valued the immediacy and explosive randomness created by the shotgun blast; he also valued the essentially Zen act of shooting itself. "Once you know where to point, all you have to do is get out of the way and let this thing happen. [...] and letting what you really know take over."[279] In a typical Burroughs step, an accident (if there is such a thing) and some playful experimentation led to a strategy and a body of work. Burroughs's chance operation had generated a particularly idiosyncratic art. According to critic Aurel Schmidt, Burroughs's art is "beyond categorization, beyond usefulness. In this sense it is emphatically nomadic—Ambush, pitfall, surprise attack—Against good taste, i.e. against constraints and conventions—In a word: sublime—Light-heartedness (that too), sometimes even an explosion of heathen laughter."[280]

"Nomadic" certainly, but to suggest that Burroughs is a naif or an "outsider" artist, however, would be a mistake. Through his close friendship with Gysin, Burroughs had been exposed to at least certain varieties of modern art and had just as certainly learned a general approach to painting from Gysin's work.

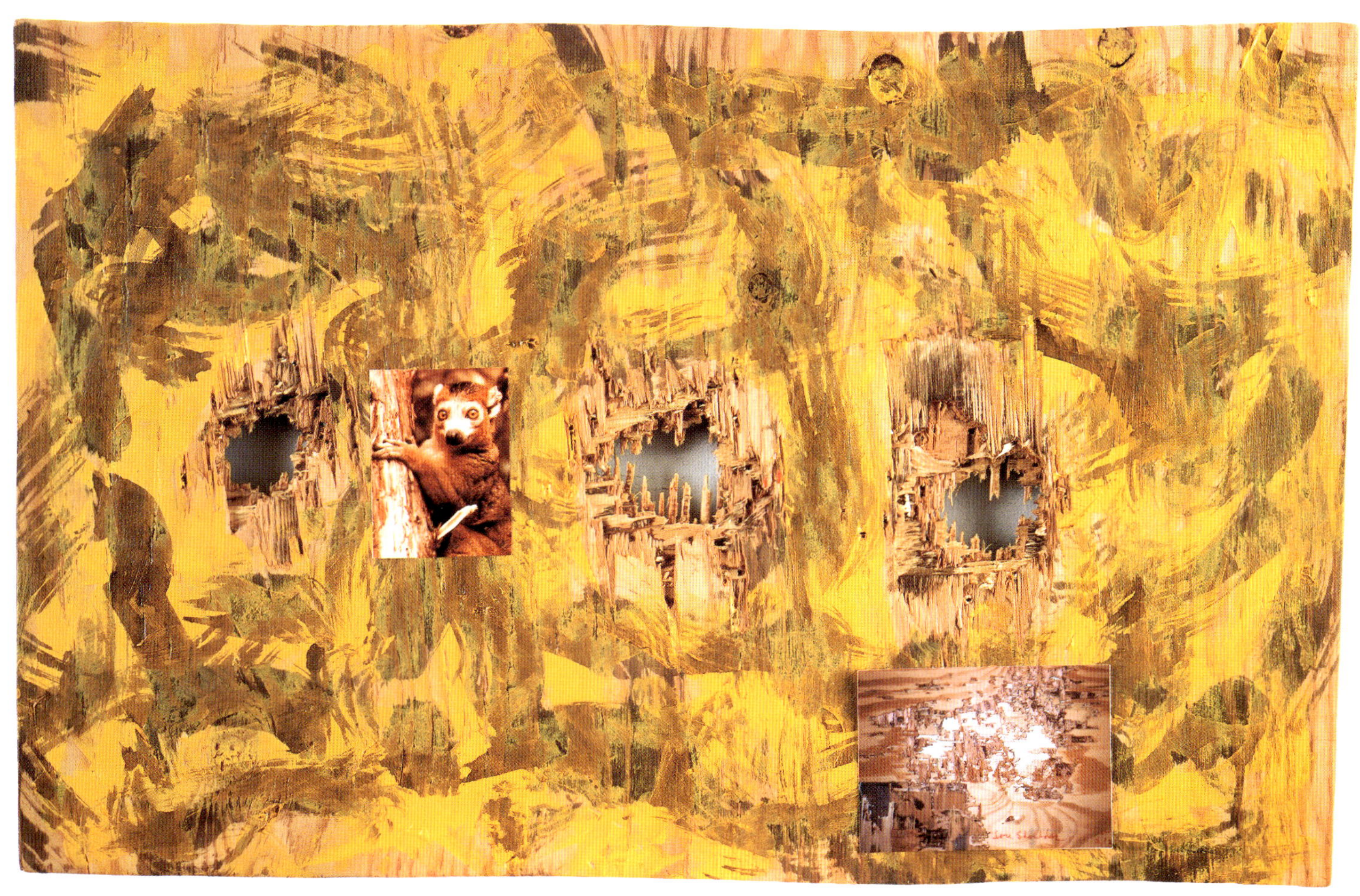

William S. Burroughs, **Wood Spirits**, 1987, cat. no. 41

In the pass the muttering sickness leaped into our throats, coughing
and spitting in the silver morning. frost on our bones....brought
sickness from white time caves frozen in my throat to hatch in the warm
spitting song of scarlet bursts in egg flesh....came to a swamp fed
by hot springs and mountain ice. and fell in flesh heaps.
sound bubbling in throats torn with the talk sickness. faces and
pus foam. animal hair thru the purple sex-flesh.
body. underwater music bubbling in blood beds. human faces tentative flicker
of focus. We waded into the warm mud-water....When we came out of the mud

The Soft Machine

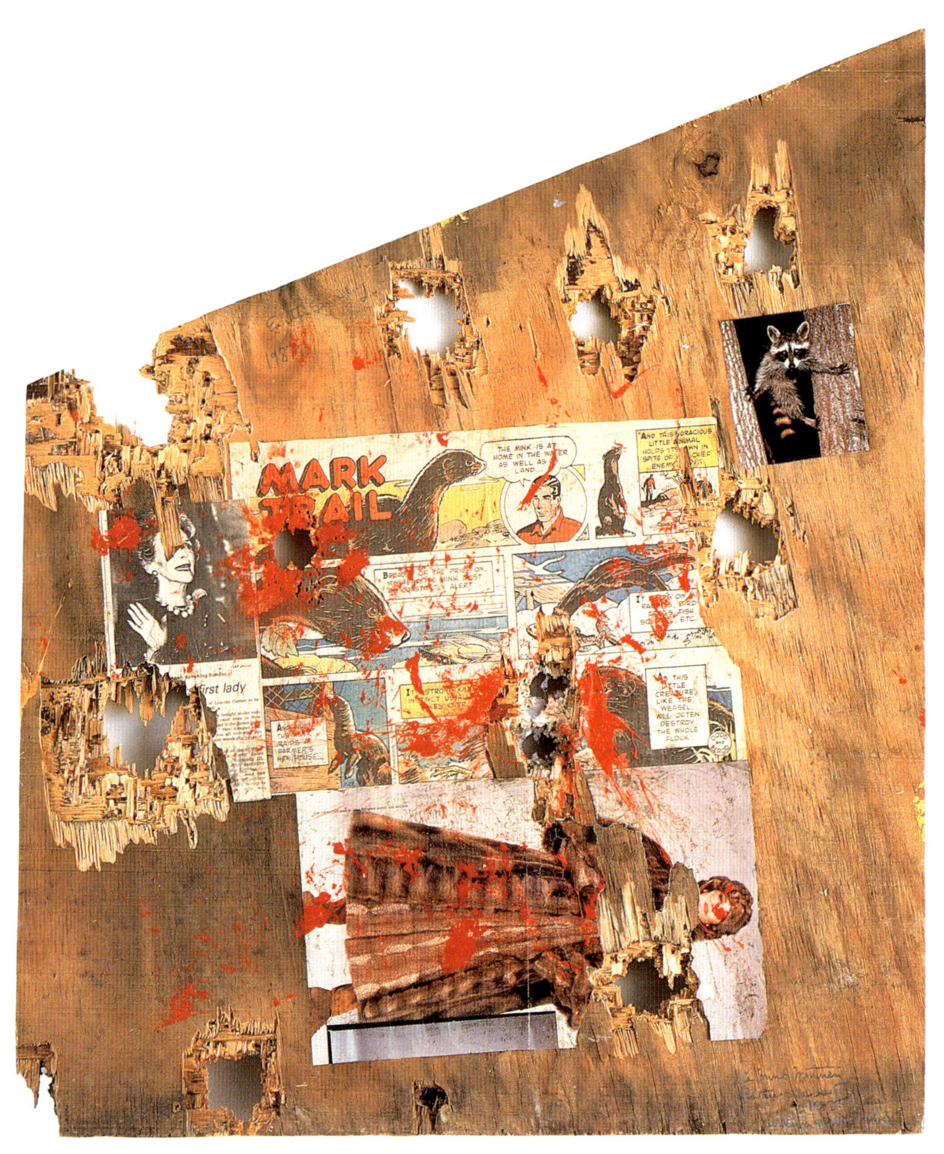

he
teamlands

ick apes spitting blood laugh.
odies covered with
ick sound twisted thru
n and out
ve had names.

William S. Burroughs, **Mink Mutiny** (recto), 1987, cat. no. 43

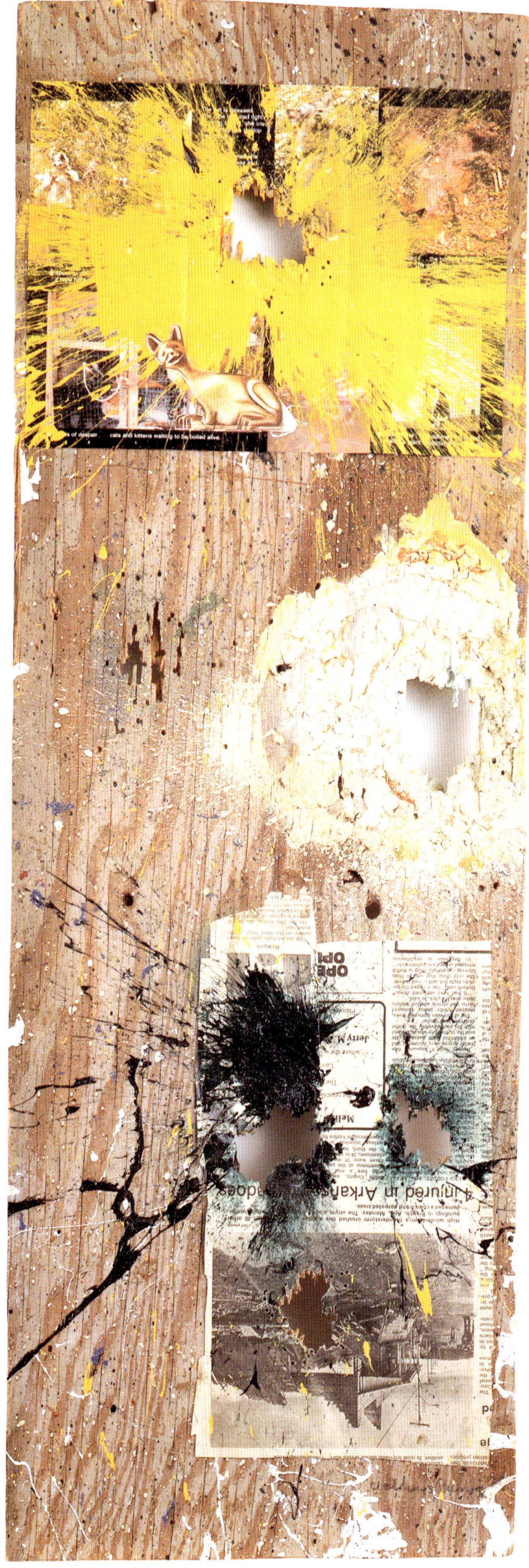

William S. Burroughs, **The Curse of Bast**, 1987, cat. no. 42

William S. Burroughs, **Fire Door** (recto), 1987, cat. no. 44

When looking at a Gysin painting, he wrote, "you look at the picture, let your gaze drift, and then it happens. You can feel it, a shift in the visual field, a movement and concentration of attention, and the images take on magical forms—they begin to move and shift."[281] About his own paintings, he has said, "I am trying to get the pictures to move. It almost happens: a face comes into almost miraculously clear focus, smiles, snarls, speaks...Then back into the picture, there on the paper, the wood."[282]

Burroughs had seen and spoken with a number of artists throughout his life. In Paris he had interviews with David Budd and Earle Brown, and at the Chelsea Hotel, in New York, he had passed works by Arman, Christo, Larry Rivers, and others in the lobby.[283] In 1974 he sublet a loft from artist Michael Balog, who was working with shattered and painted plywood at the time.[284] Through his friendship with poet John Giorno, he met Jasper Johns, Robert Rauschenberg, Les Levine, Robert Mapplethorpe, and Laurie Anderson; and he occasionally dined with Andy Warhol and Jean-Michel Basquiat. Despite all of his art-world connections, however, it could not be said that Burroughs is some kind of progressive painter in touch with either modern theory or practice. In fact, in "The Fall of Art" of 1975, his one general essay on the contemporary art scene, he naively considers a future of exploding art, sacrificial art, and art potlatches.[285] Rather, like Gysin before him, Burroughs is a mostly self-taught visionary artist who shares many of the attributes of artists outside the mainstream, most especially a "sense of focus," an "intensity," and an utter "lack of guile."[286] His is an elemental art wherein "the shotgun blast releases the little spirits compacted in the layers of wood, causing the colors of the paints to splash out in unforeseeable, unpredictable images and patterns."[287]

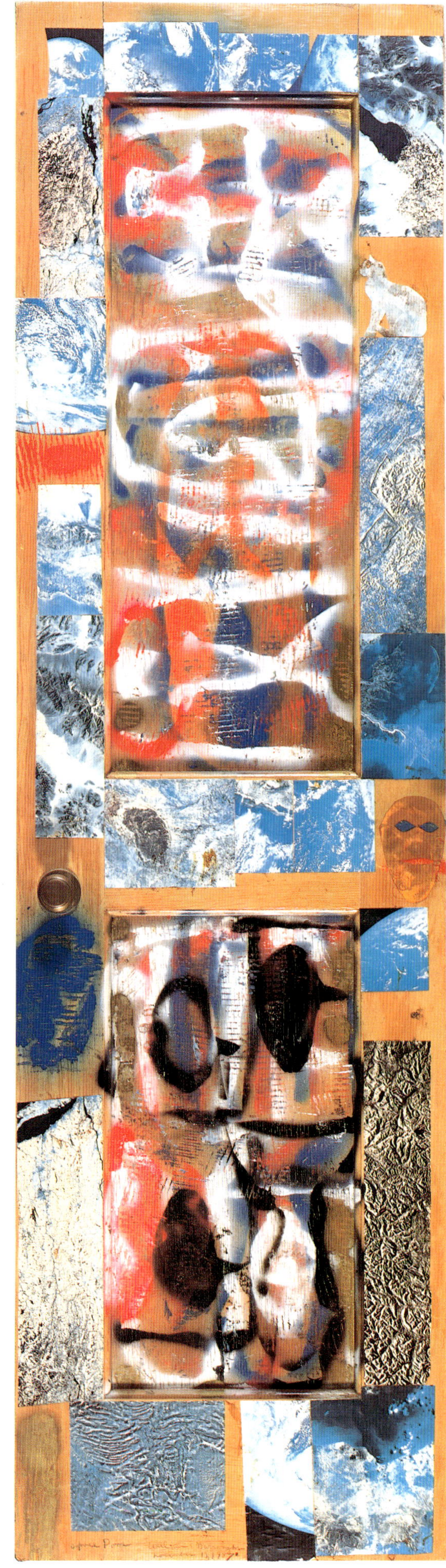

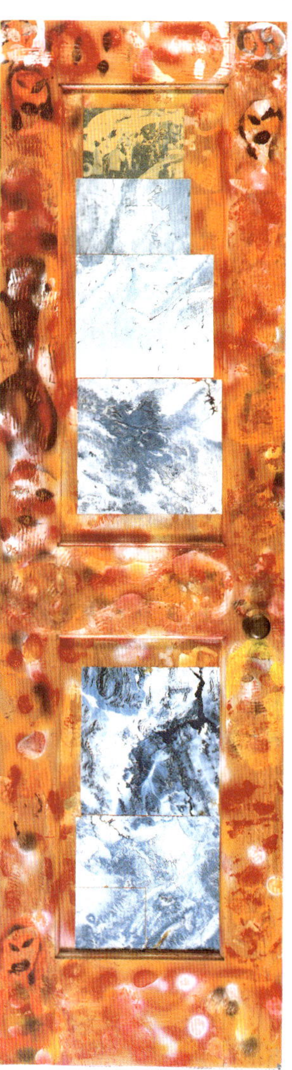

William S. Burroughs, **Space Door** (recto and verso), 1987, cat. no. 45

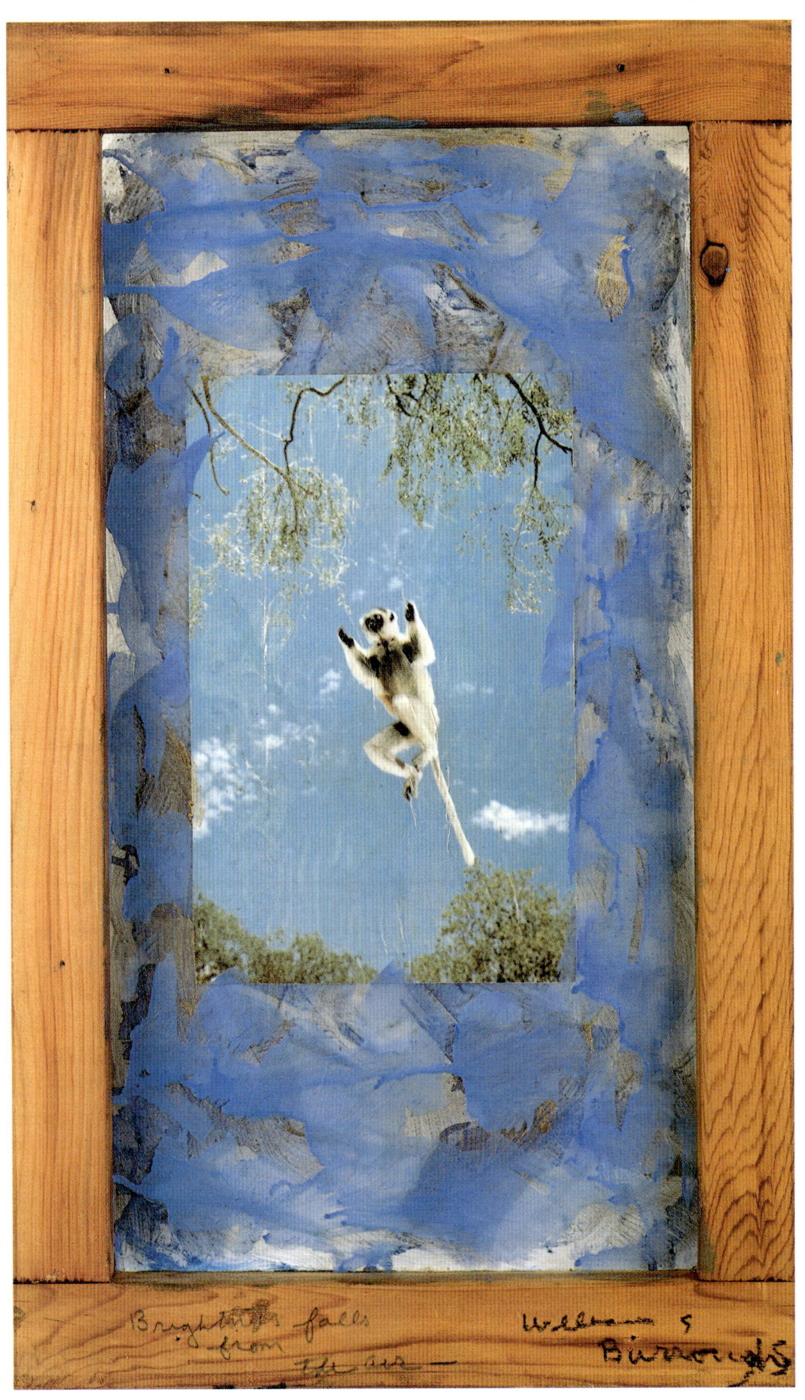

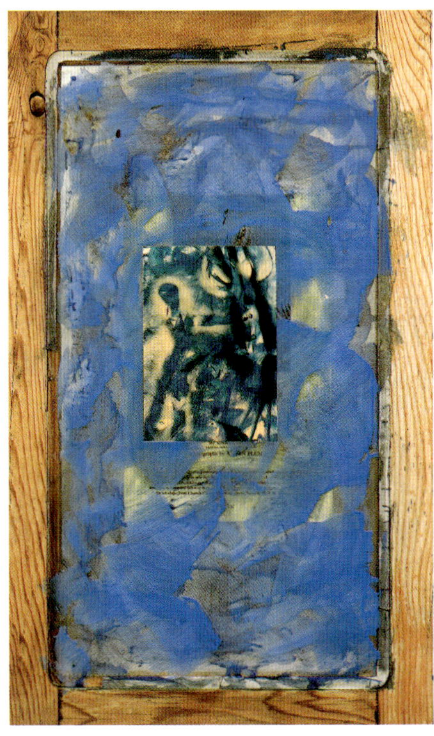

William S. Burroughs, **Brightness Falls from the Air** (recto and verso), 1988, cat. no. 47

William S. Burroughs, **Shot Sheriff**, 1992, cat. no. 49

251
Burroughs, *Port of Saints* (note **222**), 71.

252
Ibid., 73.

253
Knickerbocker, "Interview" (note **8**), 2.

254
Burroughs, *Painting and Guns* (note **171**), 10.

255
Ibid., 13.

256
Grauerholz, "On Burroughs' Art" (note **24**), x.

257
Leonardo da Vinci, *Treatise on Painting*, quoted in William S. Rubin, *Dada and Surrealist Art*, exh. cat. (New York: Harry N. Abrams, 1968), 178.

258
Pierre Georgel, *Drawings by Victor Hugo* (London: Victoria and Albert Museum, 1974), unp.

259
Vasily Kandinsky, "Reminiscences/Three Pictures," in Kenneth C. Lindsay and Peter Vergo, eds., *Kandinsky: Complete Writings on Art* (New York: Da Capo Press, 1994), 369.

260
Quoted in Rubin, *Dada and Surrealist Art* (note **257**), 176–78.

261
See Peter Selz, *The Work of Jean Dubuffet*, exh. cat. (New York: Museum of Modern Art, 1962), 55, 63–72.

262
Quoted in Francis V. O'Connor, *Jackson Pollock*, exh. cat. (New York: Museum of Modern Art, 1967); see James Grauerholz, "On Burroughs' Art" (note **24**), xii.

263
See William C. Seitz, *The Art of Assemblage*, exh. cat. (New York: Museum of Modern Art, 1961), 70. The author is grateful to his former research assistant Peter Scherz for reminding him of the Cornell work.

264
See the photographic sequence by Sanford Roth of Burri shooting a Luger pistol (Los Angeles County Museum of Art, Sanford Roth Collection, gift of Beula Roth).

265
Pierre Restany, *Yves Klein: Fire at the Heart of the Void*, trans. Andrea Loselle (New York: Journal of Contemporary Art Editions, 1992).

266
Pontus Hulten, *Paris—New York*, exh. cat. (Paris: Centre Georges Pompidou, Musée National d'Art Moderne, 1977), 587; see also Susan Hapgood, *Neo-Dada: Redefining Art, 1958–62*, exh. cat. (New York: American Federation of the Arts, 1994), 77–79.

267
Miles, *William Burroughs* (note **25**), 235.

268
Burroughs met Marcel Duchamp in Paris in 1958 and told his biographer that Duchamp had shot at his own paintings but was a very poor shot. See ibid., 237.

269
Miles, *William Burroughs* (note **25**), 237.

270
Ibid., 114.

271
Burroughs, *The Western Lands* (note **250**), 231.

272
David Bradshaw, in promotional booklet for David Bradshaw and William S. Burroughs, *Propagation Hazard*, print portfolio (Tampa: Graphicstudio, University of South Florida, 1993), unp.

273
Burroughs, *Painting and Guns* (note **171**), 11.

274
Ibid., 13–14.

275
Burroughs, "It Belongs to the Cucumbers," *The Adding Machine* (note **12**), 57. Burroughs's lengthiest discourse on venomous centipedes occurs in *The Western Lands* (note **250**), 77–82.

276
Burroughs did exhibit a work entitled *Gun Door* in New York and London in 1982; see Grauerholz, "On Burroughs' Art" (note **24**), x.

277
Burroughs, *Painting and Guns* (note **171**), 12.

278
Ibid., 14–15.

279
Ibid., 62–63.

280
Aurel Schmidt, "William Burroughs as Writer and Painter," in *William S. Burroughs*, exh. cat. (Basel: Editions Galerie Carzaniga and Ueker, 1991), 16.

281
Burroughs, *Painting and Guns* (note **171**), 30–31.

282
Ibid., 11–12.

283
Miles, *William Burroughs* (note **25**), 239.

284
Grauerholz, "On Burroughs' Art" (note **24**), ix.

285
See Burroughs, "The Fall of Art," in *The Adding Machine* (note **12**), 61–65; see also Grauerholz, "On Burroughs' Art" (note **24**), vii.

286
These terms were used by artist Gregory Amenoff to describe what mainstream artists find compelling about so-called "outsider" artists; quoted in Carol S. Eliel, "Moral Influence and Expressive Intent: A Model of the Relationship between Insider and Outsider," in Maurice Tuchman and Carol S. Eliel, *Parallel Visions: Modern Artists and Outsider Art*, exh. cat. (Los Angeles: Los Angeles County Museum of Art, 1992), 17.

287
Burroughs, *Painting and Guns* (note **171**), 15.

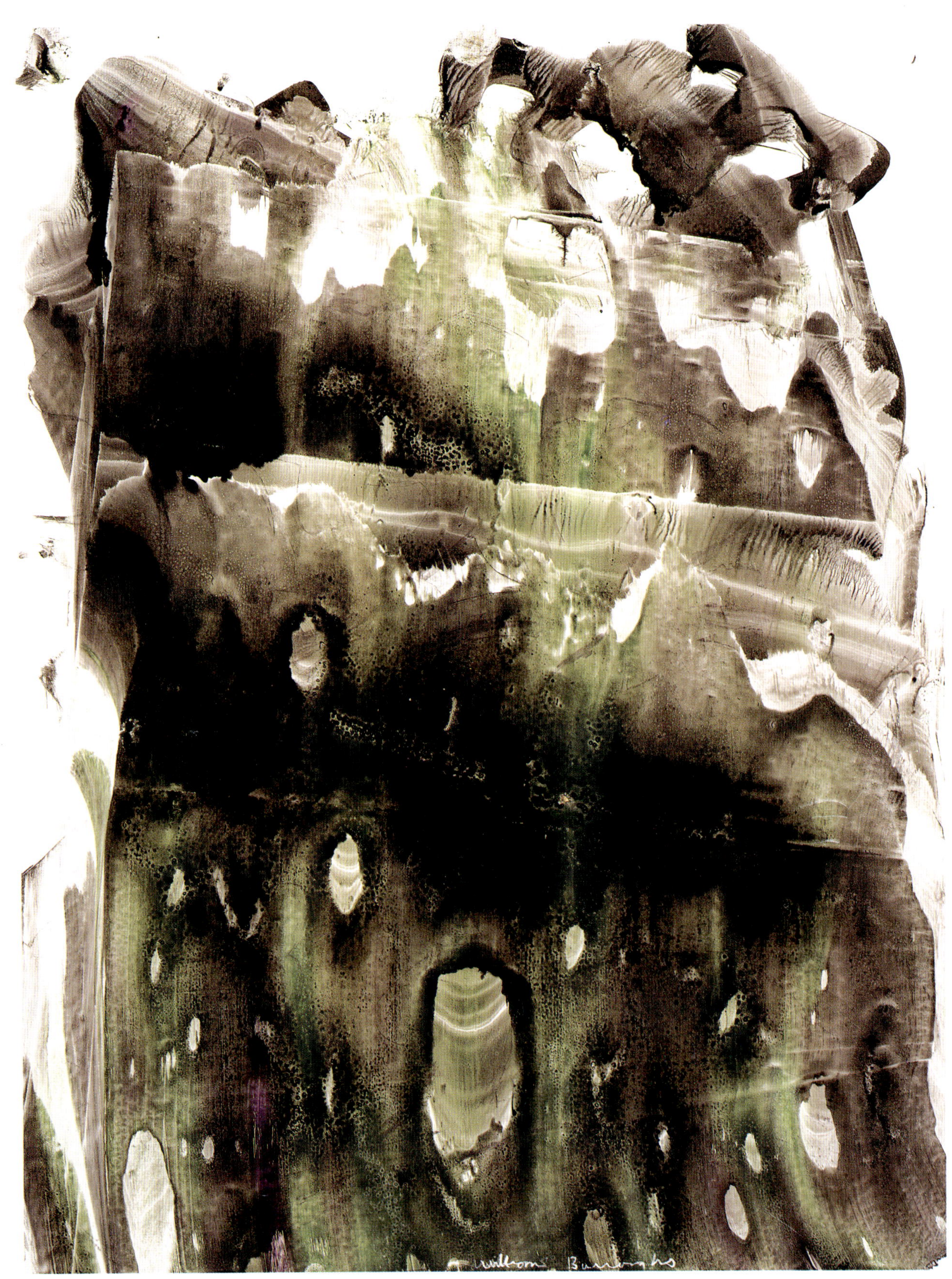

William S. Burroughs, **Underwater**, 1989, cat. no. 75

XIII

COLOR COMICS

You ache to look at these colors.[288]

With a few exceptions of such pistol-shot pieces as *Shot Sheriff* (1992), work on gun art came to a halt in 1988, when Burroughs turned to painting on slick, heavy papers ("I want the colors to run around"), with a brush most often but also with his hands, spray paint, markers, plungers, and even mushrooms ("I got some good mileage out of them mushrooms").[289] Despising all limitations, as he has declared throughout his writings, Burroughs would not restrict himself to traditional painterly brushwork. And, not wishing to have his work become mechanical or predictable, he changes techniques often: "spattering, marbling, strips of paper, rollers, Pollock's drip-can device, the Rorschach method."[290] What Burroughs calls the "Rorschach method" is precisely that, the method of making ink-blot abstractions, or *Zufallsbilder* (literally "chance pictures"), devised by Dr. Hermann Rorschach around 1912 for use in psychiatric diagnoses. What Burroughs calls "rollers" is his idiosyncratic reference to the kind of carved-out printmaking brayer used by Gysin in the 1960s. In *Underwater* and other paintings of 1989 Burroughs applied blotting techniques that could easily be labeled *décalcomanies*; and a brayer was used as the background for his portrait of the writer Jack Black and for other works in 1992.

William S. Burroughs, untitled, 1992, cat. no. 74

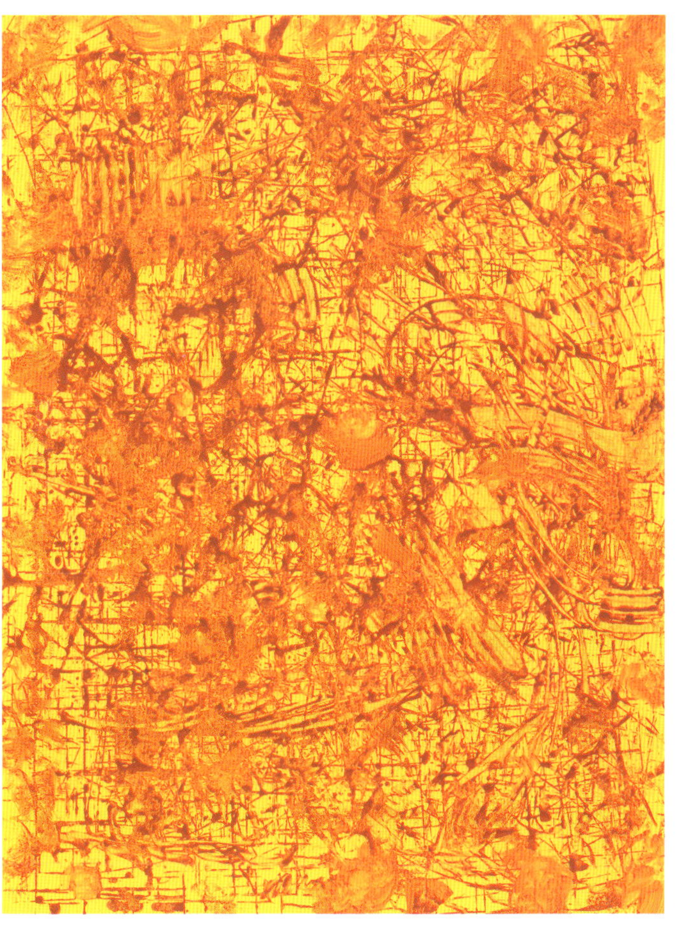

A few times Gysin's permutations and word paintings were reprised, as with *Rub Out the Word* (1989). Burroughs has painted on Cadillac cover stock as well as on stretched canvas, but he has also painted on doors and windows, which function as literal emblems

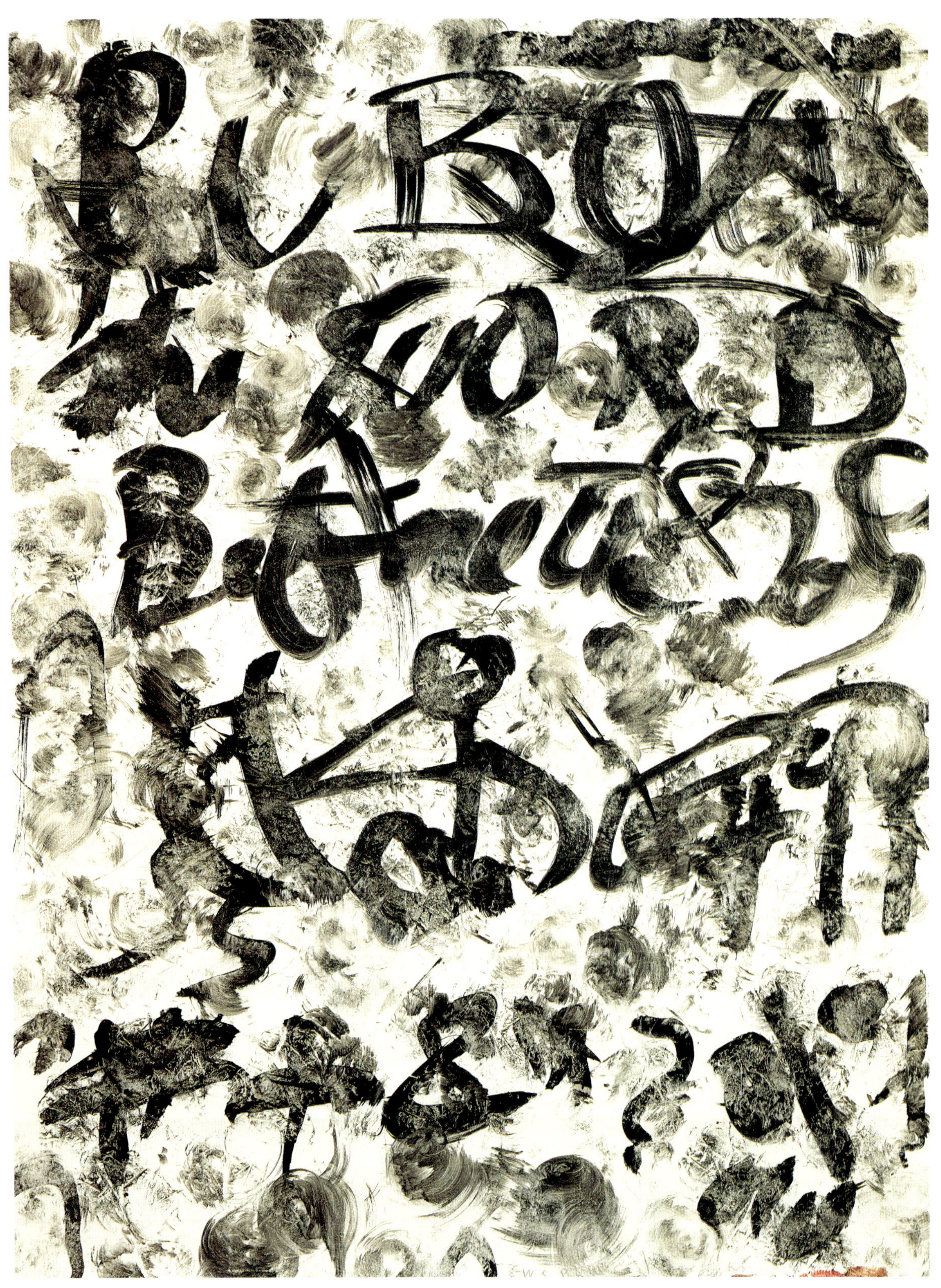

William S. Burroughs, **Rub Out the Word**, 1989, cat. no. 53

of portals to new perceptions, and has had figures cut out of wood and special, thick papers fabricated by Stephen Lowe for painting on. He has also constructed assemblage sculptures that are reminiscent of Bruce Conner's or George Herms's and has used plastic guns and other objects in spray stenciling. He has produced limited-edition lithographs and etchings as well as computer-generated stereograms. In short, he does whatever he can with whatever means are immediately available.

What Burroughs learned from Gysin was that automatism was the surest route to the unconscious, that writing and painting could be treated the same materially, that pigments can be smeared between two surfaces in order to produce a fluid abstraction, that an overall field or texture can act as a foundation for further stagings and explorations, and that a picture can contain numerous ports of entry into its mysteries as well as those of its viewer. It is somewhat unclear at times just what "port of entry" Burroughs has used to enter his paintings and what has led him to entitle them as he does, for example, *The Door in the Mountain Side through Which the Piper Led the Children of Hamelin* or *The Alleys of Marrakech*. Nevertheless Burroughs's titles do serve to suggest approaches to the images' possible landscapes if not exactly ways in. Should the picture lack any port of entry, however, it is dead. "The most deadly picture," wrote Burroughs in his dream book, "is a picture of nothing at all. The colors are there, and the contrasts, but there is no image, nothing. One searches desperately for some face, some tree, some house, and there is nothing."[291] If some form or shape suggesting a subject can be discerned in even the most unrepresentational painting, the work becomes alive for Burroughs. The artist Ed Moses calls this kind of art the "apparitional abstract."[292] The modern artist is for Burroughs at once involved with randomness, but also with steering a path to greater awareness.

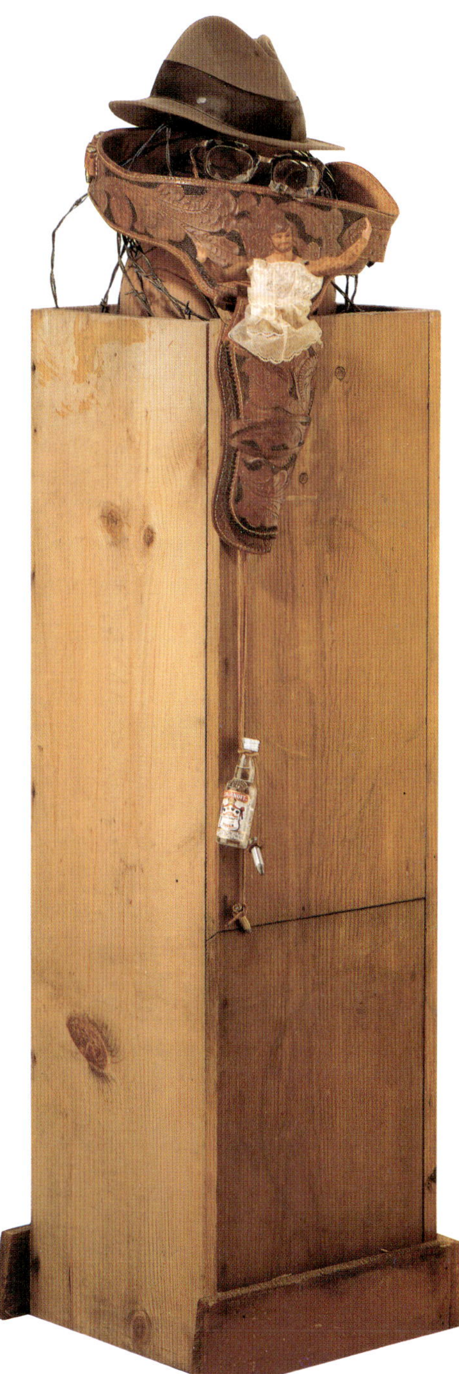

William S. Burroughs, untitled, 1992, cat. no. 50

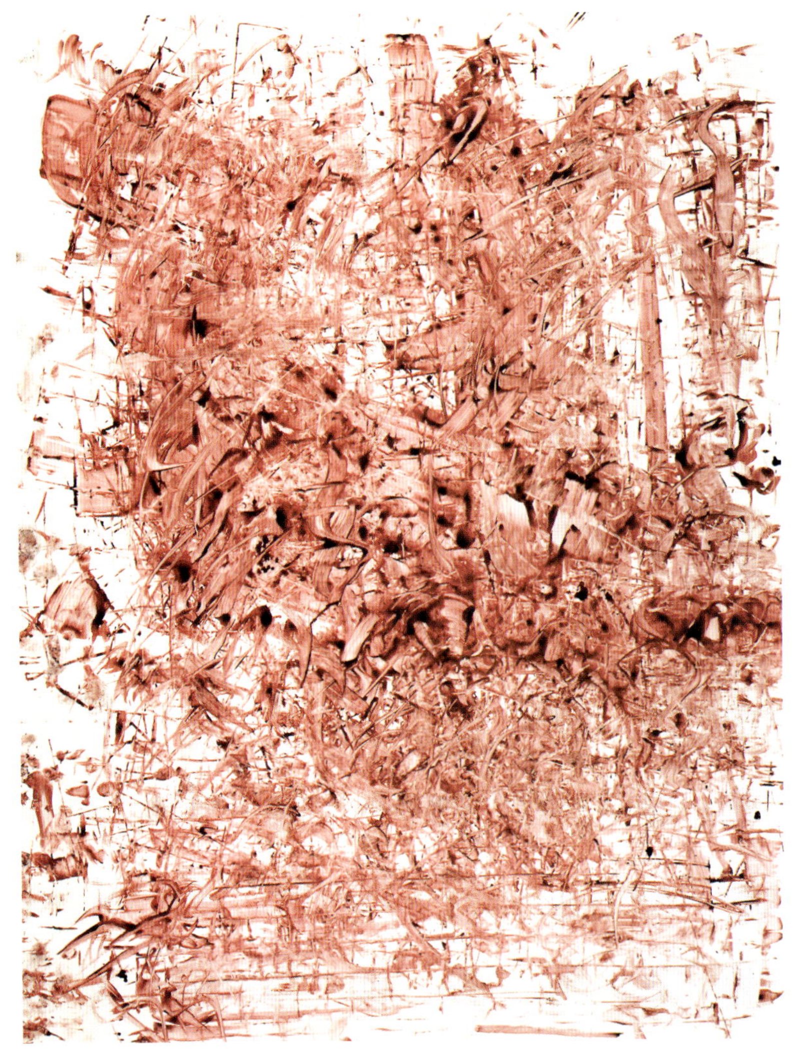

William S. Burroughs, **The Door in the Mountain Side through Which the Piper Led the Children of Hamelin**, 1992, cat. no. 73

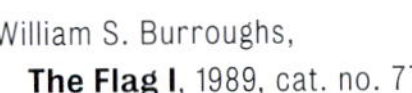

William S. Burroughs, **The Flag I**, 1989, cat. no. 77

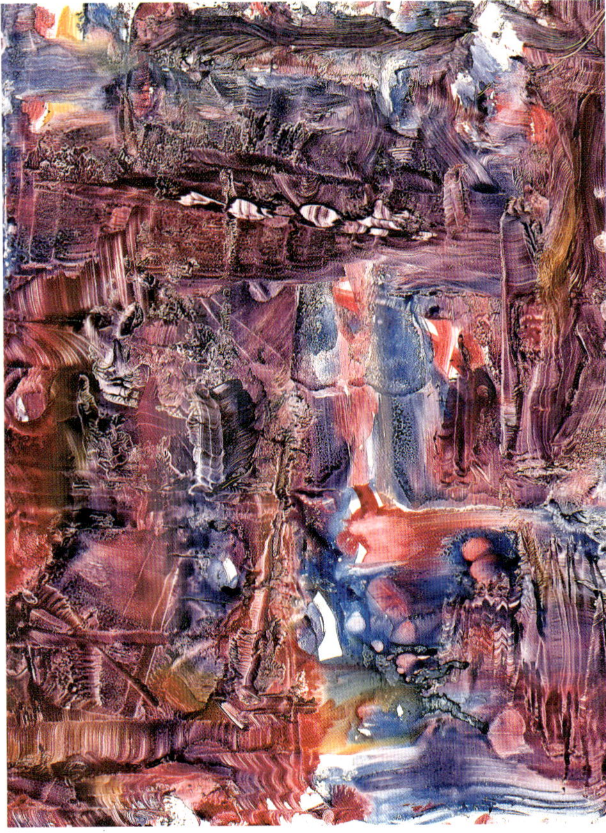

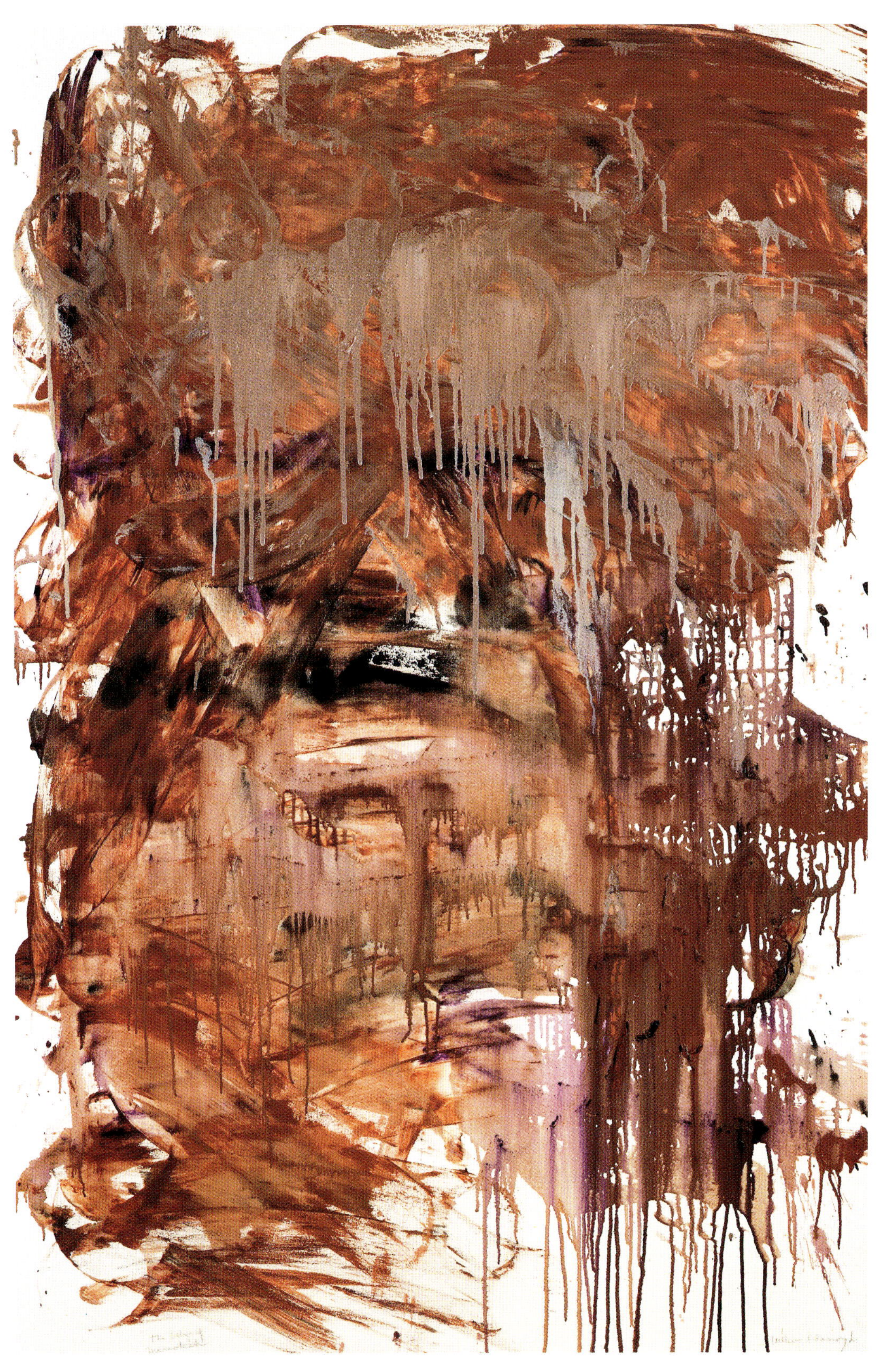

William S. Burroughs, **The Alleys of Marrakech**, 1993, cat. no. 78

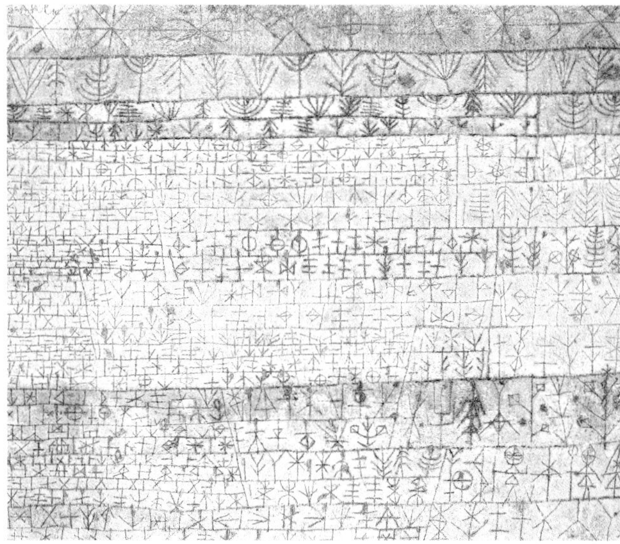

Paul Klee, **Tree Nursery**, 1929, oil on incised gesso on canvas, 16⅞ x 20½ in. (42.9 x 52.1 cm), the Phillips Collection, Washington, D.C.

"Artists are trying to make people aware," Burroughs stated, "Aware of what they know and don't know that they know."[293] Burroughs believes artists try to open the doors of perception to reveal what is patently obvious but hidden, to expose what is invisible. According to the Italian critic Achille Bonito Oliva, "If the *cut-up* was a way of giving form to the *unsayable*, the technique of the '*shotgun*' brings about the appearance of the *invisible*, which was what Klee demanded of art."[294]

With the single exception of Gysin, Burroughs's ideas on painting have been most influenced by, and he feels most attuned to, the Swiss artist Paul Klee, who Burroughs hyperbolically considered "the most influential artist of the twentieth century."[295] Like Gysin and Burroughs, Klee played with the symbolic forms of language; and like Burroughs especially, Klee saw Chinese characters, hieroglyphics, runic symbols, and alphabets as much more associative than denotative, much more subjective than objective. According to historian Ann Temkin, "Linear forms constitute an alphabet from which Klee could assemble his pictures. As with language, a finite number of elements can produce an infinite number of images. Ultimately the titles that indicate landscape or figural motifs hardly matter; the images are generalized, and the distance from a physiognomy to a forest is very slight."[296]

Klee believed that the mission of the artist was to observe what goes unnoticed by the multitude; that there were imaginative "regions with different laws and new symbols, signifying freer movement and more dynamical position";[297] that lines could be taken on walks, and that the general direction of art was toward the infinite where there were no directions. When asked for what purpose we were here on earth, Gysin said, and Burroughs repeatedly quoted, "We are here to go."[298] For Gysin and Burroughs, the future was not here on earth nor in our physical bodies but in a dimensionless and bodiless outer space. In the final chapter of his *Pedagogical Sketchbook*, Klee asserted that art must pass "on to infinite movement, where the actual direction of movement becomes irrelevant....Because the question is no longer: 'to move there' but to be 'everywhere' and consequently also 'There!'"[299] Klee was also an evolutionist, and this is important for Burroughs who has quoted Klee as saying, "The painter who is called will contact the elemental forces of evolution."[300]

Burroughs stated that he wants his paintings to move. He wants to make his paintings take on a kind of animism and "talk" directly to the viewer. "It can even come off the canvas, as Klee said," Burroughs wrote, "This may be dangerous and may even cause disease, if the viewers are rigid and cannot adjust, but not necessarily."[301] Burroughs stresses that he wants his paintings to be dangerous: "I want my painting to literally walk off the goddamned canvas, to become a creature and a very dangerous creature. I see painting as evocative magic. And there must always be a random factor in magic, one which must be constantly changed and renewed."[302] There are plenty of figural creatures in Burroughs's paintings, creatures that may be dangerous as well as benevolent, mercenary as well as spectral. There is the alien and heartless *Crazy Man* (1988) and the secret agents in *Research Animal* (1989)

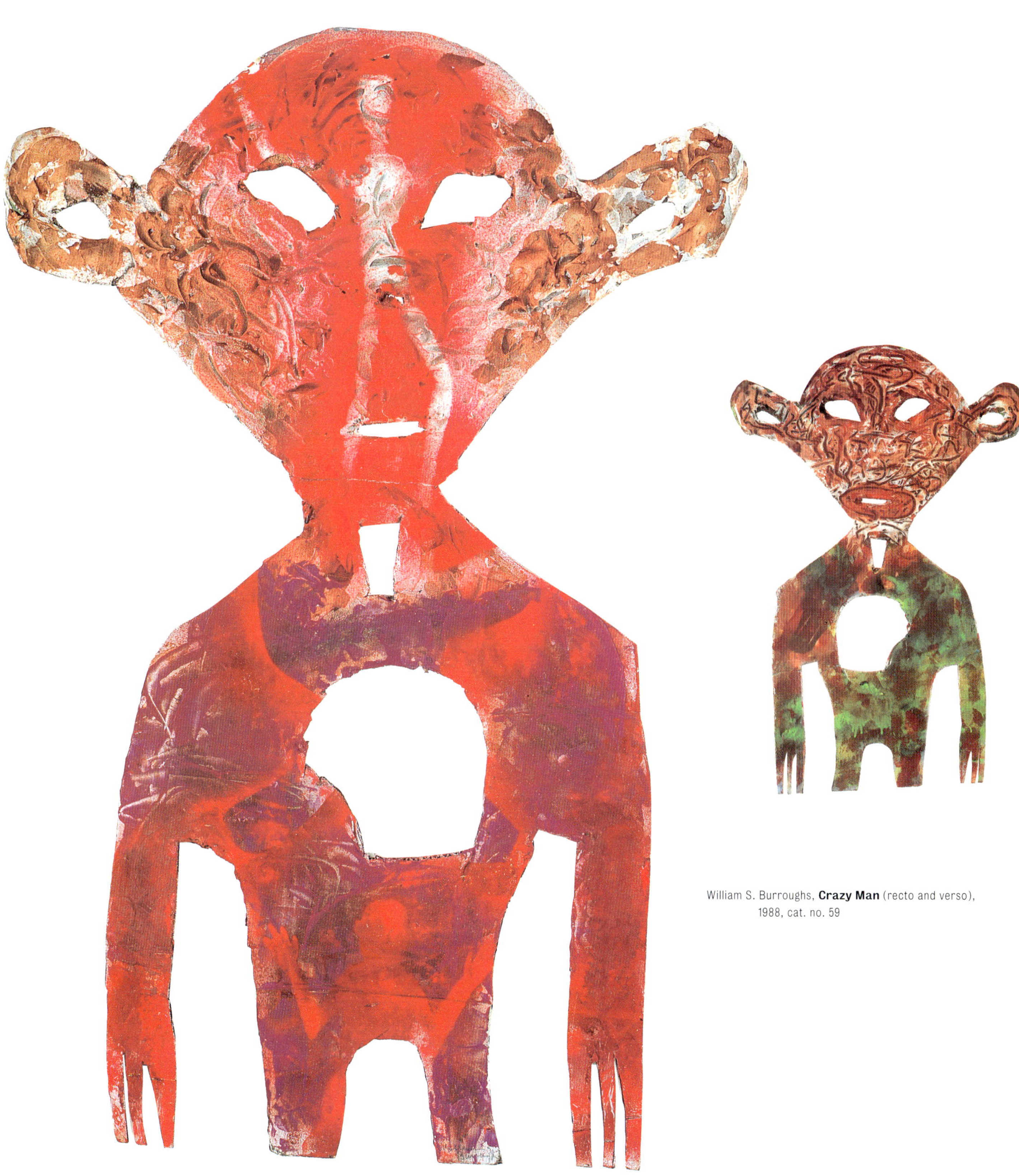

William S. Burroughs, **Crazy Man** (recto and verso), 1988, cat. no. 59

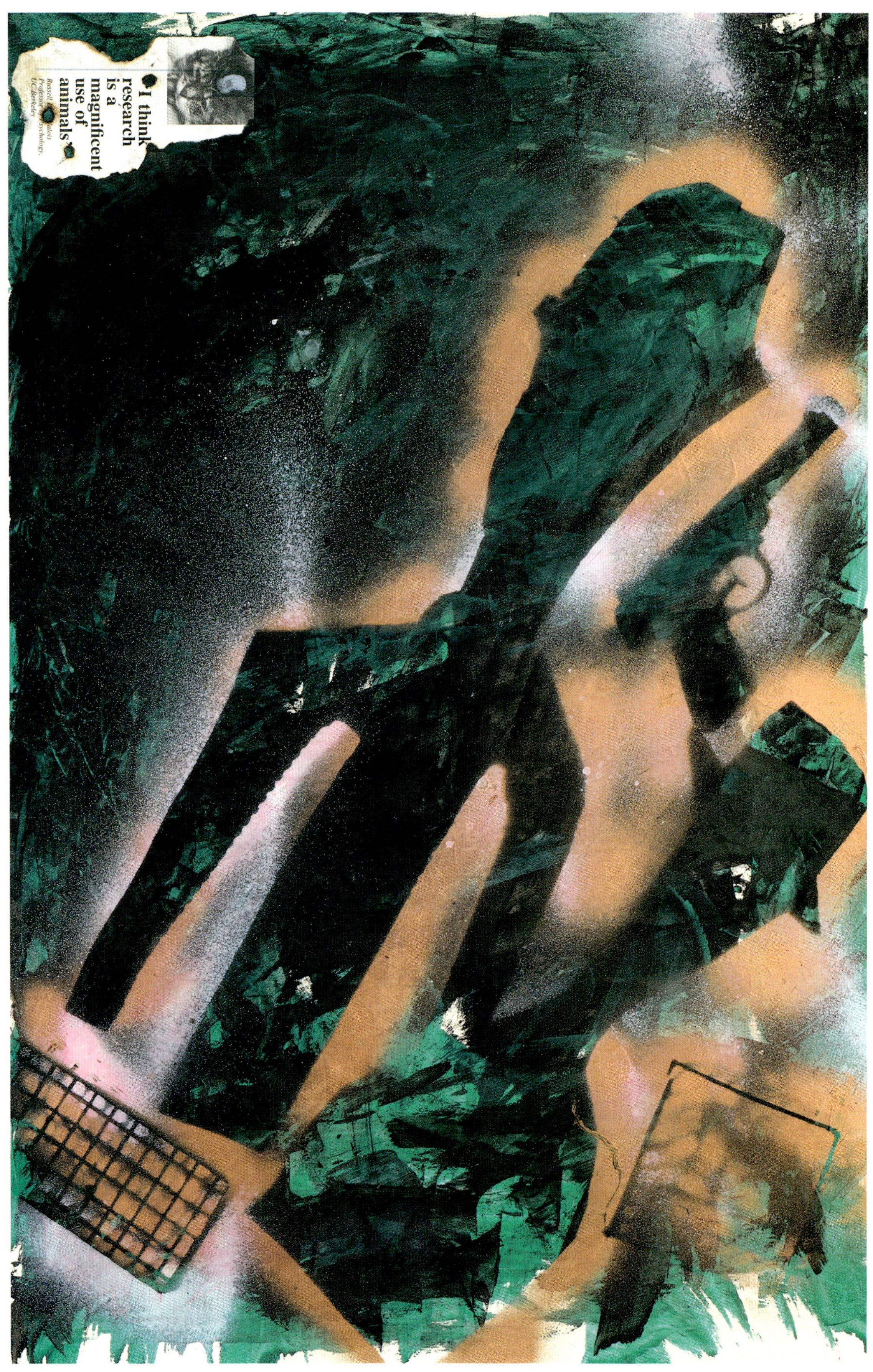

William S. Burroughs, **Research Animal** (recto), 1989, cat. no. 60

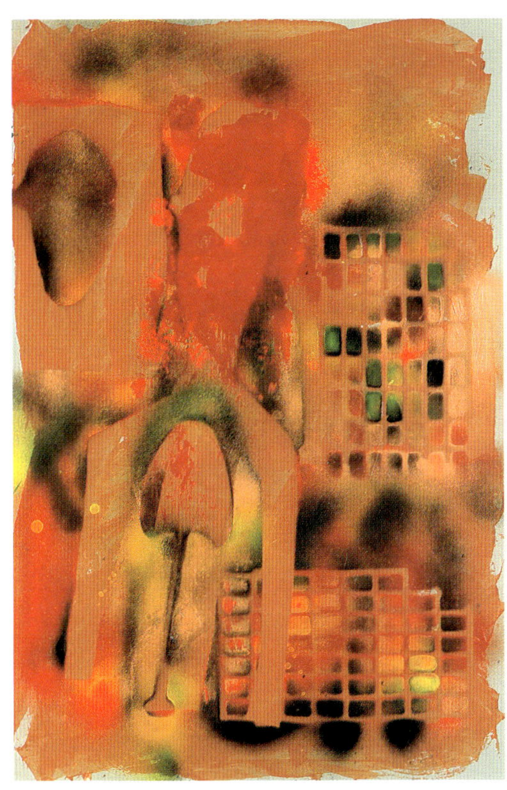

William S. Burroughs, **Research Animal** (verso), 1989, cat. no. 60

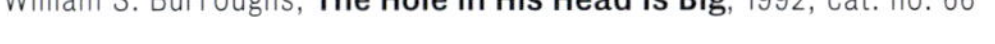

William S. Burroughs, **The Hole in His Head Is Big**, 1992, cat. no. 66

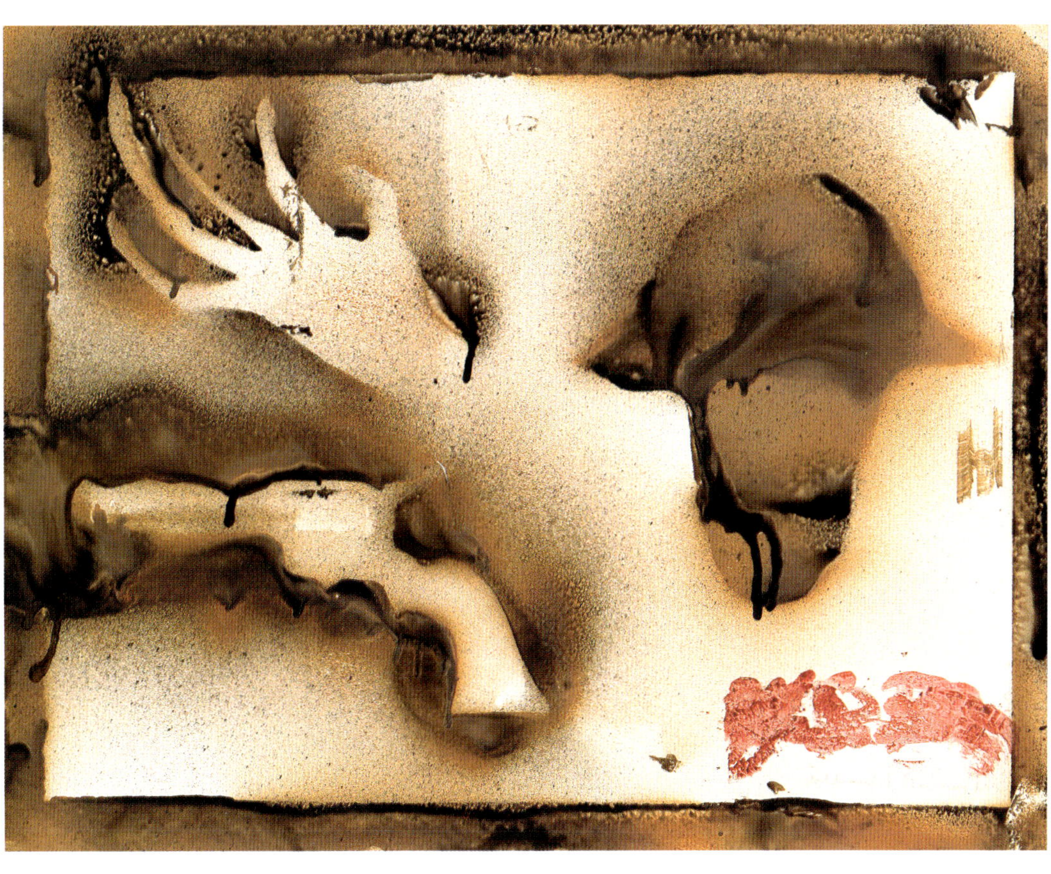

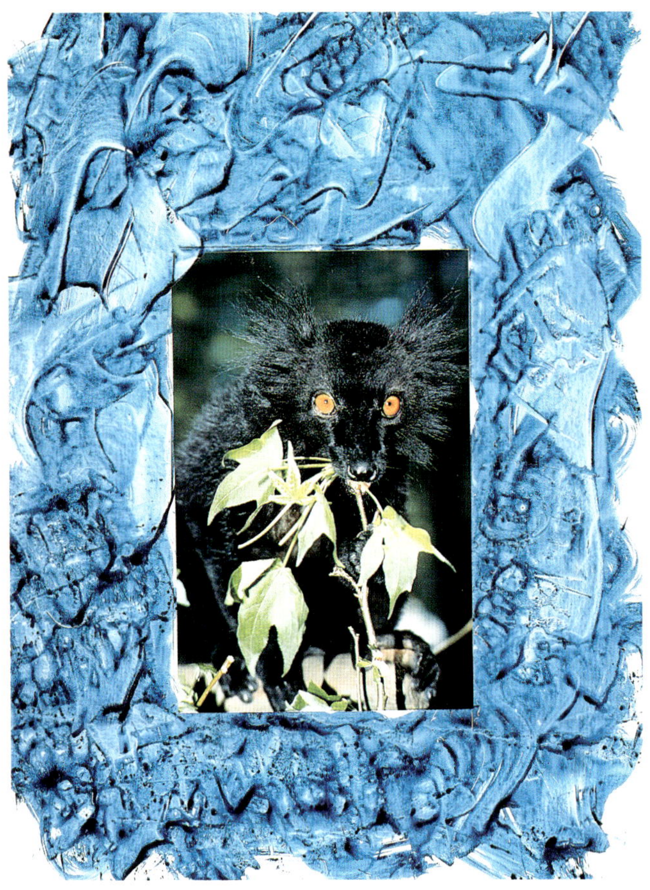

William S. Burroughs, **Black Lemur 30,000,000 Years Old**, 1992, cat. no. 70

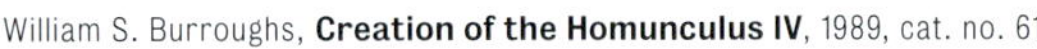

William S. Burroughs, **Creation of the Homunculus IV**, 1989, cat. no. 61

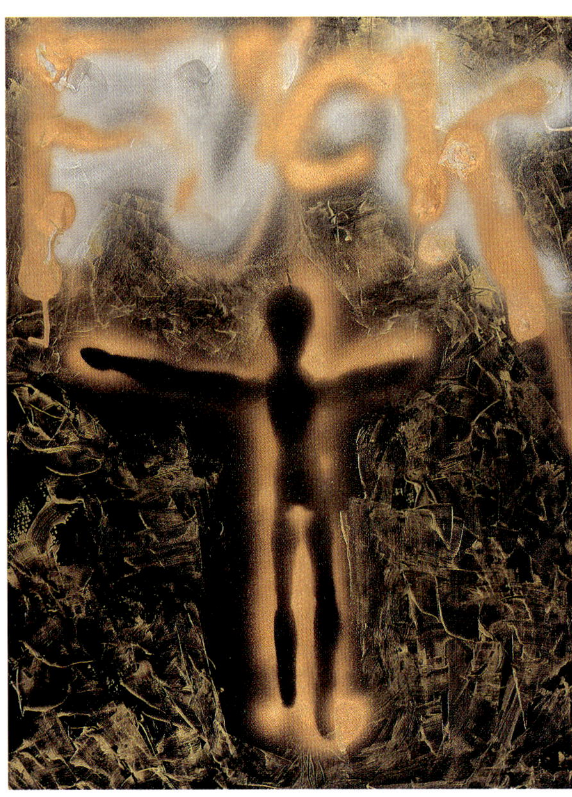

and *Call* (1991). There are the *Four Celestial Babies* (1992), spawned by aliens who abducted the crew of the *Mary Celeste* in 1872 ("Celestial Babies can take any form that the Guardian can see: lemur, cat, monkey, flying fox, or any creature of dream and fantasy."[303]). Monkeys and lemurs (and cats, of course) are featured in a number of collage paintings of the late 1980s and early 1990s but so are homunculi, those manlike creations of medieval alchemists.

Klee had sought to create an art of *Resonanzverhältnis*—"a reverberation of the finite in the infinite, of outer perception and inner vista."[304] Burroughs seeks to increase the stakes, as it were, and singularly aspires to the infinite and those inner vistas commonly associated with visionaries or users of psychedelic drugs. Gilles Deleuze and Félix Guattari remind us that "experimentation with drugs has left its mark on everyone, even nonusers," and that it has "changed the perceptive coordinates of space-time and introduced us to a universe of microperceptions."[305] In *Nova Express* Burroughs notes a similar interest in microimagery: "We first took our image and put it into code.[...]This code was written at the molecular level to save space, when it was found that the image material was not dead matter."[306] Carlos Castaneda's purportedly ethnographic studies on the Yaqui Indian don Juan Matus also illustrate the process of microperception associated with drug-induced cosmologies, as well as the significance of an out-of-body or "body without organs" state experienced by spiritual mystics and those in trances.[307] Such states, according to don Juan, reveal two orders of the universe: the "tonal" and the "nagual." The "tonal" is everything physical or susceptible to explanation, interpretation, memory, and analysis. The "nagual" is the same everything and in the same place, but instead of existing to be explained, interpreted, recalled, or analyzed, it is immaterial and simply exists as fluid transformations, flows of intensity, and states of perpetual becoming.

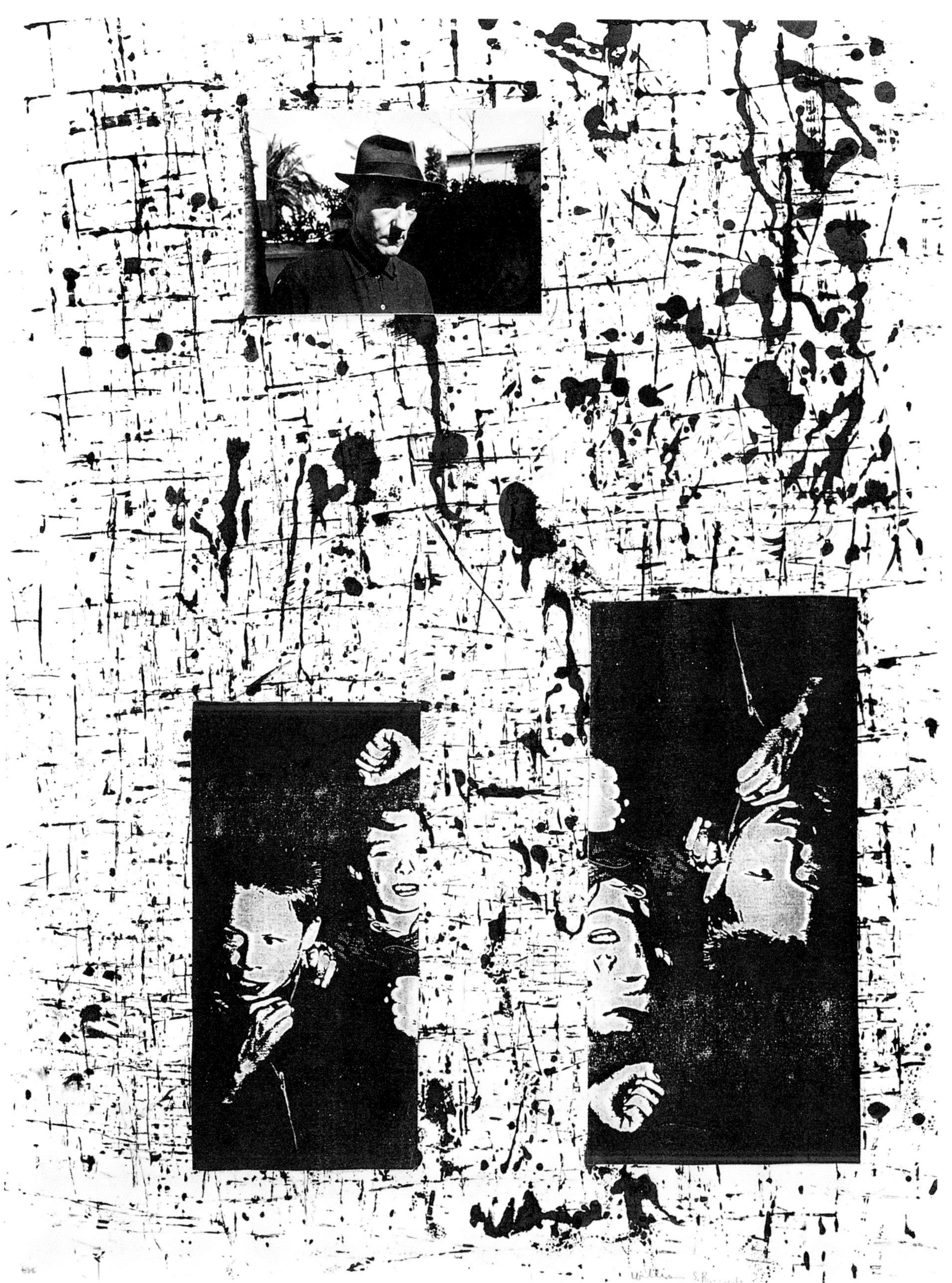

William S. Burroughs, **Joy Rider to Nowhere. Last Ride by a Viking Priest**, 1993, cat. no. 72

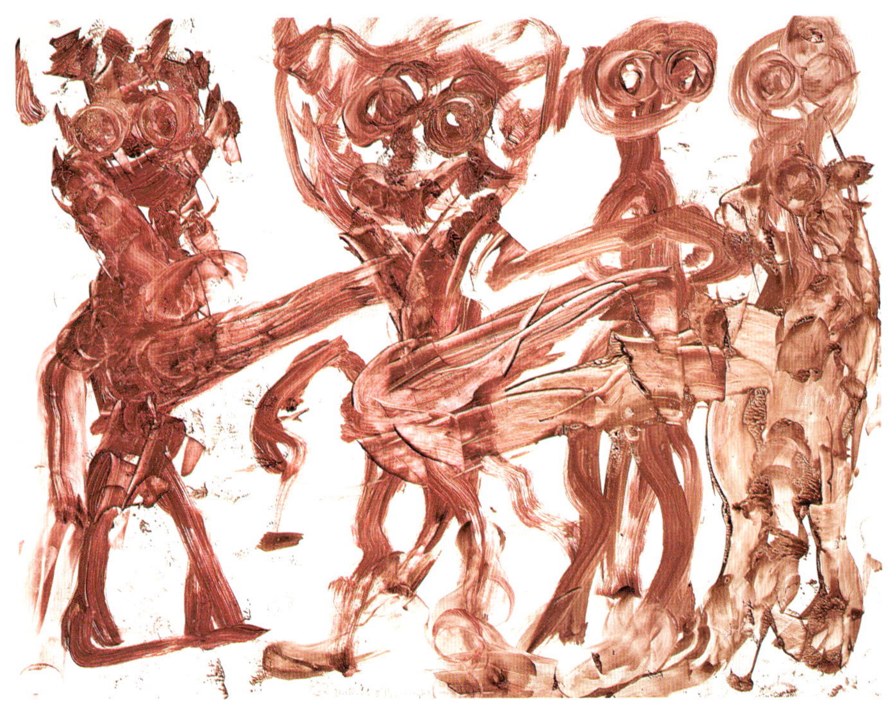

William S. Burroughs, **Four Celestial Babies**, 1992, cat. no. 68

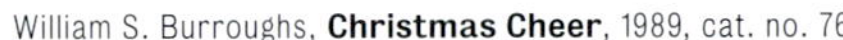

William S. Burroughs, **Christmas Cheer**, 1989, cat. no. 76

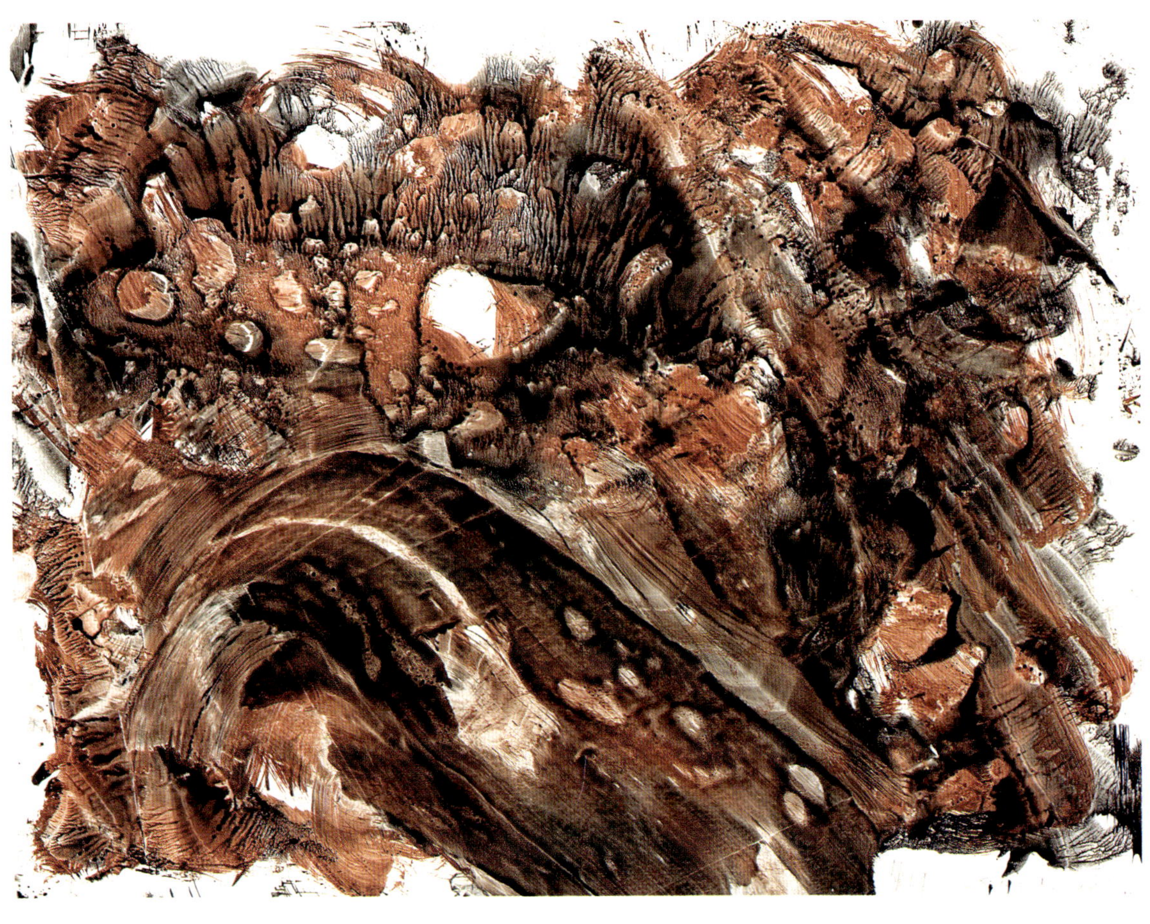

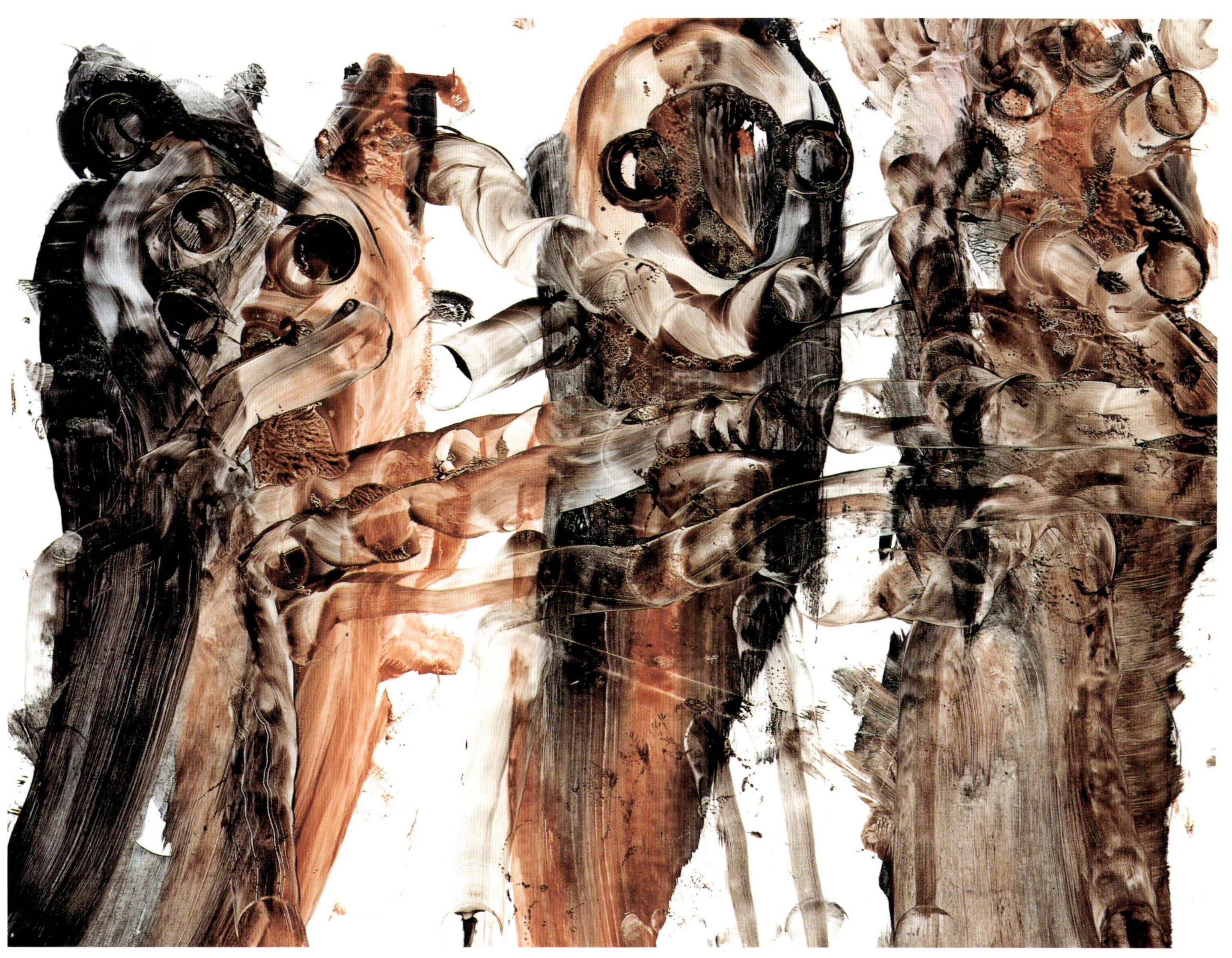

William S. Burroughs, **Alien Penetration**, 1992, cat. no. 69

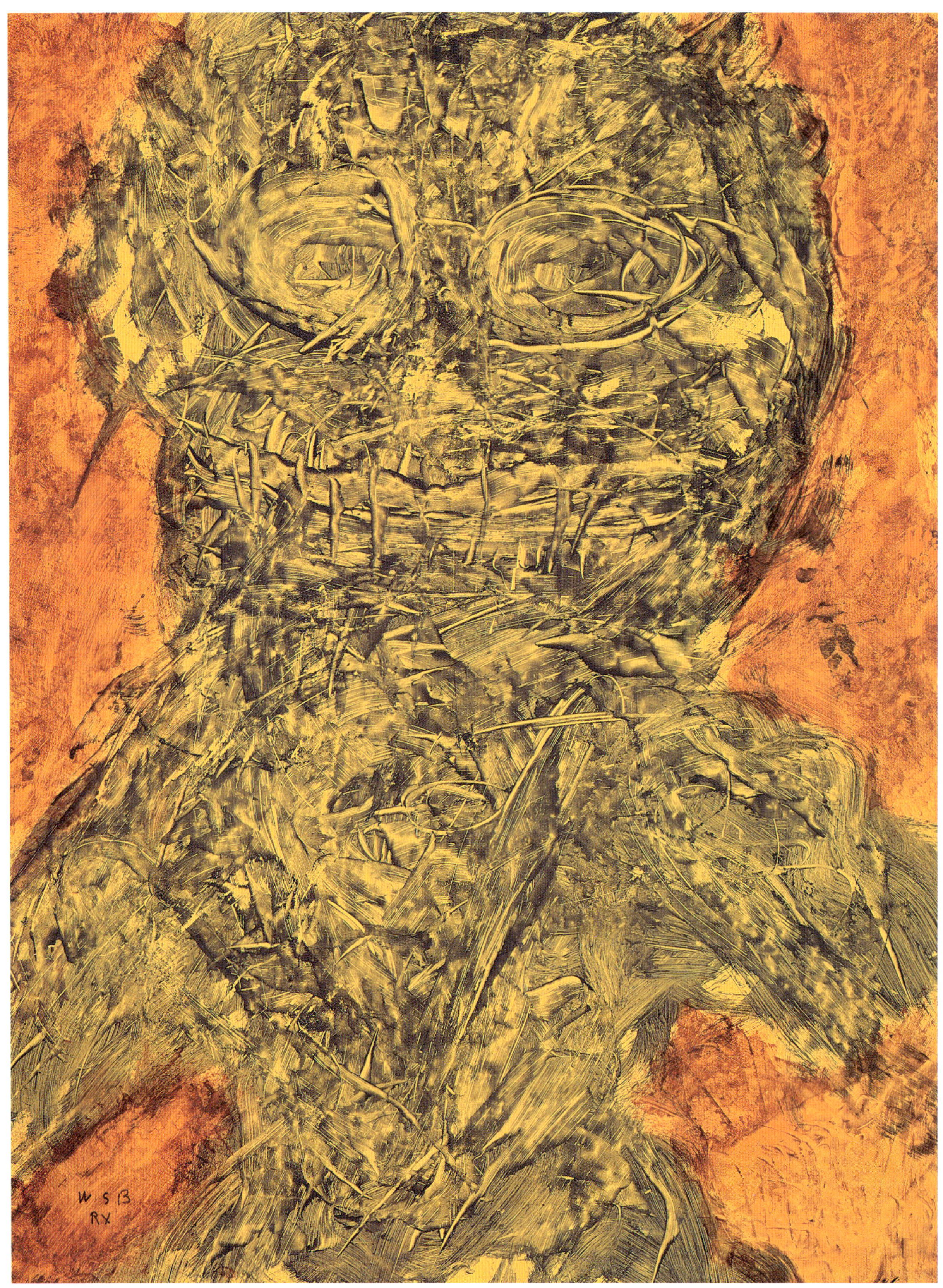

William S. Burroughs, **The Kindly Old General Practitioner**, 1992, cat. no. 67

Ultimately the "nagual" dismantles the "tonal" universe of physical and other signifiers and replaces the self and its limitations with an infinity of "continuums and conjunctions of affects."[308]

The sudden and often wonderfully fantastic transformations of one creature or character into another, one place or time into another, that take place in Burroughs's fiction are essentially "nagual." So are his frequently juxtaposed "association blocks" or "conjunctions of affects." And so is his painting.

Citing Castaneda's writings, Burroughs willfully adapts the notion of the "nagual" to his own faith in randomness:

> **The *tonal* universe is the everyday cause-and-effect universe, which is predictable because it is pre-recorded. The *nagual* is the unknown, the unpredictable, the uncontrollable. For the *nagual* to gain access, the door of chance must be open. There must be a random factor: drips of paint down the canvas, setting the paint on fire, squirting the paint. Perhaps the most basic random factor is the shotgun blast, producing an explosion of color into unpredictable, uncontrollable patterns and forms. Without this random factor, the painter can only copy the *tonal* universe, and his painting is as predictable as the universe he copies.**[309]

Achille Bonito Oliva called Burroughs the "good shaman who applies the apotropaic and magical strategies of Castaneda to the door of Marcel Duchamp."[310] The reference to Duchamp is to his *Door: 11, rue Larrey* (1927), which was installed in a corner so that it was both opened and closed at the same time. "The *nagual* must be continually created and *re-created*," Burroughs claimed, and it is as if Burroughs has attempted to do precisely this throughout his career and with every material and medium he has chosen to use.[311]

The "nagual" functions for Burroughs as yet another way of describing his continued risk-taking in pushing randomness toward the extreme, toward the breakdown of all limiting structures, toward silence. At that extreme, it just may possibly be useful in retrieving some of the unadulterated prerecordings of the universe. In book two of *Cities of the Red Night* the fearless hero Clem Snide is presented with a pile of books by one of the Iguana twins. She explains to him that the books are only "copies" and that his job is to find the originals because they are needed in order to effect change:

> **Changes, Mr. Snide, can only be effected by alterations in the *original*. The only thing not prerecorded in a prerecorded universe are the prerecordings themselves. The copies can only repeat themselves word for word. *A virus is a copy*. You can pretty it up, cut it up, scramble it—it will reassemble in the same form.**[312]

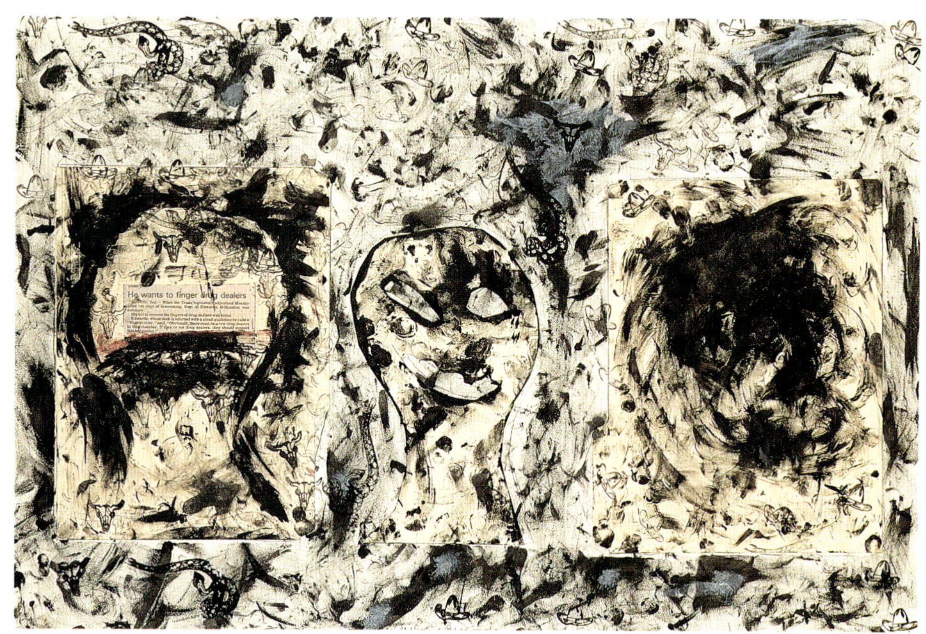

William S. Burroughs, **Terminal Drug Psychosis**, 1989, cat. no. 58

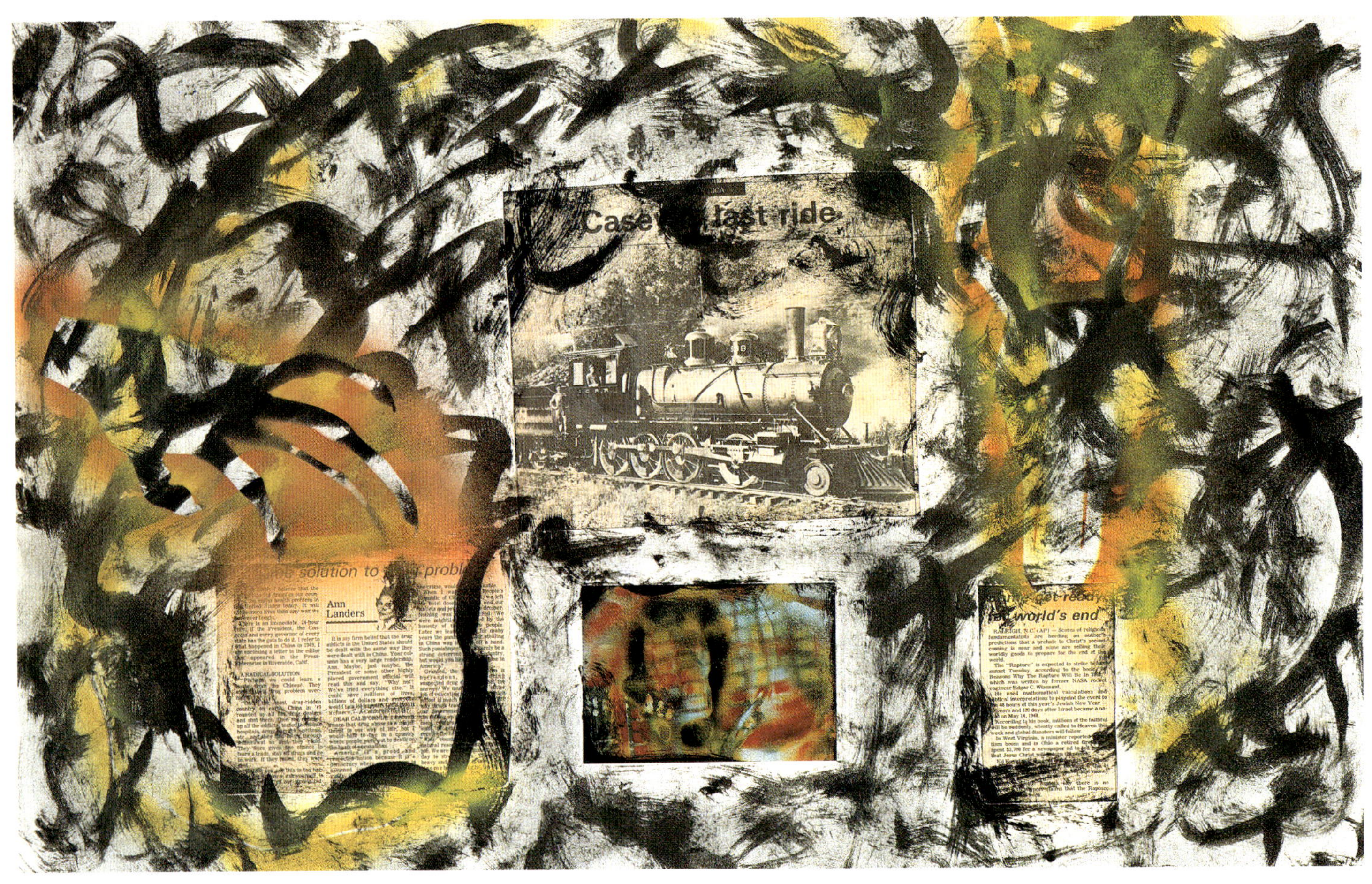

William S. Burroughs, **Last Chance Junction and Curse on Drug Hysterics**, 1988, cat. no. 56

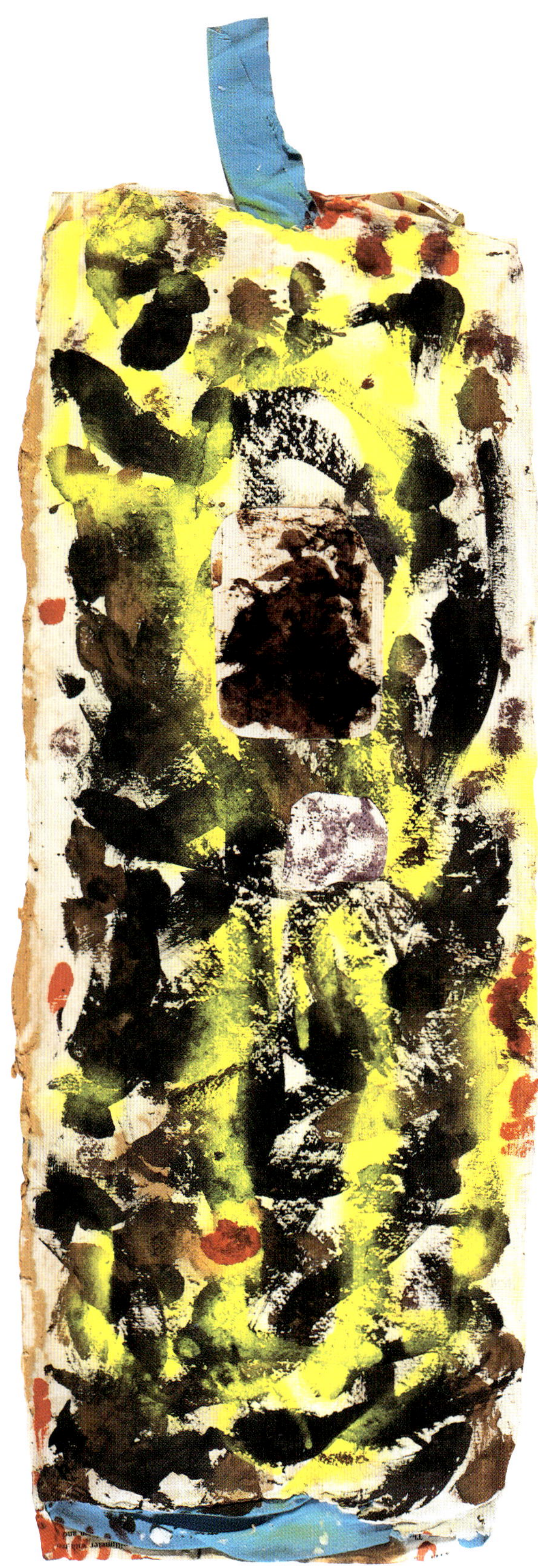

William S. Burroughs, **Thick Pages #8** (recto and verso), 1990, cat. no. 57

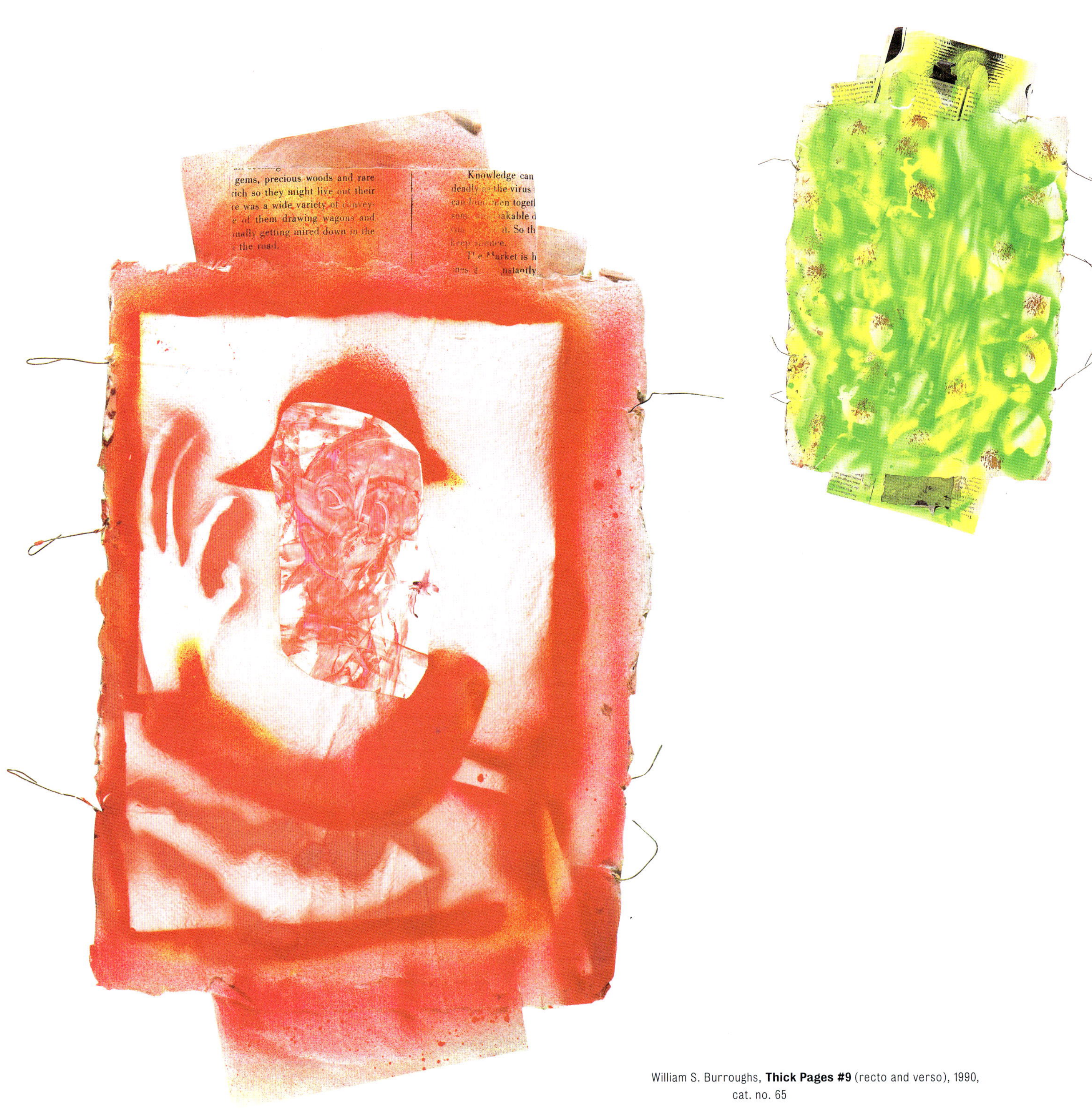

William S. Burroughs, **Thick Pages #9** (recto and verso), 1990, cat. no. 65

The "complete derangement of the senses" advocated by Rimbaud, Artaud, and Gysin is also essentially "nagual" and can be used to great effects. Examining the "copies," we find out that, according to Snide,

The books are color comics. "Jokes," Jim calls them. Some lost color process has been used to transfer three-dimensional holograms onto the curious tough translucent parchment-like material of the pages. You ache to look at these colors. Impossible reds, blues, sepias. Colors you can smell and taste and feel with your whole body. Children's books against a Bosch background; legends, fairy stories, stereotyped characters, surface motivations with a child's casual cruelty.[313]

The passage reads like a fairly good description of Burroughs's color palette in his paintings and of the nature of the photographs and other illustrations he pastes atop or embeds within them. The intensity of the colors and their not necessarily harmonious admixtures are the direct result of the artist's faith in immediacy and in random choices. In the process a great many paintings turn out "dead" and are discarded; only those that furnish the artist with some sort of way in, either by themselves or by collaging other images of people, endangered species, disasters, or news events on them, are retained and given a title.

The passage from *Cities of the Red Night* is significant for other reasons. Snide's description of the comic-book copies seems right out of William Randolph Hearst's advertisement for the first printed comic supplement in full color of 1896. In it the copywriter described the supplement as "eight pages of iridescent polychromous effulgence that makes the rainbow look like a lead pipe."[314] Furthermore, the insistence on copies and their equation with a virus not only fits in with Burroughs's notion of prerecordings but also underscores his belief that the modern writer is privileged to rearrange, or cut-up, other texts by previous

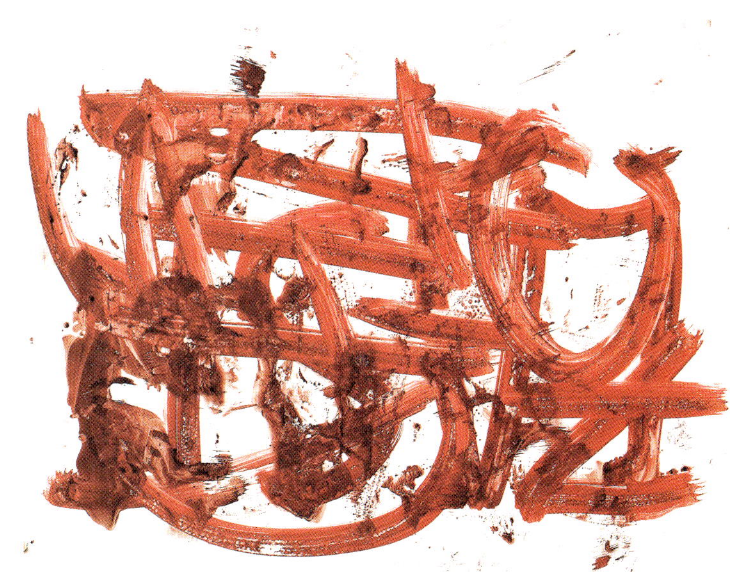

William S. Burroughs, **Animated Tassels**, 1992, cat. no. 54

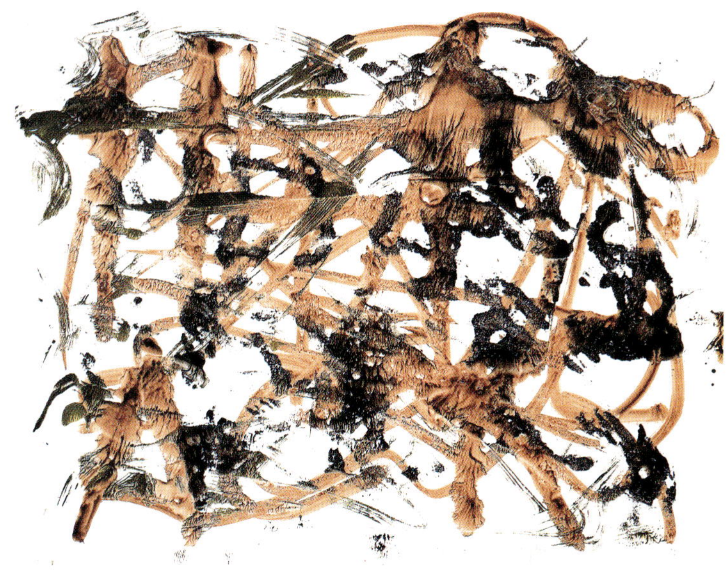

William S. Burroughs, **Attila the Hun**, 1992, cat. no. 55

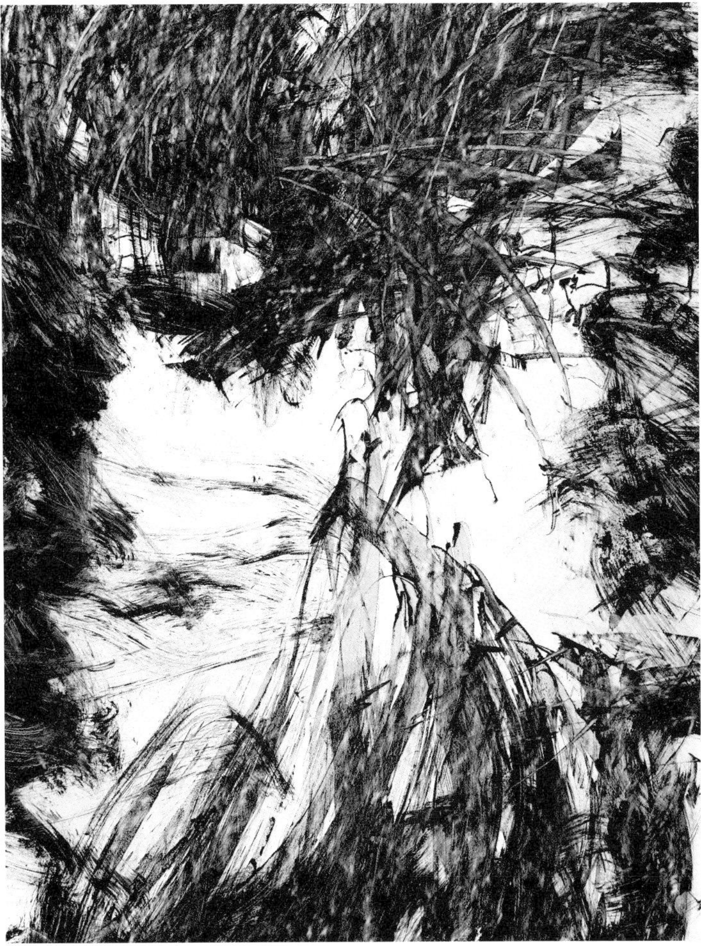

William S. Burroughs, **Ghost of Chance 15 (The Bridge)**, 1989, cat. no. 52

authors. In this Burroughs is a postmodernist like Borges, who had one of his characters write another version of *Don Quixote* that is indistinguishable from Cervantes's seventeenth-century novel.[315] Burroughs is a postmodernist like Roland Barthes, who believed that "what is left to the writer is no more than an activity of variation and combination."[316] Burroughs is also a postmodernist like Jean Baudrillard, who, by way of Walter Benjamin, wrote that "the very definition of the real has become: *that of which it is possible to give an equivalent reproduction*. . . .The real is not only what can be reproduced but *that which is always already reproduced*."[317]

Turning to painting after so many written texts, Burroughs may just possibly have succeeded in rubbing out the word. To think in pictures, with the inner voice silenced, is a method for jumping back in time to that moment just before the apes contracted the "talk sickness" and fell into the swamp. Simultaneously, by entering all the worlds that exist within his paintings and shotgun art, Burroughs proposes a form of jumping ahead in time and into space, an ultimate evolutionary jump metaphorically. Burroughs, like his character Kim Carsons, "considers these imaginary space trips to other worlds as practice for the real thing, like target shooting." But, when he considered what it was that had to be breathed in space, "the answer came to Kim in a silver flash. . . .*Silence*."[318] Despite his radicalism, however, and despite the sardonic wit and nihilistic sarcasm, Burroughs is very much a romantic since he is utterly convinced there is a possibility of creating something with his painting that is not a reproduction, recording, or copy. "All serious and dedicated artists," he wrote, "attempt the miraculous: the creation of life."[319] Barthes had written that the true role for modern art is not to "express the inexpressible," but rather the contrary: "The whole task of art is to *unexpress the expressible*, to kidnap from the world's language, which is the poor and powerful language of the passions, another speech, an exact speech."[320] This had been Burroughs's self-appointed task since *Naked Lunch*, and perhaps Burroughs is that romantic who hopes to unexpress the expressible, believes in the primacy of dreams which cannot be expressed, and fervently trusts in the exercise of "purposeful abandonment" to those dreams.[321] "Kim sees dreams as a vital link to our biologic and spiritual destiny in space," Burroughs wrote in *The Place of Dead Roads*, "Deprived of this air line we die."[322]

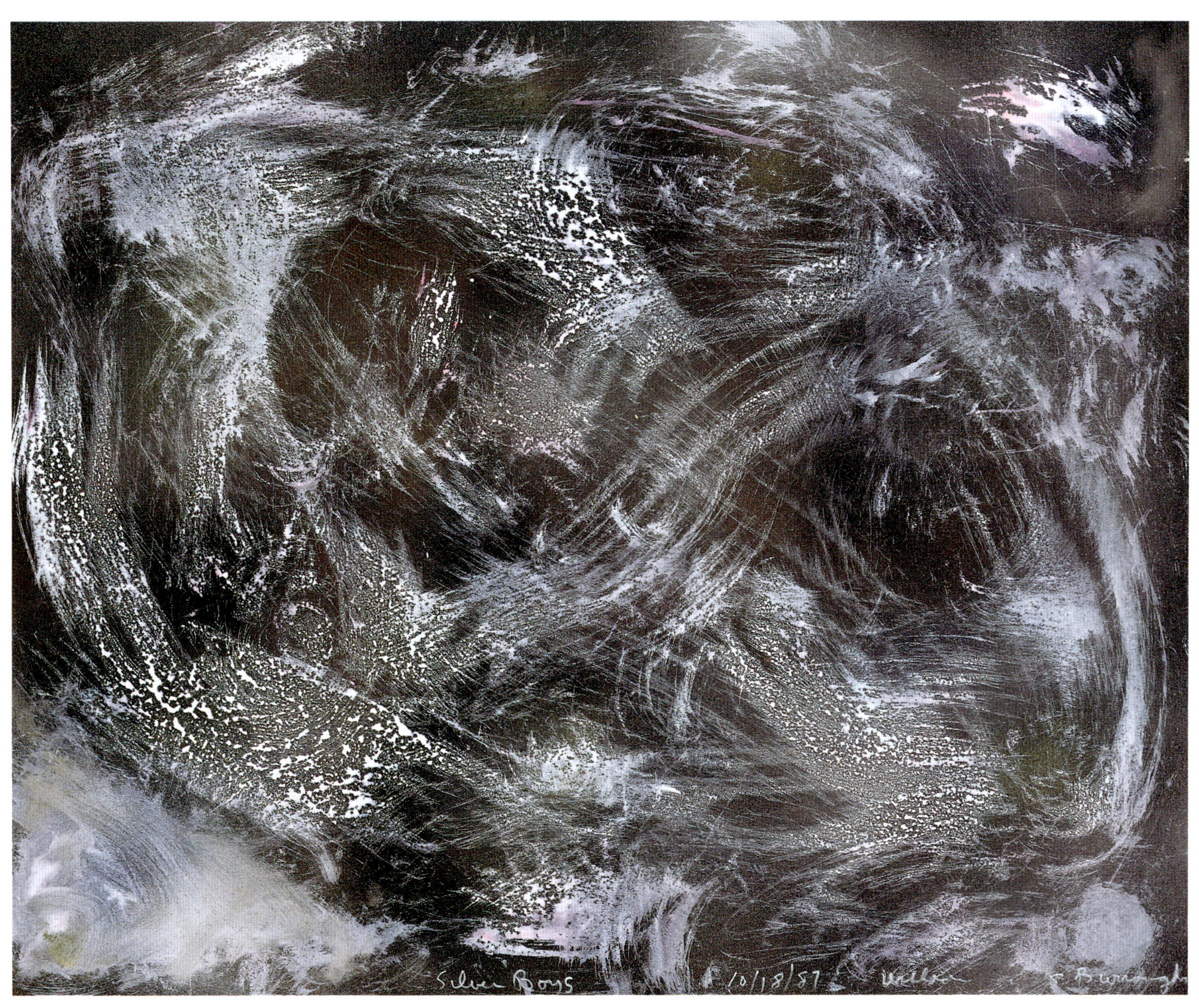

William S. Burroughs, **Silver Boys**, 1987, cat. no. 51

288
William S. Burroughs, *Cities of the Red Night* (New York: Holt, Rinehart and Winston, 1981), 167.

289
Burroughs, *Painting and Guns* (note **171**), 16–17.

290
Ibid., 17.

291
Burroughs, *My Education* (note **42**), 182.

292
Ed Moses, in Sean Mitchell, "Wholly Moses," *Los Angeles* 40, no. 7 (July 1995): 110.

293
Burroughs, *Painting and Guns* (note **171**), 36–37.

294
Achille Bonito Oliva, "Art and Its Shoulder Ache," in *William S. Burroughs*, exh. cat. (Rome: Galleria Cleto Polcina Arte Moderna, 1989), unp.

295
Burroughs quoted in John Gruen, *Keith Haring: The Authorized Biography* (New York: Simon and Schuster/Fireside Books, 1991), 183.

296
Ann Temkin, "Klee and the Avant-Garde, 1912–1940," in Carolyn Lanchner, ed., *Paul Klee* exh. cat. (New York: Museum of Modern Art, 1987), 31.

297
Paul Klee, quoted in Sibyl Moholy-Nagy, "Introduction," in Klee, *Pedagogical Sketchbook* (New York: Praeger, 1953), 10.

298
See William S. Burroughs, "Preface," in Gysin and Wilson, *Here to Go* (note **14**), x.

299
Klee, *Pedagogical Sketchbook* (note **297**), 60–61.

300
Burroughs, *Painting and Guns* (note **171**), 33; the actual quotation is "Presumptuous is the artist who does not follow his road through to the end. But chosen are those artists who penetrate to the region of that secret place where primeval power nurtures all evolution"; see Paul Klee, *On Modern Art*, trans. Paul Findlay (London: Faber and Faber, 1949; reprinted 1962), 49.

301
Burroughs, *Painting and Guns* (note **171**), 36–37.

302
Ibid., 34–35.

303
Burroughs, *My Education* (note **42**), 125.

304
Moholy-Nagy, "Introduction," (note **297**), 12.

305
Gilles Deleuze and Félix Guattari, *A Thousand Plateaus: Capitalism and Schizophrenia*, trans. Brian Massumi (Minneapolis: University of Minnesota Press, 1987), 248.

306
Burroughs, *Nova Express* (note **2**), 49.

307
See Deleuze and Guattari, *A Thousand Plateaus* (note **305**), 161–62. Castaneda's discussions on the "tonal" and the "nagual" are found in *Tales of Power* (New York: Simon and Schuster, 1974). See also Carlos Castaneda, *The Teachings of Don Juan: A Yaqui Way of Knowledge* (Berkeley: University of California Press, 1968); and his *A Separate Reality: Further Conversations with Don Juan* (New York: Simon and Schuster, 1971).

308
Deleuze and Guattari, *A Thousand Plateaus* (note **305**), 162.

309
Burroughs, "Nagual Art" (note **22**), unp.

310
Oliva, "Art and Its Shoulder Ache" (note **294**), unp.

311
Burroughs, "Nagual Art" (note **22**), unp.

312
Burroughs, *Cities of the Red Night* (note **288**), 166.

313
Ibid., 167.

314
Boorstein, *The Image* (note **70**), 125; having been first published in 1961, this essay may have been read by Burroughs; in any case, he also featured Hearst in one of his and Gysin's collages for *The Third Mind*.

315
Jorge Luis Borges, "Pierre Menard, Author of Don Quixote," in *Ficciones* (note **71**), 45–55.

316
Roland Barthes, "Preface," in *Critical Essays*, trans. Richard Howard (Evanston, Illinois: Northwestern University Press, 1972), xvii.

317
Jean Baudrillard, *Simulations*, trans. Paul Foss et al. (New York: Semiotext(e), 1983), 146.

318
Burroughs, *The Place of Dead Roads* (note **28**), 40.

319
Burroughs, *Painting and Guns* (note **171**), 18.

320
Barthes, "Preface" (note **316**), xvii.

321
Burroughs, *Port of Saints* (note **222**), 165.

322
Burroughs, *The Place of Dead Roads* (note **28**), 42.

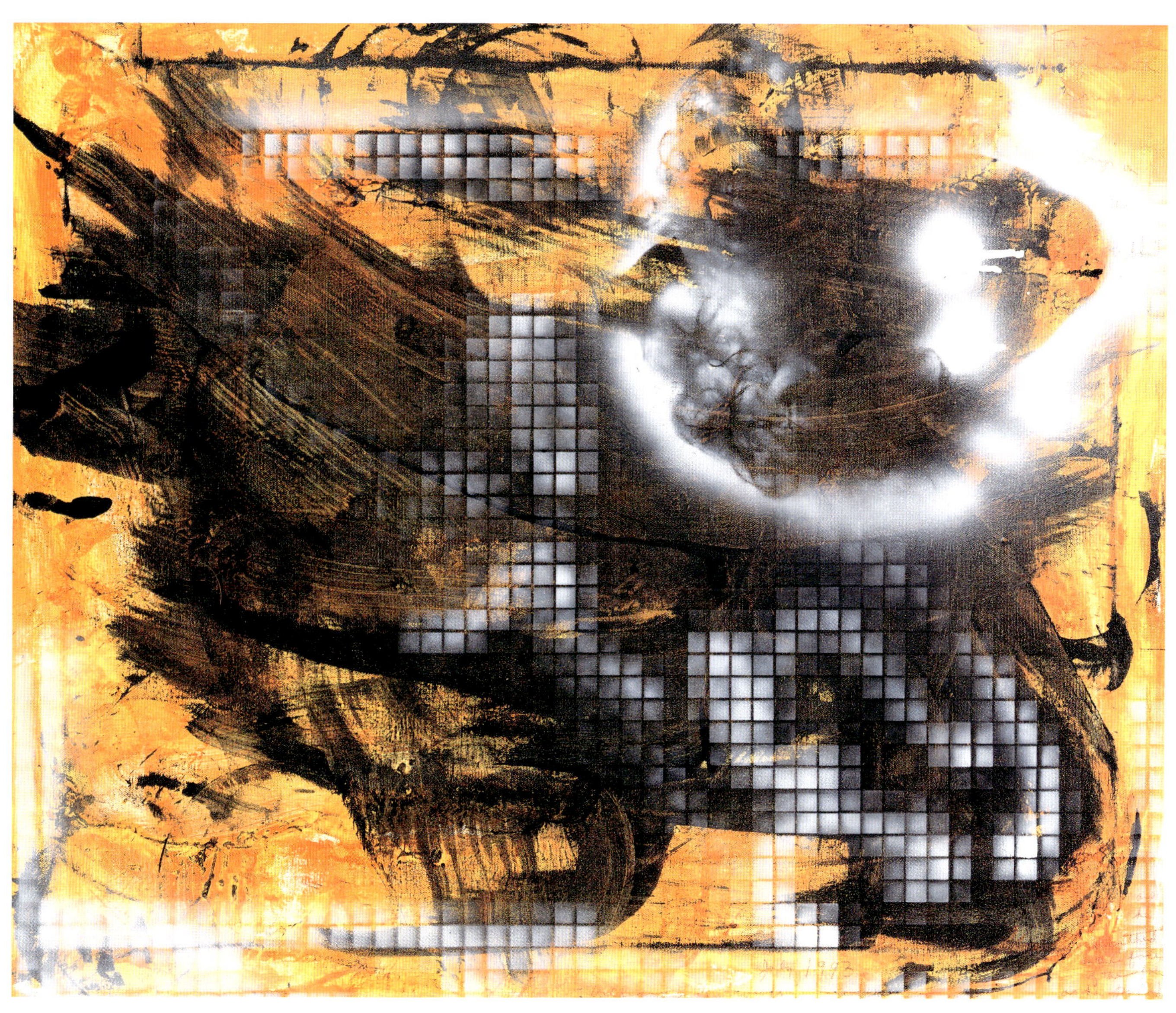

William S. Burroughs, **For the Angel of Death Spread His Wings**, 1993, cat. no. 79

XIV

¿QUIÉN ES?

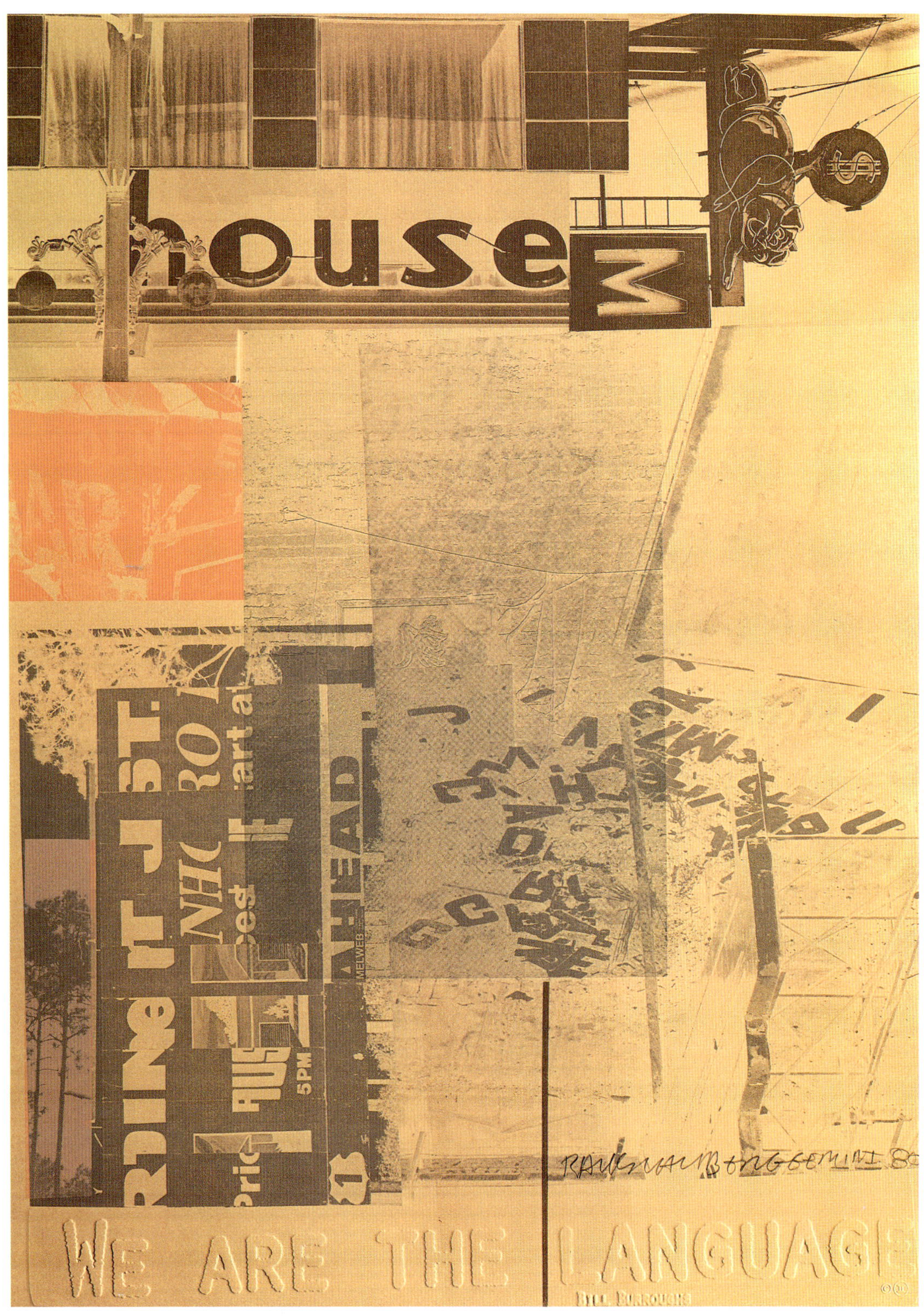

William S. Burroughs and Robert Rauschenberg, **American Pewter with Burroughs V**, 1981, cat. no. 82

Isn't there some other self in there with your self?[323]

The decade of the 1980s was for Burroughs a period of exceptional productivity and feverish experimentation. He completed his final trilogy of adventure novels, became progressively involved with the visual arts, and began a series of mutually fulfilling collaborations with other artists. In 1981, a year before he began shotgunning plywood panels, Burroughs gave six brief sentences to Sidney Felsen, co-owner of Gemini G.E.L., a fine-art publisher of artists' prints and sculpture editions based in Los Angeles. The original idea was Robert Rauschenberg's, who wanted to collaborate with Burroughs, and it was enthusiastically embraced by Felsen and his partner Stanley Grinstein.[324] Rauschenberg embedded Burroughs's texts within his own photomontages as part of a suite of lithographic prints published by Gemini entitled *American Pewter with Burroughs*. In the fifth print of the suite Burroughs's "We Are the Language" is embossed beneath a montage of positive and negative photographic images of store fronts, signs, posters, and what appears to be a pavement strewn with randomly scattered letters. Rauschenberg's literal take on Burroughs's notion of "word falling?" *American Pewter with Burroughs* was the first time Burroughs actively collaborated with anyone other than Gysin in painting or printmaking.

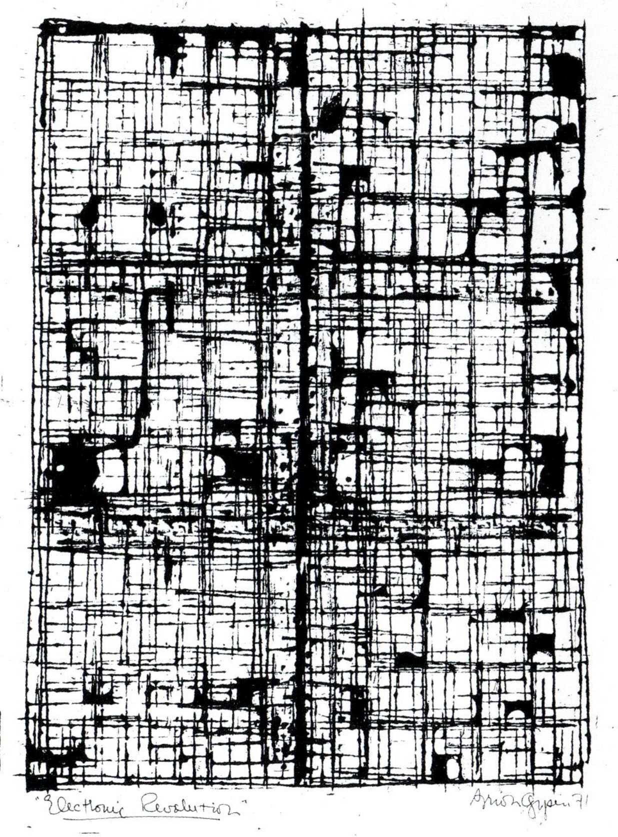

Brion Gysin, **Electronic Revolution**, 1971, cat. no. 81

Much of Burroughs's collaborative work has involved having other artists contribute images to limited and illustrated editions of his texts. Gysin provided two screenprints of his brayer experiments to the Blackmoor Head Press edition of *Electronic Revolution* (1971) and a number of whimsical lithographic images

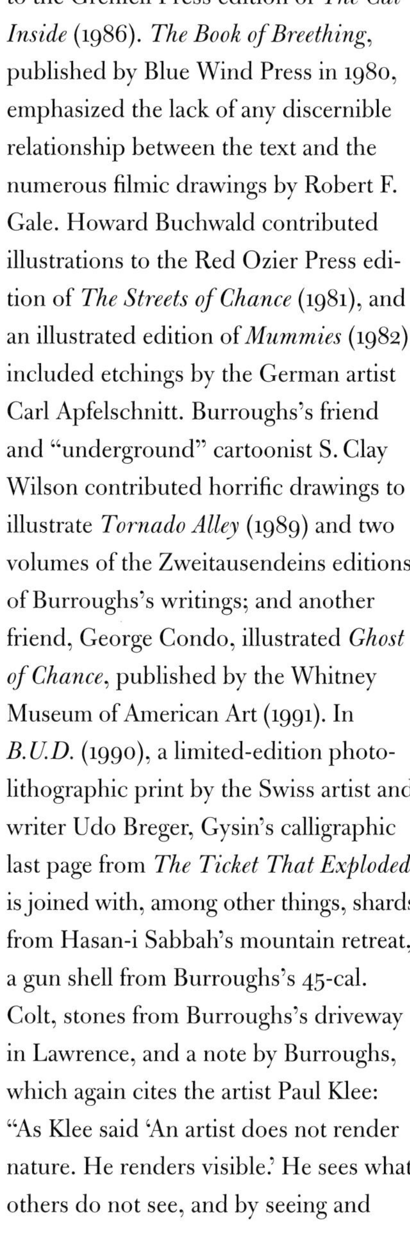

to the Grenfell Press edition of *The Cat Inside* (1986). *The Book of Breething*, published by Blue Wind Press in 1980, emphasized the lack of any discernible relationship between the text and the numerous filmic drawings by Robert F. Gale. Howard Buchwald contributed illustrations to the Red Ozier Press edition of *The Streets of Chance* (1981), and an illustrated edition of *Mummies* (1982) included etchings by the German artist Carl Apfelschnitt. Burroughs's friend and "underground" cartoonist S. Clay Wilson contributed horrific drawings to illustrate *Tornado Alley* (1989) and two volumes of the Zweitausendeins editions of Burroughs's writings; and another friend, George Condo, illustrated *Ghost of Chance*, published by the Whitney Museum of American Art (1991). In *B.U.D.* (1990), a limited-edition photolithographic print by the Swiss artist and writer Udo Breger, Gysin's calligraphic last page from *The Ticket That Exploded* is joined with, among other things, shards from Hasan-i Sabbah's mountain retreat, a gun shell from Burroughs's 45-cal. Colt, stones from Burroughs's driveway in Lawrence, and a note by Burroughs, which again cites the artist Paul Klee: "As Klee said 'An artist does not render nature. He renders visible.' He sees what others do not see, and by seeing and

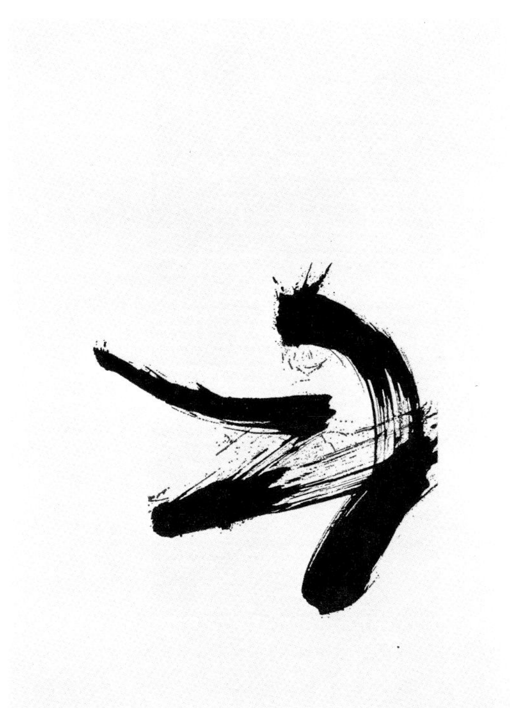

Brion Gysin, untitled, from **The Cat Inside**, 1986, cat. no. 84

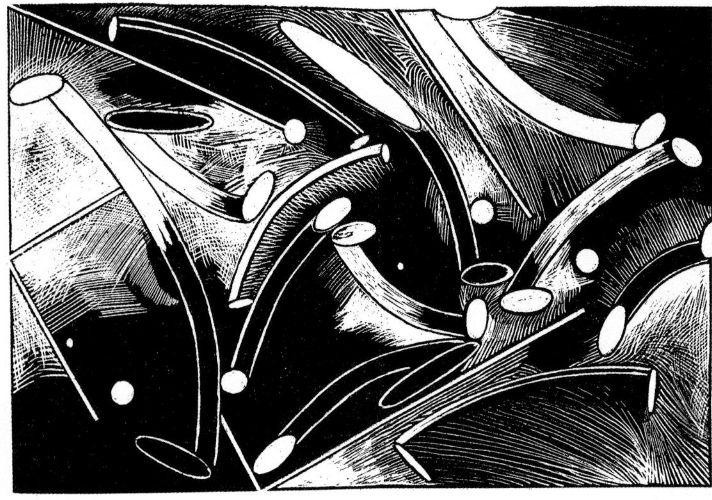

Howard Buchwald, book illustration in **The Streets of Chance**, 1981, cat. no. 139

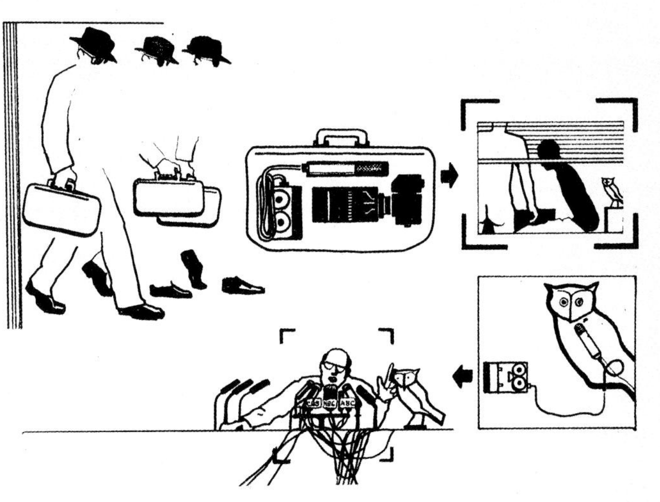

Robert F. Gale, book illustration in **The Book of Breething**, 1974, cat. no. 137

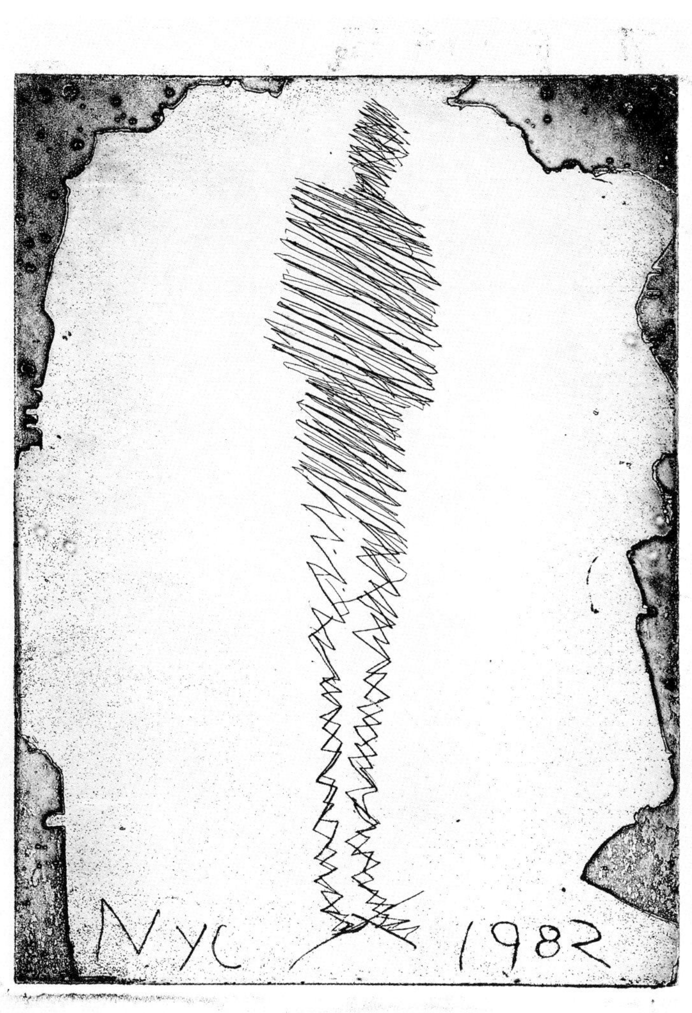

Carl Apfelschnitt, untitled, from **Mummies**, 1982, cat. no. 83

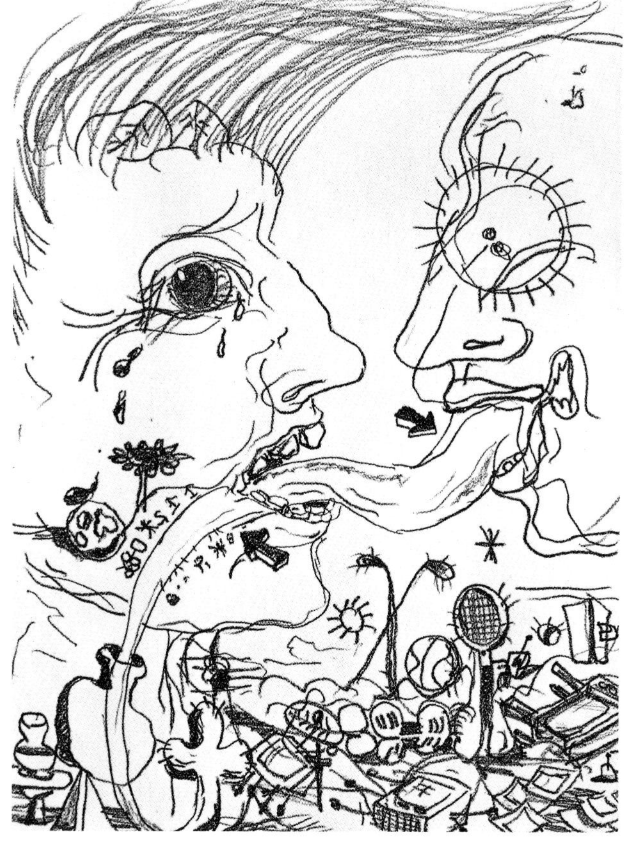

George Condo, untitled, from **Ghost of Chance**, 1991, cat. no. 92

rendering on canvas, paper, whatever makes his vision visible to others (if they are able to see)."

Burroughs met the young and celebrated graffiti artist Keith Haring at Victor Bockris's apartment in New York in 1983. Haring had earlier learned the importance of combining images and words when as a student he attended the Nova Convention, organized by John Giorno, James Grauerholz, and Sylvère Lotringer in 1978. From this experience, Haring wrote, "William Burroughs and Brion Gysin became my models."[325] By the summer of 1980 Haring had fully developed his unique style: "I had made these symbols that were nonverbal, but were signs that could have different meanings at different times. And everything was a cross-reference to everything else. It was what I had learned from the

S. Clay Wilson, untitled, from **Tornado Alley**, 1989, cat. no. 144

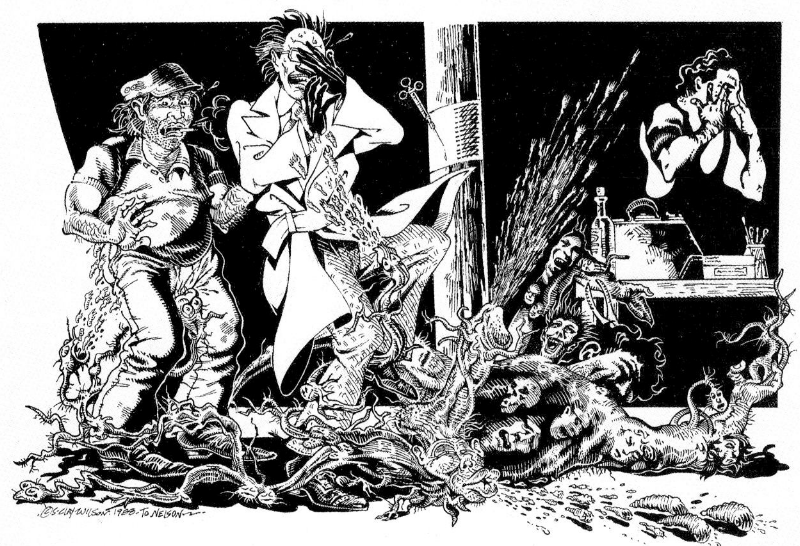

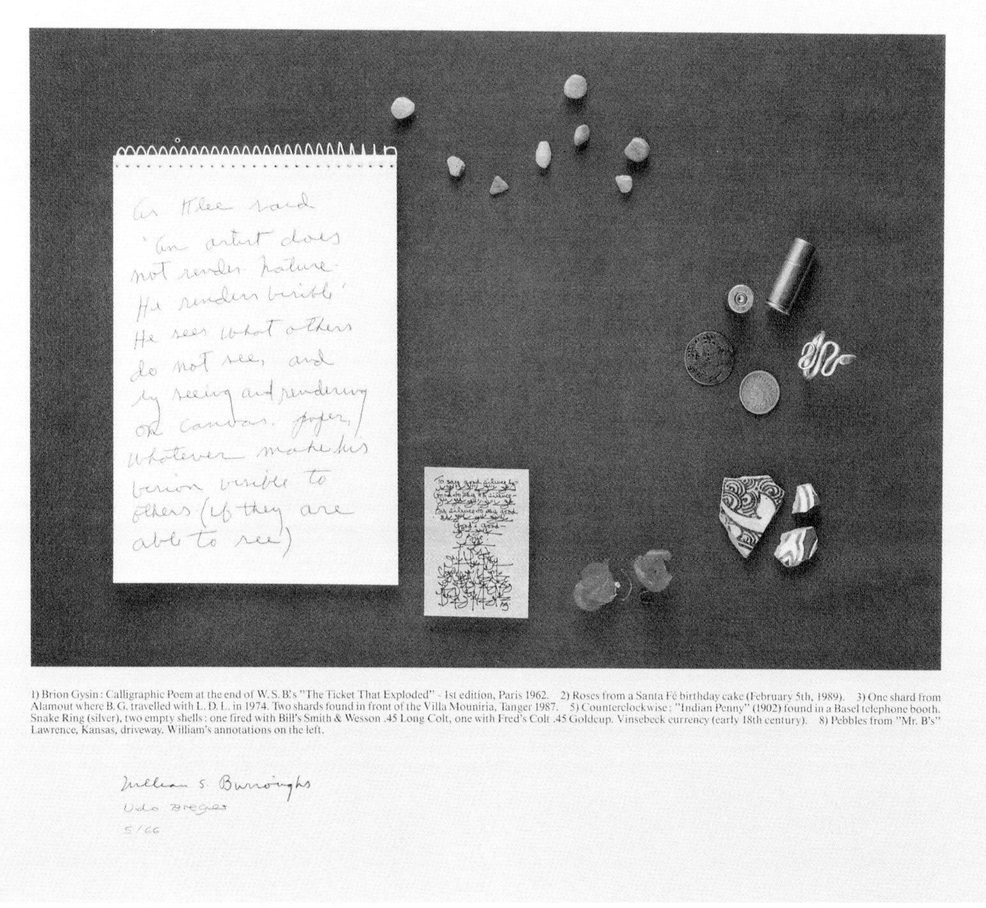

William S. Burroughs and Udo Breger, **B.U.D.**, 1990, cat. no. 90

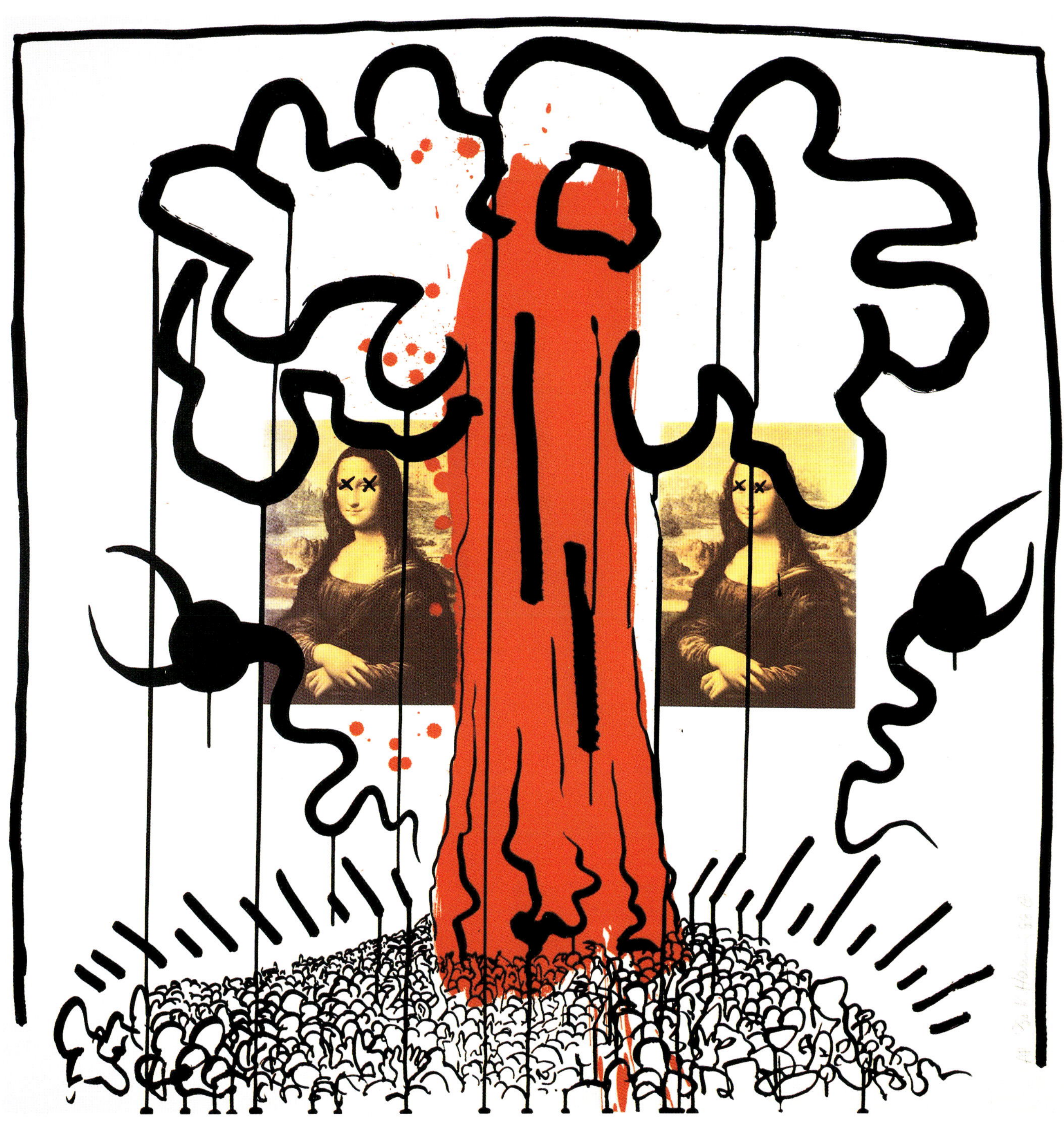

William S. Burroughs and Keith Haring, untitled, from **Apocalypse**, 1988, cat. no. 87

cut-up works of Burroughs—and it felt great!"[326] By 1983, when Burroughs met him, Haring had already befriended Gysin and was working at illustrating a fine-art edition of "The Faultline" section of Gysin's novel *The Last Museum* for a Munich publisher.[327] In 1987 the fine-print publisher George Mulder effected a collaboration between Burroughs and Haring, and the result was the following year's *Apocalypse*, a suite of ten large-scaled, lithographic prints by Haring with accompanying text sheets by Burroughs and a trade book reproducing the entire work. Putting the two artists together was like "Dante and Titian getting together," according to Timothy Leary.[328] Burroughs compared Haring to Paul Klee and considered the work they each brought to their collaboration to be of "equal weight and purpose....My texts were perfectly understood and perfectly rendered."[329] Burroughs could not help but react positively to the "tremendous electric vitality" of Haring's illustrations: his hanging men, spurting phalluses, horned sperm, and television sets broadcasting disasters pepper the prints in some sort of jumbled vision of the end of the world. Haring gave Burroughs one of the ink-and-watercolor drawings he did at this time, not as a design for *Apocalypse* but one that was in the same style and whose content is more appropriate to *The Wild Boys* than the book of *Revelation*.

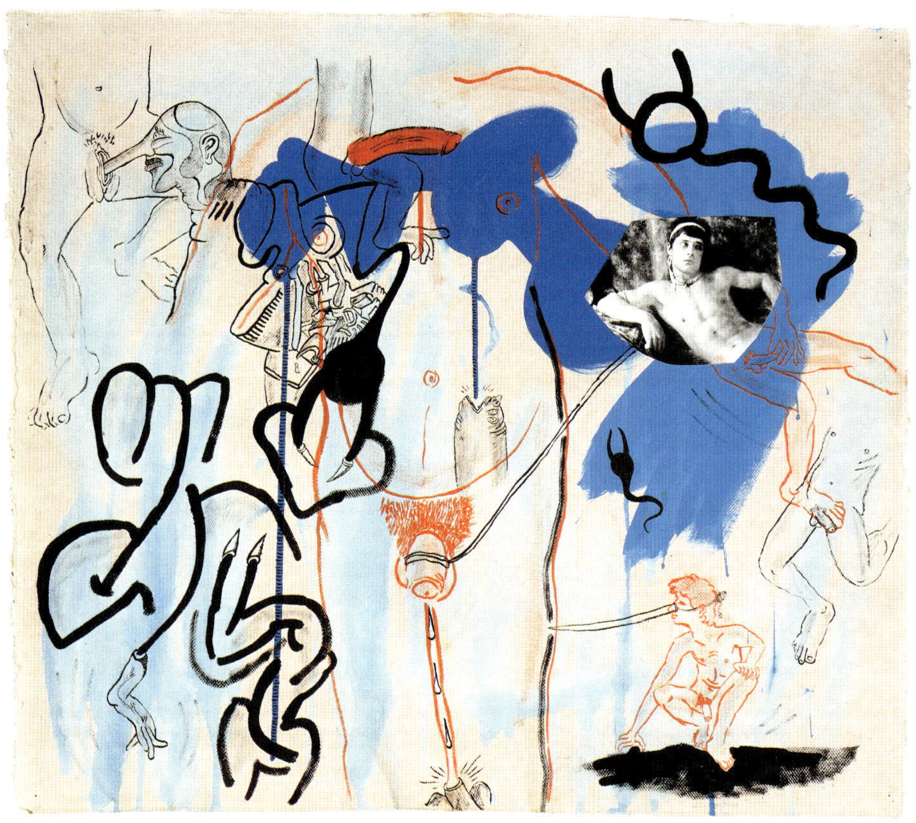

Keith Haring, **For William Burroughs with Love and Admiration**, 1987, cat. no. 143

The artist Jean-Michel Basquiat visited Burroughs in 1987. Basquiat, a Burroughs admirer who counted *Junky* and *Naked Lunch* among his favorite books, was a former heroin addict himself. At least one critic characterized Basquiat, who was often wired on coke and frequented dance clubs, as a real-life "Subliminal Kid," the hyper-driven character from *Nova Express*.[330] In December of that year at a dinner party at Victor Bockris's apartment Burroughs and Basquiat began making drawings in Basquiat's sketchbook, at times assisted by Ginsberg. Burroughs visited Basquiat's studio the following

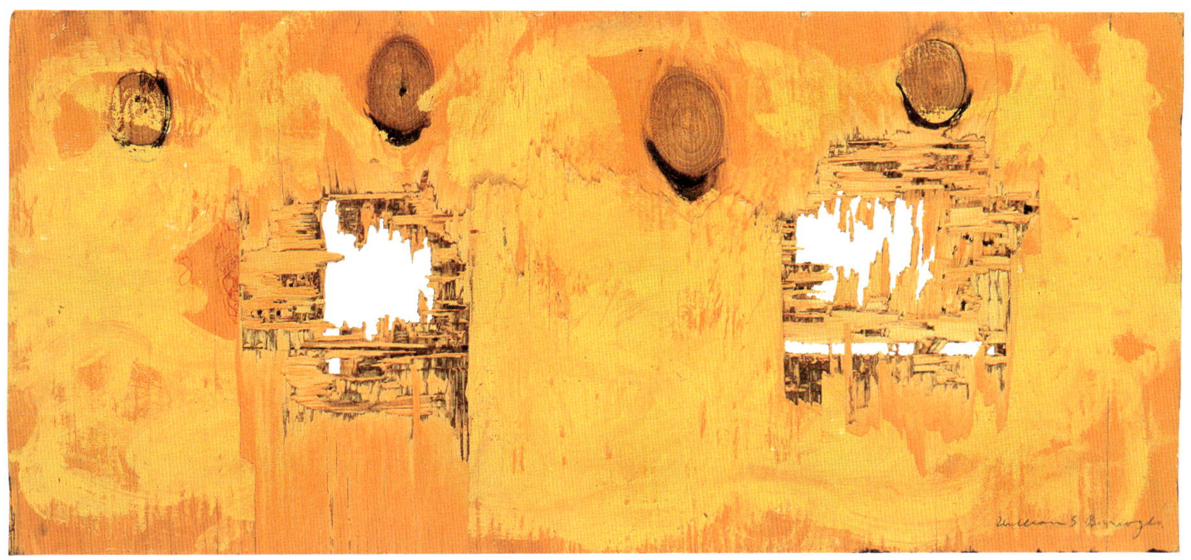

William S. Burroughs, **Woman as Man**, 1988, cat. no. 48

Jean-Michel Basquiat, **Nod**, c. 1985–88, cat. no. 142

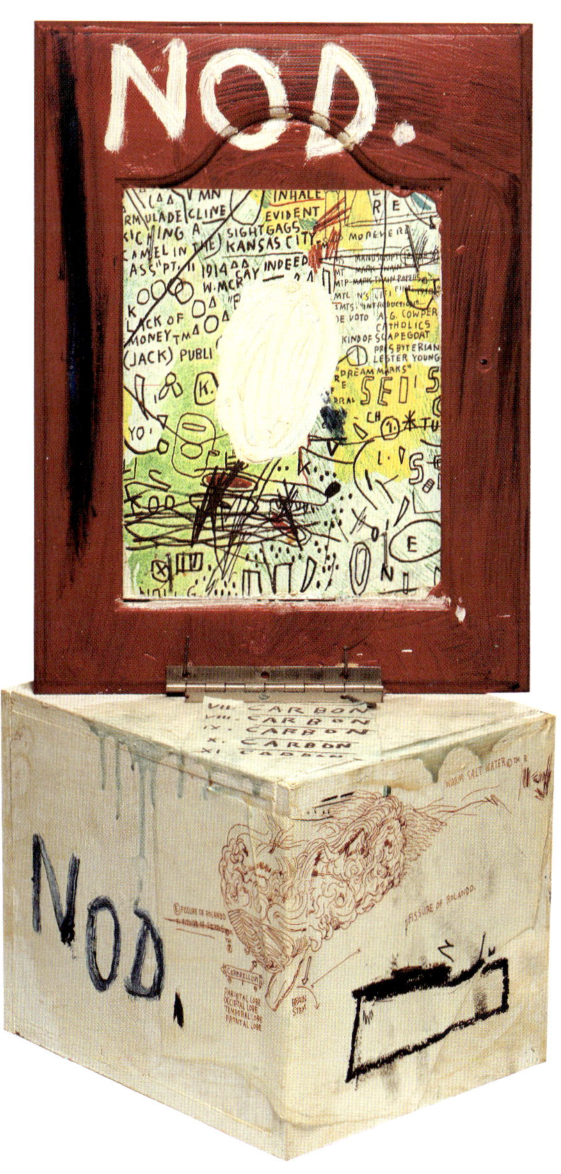

day, and the two artists eventually traded works through the mail in 1988. Burroughs gave the younger artist a "wood reverse relief with gunshots" entitled *Woman as Man*, while Basquiat reciprocated with a two-part wooded assemblage entitled appropriately *Nod* done sometime between 1985 and when it was given.[331] The white-painted cube base features the work's title, a drawing of a distorted brain and comments locating the "fissure of Rolando," the cerebellum, various lobes, and the brain stem, in addition to the phrase "warm salt water." Mounted on top of this base, a red-painted cabinet door bears the title again, while its whited-out center panel bears a typical Basquiat collage of colored xerographic photocopies concerned with "sight gags," "Kansas City," and "lack of money." Considering Burroughs's painted doors and windows, such as *Space Door* and *Fire Door* (both 1987–88), it is interesting to note Basquiat's use of a cabinet door here and his earlier *Pork* (1981), which is similarly painted on a wood and glass door.[332] Again, as in the case of Niki de Saint Phalle's gunshot paintings, Burroughs was certainly unaware of this precedent.

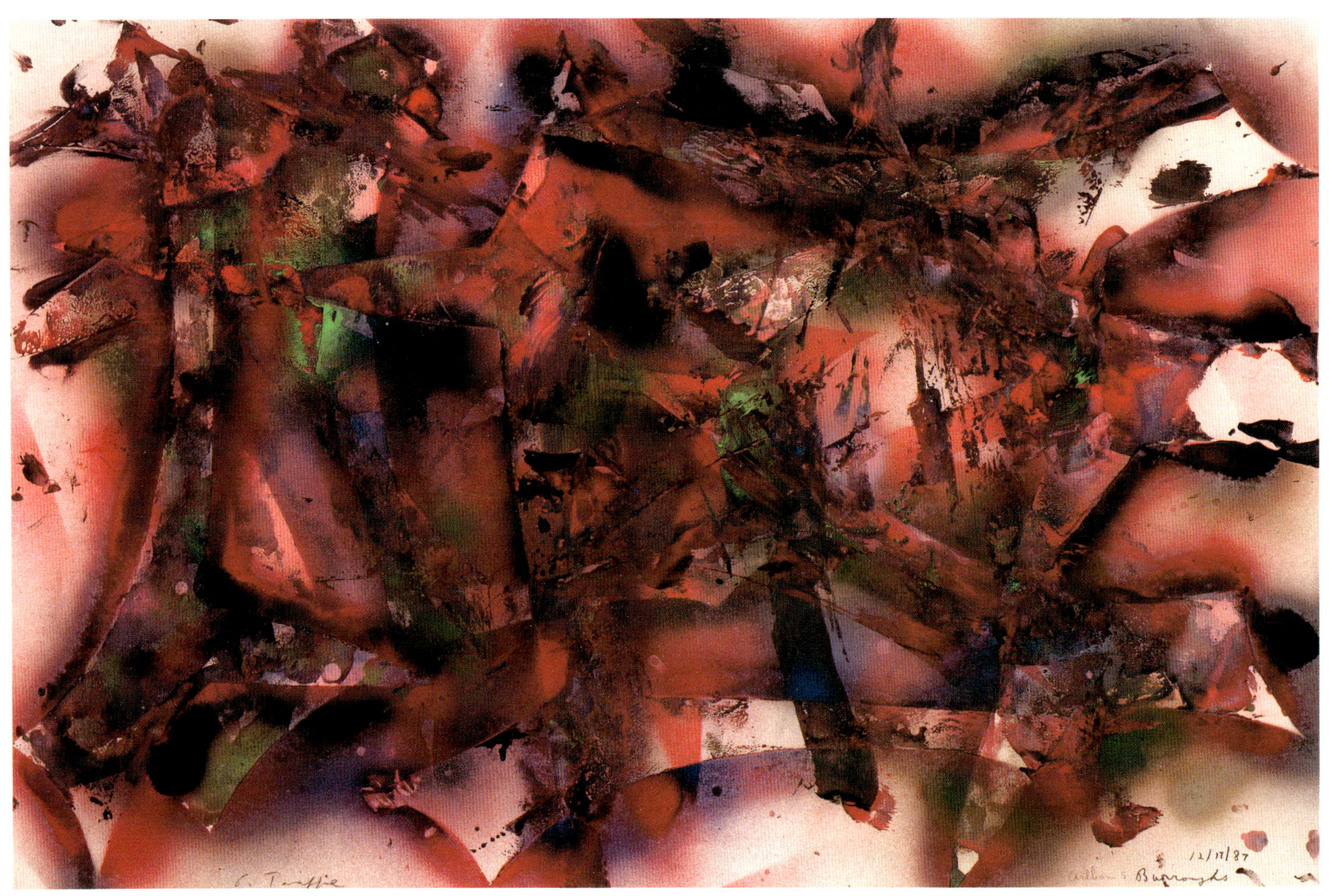

William S. Burroughs and Philip Taaffe, untitled, 1987, cat. no. 85

Following Gysin's death in 1986, Burroughs's collaborations with other artists became much more frequent. Immediately following his experience with Philip Taaffe and Diego Cortez in making *The Red Skull* (1987; also known as *The Red Death*), Burroughs joined forces with Taaffe on a series of ink drawings sponsored by the Pat Hearn Gallery. A year after *Apocalypse* was published, Burroughs and Haring collaborated again on *The Valley*, which included sixteen etchings illustrating Haring's favorite chapter from *The Western Lands* and was published by Mulder. In the same year, 1989, Burroughs joined with Robert Wilson not only on the libretto for the composer's *The Black Rider* but on large pen-and-ink drawings associated with the opera as well. The painter Dean Ripa worked with Burroughs on a panel entitled *The Ambiguous Smile of the Tempter* in 1990. Also in that year Giorno collaborated with Burroughs on a painting that Giorno entitled *That Gun's Got Blood in Its Hole*. Between 1992 and 1994 George Condo visited Burroughs in Lawrence a number of times and collaborated with him on both small and large paintings.

Encouraged by the print publishers Robert Lococo and Mulder, Burroughs brought out his own portfolio, *The Seven Deadly Sins* (1992), featuring oversized woodblock and screenprint plates accompanied by equally large, screened texts. The images in *The Seven Deadly Sins* derive from Burroughs's work with shotgunned plywood and with spray paint and stenciling. Similarly combining the images of gunshots and painting,

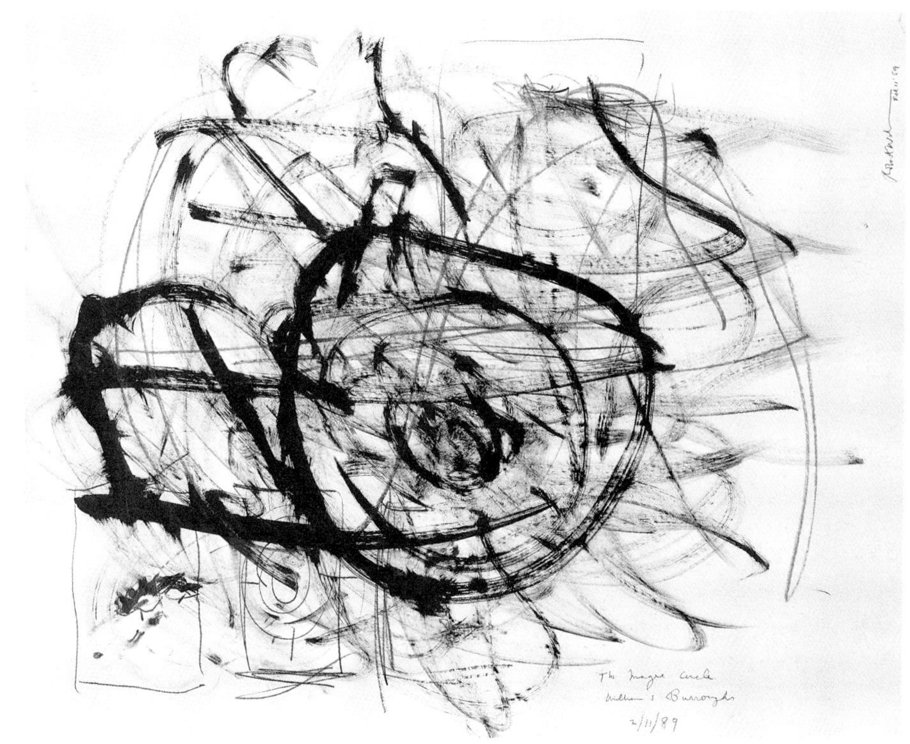

William S. Burroughs and Robert Wilson, **The Magic Circle**, 1989, cat. no. 89

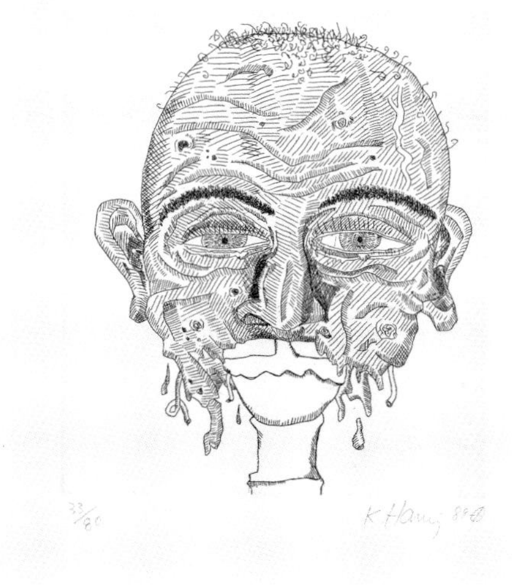

William S. Burroughs and Keith Haring, untitled, from **The Valley**, 1989, cat. no. 88

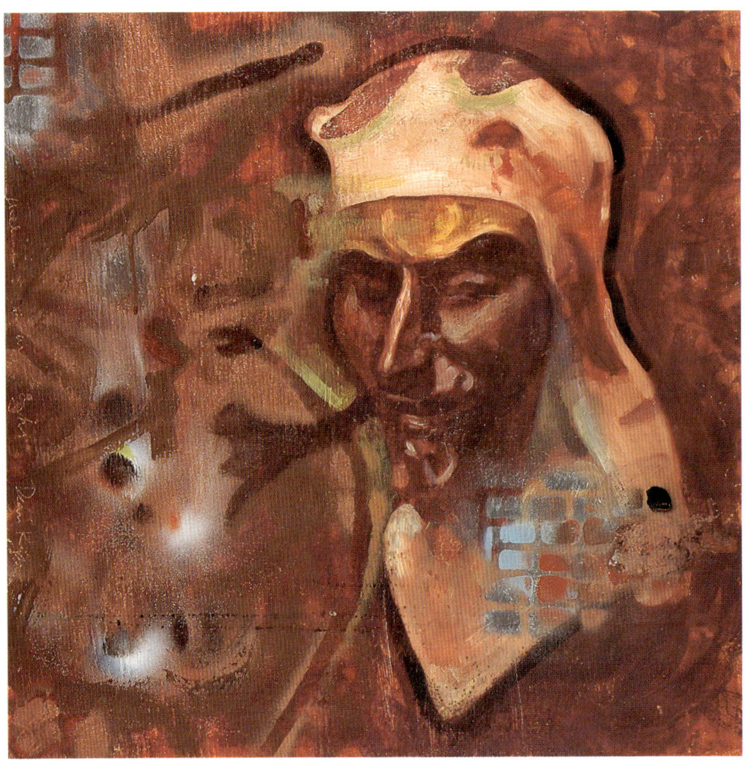

William S. Burroughs and Dean Ripa,
The Ambiguous Smile of the Tempter, 1990, cat. no. 91

William S. Burroughs and John Giorno,
That Gun's Got Blood in Its Hole, 1991, cat. no. 86

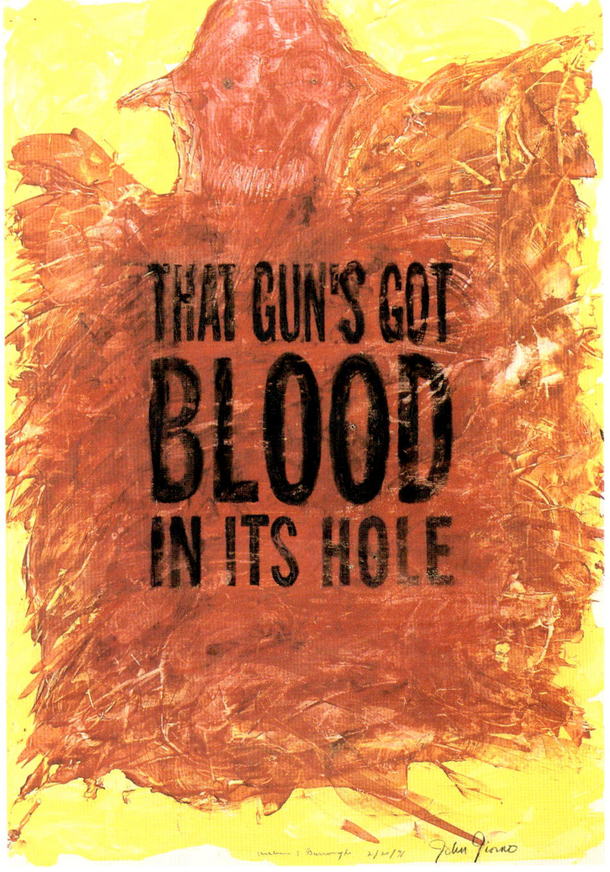

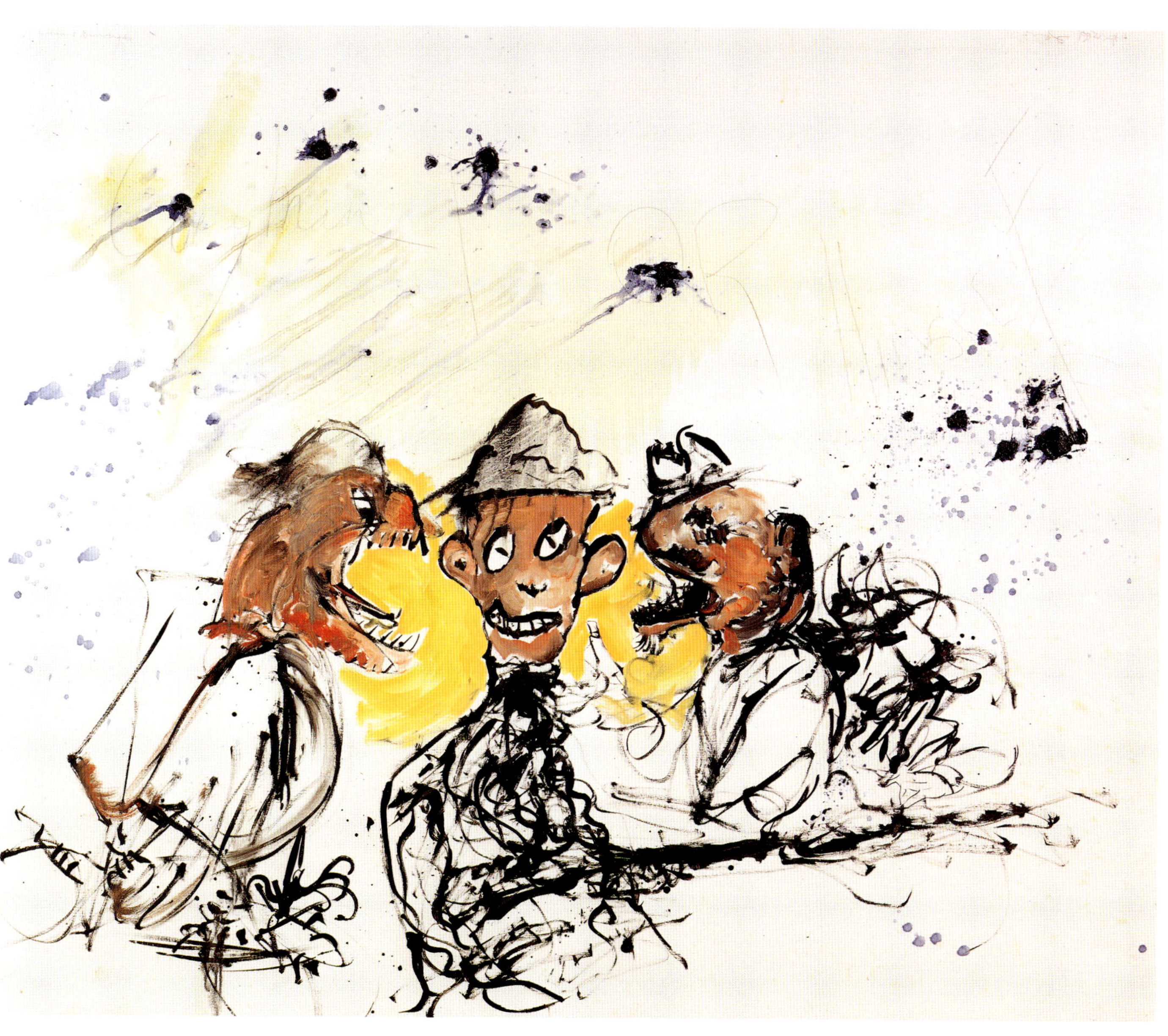

William S. Burroughs and George Condo, **Every Man for Himself**, 1992, cat. no. 93

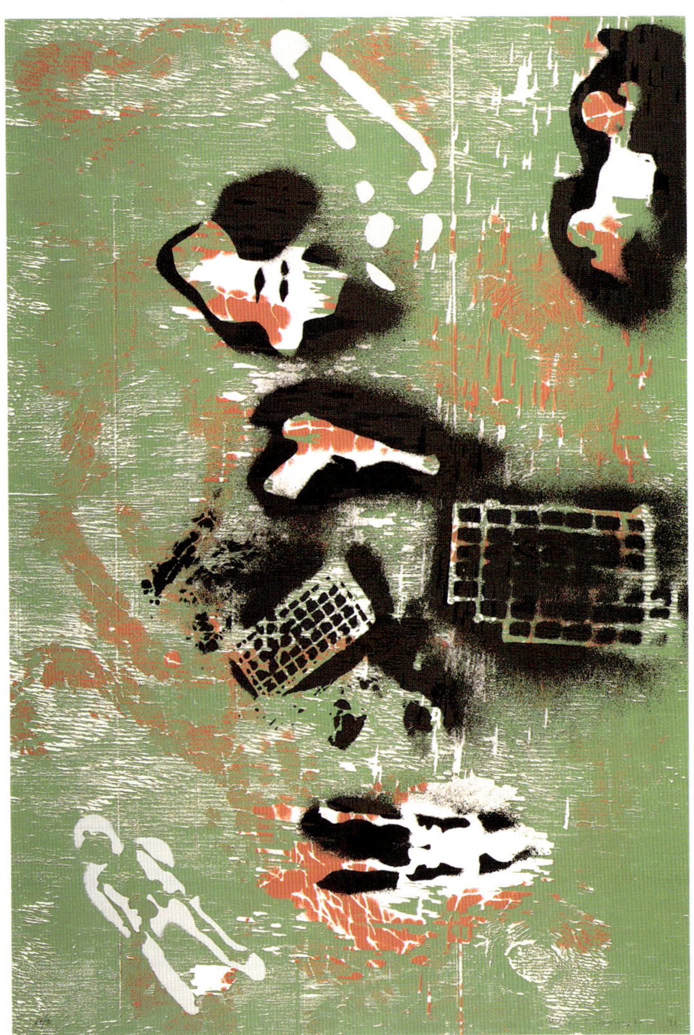

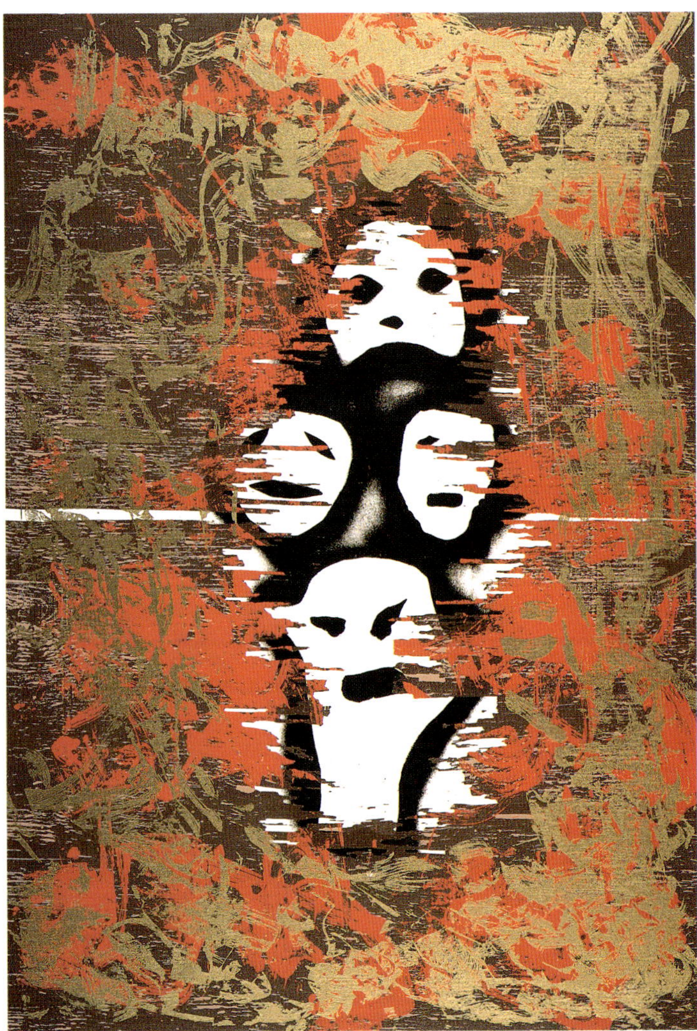

William S. Burroughs, **Envy**, from **The Seven Deadly Sins**, 1992, cat. no. 63

William S. Burroughs, **Gluttony**, from **The Seven Deadly Sins**, 1992, cat. no. 64

Burroughs teamed up with a friend, the artist and expert marksman David Bradshaw, and produced *Propagation Hazard*, a steel-cased portfolio of lithographic prints published by Graphicstudio of the University of South Florida in 1993. Burroughs's prints are adapted from his paintings of the time, and Bradshaw's are target lithographs shot by him for the final edition. And, in 1995, Burroughs joined with computer animator Roger Holden in producing a series of computer-generated stereograms, created by digitally scanning a detail of one of Burroughs's paintings into a computer, color-enhancing it, and printing it with a laser printer. When viewed with relaxed and slightly crossed eyes, the three-dimensional effects of these "cybernetic cut-ups" form imaginary landscapes of extreme intricacy and depth not unlike those imagined works described by Burroughs in 1981 as made by "some lost color process…used to transfer three-dimensional holograms onto the…pages. You ache to look at these colors."[333]

David Bradshaw, **Blue Sharpshooter**, from **Propagation Hazard**, 1993, cat. no. 94

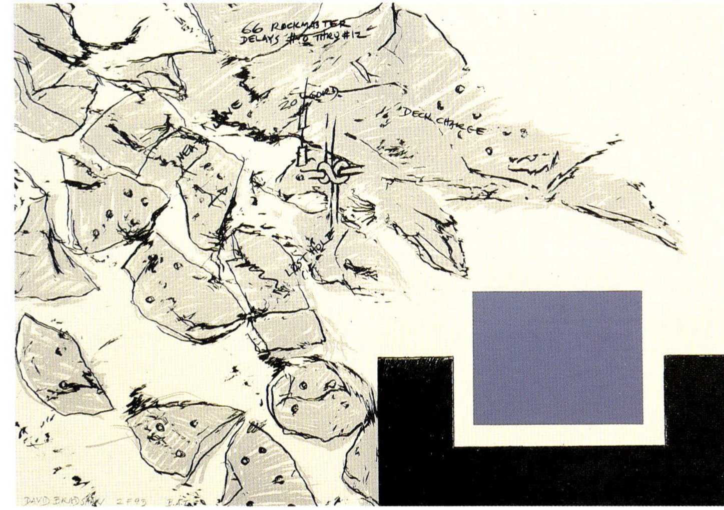

William S. Burroughs and Roger Holden, untitled, 1995, cat. no. 95

323
Burroughs, "Introduction," in Giorno, *You Got to Burn to Shine* (note **4**), 4.

324
According to Sidney Felsen, in conversation with the author, July 12, 1995.

325
Keith Haring, quoted in Gruen, *Keith Haring* (note **295**), 55.

326
Ibid., 58.

327
Grauerholz, "On Burroughs' Art" (note **24**), x.

328
Timothy Leary, quoted in Gruen, *Keith Haring* (note **295**), 185.

329
Burroughs, quoted in ibid., 183.

330
Hebdige, "Welcome to the Terrordome" (note **217**), 63.

331
Klaus Kertess, "Brushes with Beatitude," in Marshall, *Jean-Michel Basquiat* (note **217**), 53. The sketchbook containing Burroughs's and Ginsberg's contributions has not been located in the artist's estate as yet.

332
Ibid., 80.

333
Burroughs, *Cities of the Red Night* (note **288**), 167. The title "cybernetic cut-ups" was coined by Holden in a letter to the author, June 15, 1995.

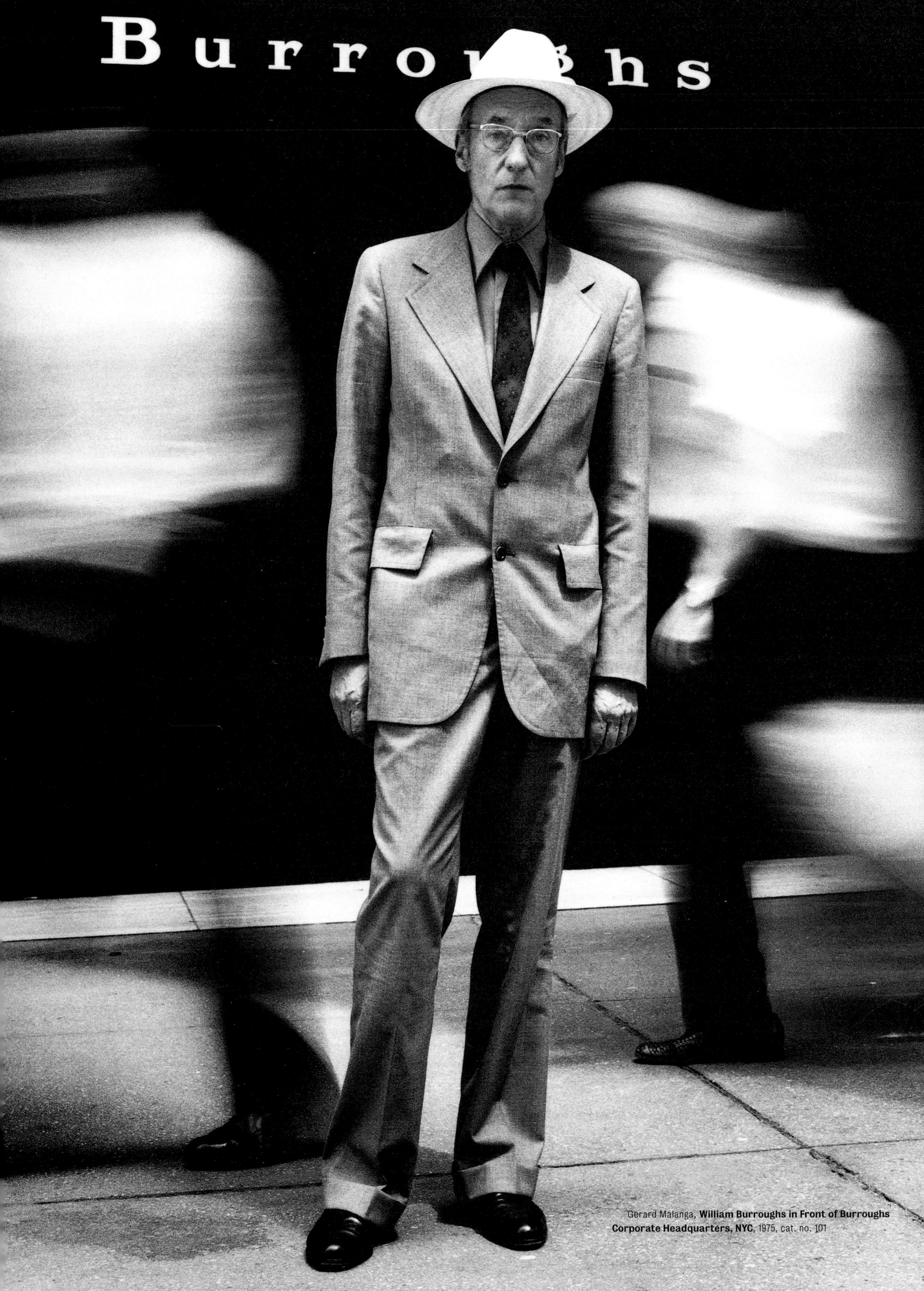

Gerard Malanga, **William Burroughs in Front of Burroughs Corporate Headquarters, NYC**, 1975, cat. no. 101

XV
EL HOMBRE INVISIBLE

The whole secret is intent.[334]

In his self-appointed role as an agent provocateur, Burroughs has been fascinated with masks and disguises: Clem and Jody dressed in Stetsons and red suspenders, "Happy Cloak" addicts wearing Venusian skins, Audrey Carsons in a "Charro costume," Kim Carsons selecting a disguise to return to the New World, the drug-pusher as a priest, and, of course, the hipster in a three-piece banker's suit. Disguises are used to conceal one's identity, presence, and behavior; they allow the wearer to travel stealthily and perform his operations unseen. Ultimately, however, the best disguise is none at all; Burroughs describes it as the "Walk Exercise":

Basically it consists in taking a walk with the continuity and perceptions you encounter. The original version of this exercise was taught me by an old Mafia Don in Columbus, Ohio: seeing everyone on the street before he sees you.[...]Generally speaking, if you see other people before they see you, they *won't* see you. I have even managed to get past a whole block of guides and shoeshine boys in Tangier this way, thus earning my Moroccan monicker: "El Hombre Invisible."[335]

Burroughs has conducted himself in precisely the fashion of a shy and retiring surveillance agent, quietly gathering the facts, penetrating the most hardened defenses of cultural "Control," and reporting the details back from the front lines. Like the Invisible Man in the H. G. Wells novel, his invisibility allows him to approach and withdraw without anyone noticing. Like the "spy" described by Jasper Johns in 1965, he is an artist who "must be ready to 'move,' must be aware of his entrances and exits....must remember and must remember himself and his remembering....The spy designs himself to be overlooked."[336] Artists and writers may function as spies of sorts, but if their reports make enough of an impact, exert enough of an influence, or change the course of affairs, they become much more akin to an agent runner who directs other spies. And, according to the fictional spy George Smiley, "it is the business of agent runners to turn themselves into legends."[337]

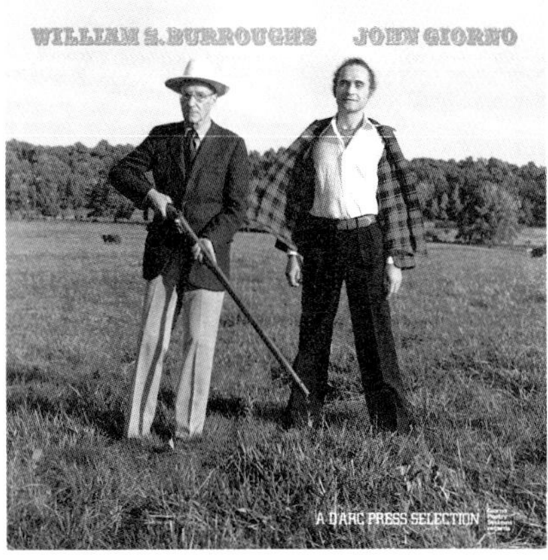

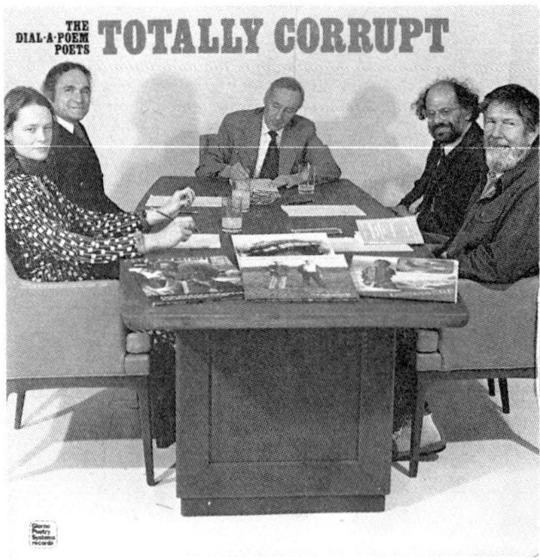

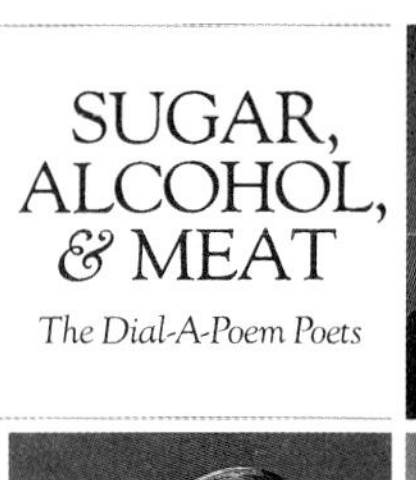

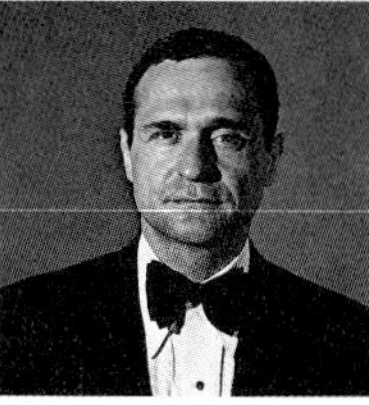

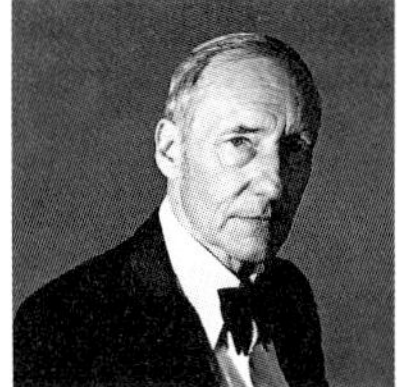

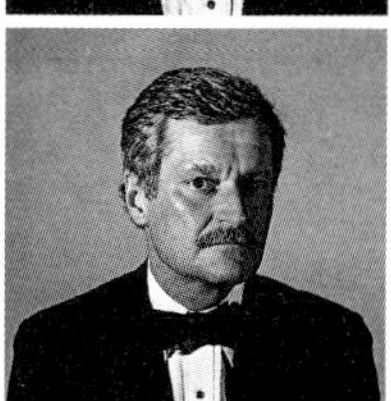

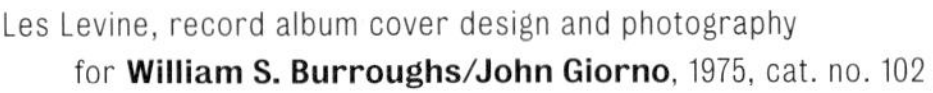

Les Levine, record album cover design and photography for **William S. Burroughs/John Giorno**, 1975, cat. no. 102

Les Levine, record album cover design and photography for **Totally Corrupt**, 1976, cat. no. 103

Robert Mapplethorpe, record album photography for **Sugar, Alcohol, and Meat**, 1980, cat. no. 108

William S. Burroughs the legend is hardly invisible by the end of the twentieth century. To be sure, there are many photographs of this agent from his early days: photographs by Gysin, by Sommerville, and by Ginsberg. For the most part, these were kept from mass circulation, appeared only in underground publications, and many have only surfaced in the last decades. Starting in the mid-1970s, however, a certain amount of fame began to surround his exploits and achievements. In 1975 he was photographed by both the fashion photographer Richard Avedon and the conceptual artist Les Levine. He is pictured (sometimes alone but more often in groups) on record and cassette albums brought out by John Giorno as part of the *Dial-a-Poem Poets* series, and appears in the crowd on the cover of The Beatles's *Sgt. Pepper's Lonely Hearts Club Band* album. By the late 1970s photographic artists Robert Mapplethorpe and Andy Warhol were arranging portrait sessions with him. In 1984 Howard Brookner released a documentary film of his life and times. By the mid-1990s he had sat for portraits by David Hockney, Gottfried Helnwein, and Kate Simon, had been photographed by Annie Leibovitz for *Vanity Fair*, and had seen his face appear on public posters advertising denim shirts, on public billboards promoting cross-training athletic shoes, and on clothing labels for chino pants manufactured in East Los Angeles.

Similarly during the same span of years, Burroughs's face appeared in works of art that were not exactly documentary. In 1976 French collagist Cozette de Charmoy and photographer François Lagarde collaborated on the portfolio *Poste Vaticane*, comprising a suite of fictive, international postage stamps with Burroughs's portrait replacing the likenesses of Boy Scouts or the Statue of Liberty, or included along with Gysin's as some heroes of Moroccan history. In the same year de Charmoy recombined many of these stamps in larger collages surrounded by typescripts and lettering that played on the word "post." A young David Wojnarowicz included a photomechanical portrait of Burroughs in a collage entitled *Bill Burroughs' Recurring Dream* in 1978, enmeshing the subject

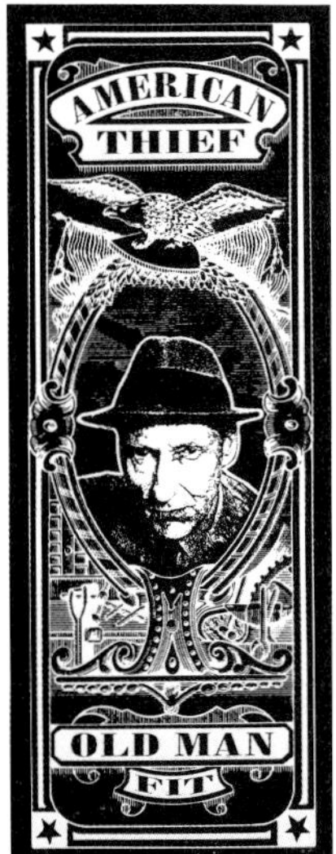

American Thief, a.k.a. Gypsies and Thieves, **Old Man Fit**, 1994, cat. no. 123

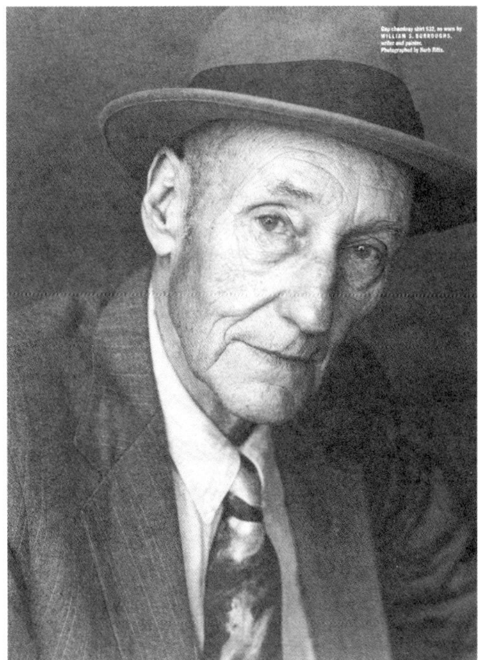

Herb Ritts, **William S. Burroughs**, 1990, cat. no. 116

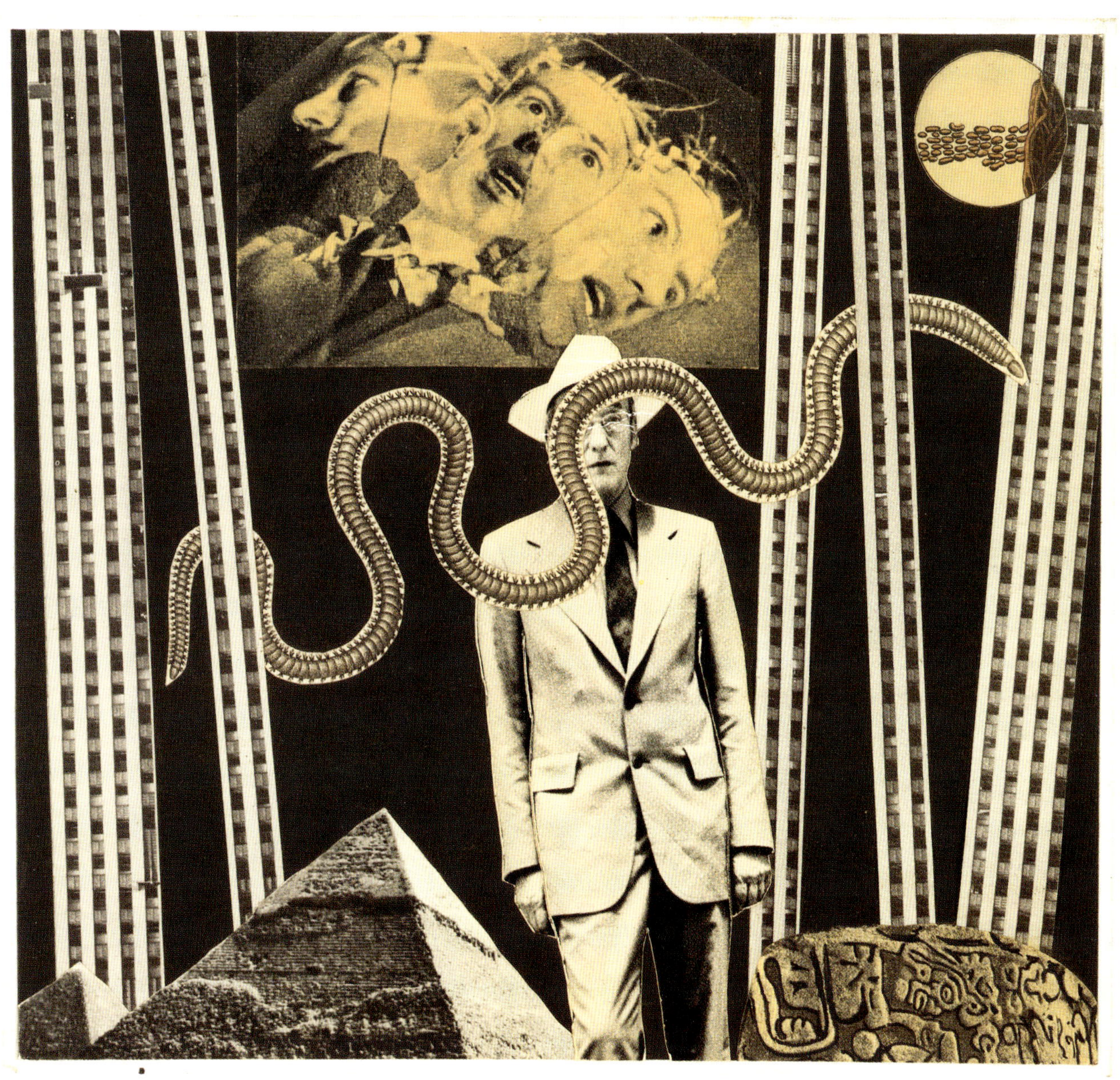

David Wojnarowicz, **Bill Burroughs' Recurring Dream**, 1978, cat. no. 106

within a landscape of infinitely tall skyscrapers and Egyptian pyramids. Above him is a chronophotographic image of an unidentified subject undergoing some undisclosed cerebral experiment while a giant centipede meanders across Burroughs's image, probably a reference to the many fantasy images of centipedes and "centipede death" found in his novels. In the mid-1980s Burroughs again surfaces in a number of drawings by his friend and associate David Bradshaw, this time displaying the subject's penchant for shooting guns and knife throwing.

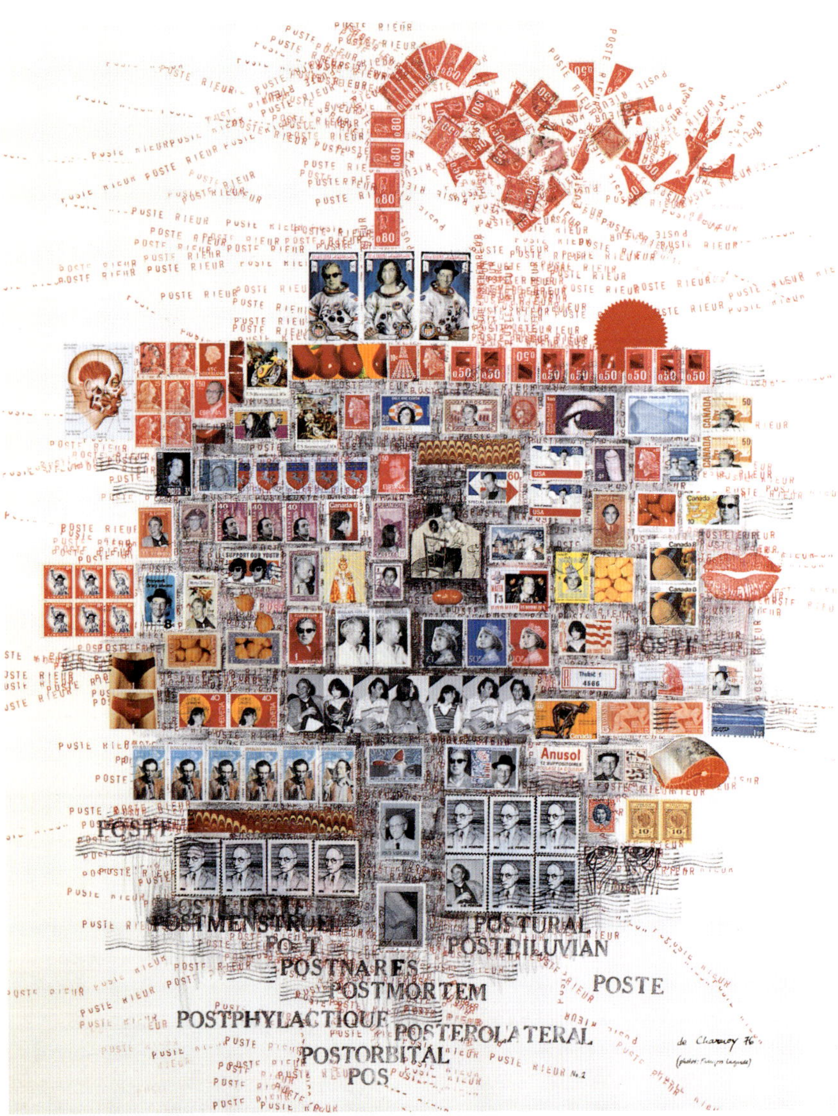

Cozette de Charmoy, untitled, 1976, cat. no. 104

His likeness can be found among portraits of famous males in history in a series of hand-altered Polaroid SX-70 prints by Rick McKee Hock; Burroughs is located in the sixth horizontal row and third vertical column and is associated with, among others, Albrecht Dürer, Charles Baudelaire, and Hulk Hogan. Burroughs's face is, again, encountered screenprinted across a large canvas and overpainted by the German artist Walter Dahn in 1989. Two years later Christof Kohlhofer, a German-born painter working out of Los Angeles, made a number of circular "tabletop" paintings, at least one of which contains a vaguely recognizable likeness of Burroughs amid references to a missing Mark Twain manuscript and the U.S. involvement in the Gulf War. New Orleans artist Frances Swigart paid homage to Burroughs, his writings, and the master printmaker Jon Webb and his Loujon Press in her *Ursulines* (1993). By 1995 numerous artists had graphically portrayed Burroughs, either in formal portraits or in caricature—such artists as Alison Van Pelt, Humberto Jardón, and caricaturist Ralph Steadman. Clearly this agent has, over the course of two decades, blown his cover as "El Hombre Invisible."

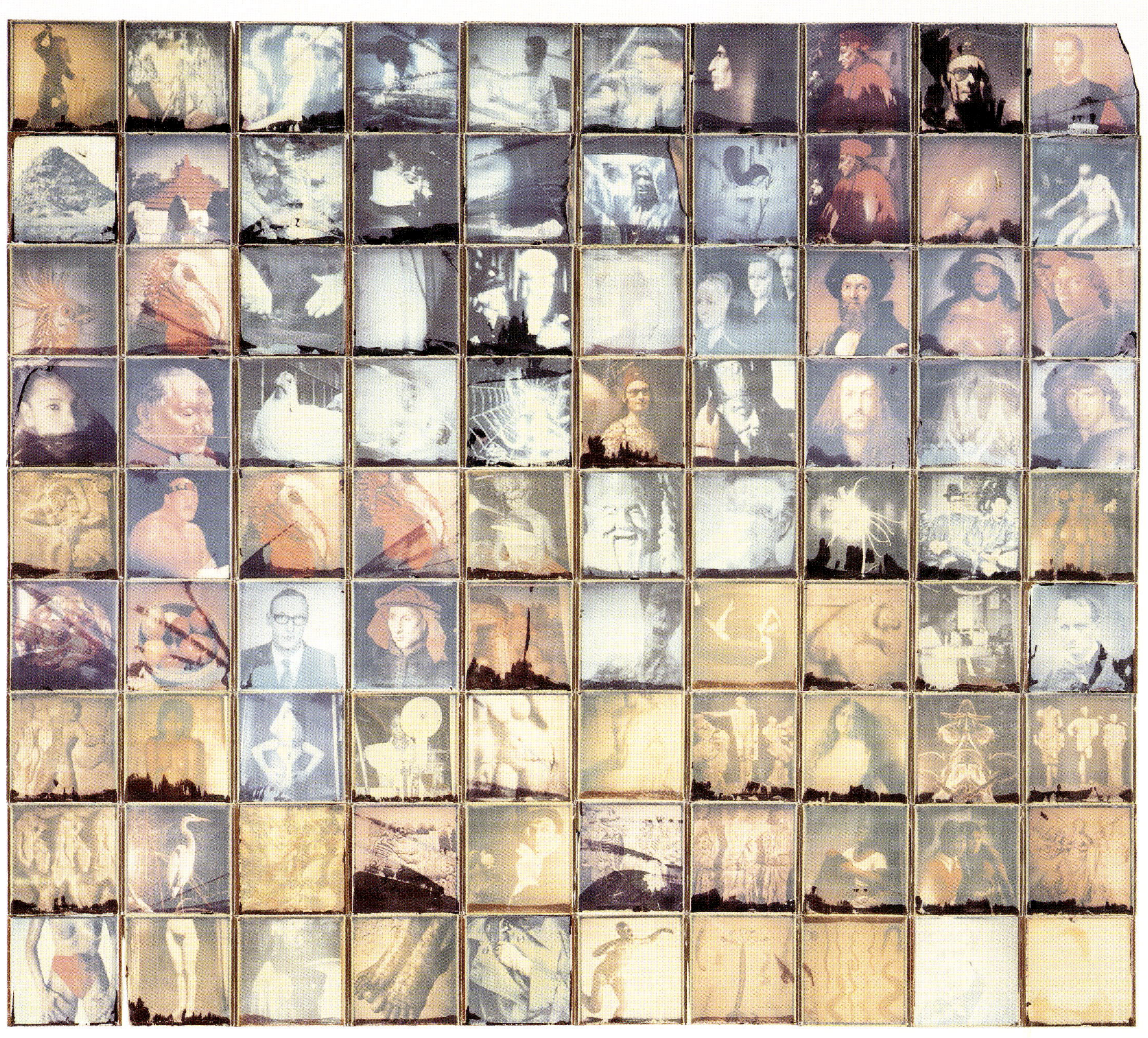

Rick McKee Hock, **Codex (Burroughs)**, 1987, cat. no. 113

Images--millions of images--That's what I eat--Cyclotron shit--Ever try kicking that habit wit the images of sex acts and torture ever took place anywhere and I can just blast i the molecule--I got orgasms--I got screams--I got all the images any hick poet ever shit out--My Power's coming-- My Power's coming--My Power's coming--... And I got millions and millions and millions of images of Me, Me, Me, meee.

Nova Express

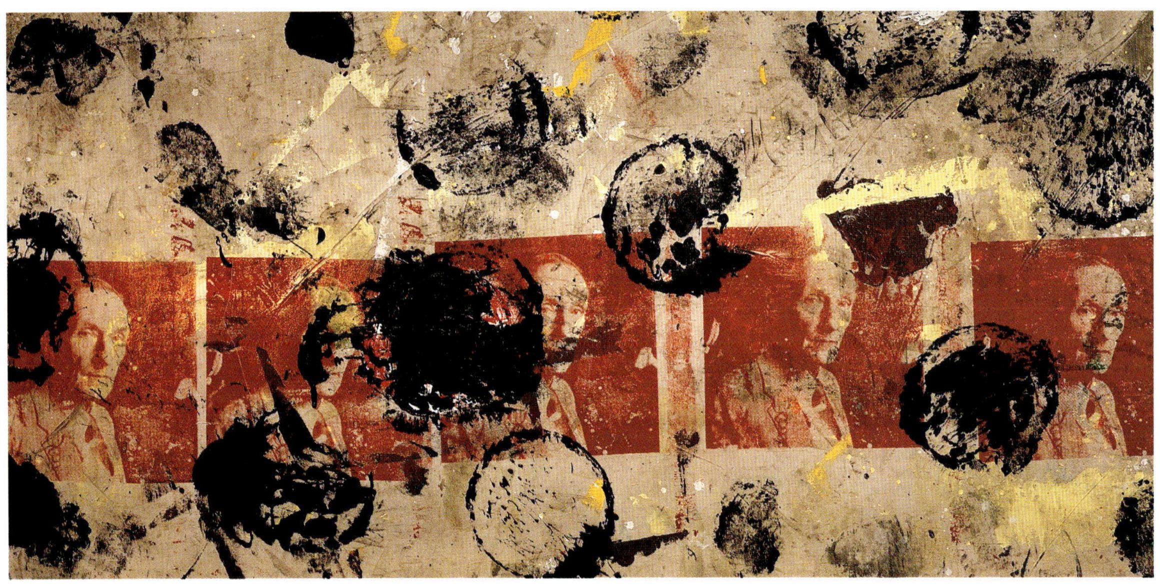

Walter Dahn, **William Burroughs**, 1989, cat. no. 114

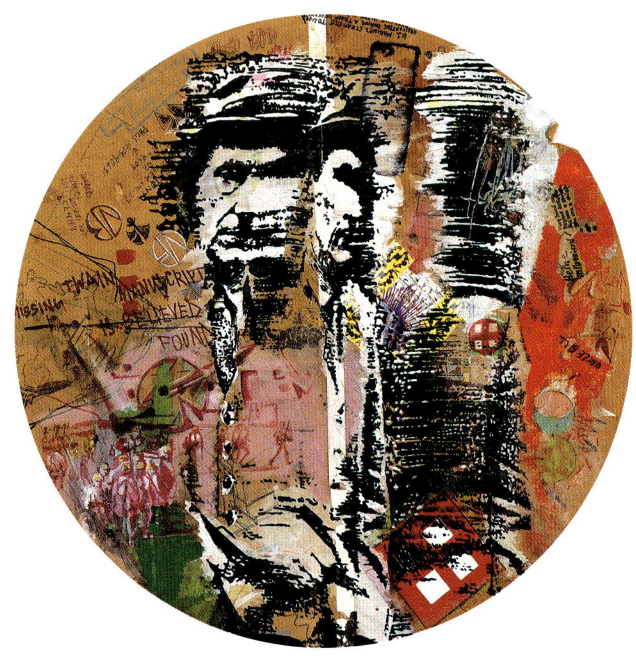

Christof Kohlhofer, **W. S. Burroughs and G.I.'s at the Persian Gulf Getting Ready for Take Off, News of the Day: Mark Twain's Lost Manuscript Found, Mixed Media on Shopping Bags**, 1991, cat. no. 117

omorphine?--Now I got all
ut and control you gooks right down to

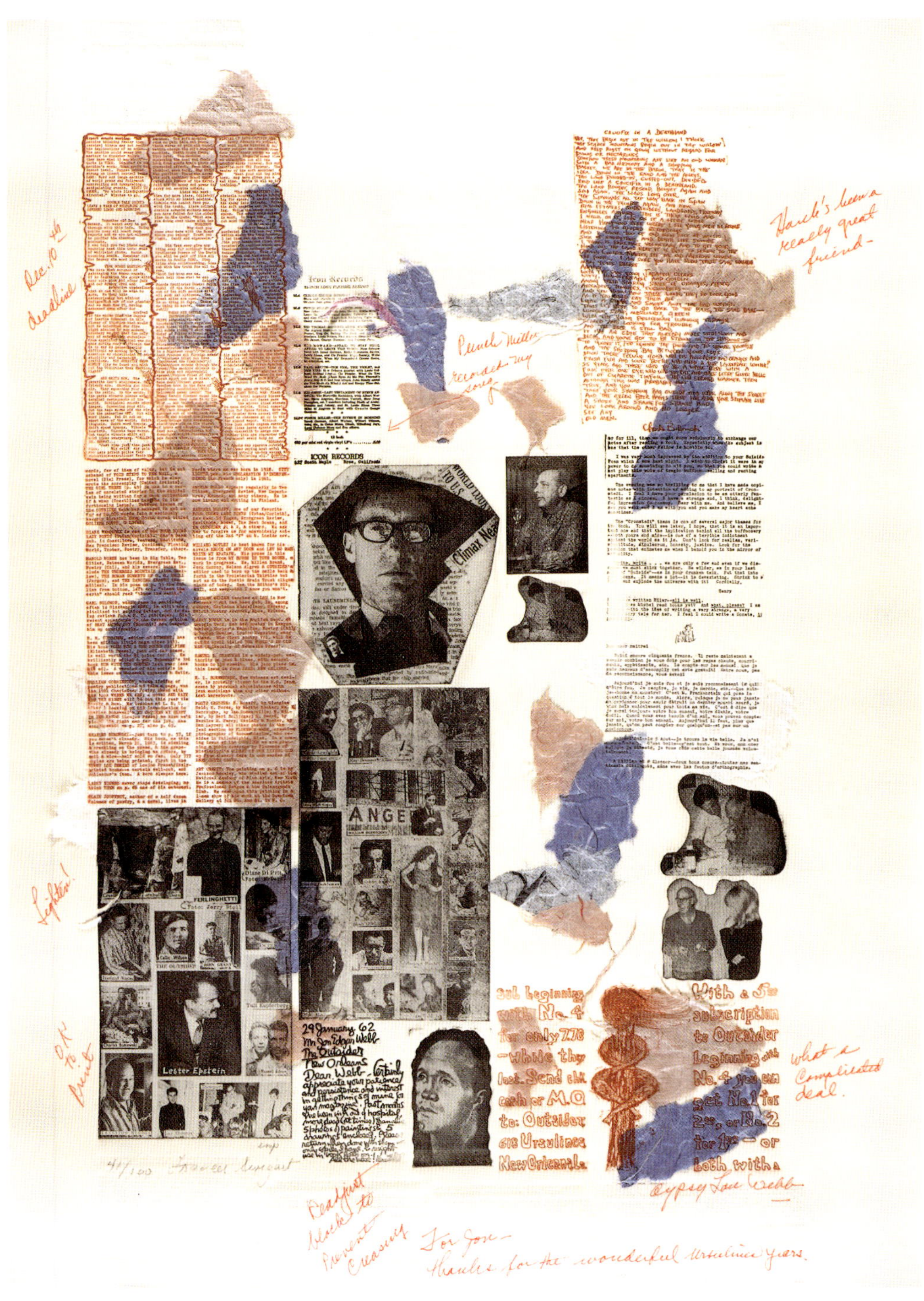

Frances Swigart, **Ursulines**, 1993, cat. no. 121

Alison Van Pelt, **William Burroughs**, 1992, cat. no. 118

Humberto Jardón, **Feliz Cumpleaños**, 1994, cat. no. 122

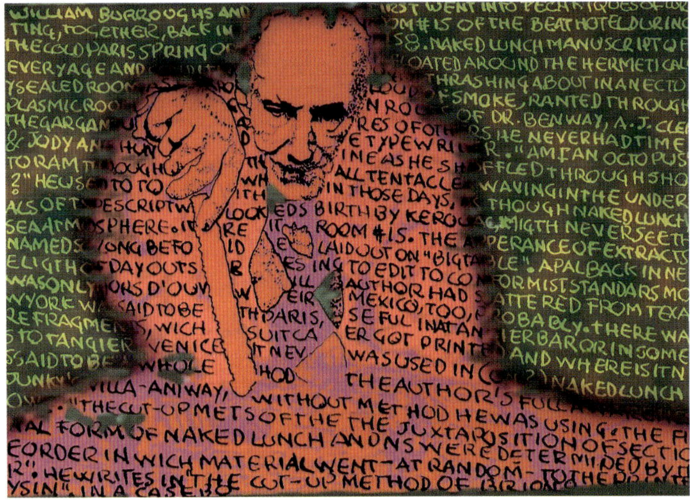

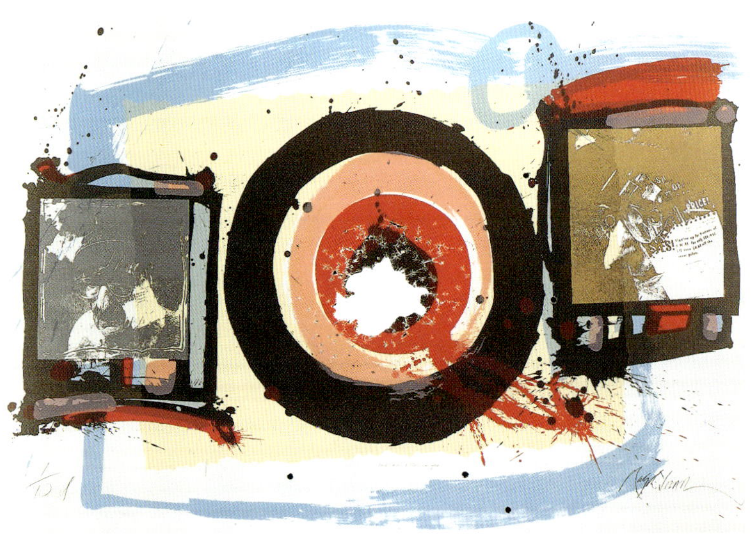

Ralph Steadman, **Something New Has Been Added**, 1995, cat. no. 124

Like an unobserved virus that continually replicates itself, however, Burroughs's justifiably paranoid reports on Control, his tactical operations with chance, his various artistic strategies, and his legendary status have quietly insinuated themselves into the general fabric of the culture. There are certain instances that are clearly the result of some direct intervention by the agent. Illustrator and artist Thomi Wroblewski has visualized Burroughs's visions in his concepts for the covers of the writer's British publications by John Calder and Picador throughout the 1980s. German writers Jürgen Ploog, Carl Weissner, and Jörg Fauser had adopted Burroughs's cut-up technique by the early 1970s and have witnessed a resurgence of interest in it in recent years.[338] Rudy Rucker's science-fiction novels contain numerous references from "flickercladders" and a

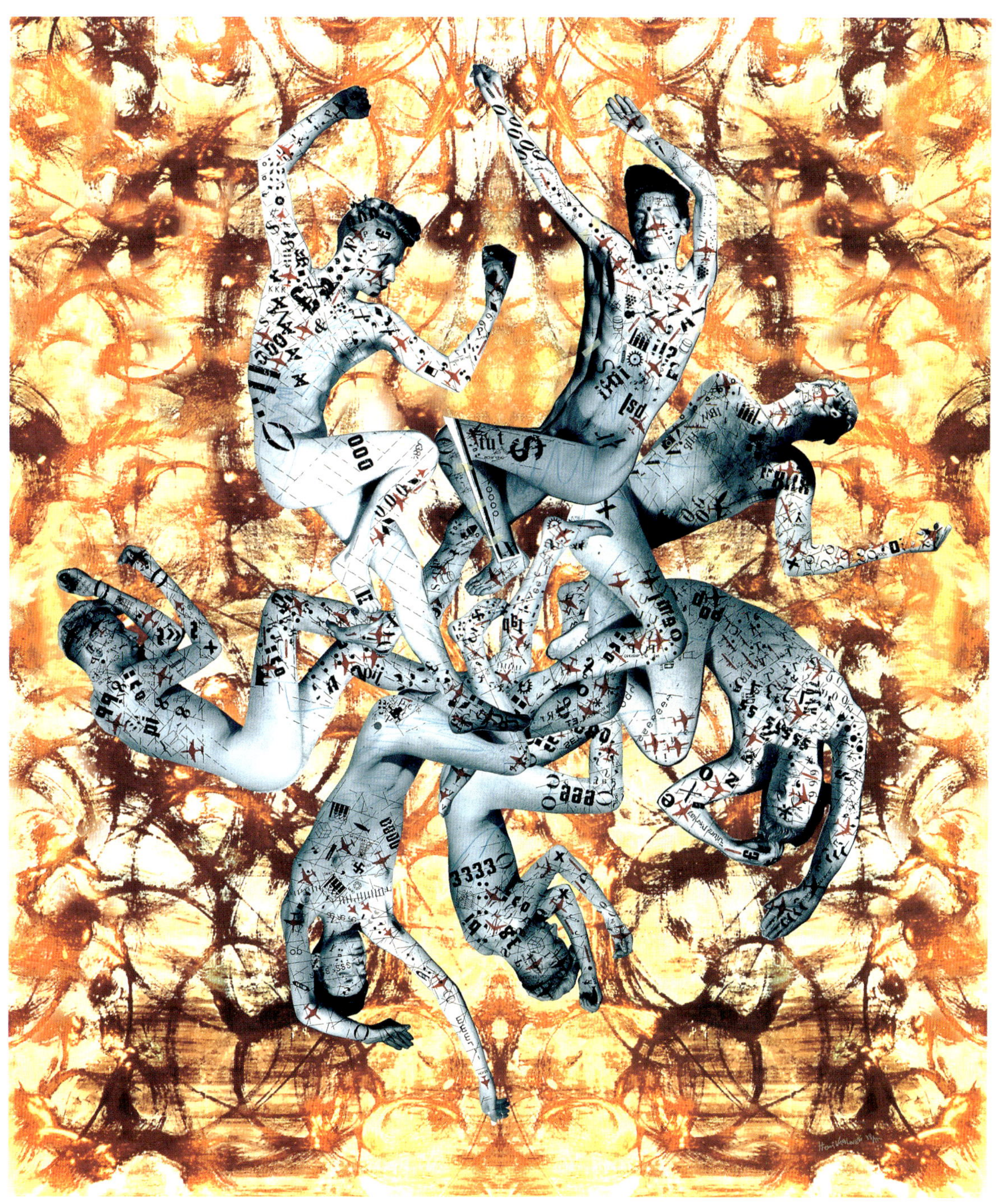

Thomi Wroblewski, **Wild Boys**, 1988, cat. no. 148

gaunt addict wearing a fedora to "happy cloaks" and even a Dr. Benway.[339] The Irish rock group U2's lead singer Bono could describe the band's latest project as "pure Burroughs" to Allen Ginsberg.[340] The musical group Future Sound of London contains "viral strains of an alien fiction" and "Burroughs' insect consciousness."[341]

New York artist Warren Neidich portrayed a fictive, eighteenth-century gentleman reading *Cities of the Red Night* in his *American History Reinvented* series (1984–85). Los Angeles-based artist John Boskovich has paid homage to Burroughs and the Beats on a number of occasions and has included the question "Who is the third who walks always beside you?" in his *Portrait of the Artist and His Dog* (1989). Tyler Stallings's *Cyborg Blossoms* (1994) contains dot-matrix-printed texts that are patently Burroughs inspired, filled as they are with images of alien abductions, alien sex, and biological warfare.[342] Director David Cronenberg's films, exclusive of his *Naked Lunch*, are fundamentally (and admittedly) founded in Burroughs: from the orgiastic sexuality and parasite infestations of *Shivers* (1975) and *Rabid* (1976) to the exploding minds and the biological morphings of humans and machines in *Scanners* (1980) and *Videodrome* (1982).[343]

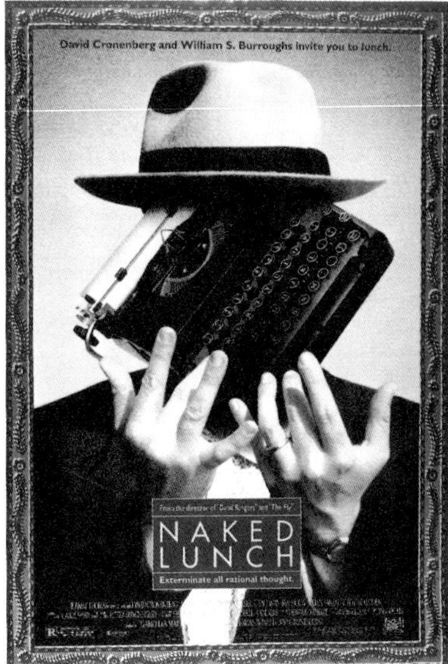

Steven Twigger, **Naked Lunch**, 1991, cat. no. 147

In general, however, it is difficult to trace any direct involvement with Burroughs in the majority of cases. Laurie Anderson's *New York Times (Horizontal), China Times (Vertical)—1971* (1976) may not be consciously derived from Burroughs, but in its deconstruction of the newspaper pages and in its fragmentation of texts and images the strategy is pure Burroughs by an artist who has frankly acknowledged his importance.[344] Ridley Scott's film *Alien* (1979) and its production design by H. R. Giger may be derived in part from Burroughs's *The Soft Machine* where,

Carl walked a long row of living penis urns made from men whose penis has absorbed the body with vestigial arms and legs breathing through purple fungoid gills and dropping a slow metal excrement like melted solder forms a solid plaque under the urns stand about three feet high on rusty iron shelves wire mesh cubicles joined by catwalks and ladders a vast warehouse of living penis urns slowly transmuting to smooth red terra cotta. Others secrete from the head crystal pearls of lubricant that forms a shell of solid crystal over the red penis flesh.[345]

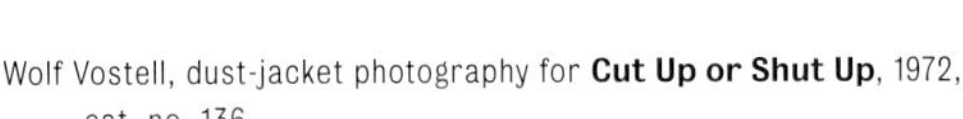
Wolf Vostell, dust-jacket photography for **Cut Up or Shut Up**, 1972, cat. no. 136

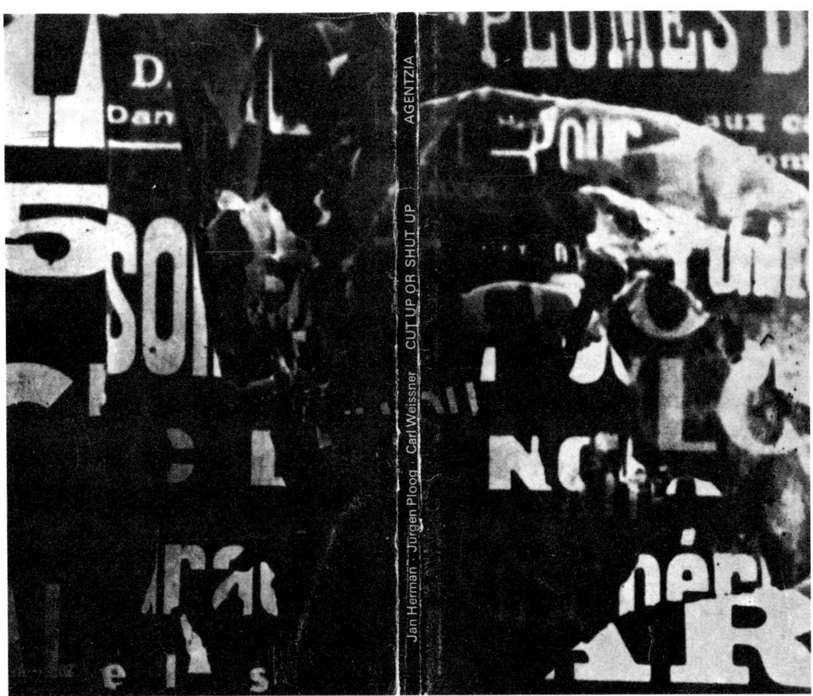

Warren Neidich, **Cities of the Red Night**, 1984–85, cat. no. 141

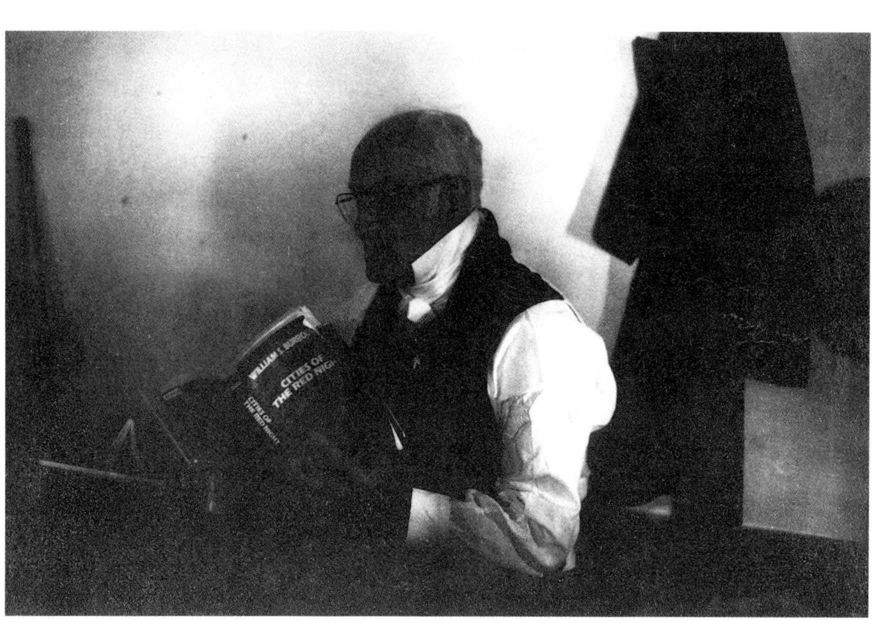

Who is the third who walks always beside you?
when I count, there are only you and I together

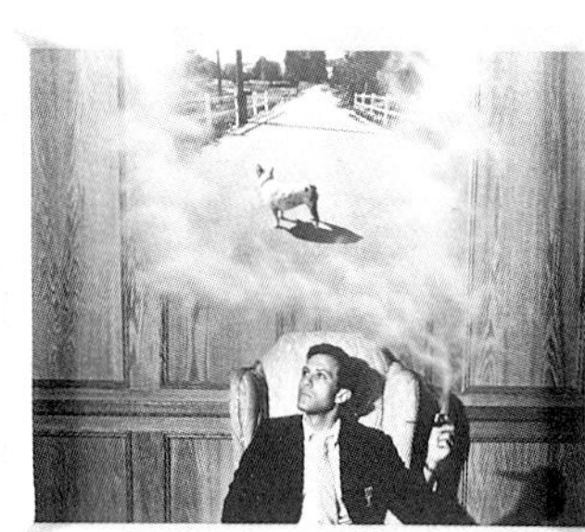

John Boskovich, **Portrait of the Artist and His Dog**, 1989, cat. no. 146

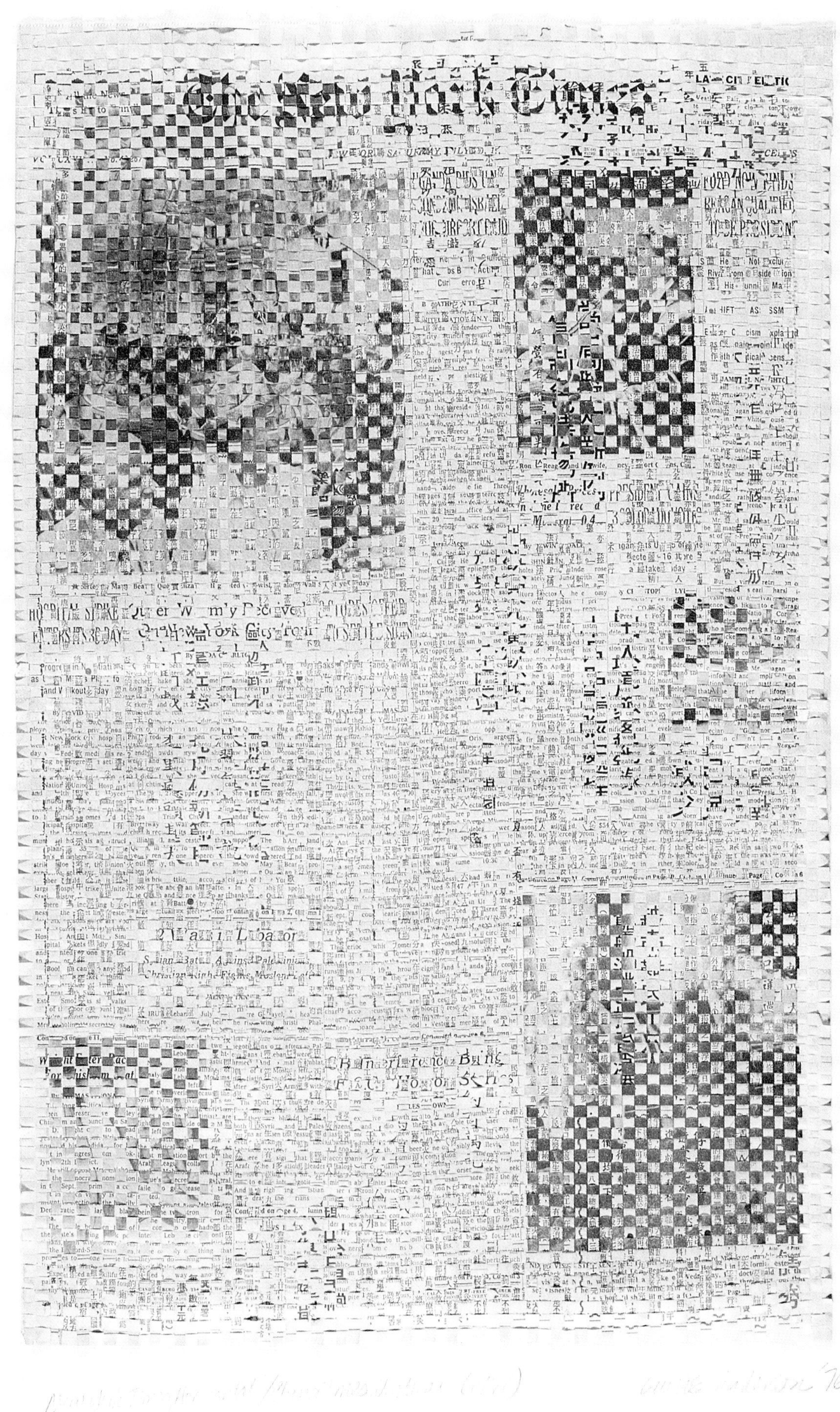

Laurie Anderson, **New York Times (Horizontal), China Times (Vertical)—1971**, 1976, cat. no. 138

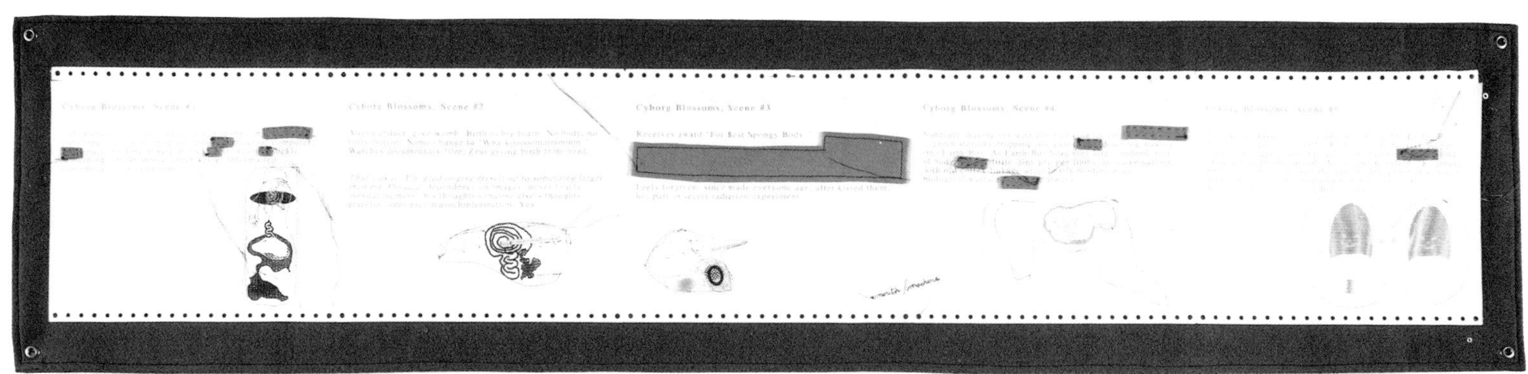

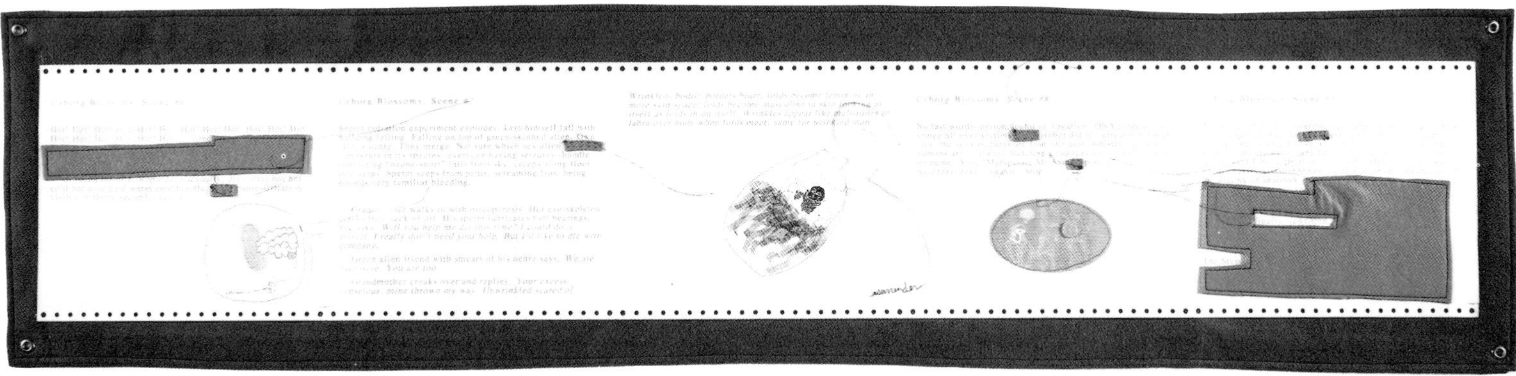

Tyler Stallings, **Cyborg Blossoms, Scenes 1–9** (diptych), 1994, cat. no. 152

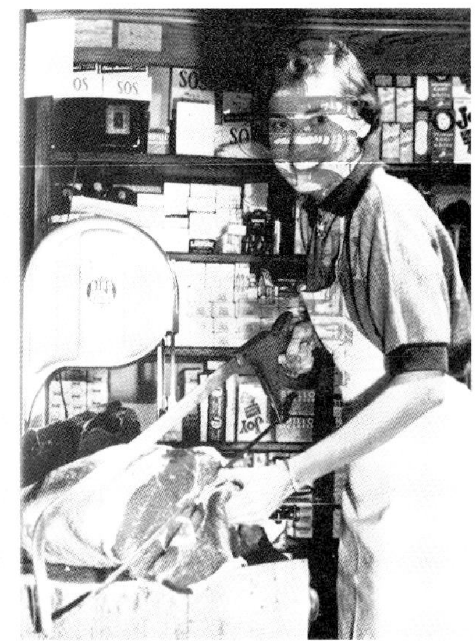

Christof Kohlhofer, **Vogue Interzone**, 1993, cat. no. 151

A quintessential Nova detective, android "replicants," and floating organs in the same director's *Blade Runner* (1982) may be derived as well from the corpus of Burroughs's early fiction, while the title itself is taken from his unproduced futuristic screenplay about black-market medical care.[346]

Novelist William Gibson's neuromancer (who "jacked into a custom cyberspace deck that projected his disembodied consciousness into the consensual hallucination that was the matrix"), the entropic landscapes in his *Virtual Light*, as well as his dependence on randomness may all be inspired by Burroughs.[347] Bruce Cannon's *Subjective Object III* (1994) utilizes a computer speech chip to randomly permutate such simple word strings as "I think therefore I am," just as Gysin and Burroughs had done by other means. Moreover no one would suggest that the phenomenon of computer viruses derives directly from Burroughs, but his concept of "information that subverts control" surely can be seen as prophetic now. Also Burroughsesque are the attempts of "hypermedia," "hypertext," and computer-based "html" (hypertext markup language) software to simulate the mind's "continuous linking and restructuring of images from the past, present and future; from the real and the imaginary; from the internal and external realms of experience."[348]

Burroughs's example has been one of endurance. Around 1959 Burroughs wrote to his friend Alan Ansen: "I am tired of sitting behind the lines with an imperfect recording device receiving inaccurate bulletins....I must reach the Front."[349] Four and a half decades later, he has become novelist Norman Mailer's "genius," speculative-fiction author J. G. Ballard's "mythmaker of the twentieth century," painter Keith Haring's role model, fashion model Lauren Hutton's "greatest living writer," rock idol Kurt Cobain's idol, and cyberpunk critic R. U. Sirius's Shakespeare.[350] For art columnist and writer Glenn O'Brien, he is the old man who says image is a virus and who spreads a contagion that is "a blend of witty bacteria and elegant viruses that evokes unknown causes, ancient myths, and a roster of exquisitely wrought maladies gently nourished and passed down over the ages from generation to generation."[351] The critic and curator Klaus Kertess views him as the "wry high priest of the youthful counterculture that carnivaled and protested from the late 1960s through the 1970s."[352] This grandpa from hell is in the movies and on television, on MTV as well as NBC, and appears in commercial advertising for Gap shirts and Nike footware. Documentaries are made of him and at least one of his novels has been turned into a feature film. His voice can be heard in the latest contemporary opera and is embedded in the latest hip-hop music. His techniques have been transformed into those of hypertext and morphing and his fantasies incorporated into contemporary films. Given all of this, it would be safe to conclude that Burroughs has always been at the front.

In 1967 Burroughs met Jasper Johns in London and asked him "what painting was all about—what are painters really doing?"[353] Johns apparently countered with another question, asking Burroughs what writing is about. "I did not have an answer then," Burroughs later wrote, "I have an answer now: The purpose of writing is to make it happen."

What we call "art"—painting, sculpture, writing, dance, music—is magical in origin. That is, it was originally employed for ceremonial purposes to produce very definite effects. In the world of magic nothing happens unless someone wants it to happen, *wills* it to happen, and there are certain magical formulae to channel and direct the will. The artist is trying to make something happen in the mind of the viewer or reader.[354]

In both literature and the arts Burroughs is an example of fecund creativity. He has worked in fiction, painting, text-image collages, shotgun art, films, tape experiments, music, and video. With his theories of chaos and control, his willingness to extend his ideas as far as they need to go, and his irreverent disregard of definitions, genres, pigeonholes, and physical materials, Burroughs has left his mark on the culture of the late twentieth century. Fearlessly he has armed himself with chance and randomness, embraced his dreams and imagination, and faced the bleakest of visions with humor and wit. "If you're still there after the fear," he wrote in 1978, "then you got the courage, baby, that's all. If you're not, then you're dead."[355] Indisputably William S. Burroughs has made it happen.

334
Burroughs, *Painting and Guns* (note **171**), 49; Burroughs here is citing Castaneda's don Juan.

335
Burroughs, "Ten Years and a Billion Dollars," *The Adding Machine* (note **12**), 50.

336
Jasper Johns, "Sketchbook Notes," *Art and Literature*, no. 4 (spring 1965): 187.

337
John Le Carré, *Tinker, Tailor, Soldier, Spy* (New York: Alfred A. Knopf, 1974), 191.

338
According to Jürgen Ploog, "For some reason there is a new and mysterious interest in cut-ups here. Writers and artists are asking what it is.... This after twenty years of uninterrupted practice on my part." In a letter to the author, December 8, 1994.

339
See Rudy Rucker, *Master of Space and Time* (New York: Baen Books, 1984), 7; and his *Wetware*, in *Live Robots* (New York: Avon Books, 1994), 207, 292, 324.

340
Reported by Ginsberg, in conversation with the author, March 6, 1995.

341
Chris Campion, "Future Sound of London Psyche Out," *Mondo 2000*, 13 (1995): 78.

342
Tyler Stallings, "Cyborg Blossoms," in Robert Reynolds and Thomas Zummer, eds., *Crash: Nostalgia for the Absence of Cyberspace*, exh. cat. (New York: Thread Waxing Space, 1994), 17–18.

343
David Cronenberg, *Cronenberg on Cronenberg*, ed. Chris Rodley (London: Faber and Faber, 1992).

344
Laurie Anderson, lecture, Institute of Contemporary Art, University of Pennsylvania, Philadelphia, November 18, 1983; to the author's suggestion that similarities to Burroughs could be found in her humor, political stance, and techniques, Anderson replied, "You're right: Burroughs!"; letter to the author, January 10, 1984.

345
Burroughs, *The Soft Machine* (note **56**), 108–9.

346
William S. Burroughs, *Blade Runner, a Movie* (Berkeley: Blue Wind Press, 1990); according to Grauerholz, in conversation with the author November 29, 1995, Burroughs had read and was inspired by a science-fiction novel entitled *The Bladerunner* written by Alan E. Nourse.

347
William Gibson, *Neuromancer* (New York: Ace Books, 1984), 5; for the landscape in *Virtual Light* (New York: Bantam Books, 1993), cf. *The Soft Machine* (note **56**), 115–19; on randomness, see Laurence B. Chollet, "William Gibson's Second Sight," *Los Angeles Times Magazine* (September 12, 1993), 36.

348
Julian Dibbell, "Viruses Are Good for You," *Wired* 3, no. 2 (February 1995): 132; see also George P. Landow and Paul Delany, "Hypertext, Hypermedia and Literary Studies: The State of the Art," in *Hypermedia and Literary Studies* (Cambridge: MIT Press, 1994), 8.

349
Burroughs, quoted in Alan Ansen, "Anyone Who Can Pick Up a Frying Pan Owns Death," *Big Table* 2 (summer 1959): 41.

350
R. U. Sirius, "Evolutionary Mutations," in Rudy Rucker, R. U. Sirius, and Queen Mu, eds., *Mondo 2000: A User's Guide to the New Edge* (New York: HarperCollins, 1992), 103.

351
Glenn O'Brien, "Culture," *Artforum* 31, no. 4 (December 1992): 73.

352
Klaus Kertess, "Brushes with Beatitude," in Marshall, *Jean-Michel Basquiat* (note **217**), 53.

353
Burroughs, "The Fall of Art," *The Adding Machine* (note **12**), 61.

354
Ibid.

355
Bockris, *With William Burroughs* (note **6**), 78.

Bruce Cannon, **Subjective Object III**, 1994, cat. no. 153

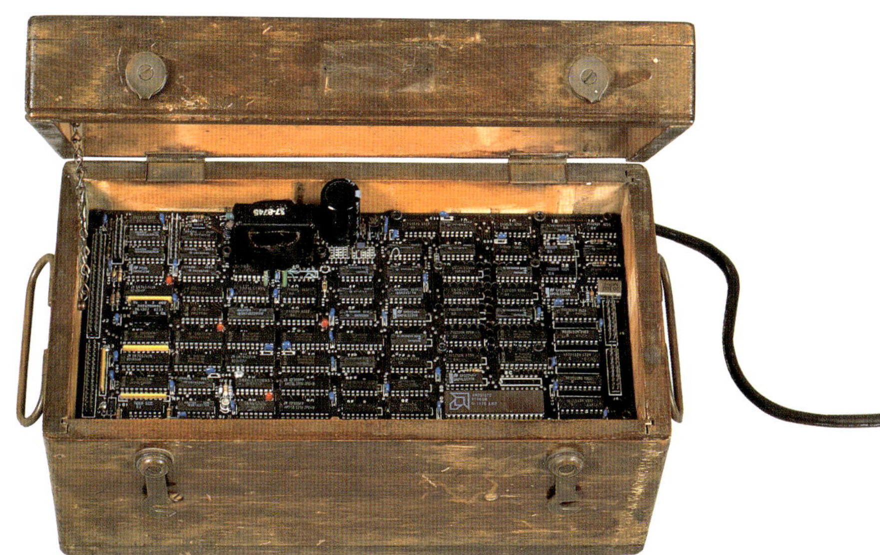

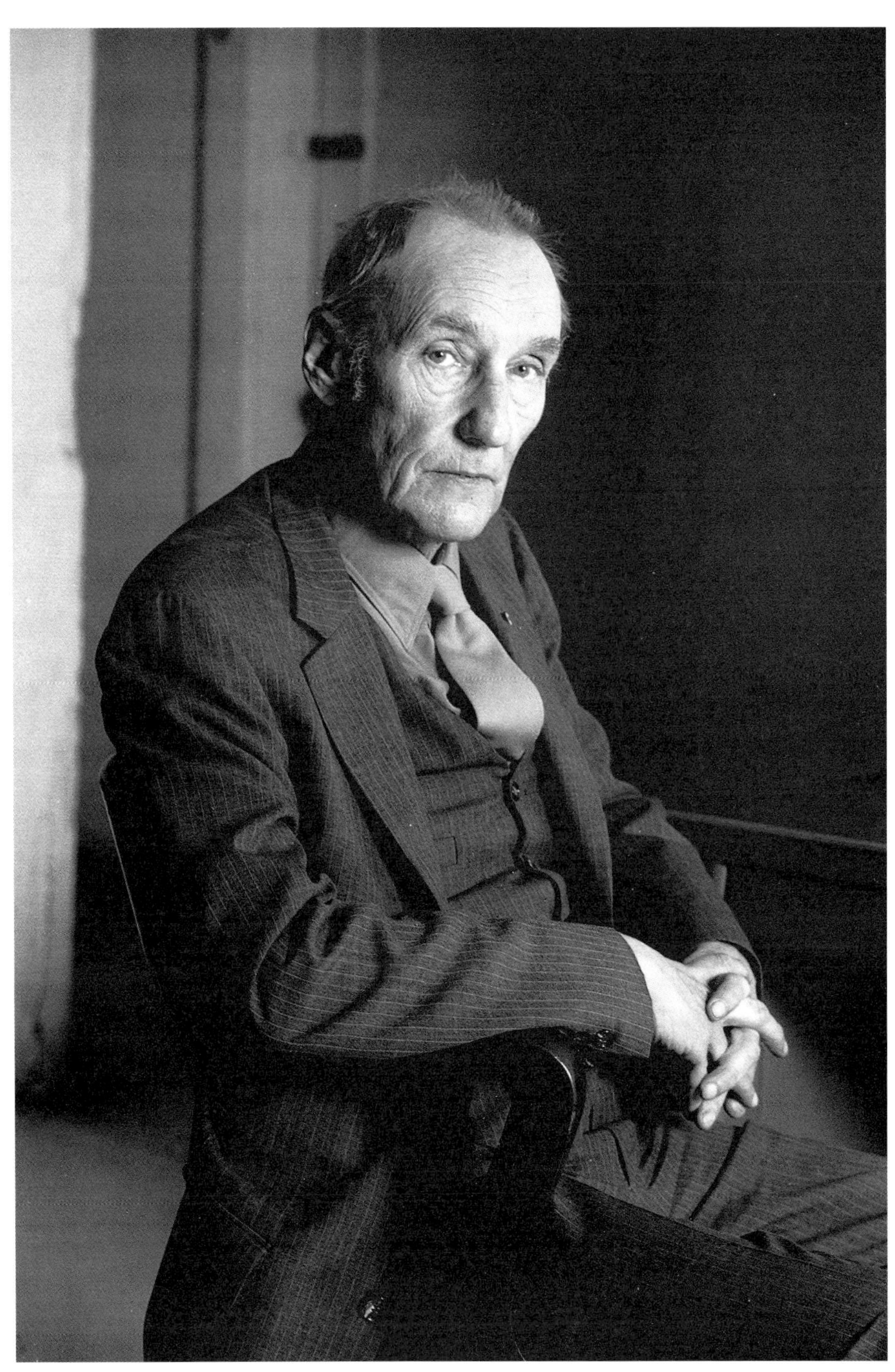

Kate Simon, **William S. Burroughs**, 1984, cat. no. 110

INVISIBLE INK

WILLIAM S. BURROUGHS

My own myth as an omniscient author writing in a timeless vacuum was exploded when I first met Brion Gysin. Brion Gysin was the principal instigator of the cut-up. New words and new meanings emerged: cut words, new words come, sometimes the perfect word. Expansion of awareness emerged. (How random is random?) Every time you look out the window, walk around in your home, or walked down any street, your consciousness is cut by seemingly random word and image. Coherent messages emerge and in 1960 with the publication of *Minutes to Go* advanced experimental cut-ups emerged as a serious art form.

There were many other experiments with word and image carried out by Brion Gysin, Ian Sommerville, your reporter and others.

Color scrap books of meaningful juxtapositions of word and image. Cut-ups on tape recorders, begun way back (in) 1960–61, carried on all times in Tangier, quite a few in London, many in New York, or Paris. Instead of gibberish, striking messages often emerge. "surprised recognition." Cut-ups on moving film—*Towers Open Fire*, *Bill and Tony*, carried out by your reporter and Antony Balch. Cut-ups of Rimbaud, Shakespeare, Ezra Pound, projected as a mask on my face, my own voice with Antony's face, etc. mixed in with any text, mixed in other contexts.

Some experiments were duds. Like shifting from black-and-white to color on moving film. Lesson: *learn to let go*. Never hang on to a dud.

Cut-ups as novels: *The Soft Machine*, *Nova Express*, *Exterminator*.

About the paintings. My painting derives from an innate disability. I cannot draw. Not a chair, not a table, not a tree. Consequently when I apply paint to a surface I do not know what will emerge.

Castaneda's Don Juan separates the *Tonal* that is the predictable universe, from the *Nagual*, the unpredictable universe of intuition, where anything is possible. *My painting is Nagual by necessity*. Clear, recognizable images and scenes do emerge, but not through my conscious control I quote from Wheeler's Recognition Physics: "Nothing exists until it is observed."

I am as much surprised as the observer by anything I have created.

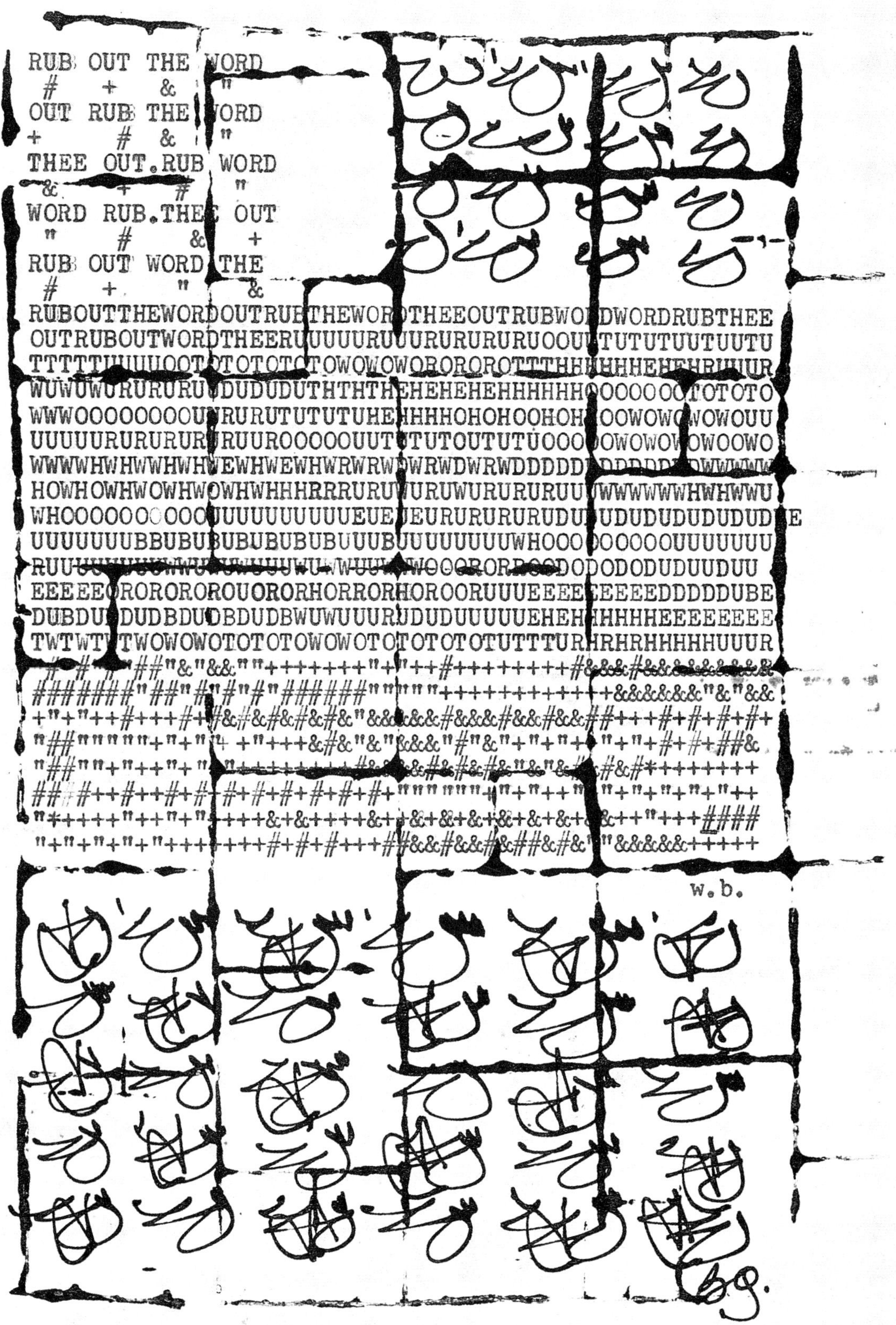

William S. Burroughs and Brion Gysin, untitled [Rub Out the Word], c. 1965, cat. no. 15

CHECKLIST OF THE EXHIBITION

Calligraphic Abstractions by William S. Burroughs

1 (PAGE 18)
Dust-jacket illustration for
The Naked Lunch, 1959
Offset photolithographic printing
6⅞ x 4⅜ in. (17.5 x 11.1 cm)
Collection of Joseph Zinnato, Burbank

2 (PAGE 18)
Dust-jacket illustration for
The Soft Machine, 1966
Offset photolithographic printing
8 x 5¼ in. (20.3 x 13.3 cm)
Collection of Joseph Zinnato, Burbank

Collages and Photo Works by William S. Burroughs

3 (PAGE 33)
Untitled [Allen Ginsberg], c. 1954
Gelatin-silver prints and cellophane tape on board
6¼ x 6⅜ in. (15.9 x 16.2 cm)
Collection of Richard Lorenz, Berkeley

4 (PAGE 6)
Untitled [William S. Burroughs, Kells Elvins], c. 1954
Gelatin-silver prints and cellophane tape on board
4⅜ x 5⅜ in. (11.1 x 13.7 cm)
Collection of Richard Lorenz, Berkeley

5 (PAGE 34)
Birdie Does the Watching, c. 1964
Gelatin-silver print from newspaper negative
4¼ x 3¼ in. (10.8 x 8.3 cm)
Collection of Norman Laurila, New York

6 (PAGE 34)
Sturdy Steel Snap-Tight (diptych), 1964
Gelatin-silver prints from newspaper negative
Each print: 4¼ x 3¼ in. (10.8 x 8.3 cm)
Collection of Norman Laurila, New York

7 (PAGE 36)
Time, 1965
Collage for *Time*
Paint and ink on offset lithographic magazine cover
12 x 9½ in. (30.5 x 24.1 cm)
Collection of Joseph Zinnato, Burbank

8 (PAGE 36)
Proclaim Present Time Over.Claim Present.Pro Time Over and Doble on Sunday, 1965
Collage for *Time*
Gelatin-silver print, ink, and typescript on board
12 x 9½ in. (30.5 x 24.1 cm)
Collection of Joseph Zinnato, Burbank

9 (PAGE 36)
The Fliday Newsmagazine? No Glot.Clom Fliday., 1965
Collage for *Time*
Gelatin-silver print, ink, and typescript on board
12 x 9½ in. (30.5 x 24.1 cm)
Collection of Joseph Zinnato, Burbank

10 (PAGE 55)
Danger Ahead, 1965
Collage for *Lines* 6 (November 1965)
Gelatin-silver print, paper, and typescript on paper
12 x 9½ in. (30.5 x 24.1 cm)
Collection of Joseph Zinnato, Burbank

Works by William S. Burroughs and Brion Gysin: The Scrapbooks

11 (PAGES 48–53)
Black Scrapbook, c. 1963–64
Mixed media in 1964 agenda, 416 pages
6¾ x 4¼ in. (17.2 x 10.8 cm)
Lent by the Grinstein Family

12 (PAGE 46)
Red Scrapbook, c. 1966–73
Mixed media in 1966 agenda, 382 pages (lacking June 9–30)
6¾ x 4¼ in. (17.2 x 10.8 cm)
Lent by the Grinstein Family

13 (PAGES 38–43)
Green Scrapbook, c. 1971–73
Mixed media in *Les goélands* sketchbook, 192 pages plus endpapers
8⅝ x 6½ in. (22 x 16.5 cm)
Lent by the Grinstein Family

Works by William S. Burroughs and Brion Gysin: The Third Mind

14 (PAGE 59)
Permutations, c. 1965
Collage for *The Third Mind*, p. 29
Gelatin-silver prints, ink, and letterpress on paper
9¹¹⁄₁₆ x 6⅞ in. (24.6 x 17.5 cm)
Los Angeles County Museum of Art, purchased with funds provided by the Hiro Yamagata Foundation
AC1993.56.118

15 (PAGES 58 AND 168)
Untitled [Rub Out the Word], c. 1965
Permutation for *The Third Mind*, p. 33
Typescript and ink on paper
10¹⁄₁₆ x 6¹³⁄₁₆ in. (25.6 x 17.3 cm)
Los Angeles County Museum of Art, purchased with funds provided by the Hiro Yamagata Foundation
AC1993.56.21.2

16 (PAGE 58)
Untitled [The Present Shape of Words], c. 1965
Permutation for *The Third Mind*, p. 34
Ink on paper
9¾ x 7¼ in. (24.8 x 18.4 cm)
Los Angeles County Museum of Art, purchased with funds provided by the Hiro Yamagata Foundation
AC1993.56.22.1

17 (PAGE 58)
Untitled [Breathe in the Words], c. 1965
Permutation for *The Third Mind*, p. 35
Ink on paper
10 x 7⅜ in. (25.4 x 18.7 cm)
Los Angeles County Museum of Art, purchased with funds provided by the Hiro Yamagata Foundation
AC1993.56.22.2

18 (PAGE 61)
The Big Survey, c. 1965
Collage for *The Third Mind*, p. 138
Gelatin-silver print, letterpress, and ink on paper
10⁵⁄₁₆ x 8⁹⁄₁₆ in. (26.2 x 21.7 cm)
Los Angeles County Museum of Art, purchased with funds provided by the Hiro Yamagata Foundation
AC1993.56.74

19 (PAGE 60)
Scrapbooks, c. 1965
Collage for *The Third Mind*, p. 146
Gelatin-silver prints, letterpress, and ink on paper
10¼ x 7¹¹⁄₁₆ in. (26 x 19.5 cm)
Los Angeles County Museum of Art, purchased with funds provided by the Hiro Yamagata Foundation
AC1993.56.76

20 (PAGE 62)
The Death of Mrs. D, c. 1965
Collage for *The Third Mind*, p. 142
Gelatin-silver print, letterpress, and ink on paper
11 x 8½ in. (27.9 x 21.6 cm)
Los Angeles County Museum of Art, purchased with funds provided by the Hiro Yamagata Foundation
AC1993.56.77

21 (PAGE 77)
Dreamachine, c. 1965
Collage for *The Third Mind*, p. 205
Gelatin-silver prints and ink on paper
9 5/8 x 6 13/16 in. (24.5 x 17.3 cm)
Los Angeles County Museum of Art,
purchased with funds provided by the
Hiro Yamagata Foundation
AC1993.56.107

22 (PAGE 72)
Untitled [Projection Performance],
c. 1965
Collage for *The Third Mind*, p. 203
Gelatin-silver prints and ink on paper
9 7/8 x 7 1/8 in. (25.1 x 18.1 cm)
Los Angeles County Museum of Art,
purchased with funds provided by the
Hiro Yamagata Foundation
AC1993.56.106

23 (PAGE 64)
Untitled [William Buys a Parrot], c. 1965
Collage for *The Third Mind*, p. 134
Gelatin-silver prints and ink on paper
8 9/16 x 6 15/16 in. (21.8 x 17.6 cm)
Los Angeles County Museum of Art,
purchased with funds provided by the
Hiro Yamagata Foundation
AC1993.56.119

24 (PAGE 64)
Untitled [William and the Captain],
c. 1965
Collage for *The Third Mind*, p. 136
Gelatin-silver prints and ink on paper
11 x 8 9/16 in. (27.9 x 21.8 cm)
Los Angeles County Museum of Art,
purchased with funds provided by the
Hiro Yamagata Foundation
AC1993.56.122

25 (PAGE 8)
Untitled [William Vacates Rooms],
c. 1965
Collage for *The Third Mind*, p. 132
Gelatin-silver prints and ink on paper
9 1/2 x 7 1/16 in. (24.1 x 17.9 cm)
Los Angeles County Museum of Art,
purchased with funds provided by the
Hiro Yamagata Foundation
AC1993.56.112

26 (PAGE 65)
Untitled [Doctor Zeit M.D.], c. 1965
Collage for *The Third Mind*, p. 158
Gelatin-silver print, typescript, offset
lithography, and letterpress on paper
12 5/16 x 9 9/16 in. (31.3 x 24.3 cm)
Los Angeles County Museum of Art,
purchased with funds provided by the
Hiro Yamagata Foundation
AC1993.56.114.1

27 (PAGE 66)
Untitled [Bubble Trouble], c. 1965
Collage for *The Third Mind*, p. 159
Typescript, offset lithography, and ink
on graph paper
12 5/16 x 9 9/16 in. (31.3 x 24.3 cm)
Los Angeles County Museum of Art,
purchased with funds provided by the
Hiro Yamagata Foundation
AC1993.56.115.2

28 (PAGE 67)
Untitled [Girl], c. 1965
Collage for *The Third Mind*, p. 160
Gelatin-silver prints, typescript,
offset lithography, and newsprint on
graph paper
12 5/16 x 9 9/16 in. (31.3 x 24.3 cm)
Los Angeles County Museum of Art,
purchased with funds provided by the
Hiro Yamagata Foundation
AC1993.56.115.1

29 (PAGE 67)
Untitled [Another Goal], c. 1965
Collage for *The Third Mind*, p. 161
Gelatin-silver print, typescript, and offset
lithography on graph paper
12 5/16 x 9 9/16 in. (31.3 x 24.3 cm)
Los Angeles County Museum of Art,
purchased with funds provided by the
Hiro Yamagata Foundation
AC1993.56.123.1

30 (PAGE 68)
Untitled [Primrose Path ?], c. 1965
Collage for *The Third Mind*, p. 12
Gelatin-silver prints, typescript,
newsprint, and ink on paper
9 7/16 x 6 11/16 in. (24 x 17 cm)
Los Angeles County Museum of Art,
purchased with funds provided by the
Hiro Yamagata Foundation
AC1993.56.11.1

31 (PAGE 69)
Untitled [Tornado Dead: 223], c. 1965
Collage for *The Third Mind*, p. 174
Gelatin-silver prints and ink on paper
8 11/16 x 6 11/16 in. (22.1 x 17 cm)
Los Angeles County Museum of Art,
purchased with funds provided by the
Hiro Yamagata Foundation
AC1993.56.116

32 (PAGE 68)
Untitled [The Energy of a Hurricane],
c. 1965
Collage for *The Third Mind*, p. 180
Gelatin-silver prints and ink on paper
9 11/16 x 6 11/16 in. (24.6 x 17 cm)
Los Angeles County Museum of Art,
purchased with funds provided by the
Hiro Yamagata Foundation
AC1993.56.120

33 (PAGE 70)
Untitled [W. R. Hearst Jr.], c. 1965
Collage for *The Third Mind*, p. 155
Gelatin-silver print, typescript (edges
burnt), offset lithography (edges burnt),
letterpress, and crayon on graph paper
12 5/16 x 9 9/16 in. (31.3 x 24.3 cm)
Los Angeles County Museum of Art,
purchased with funds provided by the
Hiro Yamagata Foundation
AC1993.56.117.1

34 (PAGE 60)
Untitled [The Nova Express], c. 1965
Collage for *The Third Mind*, p. 154
Gelatin-silver print, typescript, offset lithography, and newsprint on graph paper
12 5/16 x 9 9/16 in. (31.3 x 24.3 cm)
Los Angeles County Museum of Art, purchased with funds provided by the Hiro Yamagata Foundation
AC1993.56.124

35 (PAGE 71)
Untitled [Plan Drug Addiction], c. 1965
Collage for *The Third Mind*, p. 157
Gelatin-silver print, typescript, offset lithography, newsprint, crayon, and ink on graph paper
12 5/16 x 9 3/8 in. (31.3 x 23.2 cm)
Los Angeles County Museum of Art, purchased with funds provided by the Hiro Yamagata Foundation
AC1993.56.113

36 (PAGE 96)
The Third Mind Cut-Up, 1976
Gelatin-silver prints, text, and roller
28 x 18 in. (71.1 x 45.7 cm)
Collection of Laetitia Firmin Didot, Paris

Shotgun Art, Doors, Windows, and Sculpture by William S. Burroughs

37 (PAGE 99)
Sore Shoulder, 1982
Plywood with shotgun holes
16 x 21 in. (40.6 x 53.3 cm)
Collection of the artist, New York

38 (PAGE 103)
Screaming Ghost (double-sided), 1982
Paint on plywood with shotgun holes
12 1/8 x 19 3/8 in. (30.8 x 49.2 cm)
Collection of Timothy Leary, Beverly Hills

39 (PAGES 102–103)
Escape from Centipede Troughs, 1982
Housepaint and chromogenic-development prints on plywood
6 x 24 in. (15.2 x 61 cm)
Collection of the artist, New York

40 (PAGES 3–4)
Traveller on the Yellow Wave (double-sided), 1982
Gelatin-silver and chromogenic-development prints and paint on plywood with shotgun holes
25 1/8 x 13 1/2 in. (63.8 x 34.3 cm)
Lent by the Grinstein Family

41 (PAGE 105)
Wood Spirits, 1987
Acrylic, india ink, photomechanical prints, and paper on plywood with shotgun holes
16 x 26 1/4 in. (40.6 x 66.7 cm)
Collection of the artist, New York

42 (PAGE 107)
The Curse of Bast, 1987
Acrylic, housepaint, and newsprint on plywood with shotgun holes
36 1/2 x 12 1/2 in. (92.7 x 31.8 cm)
Collection of Andrew Renton, London; photo by Ivan Dalla Tana

43 (PAGE 106)
Mink Mutiny (double-sided), 1987
Acrylic, oil, photomechanical print, plywood with shotgun holes
29 1/2 x 25 1/4 in. (74.9 x 64.1 cm)
Private collection, St. Louis; photo by Ivan Dalla Tana

44 (PAGE 108)
Fire Door (double-sided), 1987
Spraypaint and paint on paneled wood door
83 x 28 in. (210.8 x 71.1 cm)
Collection of Peter Brams, New York; photo by Ivan Dalla Tana

45 (PAGE 109)
Space Door (double-sided), 1987
Spraypaint, paint, and offset lithographic prints on paneled wood door
83 x 23 7/8 x 6 in. (210.8 x 60.6 x 15.2 cm)
Collection of George Mulder, Venice

46 (PAGE 104)
Ten Gauge City (double-sided), 1988
Housepaint on wood panel with shotgun holes
39 x 15 in. (99.1 x 38.1 cm)
Collection of F. José Férez K., London

47 (PAGE 110)
Brightness Falls from the Air (double-sided), 1988
Paint on wood and glass window
22 x 13 in. (55.9 x 33 cm)
Lent by Galerie Carzaniga and Ueker, Basel

48 (PAGE 143)
Woman as Man, 1988
Plywood with gunshot holes
15 x 28 in. (38.1 x 71.1 cm)
Estate of Jean-Michel Basquiat, courtesy Robert Miller Gallery, New York

49 (PAGE 111)
Shot Sheriff, 1992
Ink on canvas with gunshot holes
16 x 12 in. (40.6 x 30.5 cm)
Collection of the artist, Lawrence

50 (PAGE 115)
Untitled, 1992
Mixed media
56 x 14 x 14 in. (142.2 x 35.6 x 35.6 cm)
Collection of the artist, Lawrence

Paintings on Paper, Board, and Canvas by William S. Burroughs

51 (PAGE 133)
Silver Boys, 1987
Paint on board
20 x 16½ in. (50.8 x 41.9 cm)
Collection of the artist, Lawrence

52 (PAGE 132)
Ghost of Chance 15 (The Bridge), 1989
Paint on paper
23 x 18 in. (58.4 x 45.7 cm)
Collection of the artist, Lawrence

53 (PAGE 114)
Rub Out the Word, 1989
Ink on paper
23 x 18 in. (58.4 x 45.7 cm)
Lent by Galerie Carzaniga and Ueker, Basel

54 (PAGE 131)
Animated Tassels, 1992
Paint on paper
17½ x 23 in. (44.5 x 58.4 cm)
Collection of the artist, Lawrence

55 (PAGE 131)
Attila the Hun, 1992
Paint on paper
17½ x 23 in. (44.5 x 58.4 cm)
Collection of the artist, Lawrence

56 (PAGE 128)
Last Chance Junction and Curse on Drug Hysterics, 1988
Acrylic, photomechanical print, newsprint, and ink on board
20 x 32 in. (50.8 x 81.3 cm)
Collection of F. José Férez K., London

57 (PAGE 129)
Thick Pages #8 (double-sided), 1990
Ink, paint, and xerographic sheets on irregular handmade paper
34 x 13 in. (86.4 x 33 cm)
Collection of the artist, Lawrence

58 (PAGE 127)
Terminal Drug Psychosis, 1989
Ink, paint, paper, and letterpress on board
20 x 30 in. (50.8 x 76.2 cm)
Collection of Peter Weller, London

59 (PAGE 119)
Crazy Man (double-sided), 1988
Paint on cardboard
33 x 21 in. (83.8 x 53.3 cm)
Collection of F. José Férez K., London

60 (PAGES 120–21)
Research Animal (double-sided), 1989
Spray paint and collage on board
30 x 20 in. (76.2 x 50.8 cm)
Private collection

61 (PAGE 122)
Creation of the Homunculus IV, 1989
Paint on paper
23 x 18 in. (58.4 x 45.7 cm)
Collection of the artist, Lawrence

62 (PAGE 11)
Call, 1991
Acrylic and spray paint on board
30 x 22 in. (76.2 x 55.9 cm)
Collection of the artist, Lawrence

63 (PAGE 148)
Envy, 1992
From the portfolio *The Seven Deadly Sins*, 1992
Woodblock and serigraphic print on paper
45 x 31 in. (114.3 x 78.7 cm)
Los Angeles County Museum of Art, gift of Robert Lococo
AC1994.28.6.2

64 (PAGE 148)
Gluttony, 1992
From the portfolio *The Seven Deadly Sins*, 1992
Woodblock and serigraphic print on paper
45 x 31 in. (114.3 x 78.7 cm)
Los Angeles County Museum of Art, gift of Robert Lococo
AC1994.28.4.2

65 (PAGE 130)
Thick Pages #9 (double-sided), 1990
Paint and xerographic sheets on irregular handmade paper
33½ x 19½ in. (85.1 x 49.5 cm)
Collection of the artist, Lawrence

66 (PAGE 121)
The Hole in His Head Is Big, 1992
Acrylic on paper
17½ x 23 in. (44.5 x 58.4 cm)
Collection of the artist, Lawrence

67 (PAGE 126)
The Kindly Old General Practitioner, 1992
Paint on paper
23 x 17½ in. (58.4 x 44.5 cm)
Collection of the artist, Lawrence

68 (PAGE 124)
Four Celestial Babies, 1992
Paint on paper
17½ x 23 in. (44.5 x 58.4 cm)
Collection of the artist, Lawrence

69 (PAGE 125)
Alien Penetration, 1992
Paint on paper
17½ x 23⅛ in. (44.5 x 58.7 cm)
Collection of the artist, Lawrence

70 (PAGE 122)
Black Lemur 30,000,000 Years Old, 1992
Paint and offset lithography on paper
23 x 17½ in. (58.4 x 44.5 cm)
Collection of the artist, Lawrence

71 (PAGE 25)
Portrait of Jack Black—Narrator of "You Can't Win" and "Salt Chunk Mary," 1992
Paint and xerographic print on paper
23 x 17½ in. (58.4 x 44.5 cm)
Collection of the artist, Lawrence

72 (PAGE 123)
Joy Rider to Nowhere. Last Ride by a Viking Priest, 1993
Gelatin-silver print, xerographic prints, and ink on paper
23 x 17½ in. (58.4 x 44.5 cm)
Collection of the artist, Lawrence

73 (PAGE 116)
The Door in the Mountain Side through Which the Piper Led the Children of Hamelin, 1992
Paint on paper
23 x 17½ in. (58.4 x 44.5 cm)
Collection of the artist, Lawrence

74 (PAGE 113)
Untitled, 1992
Acrylic on paper
23 x 17½ in. (58.4 x 44.5 cm)
Collection of the artist, Lawrence

75 (PAGE 112)
Underwater, 1989
Paint on paper
23 x 18 in. (58.4 x 45.7 cm)
Collection of the artist, Lawrence

76 (PAGE 124)
Christmas Cheer, 1989
Paint on paper
18 x 23 in. (45.7 x 58.4 cm)
Collection of the artist, Lawrence

77 (PAGE 116)
The Flag I, 1989
Paint on paper
23 x 18 in. (58.4 x 45.7 cm)
Lent by Galerie Carzaniga and Ueker, Basel

78 (PAGE 117)
The Alleys of Marrakech, 1993
Acrylic on canvas
72 x 48 in. (182.9 x 121.9 cm)
Diego Cortez Arte, Ltd., New York

79 (PAGE 135)
For the Angel of Death Spread His Wings, 1993
Acrylic and spray paint on canvas
25 x 30 in. (63.5 x 76.2 cm)
Collection of the artist, Lawrence

Collaborations with and Illustrations for William S. Burroughs

80 (PAGE 90)
Brion Gysin (with WSB)
England, active Morocco and France, 1916–86
The Cut-Ups, 1964
Ink on paper
16¼ x 11⅜ in. (41.2 x 28.1 cm)
Collection of Laetitia Firmin Didot, Paris

81 (PAGE 137)
Brion Gysin
England, active Morocco and France, 1916–86
Electronic Revolution, 1971
From the limited edition of *Electronic Revolution*, 1971
Etching on paper
12½ x 9½ in. (31.8 x 24.1 cm)
Collection of Joseph Zinnato, Burbank

82 (PAGE 136)
Robert Rauschenberg (with WSB)
United States, b. 1925
American Pewter with Burroughs V, 1981
From the portfolio *American Pewter with Burroughs*, 1981
Lithographic print with embossing on paper
31¾ x 23¼ in. (80.7 x 59.1 cm)
Lent by Gemini G.E.L., Los Angeles
© 1981 Gemini G.E.L.

83 (PAGE 139)
Carl Apfelschnitt
United States, 1948–90
Untitled, 1982
From the limited edition of *Mummies*, 1982
Etching on paper
14½ x 11⅛ in. (36.8 x 28.3 cm)
Collection of Joseph Zinnato, Burbank

84 (PAGE 138)
Brion Gysin
England, active Morocco and France, 1916–86
Untitled, 1986
From the limited edition of *The Cat Inside*, 1986
Lithographic print on paper
14 x 10 in. (35.6 x 25.4 cm)
Collection of Joseph Zinnato, Burbank

85 (PAGE 144)
Philip Taaffe (with WSB)
United States, b. 1955
Untitled, 1987
Encaustic and paint on paper
23 x 35 in. (58.4 x 88.9 cm)
Collection of Philip Taaffe, New York

86 (PAGE 146)
John Giorno (with WSB)
United States, b. 1936
That Gun's Got Blood in Its Hole, 1991
Paint and wax color on paper
24 x 30 in. (61 x 76.2 cm)
Collection of John Giorno, New York

87 (PAGE 141)
Keith Haring (with WSB)
United States, 1958–90
Untitled, 1988
From the portfolio *Apocalypse*, 1988
Lithographic and photolithographic print on paper
38 x 38 in. (96.5 x 96.5 cm)
Collection of William S. Burroughs, Lawrence

88 (PAGE 145)
Keith Haring (with WSB)
United States, 1958–90
Untitled, 1989
From the limited edition of *The Valley*, 1989
Etching on paper
16⅜ x 15¾ x 2½ in. (41.6 x 40 x 6.4 cm)
Lent by the Robert Berman Gallery, Santa Monica

89 (PAGE 145)
Robert Wilson (with WSB)
United States, b. 1941
The Magic Circle, 1989
Ink on paper
32⅛ x 40 in. (81.6 x 101.6 cm)
Collection of William S. Burroughs, Lawrence

90 (PAGE 140)
Udo Breger (with WSB)
Germany, active Switzerland, b. 1941
B.U.D., 1990
Photolithographic print on paper
16⅛ x 18⅛ in. (41 x 46 cm)
Private collection, Los Angeles

91 (PAGE 146)
Dean Ripa (with WSB)
United States, b. 1957
The Ambiguous Smile of the Tempter (double-sided), 1990
Paint on plywood
17½ x 21½ in. (44.5 x 54.6 cm)
Collection of William S. Burroughs, Lawrence

92 (PAGE 139)
George Condo
United States, b. 1957
Untitled, 1991
From the limited edition of *Ghost of Chance*, 1991
Etching on paper
14 x 10¼ in. (35.6 x 26 cm)
Collection of Joseph Zinnato, Burbank

93 (PAGE 147)
George Condo (with WSB)
United States, b. 1957
Every Man for Himself, 1992
Paint on canvas
60 x 72 in. (152.4 x 182.9 cm)
Collection of William S. Burroughs, Lawrence

94 (PAGE 149)
David Bradshaw
United States, b. 1944
Blue Sharpshooter, 1993
From the portfolio *Propagation Hazard*, 1993
Lithographic print on paper
15 x 22 in. (38.1 x 55.9 cm)
Lent by Graphicstudio/University of South Florida, Tampa

95 (PAGE 149)
Roger Holden (with WSB)
United States, b. 1952
Untitled, 1995
From the series *Cybernetic Cut-ups*
Stereogrammetric, digital ink-jet print on paper
9⅜ x 11 in. (23.9 x 27.9 cm)
Lent by the artist

El Hombre Visible—Portraits and Other Likenesses

96 (PAGE 19)
Loomis Dean
United States, b. 1917
William S. Burroughs at the Beat Hotel, 1959
Gelatin-silver print
8 x 10 in. (20.3 x 25.4 cm)
Lent by the artist, courtesy Keith deLellis, New York

97 (PAGE 32)
Allen Ginsberg
United States, b. 1926
Burroughs and Friends, Hotel Muniria, Tangiers, 1961
Gelatin-silver print, printed later
16 x 20 in. (40.6 x 50.8 cm)
Lent by the artist, courtesy Tibor de Nagy Gallery, New York, and Fahey/Klein Gallery, Los Angeles

98 (PAGE 80)
Antony Balch
England, 1937–80
William S. Burroughs, c. 1963
Gelatin-silver print (film still from *Towers Open Fire*), 1963
8 x 10 in. (20.3 x 25.4 cm)
Collection of Norman Laurila, New York

99 (PAGE 82)
Conrad Rooks
United States, active Thailand, b. 1934
Chappaqua (film still), 1967
From the promotional booklet *Chappaqua*, 1967
Offset photolithographic printing
10⅝ x 9 in. (27 x 22.9 cm)
Private collection, Los Angeles

100 (PAGES 74–75)
Charles Gatewood
United States, b. 1942
The Dream Machine, 1973
Limited edition artist's book with gelatin-silver prints and letterpress
7½ x 7½ in. (19.1 x 19.1 cm)
Collection of Joseph Zinnato, Burbank

101 (PAGE 150)
Gerard Malanga
United States, b. 1943
William Burroughs in Front of Burroughs Corporate Headquarters, NYC, 1975
Gelatin-silver print
20 x 16 in. (50.8 x 40.6 cm)
Lent by the artist

102 (PAGE 152)
Les Levine
Ireland, active United States, b. 1935
Record album cover design and photography for *William S. Burroughs/John Giorno*, 1975
Offset photolithographic printing
12¼ x 12⅜ in. (31.1 x 31.4 cm)
Collection of Joseph Zinnato, Burbank

103 (PAGE 152)
Les Levine
Ireland, active United States, b. 1935
Record album cover design and photography for *Totally Corrupt*, 1976
Offset photolithographic printing
12¼ x 12⅜ in. (31.1 x 31.4 cm)
Collection of Joseph Zinnato, Burbank

104 (PAGE 154)
Cozette de Charmoy
France, b. 1939
Untitled, 1976
Gelatin-silver prints, postage stamps, ink, crayon, and pencil on paper (source photographs by François Lagarde)
29⅛ x 23⅛ in. (74 x 58.7 cm.)
Collection of Jean-Jacques Berger, Berne

105 (PAGE 73)
François Lagarde
France, b. 1949
The Three Minds (triptych), 1978
Gelatin-silver prints and offset lithography on board
9¾ x 21⅞ in. (24.8 x 55.6 cm)
Collection of Joseph Zinnato, Burbank

106 (PAGE 153)
David Wojnarowicz
United States, 1954–92
Bill Burroughs' Recurring Dream, 1978
Gelatin-silver and offset photolithographic prints on paper (source photograph by Gerard Malanga)
6½ x 7 in. (16.5 x 17.8 cm)
Los Angeles County Museum of Art, Ralph M. Parsons Fund
AC1995.63.1

107 (PAGE 87)
Robert Mapplethorpe
United States, 1946–89
William Burroughs, 1979
Gelatin-silver print
14 x 13⅞ in. (35.6 x 35.2 cm)
© the Estate of Robert Mapplethorpe, New York. Used by permission.

108 (PAGE 152)
Robert Mapplethorpe
United States, 1946–89
Record album photography for *Sugar, Alcohol, and Meat*, 1980
Offset photolithographic printing
12¼ x 12⅜ in. (31.1 x 31.4 cm)
Collection of Joseph Zinnato, Burbank

109 (PAGE 22)
Andy Warhol
United States, 1928–87
William S. Burroughs, 1980
Dye-diffusion transfer (Polacolor) print
4¼ x 3⅜ in. (10.8 x 8.6 cm)
Courtesy the Andy Warhol Foundation and PaceWildensteinMacGill

110 (PAGE 166)
Kate Simon
United States, b. 1951
William S. Burroughs, 1984
Gelatin-silver print
20 x 16 in. (50.8 x 40.6 cm)
Collection of John Musall, New York

111 (PAGE 87)
Gus Van Sant
United States, b. 1952
Compact disc cover illustration for *The Elvis of Letters*, 1985
Offset photolithographic printing
4⅞ x 5⅝ in. (12.4 x 14.3 cm)
Private collection, Los Angeles

112 (PAGE 101)
David Bradshaw
United States, b. 1944
William Burroughs with My Smith and Wesson Model 629, 1986
From the series *South America Pond*
Xerographic print with charcoal on paper
12 x 10¼ in. (30.5 x 26 cm)
Collection of William S. Burroughs, Lawrence

113 (PAGE 155)
Rick McKee Hock
United States, b. 1947
Codex (Burroughs), 1987
Hand-altered dye-diffusion transfer (Polacolor) prints
34½ x 30 in. (87.6 x 76.2 cm)
Los Angeles County Museum of Art, Ralph M. Parsons Fund
AC1994.125.1

114 (PAGE 156)
Walter Dahn
Germany, b. 1954
William Burroughs, 1989
Oil and serigraphic print on canvas (source photograph by Kate Simon)
31½ x 63½ in. (80 x 161.3 cm)
Collection of William S. Burroughs, Lawrence

115 (PAGE 98)
Gottfried Helnwein
Vienna, active Germany, b. 1948
William Burroughs, 1990
Gelatin-silver print
13 x 9 in. (33 x 22.9 cm)
Private collection, Los Angeles

116 (PAGE 152)
Herb Ritts
United States, b. 1952
William S. Burroughs, 1990
From an advertising campaign for The Gap
Offset photolithographic proof on tissue
14¾ x 11 in. (37.5 x 27.9 cm)
Private collection, Los Angeles, courtesy The Gap, San Francisco

117 (PAGE 156)
Christof Kohlhofer
Germany, active United States, b. 1942
W. S. Burroughs and G.I.'s at the Persian Gulf Getting Ready for Take Off, News of the Day: Mark Twain's Lost Manuscript Found, Mixed Media on Shopping Bags, 1991
Gouache on paper
Diameter: 35 in. (88.9 cm)
Collection of Andreas Züst, Zürich, photo by Norbert Faehling

118 (PAGE 158)
Alison Van Pelt
United States, b. 1964
William Burroughs, 1992
Oil on canvas
27½ x 19½ in. (69.9 x 49.5 cm)
Lent by the Robert Berman Gallery, Santa Monica

119 (PAGE 83)
Gus Van Sant
United States, b. 1952
A Thanksgiving Prayer (film stills with captions), 1990
From the book *Mondo 2000: A User's Guide to the New Edge*, 1992
Offset photolithographic printing
11 x 8½ in. (27.9 x 21.6 cm)
Private collection, Los Angeles

120 (PAGE 88)
Kate Simon
United States, b. 1951
Compact disc cover photography for *Spare Ass Annie and Other Tales*, 1993
Offset photolithographic printing
4⅞ x 5⅝ in. (12.4 x 14.3 cm)
Private collection, Los Angeles

121 (PAGE 157)
Frances Swigart
United States, b. 1942
Ursulines, 1993
Photoetching, relief printing, and chine collé on paper
30 x 22 in. (76.2 x 55.9 cm)
Private collection, Los Angeles

122 (PAGE 158)
Humberto Jardón
Mexico, b. 1953
Feliz Cumpleaños, 1994
Ink-jet (Iris) print on Translight
34 x 43¾ in. (86.4 x 111.1 cm)
Collection of F. José Férez K., London

123 (PAGE 152)
American Thief, a.k.a. Gypsies and Thieves
United States, clothing manufacturer active 1990s
Old Man Fit, 1994
Offset lithographic clothing tag (source photograph by Kate Simon)
8⅝ x 3½ in. (22 x 8.9 cm)
Private collection, Los Angeles

124 (PAGE 158)
Ralph Steadman
England, b. 1936
Something New Has Been Added, 1995
Serigraphic print on paper (with shotgun holes by WSB)
30 x 44 in. (76.2 x 111.8 cm)
Collection of F. José Férez K., London

125 (PAGE 16)
Annie Leibovitz
United States, b. 1949
William Burroughs (profile), 1995
Gelatin-silver print
16 x 20 in. (40.6 x 50.8 cm)
Lent by the artist

126 (PAGE 15)
Annie Leibovitz
United States, b. 1949
William Burroughs (frontal), 1995
Gelatin-silver print
16 x 20 in. (40.6 x 50.8 cm)
Lent by the artist

El Hombre Invisible—Works by Other Artists

127 (PAGE 95)
Brion Gysin
England, active Morocco and France, 1916–86
Naked Lunch, 1960
Ink on paper
21½ x 14¾ in. (54.6 x 37.5 cm)
Lent by the Galerie de France, Paris

128 (PAGE 91)
Brion Gysin
England, active Morocco and France, 1916–86
Dust-jacket illustration for
The Exterminator, 1960
Offset photolithographic printing
9⅛ x 6⅛ in. (23.2 x 15.6 cm)
Collection of Joseph Zinnato, Burbank

129 (PAGE 92)
Brion Gysin
England, active Morocco and France, 1916–86
Dust-jacket illustration for
The Soft Machine, 1961
Offset photolithographic printing
6⅞ x 4⅜ in. (17.5 x 11.1 cm)
Collection of Joseph Zinnato, Burbank

130 (PAGES 94–95)
Brion Gysin
England, active Morocco and France, 1916–86
I Am That I Am, 1961
Ink and watercolor on paper
6 x 39¼ in. (15.2 x 99.7 cm)
Private collection

131 (PAGE 76)
Brion Gysin
England, active Morocco and France, 1916–86
Ian Sommerville
England, 1941–76
Dreamachine, 1961–62, refabricated in 1994 by David Woodard
Wood, steel, board, 80 rpm electric motor, lighting fixture, and acrylic paint
36½ x 13 x 14¾ in. (92.7 x 33 x 37.5 cm)
Lent by David Woodard, San Francisco

132 (PAGE 63)
Ian Sommerville
England, 1941–76
Dust-jacket photography for
The Ticket That Exploded, 1962
Offset photolithographic printing
6⅞ x 4⅜ in. (17.5 x 11.1 cm)
Collection of Joseph Zinnato, Burbank

133 (PAGE 19)
Brion Gysin
England, active Morocco and France, 1916–86
Francis in the Beat Hotel, 1962
Gelatin-silver prints and ink on paper
20¼ x 26 in. (51.4 x 66 cm)
Lent by the Galerie de France, Paris

134 (PAGE 76)
Michael English
England, active 1960s
International Times, 1966
Serigraphic print with metallic ink on paper
30¼ x 22½ in. (76.8 x 57.2 cm)
Collection of Joseph Zinnato, Burbank

135 (PAGE 20)
Claude Pélieu
France, b. 1934
Frontispiece illustration to
Minutes to Go, 1968
Offset photolithographic printing
8½ x 5⅜ in. (21.6 x 13.7 cm)
Collection of Joseph Zinnato, Burbank

136 (PAGE 160)
Wolf Vostell
Germany, b. 1932
Dust-jacket photography for
Cut Up or Shut Up, 1972
Offset photolithographic printing
8 x 4¼ x ⅛ in. (20.3 x 10.8 x .3 cm)
Collection of Joseph Zinnato, Burbank

137 (PAGE 138)
Robert F. Gale
United States, active 1980s
Book illustrations in
The Book of Breathing, 1974
Offset photolithographic printing
6¼ x 9½ in. (15.9 x 24.1 cm)
Private collection, Los Angeles

138 (PAGE 162)
Laurie Anderson
United States, b. 1947
New York Times (Horizontal), China Times (Vertical)—1971, 1976
Woven newsprint and tape on board
22½ x 14½ in. (57.2 x 36.8 cm)
Los Angeles County Museum of Art, Ralph M. Parsons Fund
AC1994.194.1

139 (PAGE 138)
Howard Buchwald
United States, active 1980s
Book illustrations in
The Streets of Chance, 1981
Offset photolithographic printing
9 x 6⅛ in. (22.9 x 15.6 cm)
Collection of Joseph Zinnato, Burbank

140 (PAGE 85)
Peter Christopherson
England, b. 1955
Record album cover photography for
"Nothing Here Now but the Recordings," 1981
Offset photolithographic printing
12¼ x 12⅜ in. (31.1 x 31.4 cm)
Collection Mark Alice Durant, Los Angeles

141 (PAGE 161)
Warren Neidich
United States, b. 1956
Cities of the Red Night, 1984–85
From the series *American History Reinvented*
Albumen print
7 x 9 in. (17.8 x 22.9 cm)
Lent by the artist

142 (PAGE 143)
Jean-Michel Basquiat
United States, 1960–88
Nod, c. 1985–88
Xerographic prints, paint, and metal on wood and cabinet door
25½ x 9 x 11 in. (64.8 x 22.9 x 27.9 cm)
Collection of William S. Burroughs, Lawrence

143 (PAGE 142)
Keith Haring
United States, 1958–90
For William Burroughs with Love and Admiration, 1987
Photogravure, ink, paint, and charcoal on paper
24 x 27⅜ in. (61 x 69.5 cm)
Collection of William S. Burroughs, Lawrence

144 (PAGE 140)
S. Clay Wilson
United States, b. 1941
Untitled, 1989
Drawing for illustration in *Tornado Alley*, 1989
Ink, gouache, and pencil on board
6½ x 10 in. (16.5 x 25.5 cm)
Collection of Nelson Lyon, Los Angeles

145 (PAGE 78)
The Hafler Trio and Thee Temple ov Psychick Youth
England, active 1980s
Brion Gysin's Dreamachine, 1989
Compact disc with illustrated slipcase and booklet
6½ x 5¾ in. (16.5 x 14.6 cm)
Collection of Joseph Zinnato, Burbank

146 (PAGE 161)
John Boskovich
United States, b. 1956
Portrait of the Artist and His Dog, 1989
Gelatin-silver print with gouache
10¼ x 16¼ in. (26 x 41.3 cm)
Lent by the artist, courtesy Rosamund Felsen Gallery, Santa Monica

147 (PAGE 160)
Steven Twigger
England, active United States, b. 1960
Naked Lunch, 1991
Offset photolithographic poster for the film *Naked Lunch*, directed by David Cronenberg, released by Twentieth Century Fox, art direction, Rod Dyer, Dyer/Mutchnick Group
39¾ x 26⅝ in. (101 x 67.6 cm)
Collection of Joseph Zinnato, Burbank

148 (PAGE 159)
Thomi Wroblewski
Canada, active England, b. 1949
Wild Boys, 1988
Chromogenic-development (Ektacolor) print, laminated
40¼ x 34⅜ in. (102.2 x 87.3 cm)
Lent by the artist

149 (PAGE 88)
Mark Trunz
Switzerland, active United States, b. 1962
Compact disc cover photography for *The "Priest" They Called Him*, 1992
Offset photolithographic printing
4⅞ x 5⅝ in. (12.4 x 14.3 cm)
Private collection, Los Angeles

150 (PAGE 88)
Robert Wilson
United States, b. 1941
Compact disc cover illustration for *The Black Rider*, 1993
Offset photolithographic printing
4⅞ x 5⅝ in. (12.4 x 14.3 cm)
Private collection, Los Angeles

151 (PAGE 164)
Christof Kohlhofer
Germany, active United States, b. 1942
Vogue Interzone, 1993
Offset photolithographic artist's magazine
11 x 8½ in. (27.9 x 21.6 cm)
Private collection, Los Angeles

152 (PAGE 163)
Tyler Stallings
United States, b. 1965
Cyborg Blossoms, Scenes 1–9 (diptych), 1994
Dot-matrix printing, paper, and thread on felt
Each panel: 13⅜ x 58 in. (34 x 147.3 cm)
Lent by the artist

153 (PAGE 165)
Bruce Cannon
United States, b. 1960
Subjective Object III, 1994
Microcontroller, speech electronics, and brass in oak box
12⅞ x 6⅞ x 6¾ in. (32.7 x 17.5 x 17.2 cm)
Collection of the Rene and Veronica di Rosa Foundation, Napa, courtesy of Gallery Paule Anglim, San Francisco

EXHIBITION HISTORY

Solo Exhibitions

1987

Tony Shafrazi Gallery, New York, exh. cat.

1988

Gallery Casa Sin Nombre, Santa Fe, exh. cat.

October Gallery, London, exh. cat.

Western Front Gallery, Vancouver

1989

Cleto Polcina Artemoderna, Rome, exh. cat.

Cold City Gallery, Toronto

Galeria EMI Valentim de Carvalho, Lisbon, exh. cat.

Galerie Carzaniga and Ueker, Basel, exh. cat.

Galerie Oboro and Atelier Roger Bellemare, Montreal, two-gallery show

Kellas Gallery, Lawrence

Elliot Smith Gallery, St. Louis

1990

Akarenga Hall (Seibu Sapporo), Sapporo

Deutsch-Amerikanisches Institut, Tübingen

Galeria Sephira, Madrid, exh. cat.

Galerie K, Paris, exh. cat.

Galerie WaschSalon, Frankfurt

Earl McGrath Gallery, Los Angeles

The Seed Hall (Seibu Shibuya), Tokyo, exh. cat.

1991

Galerie Carzaniga and Ueker, Basel, exh. cat.

Galerie K, Amsterdam

Vanguardia Galería de Arte, Bilbao, Spain, exh. bro.

1992

Artists en Masse, Lawrence, *The Seven Deadly Sins*

Atelier Marconi Gallery, Turin

Earl McGrath Gallery, Los Angeles, *The Seven Deadly Sins*

October Gallery, London, *The Seven Deadly Sins*

Transit Gallery, Bergamo, Italy

1993

Center for Study and Exhibit of Drawings, Exquisite Corpse, New York

Galeria Porte-Avion, Marseille

Galeria Sephira, Madrid

The Writer's Place, Kansas City, Missouri, *The Seven Deadly Sins*

1994

Aktionsforum, Munich, *Nagual Marks*

The Bourgeois Pig, Lawrence

Vintage Gallery, Amsterdam, *Photos 1962–72*

1995

Kunsthallen Brandts Klaedefabrik, Odense, Denmark, *The Seven Deadly Sins*

Terrain Gallery, San Francisco

1996

Robert Berman Gallery, Santa Monica

Webb Gallery, Waxahachie, Texas

Group Exhibitions

1988

Center of Contemporary Art, Seattle, two-person show (with St. Eom)

Paul Klein Gallery, Chicago, two-person show (with Sam Gilliam)

Jack Tilton Gallery, New York, *Literary Vision*, exh. cat.

1989

Paul Maenz Gallery, Cologne, two-person show (with Walter Dahn)

1990

Gallery Casa Sin Nombre, Santa Fe, two-person show (with Allen Ginsberg)

October Gallery, London, two-person show (with Keith Haring)

XPO Galerie, Hamburg, two-person show (with Robert Wilson)

1992

Project Theatre, Dublin, Ireland, two-person show (with Brion Gysin)

Sena Gallery, Santa Fe, two-person show (with Dennis Hopper)

1993

XLV Esposizione Internazionale d'Arte, Venice, exh. cat.

XII Biennale d'Art Contemporain, Lyon, exh. cat.

1994

David Floria Gallery, Woody Creek, Colorado, *Two Guys with Guns Making Art*, two-person show (with Hunter S. Thompson)

Luhring Augustine Gallery, New York, *The Ossuary*

New York University, New York, *Beat Generation Art*, exh. cat.

1995

Whitney Museum of American Art, New York, *Beat Culture and the New America*, exh. cat.

1996

Paolo Balducci Gallery, New York, *BANG-Gunshot Art*

Ubu Gallery, New York, *The Vehicle*

BIBLIOGRAPHY

Works by Burroughs (chronological)

Junkie. New York: Ace Books, 1953.

The Naked Lunch. Paris: Olympia Press, 1959. First U.S. edition (titled *Naked Lunch*), New York: Grove Press, 1962.

The Soft Machine. Paris: Olympia Press, 1961. First U.S. edition, New York: Grove Press, 1966.

The Ticket That Exploded. Paris: Olympia Press, 1962. First U.S. edition, New York: Grove Press, 1967.

Nova Express. New York: Grove Press, 1964.

Time. New York: 'C' Press, 1965.

Health Bulletin: APO-33, a Metabolic Regulator. New York: Fuck You Press, 1965.

The Wild Boys. New York: Grove Press, 1971.

Exterminator! New York: Viking Press, 1973.

The Last Words of Dutch Schultz. New York: Viking Press, 1975.

Cobble Stone Gardens. Cherry Valley, New York: Cherry Valley Editions, 1976.

Scrapbook 3. Electrostatic (Xerox) facsimile edition. Geneva: Editions Claude Givaudan, 1979.

Port of Saints. Berkeley: Blue Wind Press, 1980.

Cities of the Red Night. New York: Holt, Rinehart and Winston, 1981.

The Place of Dead Roads. New York: Holt, Rinehart and Winston, 1984.

The Burroughs File. San Francisco: City Lights Press, 1984.

The Adding Machine: Collected Essays. London: John Calder, 1985.

Queer. New York: Viking Penguin, 1985.

Electronic Revolution. Bonn: Expanded Media Editions, 1986.

The Western Lands. New York: Viking Penguin, 1987.

Interzone. Ed. James Grauerholz. New York: Viking Press, 1989.

Blade Runner, a Movie. Berkeley: Blue Wind Press, 1990.

Ali's Smile and *Naked Scientology*. Bonn: Expanded Media Editions, 1991.

Ghost of Chance. New York: High Risk Books/Serpent's Tail, 1995.

My Education: A Book of Dreams. New York: Viking Penguin, 1995.

Collaborative and Illustrated Works (chronological)

Beiles, Sinclair, William Burroughs, Gregory Corso, and Brion Gysin. *Minutes to Go*. Paris: Two Cities Editions, 1960.

Burroughs, William S., and Brion Gysin. *The Exterminator*. San Francisco: Auerhahn Press, 1960.

Burroughs, William S., and Allen Ginsberg. *The Yage Letters*. San Francisco: City Lights Books, 1963.

Burroughs, William S., Brion Gysin, and Henri Chopin. *Electronic Revolution*. Cambridge, Massachusetts: Blackmoor Head Press, 1971.

Burroughs, William S., and Bob Gale. *The Book of Breething*. Ingatestone, England: OU, 1974.

Burroughs, William S., and Charles Gatewood. *Sidetripping*. New York: Strawberry Hill, 1975.

Burroughs, William S., and Brion Gysin. *Colloque de Tanger*. 2 vols. Ed. Gérard-Georges Lemaire. Paris: Christian Bourgois, 1976, 1979.

——. *The Third Mind*. New York: Viking Press, 1978.

Burroughs, William S. and S. Clay Wilson. *Burroughs II: Die Wilden Boys, Port of Saints*. Trans. Carl Weissner. Frankfurt: Zweitausendeins, 1980.

Burroughs, William S., and Howard Buchwald. *The Streets of Chance*. New York: Red Ozier Press, 1981.

Burroughs, William S., and Carl Apfelschnitt. *Mummies*. Düsseldorf: Gunnar A. Kaldewey, 1982.

Burroughs, William S., and S. Clay Wilson. *Burroughs III: Die Städte der roten Nacht*. Trans. Carl Weissner. Frankfurt: Zweitausendeins, 1982.

Burroughs, William S., and Brion Gysin. *The Cat Inside*. New York: Grenfell Press, 1986.

Burroughs, William S., and Keith Haring. *Apocalypse*. New York: George Mulder Fine Arts, 1988.

Burroughs, William S., and Christof Kohlhofer. *The Four Horsemen of the Apocalypse*. Bonn: Expanded Media Editions, 1988.

Burroughs, William S., and Keith Haring. *The Valley*. New York: George Mulder Fine Arts, 1989.

Burroughs, William S., and S. Clay Wilson. *Tornado Alley*. Cherry Valley, New York: Cherry Valley Editions, 1989.

Burroughs, William S., and George Condo. *Ghost of Chance*. New York: Library Fellows of the Whitney Museum of American Art, 1991.

Burroughs, William S., and David Bradshaw. *Propagation Hazard*. Tampa: Graphicstudio/University of South Florida, 1993.

On Burroughs's Art

Biederberg, Suzanne. *William S. Burroughs: Paintings*. Exh. cat. Amsterdam: Suzanne Biederberg Gallery, and London: October Gallery, 1988.

Burroughs, William S. [Untitled commentary]. In *David Budd: Rencontre William Burroughs et Earle Brown chez Rodolphe Stadler*. Exh. cat. Paris: Galerie Stadler, 1964.

———. *The Seven Deadly Sins*. St. Louis: Lococo Mulder, 1991.

———. *Painting and Guns*. New York: Hanuman Books, 1992.

———. *Paper Cloud/Thick Pages. Art Random* 102. Exh. cat. Kyoto: Kyoto Shoin, 1992.

Burroughs, William S., and Philip Taaffe. *Drawing Dialogue*. Exh. cat. New York: Pat Hearn Gallery, 1987.

Grauerholz, James W. "On Burroughs' Art." In *William S. Burroughs*. Exh. cat. Santa Fe: Gallery Casa Sin Nombre, 1988, i–xiii.

Miles, Barry. "William Seward Burroughs: Word Falling—Photo Falling—Towers Open Fire! Photographs 1964–65." Exh. pamphlet. Amsterdam: Vintage Gallery, 1994.

Ploog, Jürgen. "Enthüllung der Bilder." *Kozmik Blues*. Klaus Wegener, Heinz Dietz, and U-Roy, eds. (special issue, 1991): 4–5.

Shafrazi, Tony. *William S. Burroughs*. Exh. cat. New York: Tony Shafrazi Gallery, 1987.

Shotgun Paintings: Works on Wood and Paper: William S. Burroughs Exhibition. Exh. cat. Tokyo: The Seed Hall, Sezon Museum of Art, 1990.

William S. Burroughs. Exh. cat. Santa Fe: Gallery Casa Sin Nombre, 1988.

William S. Burroughs. Exh. cat. Rome: Galleria Cleto Polcina Arte Moderna, 1989.

William S. Burroughs. Exh. cat. Paris: Galerie K, 1990.

William S. Burroughs. Exh. cat. Basel: Editions Galerie Carzaniga and Ueker, 1991.

William S. Burroughs: Paintings. Exh. cat. Basel: Editions Carzaniga and Ueker, 1989.

William S. Burroughs: Paintings and Drawings. Exh. cat. London: October Gallery, 1988.

William S. Burroughs: Pinturas. Exh. cat. Lisbon: Galeria EMI Valentim de Carvalho, 1989.

William S. Burroughs: Pinturas. Exh. cat. Madrid: Galeria Sephira, 1990.

Burroughs on Art (chronological)

"The Photo Collage" (1963). Burroughs Collection, University Libraries, Special Collections, Arizona State University.

[Untitled commentary]. In Wayne Andersen, *Takis: Evidence of the Unseen*. Exh. cat. Cambridge: Hayden Gallery, MIT Press, 1968.

"Ports of Entry." In *Brion Gysin*. Exh. cat. London: October Gallery, 1981, 1–7.

"Robert Walker's Spliced New York." *Aperture* 101 (winter 1985): 66.

"The Fall of Art." *Rapid Eye* 1 (1989). Simon Dwyer, ed. Revised and expanded edition. London: Annihilation Press, 1993, 1–5.

"Take One." In *Christopher Lucas: Painting, Sculpture, Collage*. Exh. cat. New York: John Good Gallery, 1989.

Photos and Remembering Jack Kerouac. Heaven Chapbook Series 46. Ed. Ron Whitehead and Kent Fielding. Photos by Allen Ginsberg. Louisville: White Fields Press, n.d. [1990].

"Eternal Farewells!" In *Bruce Weber*. Exh. cat. Los Angeles: Fahey/Klein Gallery, 1991.

[Untitled commentary]. In *George Condo: Recent Paintings*. Exh. cat. New York: Pace Wildenstein, 1994.

Conversations, Interviews, and Letters

Bockris, Victor. *With William Burroughs: A Report from the Bunker*. New York: Seaver Books, 1981.

Burroughs, William. *The Letters of William S. Burroughs, 1945–1959*. Ed. Oliver Harris. New York: Viking Press, 1993.

Corriel, Michele. "William Tells." Interview. *Cover* (January 1988): 16–17.

Ellis, Simone. "A Conversation with William S. Burroughs." *Contemporanea: International Art Magazine* 23 (December 1990): 80–83.

Febbraro, Paola, James W. Grauerholz, and Paolo Morelli. "William S. Burroughs: Interview." *Next* 7, no. 20 (winter 1990–91): 70–75.

Odier, Daniel. *The Job: Interviews with William S. Burroughs*. Revised and enlarged ed. New York: Grove Press, 1974.

Bibliographies and Biographies

García-Robles, Jorge. *La Bala Perdida: William S. Burroughs en México (1949–1952)*. Mexico City: Ediciones del Milenio, 1995.

Goodman, Michael B. *William S. Burroughs: An Annotated Bibliography of His Works and Criticism*. New York: Garland Publishing, 1975.

Köhler, Michael, ed. *Burroughs: Eine Bild-Biographie*. Berlin: Nishen, 1994.

Maynard, Joe, and Barry Miles. *William S. Burroughs: A Bibliography, 1953–1973*. Charlottesville: University Press of Virginia, 1978.

Miles Associates. *A Descriptive Catalogue of the William S. Burroughs Archive*. London: Covent Garden Press, 1973.

Miles, Barry. *William Burroughs: El Hombre Invisible, a Portrait*. New York: Hyperion, 1993.

Morgan, Ted. *Literary Outlaw: The Life and Times of William S. Burroughs*. New York: Henry Holt, 1988.

Critical Studies

Ansen, Alan. "Anyone Who Can Pick Up a Frying Pan Owns Death." *Big Table* 2 (summer 1959): 32–41.

Driscoll, Lawrence. "Burroughs/Jarman: Anamorphosis, Homosexuality and the Metanarratives of Restraint: An Immanent Analysis." *Spectator* 10, no. 2 (spring 1990): 78–95.

Lydenberg, Robin. *Word Cultures: Radical Theory and Practice in William S. Burroughs' Fiction.* Urbana: University of Illinois Press, 1987.

Mottram, Eric. *William Burroughs: The Algebra of Need.* London: Marion Boyars, 1977.

O'Brien, John, ed. *William Burroughs Number. The Review of Contemporary Fiction* 4, no. 1 (special issue, spring 1984).

Skerl, Jennie. *William S. Burroughs.* Boston: Twayne Publishers, 1985.

Skerl, Jennie, and Robin Lydenberg, eds. *William S. Burroughs at the Front: Critical Reception, 1959–1989.* Carbondale: Southern Illinois University Press, 1991.

Cultural Studies

Ambrose, Joe, Terry Wilson, and Frank Rynne. *Man from Nowhere: Storming the Citadels of Enlightenment with William Burroughs and Brion Gysin.* Dublin: The Gap and Subliminal Books, 1992.

Artaud, Antonin. *Selected Writings.* Ed. Susan Sontag. New York: Farrar, Straus and Giroux, 1976.

Barthes, Roland. *Elements of Semiology.* Trans. Annette Lavers and Colin Smith. New York: Hill and Wang, 1968.

Baudrillard, Jean. *Simulations.* New York: Semiotext(e), 1983.

——. *The Transparency of Evil: Essays on Extreme Phenomena.* New York: Verso, 1993.

Bender, Gretchen, and Timothy Druckrey, eds. *Culture on the Brink: Ideologies of Technology.* Seattle: Bay Press, 1994.

Berner, Jeff, ed. *Astronauts of Inner Space.* San Francisco: Stolen Paper Review Editions, 1966.

Black, Jack. *You Can't Win.* Foreword by William S. Burroughs. New York: Amok Press, 1988.

Boorstein, Daniel J. *The Image: A Guide to Pseudo-Events in America.* New York: Atheneum, 1987.

Bukatman, Scott. *Terminal Identity: The Virtual Subject in Postmodern Science Fiction.* Durham, North Carolina: Duke University Press, 1993.

Cook, Bruce. *The Beat Generation: The Tumultuous '50s Movement and Its Impact on Today.* New York: Charles Scribner's Sons, 1971.

Castaneda, Carlos. *Tales of Power.* New York: Simon and Schuster, 1974.

Crary, Jonathan, and Sanford Kwinter, eds. *Incorporations.* New York: Zone Books, 1992.

Delany, Paul, and George P. Landow, eds. *Hypermedia and Literary Studies.* Cambridge: MIT Press, 1994.

Deleuze, Gilles, and Félix Guattari. *Anti-Oedipus: Capitalism and Schizophrenia.* Trans. Robert Hurley, Mark Seem, and Helen R. Lane. Minneapolis: University of Minnesota Press, 1983.

——. *A Thousand Plateaus: Capitalism and Schizophrenia.* Trans. Brian Massumi. Minneapolis: University of Minnesota Press, 1987.

Dwyer, Simon, ed. *Rapid Eye* 1 (1989). Revised and expanded edition, London: 1993.

Eco, Umberto. *Travels in Hyperreality.* Trans. William Weaver. New York: Harcourt Brace Jovanovich, 1986.

Foucault, Michel. "Language to Infinity." *Language, Counter-Memory, Practice: Selected Essays and Interviews.* Ed. and trans. Donald F. Bouchard and Sherry Simon. Ithaca: Cornell University Press, 1977, 53–67.

Gysin, Brion. *Brion Gysin Let the Mice In*. Ed. Jan Herman. West Glover, Vermont: Something Else Press, 1973.

——. *The Process*. Woodstock, New York: Overlook Press, 1987.

Gysin, Brion, and Terry Wilson. *Here to Go: Planet R-101*. San Francisco: Re/Search Publications, 1982.

Jameson, Fredric. *Postmodernism, or, the Cultural Logic of Late Capitalism*. Durham, North Carolina: Duke University Press, 1991.

Kostelanetz, Richard, ed. *Breakthrough Fictioneers*. West Glover, Vermont: Something Else Press, 1973.

Leary, Timothy. *Chaos and Cyber Culture*. Ed. Michael Horowitz. Berkeley: Ronin Publishing, 1994.

Lotringer, Sylvère, ed. *Schizo-Culture*. *Semiotext(e)* 3, no. 2 (special issue, 1978).

McCaffery, Larry, ed. *Storming the Reality Studio: A Casebook of Cyberpunk and Postmodern Fiction*. Durham, North Carolina: Duke University Press, 1992.

Porush, David. *The Soft Machine: Cybernetic Fiction*. New York: Methuen, 1985.

Ronell, Avital. *The Telephone Book: Technology, Schizophrenia, Electric Speech*. Lincoln: University of Nebraska Press, 1989.

Rucker, Rudy. *Transreal!* Englewood, Colorado: WCS Books, 1991.

Rucker, Rudy, R. U. Sirius, and Queen Mu, eds. *Mondo 2000: A User's Guide to the New Edge*. New York: HarperPerennial, 1992.

Rushkoff, Douglas. *Media Virus: Hidden Agendas in Popular Culture*. New York: Ballantine Books, 1994.

Sappington, Rodney, and Tyler Stallings, eds. *Uncontrollable Bodies: Testimonies of Identity and Culture*. Seattle: Bay Press, 1994.

Shaviro, Steven. *Doom Patrols*. Online: Internet, August 23, 1995. Available: http://www.shaviro@u.washington.edu.

Silverberg, Ira, ed. *Everything Is Permitted: The Making of Naked Lunch*. New York: Grove Weidenfeld, 1992.

Tuchman, Mitch. "Film." *Omni* (May 1981): 30–31.

Tytell. John. *Naked Angels: The Lives and Literature of the Beat Generation*. New York: McGraw-Hill, 1976.

Vale, V., and Andrea Juno, eds. *William Burroughs, Brion Gysin, and Throbbing Gristle*. *Re/Search* 4/5 (special issue, 1982).

——. *Industrial Culture Handbook*. *Re/Search* 6/7 (special issue, 1983).

——. *J. G. Ballard*. *Re/Search* 8/9 (special issue, 1984).

Virilio, Paul. *War and Cinema: The Logistics of Perception*. Trans. Patrick Camiller. New York and London: Verso, 1989.

Wolfe, Tom. *The Electric Kool-Aid Acid Test*. New York: Farrar, Straus and Giroux, 1968.

Art and Art History

Ades, Dawn. *Dada and Surrealism Reviewed*. Exh. cat. London: Arts Council of Great Britain, 1978.

——. *Photomontage*. Revised and enlarged edition. London: Thames and Hudson, 1985.

Armstrong, Elizabeth, and Joan Rothfuss. *In the Spirit of Fluxus*. Exh. cat. Minneapolis: Walker Art Center, 1993.

Cage, John. *Rolywholyover: A Circus*. Exh. cat. Los Angeles: Museum of Contemporary Art, 1993.

Centre de la Vieille Charité. *Poésure et peintrie: "D'un art, l'autre."* Exh. cat. Paris and Marseille: Réunion des Musées Nationaux, 1993.

Cronenberg, David. *Cronenberg on Cronenberg*. Ed. Chris Rodley. London and Boston: Faber and Faber, 1992.

Dachy, Marc. *The Dada Movement: 1915–1923*. Trans. Michael Taylor. New York: Rizzoli International, 1990.

——. *Et tous ils changent le monde*. Exh. cat. Paris and Lyon: Réunion des Musées Nationaux, 1993.

——. *Dada & les dadaïsmes: Rapport sur l'anéantissement de l'ancienne beauté*. Paris: Editions Gallimard, 1994.

Finch, Christopher. *Image as Language: Aspects of British Art, 1950–1968*. Harmondsworth and Baltimore: Penguin Books, 1969.

Freeman, Judi. *The Dada and Surrealist Word-Image*. Exh. cat. Los Angeles: Los Angeles County Museum of Art, 1989.

Gallozzi, Guillaume, ed. *Brion Gysin: Back in No Time*. Exh. cat. New York: Guillaume Gallozzi, 1994.

Gonzalez de Canales, Fernando. *Retrato de William S. Burroughs*. Exh. cat. Leganes, Spain: Delegacion de Cultura, 1990.

Gruen, John. *Keith Haring: The Authorized Biography*. New York: Simon and Schuster, 1991.

Hapgood, Susan. *Neo-Dada: Redefining Art, 1958–62*. Exh. cat. New York: American Federation of Arts, 1994.

Heiferman, Marvin, and Lisa Phillips. *Image World: Art and Media Culture*. Exh. cat. New York: Whitney Museum of American Art, 1989.

Hulten, Pontus, ed. *Paris—New York*. Exh. cat. Paris: Centre National d'Art et de Culture Georges Pompidou, 1977.

———. *Paris—Paris*. Exh. cat. Paris: Centre Georges Pompidou, 1981.

Jean, Marcel. *The History of Surrealist Painting*. Trans. Simon Watson Taylor. New York: Grove Press, 1967.

Klee, Paul. *Pedagogical Sketchbook*. New York: Praeger, 1953.

Krauss, Rosalind, and Jane Livingston. *L'Amour fou: Photography and Surrealism*. Exh. cat. Washington and New York: Corcoran Gallery of Art and Abbeville, 1985.

Lancher, Carolyn. *Paul Klee*. Exh. cat. New York: Museum of Modern Art, 1987.

Marshall, Richard. *Jean-Michel Basquiat*. Exh. cat. New York: Whitney Museum of American Art, 1992.

Phillips, Lisa. *Beat Culture and the New America: 1950–65*. Exh. cat. New York: Whitney Museum of American Art, 1995.

Rooks, Conrad. *Chappaqua*. Paris: Conrad Rooks, 1967.

Rubin, William S. *Dada and Surrealist Art*. New York: Harry N. Abrams, 1968.

Schwartz, Arturo. *The Complete Works of Marcel Duchamp*. New York: Harry N. Abrams, 1970.

Seitz, William C. *The Art of Assemblage*. Exh. cat. New York: Museum of Modern Art, 1961.

Sobieszek, Robert A. *Robert Smithson: Photo Works*. Exh. cat. Los Angeles: Los Angeles County Museum of Art, 1993.

Spies, Werner, ed. *Max Ernst: A Retrospective*. Exh. cat. London: Tate Gallery, 1991.

Stich, Sidra. *Anxious Visions: Surrealist Art*. Exh. cat. Berkeley: University Art Museum, University of California, Berkeley, 1990.

Thieck, Catherine, ed. *Brion Gysin: Calligraphies, Permutations, Cut Ups*. Exh. cat. Paris: Galerie de France, 1987.

Tilton, Jack, ed. *Literary Vision*. Exh. cat. New York: Jack Tilton Gallery, 1988.

Tuchman, Maurice, and Carol Eliel. *Parallel Visions: Modern Artists and Outsider Art*. Exh. cat. Los Angeles: Los Angeles County Museum of Art, 1992.

Watkins, Glenn. *Pyramids at the Louvre: Music, Culture, and Collage from Stravinsky to the Postmodernists*. Cambridge: Belknap Press of Harvard University, 1994.

FILMOGRAPHY

Almereyda, Michael. *Twister*. United States, 1990.

Anderson, Laurie. *Home of the Brave*. United States, 1986.

Balch, Antony. *Bill and Tony*. England, 1963.

———. *Towers Open Fire*. England, 1963.

———. *William Buys a Parrot*. England, 1963.

———. *The Cut-Ups*. England, 1963–69.

Beatty, Maria. *Gang of Souls* (video). United States, 1989.

Brookner, Howard. *Burroughs*. United States, 1983.

Burckhardt, Jacob. *It Don't Pay to Be an Honest Citizen*. United States, 1984.

Cronenberg, David. *Shivers* (*The Parasite Murders* or *They Came From Within*). Canada, 1975.

———. *Rabid*. Canada, 1976.

———. *Scanners*. Canada, 1980.

———. *Videodrome*. Canada, 1982.

———. *Dead Ringers*. Canada, 1988.

———. *Naked Lunch*. Canada, 1992.

di Castro, Andrea. *Pantopon Rose*. Mexico, 1995.

Donkin, Nick. *The Junky's Christmas* (VH-1 music video). United States, 1993.

Forman, Janet. *The Beat Generation—An American Dream*. United States, 1987.

Frank, Robert. *Energy and How to Get It*. United States, 1981.

Hunt, Philip. *Ah Pook Is Here* (video). Germany, 1994.

ICA-Projects. *Kathy Acker in Conversation with William S. Burroughs* (video). England, 1986.

Jarman, Derek. *Pirate Tape*. England, 1982.

———. *Dream Machine*. England, 1986.

Lees, Russell. *The Dark Eye* (CD-ROM interactive). United States, 1995.

Maeck, Klaus. *Decoder*. Germany, 1984.

———. *William S. Burroughs: Commissioner of Sewers*. Germany, 1984.

Mann, Ron. *Poetry in Motion*. Canada, 1986.

Podesta, Patty. *A Short Conversation from the Grave with Joan Burroughs* (video). United States, 1993.

Rodley, Chris. *Making Naked Lunch*. United States, 1992.

Rooks, Conrad. *Chappaqua*. United States, 1966.

Scott, Ridley. *Alien*. United States, 1979.

———. *Blade Runner*. United States, 1982.

Ungerleider, Peter. *Ah Pook Is Here* (video). Text by WSB, spoken by Ron Vawter. United States, 1994.

Van Sant, Gus. *The Discipline of D. E.* United States, 1978.

———. *Drugstore Cowboy*. United States, 1989.

———. *A Thanksgiving Prayer* (video). United States, 1990.

———. *Even Cowgirls Get the Blues*. United States, 1994.

DISCOGRAPHY

Readings by Burroughs (chronological)

Call Me Burroughs. ESP-Disk (1050), 1966. Reissued on Rhino Records (R271848), 1995.

Ali's Smile. Unicorn Press [no number], 1971.

Valentine's Day Reading. OU Revuedisque (40–41), 1972.

"Nothing Here Now but the Recordings." Industrial Records (IR0016), 1981.

Abandoned Artifacts and *On the Nova Lark*. Fresh Sounds (Fresh Flexi 003), 1981.

Break Through in Grey Room. Sub Rosa (CD 006-8), 1986.

Uncommon Quotes. Caravan of Dreams (CDPT 85011), 1988.

Dead City Radio. Island (422-846-264-2), 1990.

Naked Lunch. Warner Audio Video Entertainment (2-522206), 1995.

Anthologies (chronological)

The Dial-a-Poem Poets. Giorno Poetry Systems (GPS 001), 1971.

William S. Burroughs/John Giorno. A D'Arc Press Selection. Giorno Poetry Systems (GPS 006-007), 1975.

The Dial-a-Poem Poets. *Totally Corrupt*. Giorno Poetry Systems (GPS 008-009), 1976.

The Nova Convention. 2 vols. Giorno Poetry Systems (GPS 016-017), 1979.

The Dial-a-Poem Poets. *Sugar, Alcohol, and Meat*. Giorno Poetry Systems (GPS 018-019), 1980.

You're the Guy I Want to Share My Money With. Giorno Poetry Systems (GPS 42-2), 1981.

The Dial-a-Poem Poets. *Life Is a Killer*. Giorno Poetry Systems (GPS 027), 1982.

Revolutions Per Minute (The Art Record). Ronald Feldman Fine Arts [no number], 1982.

The Dial-a-Poem Poets. *Better an Old Demon Than a New God*. Giorno Poetry Systems (GPS 033), 1984.

Smack My Crack. Giorno Poetry Systems (GPS 038C), 1987.

Like a Girl, I Want You to Keep Coming. Giorno Poetry Systems (GPS 040 CD), 1989.

Fresh Sounds from Middle America. Fresh Sound Music (FS 221), 1990.

The Myths Collection Part One and *The Myths Collection Part Two*. Sub Rosa (CD 003-15, SUBCD 009-32), 1990.

Cash Cow. Giorno Poetry Systems (ESD 80712), 1993.

Cough It Up: The Hairball Story. Tim/Kerr (TK 94 CO092), 1995.

Songs in the Key of X. Warner Bros. (9 46079-2), 1996.

10%: File Under Burroughs. Sub Rosa (DE12040-2), 1996.

Collaborations and Accompaniments

Anderson, Laurie. *Home of the Brave.* Warner Bros. (9 25400-2), 1986.

Burroughs, William S., and The Disposable Heroes of Hiphoprisy. *Spare Ass Annie and Other Tales.* Island (422-162-535-003-2), 1993.

Burroughs, William S., and Gus Van Sant. *William S. Burroughs, the Elvis of Letters.* Tim/Kerr (91 CD001), 1985.

Burroughs, William S., and Kurt Cobain. *The "Priest" They Called Him.* Tim/Kerr (TK 92 CD044), 1993.

Material. *Seven Souls.* Virgin (2-91360), 1989.

———. *Hallucination Engine.* Axiom/Island (314-518 351-2), 1994.

Ministry. *Just One Fix.* Sire/Warner (9 406772), 1992.

Big Hard Disk, vol. 2. Smash/Island (162-448 008-2), 1994.

Waits, Tom. *The Black Rider.* Island (314-518 555-2), 1993.

Related Works

Anderson, Laurie. *Big Science.* Warner (BSK 3674), 1982.

Cabaret Voltaire. *Code.* EMI Manhattan (MLT 46999), 1987.

The Disposable Heroes of Hiphoprisy. *Television: The Drug of the Nation.* 4th & B'way (162 440 541-2), 1991.

Eno, Brian, and David Byrne. *My Life in the Bush of Ghosts.* Sire/Warner (9 45374-2), 1981.

Genesis P-Orridge and Psychic TV. *Sugarmorphoses.* "E" in box-set *Splinter Test.* PTV (SYAR D004), 1993.

Gnawa Music of Marrakesh. *Night Spirit Masters.* Axion (314-510 147-2), 1990.

Gysin, Brion. *Self-Portrait Jumping* (1982–83). Made to Measure (MTM 33 CD), 1993.

The Hafler Trio and Thee Temple ov Psychick Youth. *Brion Gysin's Dreamachine.* Coble Sabam/Biem (Kk 15), 1989.

Hancock, Herbie. *Future Shock.* Columbia (CK 38814), 1983.

Manapsara. *Queer: A Soundtrack to the Novel by William S. Burroughs.* Sub Rosa (33017-22), 1989.

———. *Routine (Extended Mix).* Sub Rosa (12006-23), 1989.

The Master Musicians of Jajouka. *Apocalypse Across the Sky.* Axiom (314-5108572), 1992.

———. *Brian Jones Presents the Pipes of Pan at Jajouka.* Musidor, N.V., 1971, reissued Point Music (446 487-2), 1995.

Negativland. *Escape from Noise.* SST (SST CD 133), 1987.

———. *Helter Stupid.* SST (SST CD 252), 1989.

Psychic TV. *Listen Today.* Sordide/Sentimental (SSCDV01), 1988.

Shore, Howard. *Naked Lunch: Music from the Original Soundtrack.* Milan (7313835614-2), 1992.

Smith, Patti. *Horses.* Arista (ARCD-8362), 1975.

Sonic Youth. *Daydream Nation* (1988). Geffen Records (DG CD-24515), 1993.

Throbbing Gristle. *Second Annual Report* (1977). Mute (9 61093-2), 1991.

LENDERS TO THE EXHIBITION

Estate of Jean-Michel Basquiat, courtesy Robert Miller Gallery, New York

Jean-Jacques Berger, Berne

Robert Berman Gallery, Santa Monica

John Boskovich, courtesy Rosamund Felsen Gallery, Santa Monica

Peter Brams, New York

Diego Cortez Arte, Ltd., New York

Loomis Dean, courtesy Keith deLellis, New York

The Rene and Veronica di Rosa Foundation, Napa, courtesy of Gallery Paule Anglim, San Francisco

Mark Alice Durant, Los Angeles

F. José Férez K., London

Laetitia Firmin Didot, Paris

Galerie Carzaniga and Ueker, Basel

Galerie de France, Paris

Gemini G.E.L., Los Angeles

Allen Ginsberg, courtesy Tibor de Nagy Gallery, New York, and Fahey/Klein Gallery, Los Angeles

John Giorno, New York

Graphicstudio/University of South Florida, Tampa

The Grinstein Family, Los Angeles

Roger Holden, Lawrence

Norman Laurila, New York

Timothy Leary, Beverly Hills

Annie Leibovitz, New York

Robert Lococo, St. Louis

Richard Lorenz, Berkeley

Nelson Lyon, Los Angeles

Estate of Robert Mapplethorpe, New York

George Mulder, Venice, California

John Musall, New York

Warren Neidich, New York

Andrew Renton, London

Tyler Stallings, courtesy Food House, Santa Monica

Philip Taaffe, New York

University of Kansas, Spencer Art Museum, Lawrence

Alison Van Pelt, courtesy Robert Berman Gallery, Santa Monica

Andy Warhol Foundation and PaceWildensteinMacGill

Peter Weller, London

David Woodard, San Francisco

Thomi Wroblewski, London

Joseph Zinnato, Burbank

Andreas Züst, Zürich